The

GUINNESS BOOK

of

SUPERLATIVES

THE ORIGINAL BOOK OF
FASCINATING FACTS

CLYDESDALE

First published in 1956 by Superlatives, Inc., New York

First Clydesdale Press Edition 2017

Clydesdale Press books may be purchased in bulk at special discounts for sales promotion, corporate gifts, fund-raising, or educational purposes. Special editions can also be created to specifications. For details, contact the Special Sales Department, Skyhorse Publishing, 307 West 36th Street, 11th Floor, New York, NY 10018 or info@skyhorsepublishing.com.

Clydesdale Press™ is a pending trademark of Skyhorse Publishing, Inc.®, a Delaware corporation.

Visit our website at www.skyhorsepublishing.com.

10 9 8 7 6 5 4 3 2 1

Library of Congress Cataloging-in-Publication Data is available on file.

Cover photograph: iStockphoto

Print ISBN: 978-1-945186-44-8
Ebook ISBN: 978-1-945186-45-5

Printed in China

CONTENTS

LIST OF ILLUSTRATIONS

FOREWORD

Wherever people congregate to talk, they will argue, and sometimes the joy lies in the arguing and would be lost if there were any definite answer. But more often the argument takes place on a dispute of fact, and it can be very exasperating if there is no immediate means of settling the discussion. Who was the tallest President? Who is the richest man and the most married woman? Where is the highest point in our state? How many died in the world's worst earthquake? Who hit the longest measured home run? Who holds the corn-husking record? And so on. How much heat these innocent questions can raise! The House of Guinness in producing this book hopes that it may assist in resolving many such disputes, and may, we hope, turn heat into light.

RUPERT GUINNESS

Rupert Guinness
Earl of Iveagh

Earl of Iveagh

September 1956

PREFACE

This book is a collection of facts—finite facts expressed in quantitative terms, predominantly those which by measurement are superlative or are records in their respective fields. The world's greatest man is, for this book, the man with the greatest girth rather than the man with the greatest intellect.

Many of the data contained within these pages are by their very nature constantly changing. In 1953 the Nebula Andromeda, the most distant heavenly body visible to the naked eye, was discovered to be twice as far away as had hitherto been thought. In February 1955, the Russians announced the discovery of a new mountain in Siberia higher than any in America, Europe or Africa. No reference book such as this can ever claim to have said the last word.

It would be impracticable to mention all the vast number of sources and references which attach to each of the items included in this volume. In the event of rival claims for a particular superlative, it has been the sole responsibility of the compilers to weigh up the evidence and to come to a decision.

We wish to acknowledge the generous assistance of countless experts from all over the world who have aided us, and we shall greatly welcome comments and suggestions from our readers who have reason for criticizing our researches or can add to our information. In that way, we can hope to improve and enlarge any future editions.

THE COMPILERS.

SUPERLATIVES INC.
270 Madison Avenue
New York 16
MUrray Hill 3-7634/5

ACKNOWLEDGMENTS

The American Astronomical Society
The American Battle Monuments Commission
The American Dahlia Society, Inc.
The American Forestry Assoc.
American Railway Eng. Assoc.
The American Red Cross
The American Soc. of Agronomy
American Telephone & Telegraph Co.
Bell Aircraft Corp.
Billy Graham Evangelistic Team
The British Admiralty
The British Air Ministry
The British Broadcasting Corp.
British Central Office of Information
The British Museum
British Railways
The British Transport Commission
The British Travel and Holidays Assoc.
Burke's Peerage, Ltd.
Calaveras County Fair, Calif.
The Chemical Society (U.K.)
Chicago Midway Airport
Clerk of Dial Eireann (Eire)
The Democratic National Committee
Dept. of the Army
Dept. of Health, Education and Welfare
Dept. of the Navy
National Lead Co. (Doehler-Jarvis Division)
The Fairey Aviation Co., Ltd.
Federal Bureau of Prisons
Fed. Aéronautique Internationale
Fed. Internationale de l'Automobile
Fed. Internationale des Hôpitaux
Ford Foundation, U.S.
The Fur Trade Information Center
General Electric Co.
General Motors Corp.
Government Printing Office (U.S.)
John I. Haas, Inc.
The Home Office (U.K.)
The J. L. Hudson Co.
Imperial Chemical Industries
The Ingersoll Milling Machine Co.
Institut International des Châteaux Historiques

The Institute of Metals
The International Association of Volcanology
The International Civil Aviation Organization
The Embassy of Japan
Jones & Laughlin Steel Corp.
The Kennel Club
Kodak, Inc.
KWTV, Oklahoma
The Library of Congress, Washington, D. C.
The Liverpool Observatory and Tidal Institute
London County Council
The Meteorological Office (U.K.)
The Metropolitan Museum of Art
Metropolitan Opera Association, Inc.
Miss America Pageant
The Mountaineers, Inc.
National Fire Protection Assoc.
The National Geographic Society
National Physical Laboratory
The New York Times
New York Zoological Society
Outdoor Advertising Assoc.
Port of London Authority
Press Association—Reuters
Radio City Music Hall
Republican National Committee
The Royal Botanic Gardens
Sears, Roebuck and Co.
Société Nationale des Chemins de Fer Français
Benjamin Sonnenberg
The Timberman
The Treasury Department
U. N. E. S. C. O.
U. S. Bureau of Census
U. S. Bureau of Mines
U. S. Bureau of Public Roads
U. S. Coast Guard
U. S. Coast and Geodetic Survey
U. S. Dept. of Commerce—Weather Bureau
U. S. Dept. of the Interior
The War Office (U.K.)
The World Health Assoc.
Zoological Society of London

ACKNOWLEDGMENTS are made for the following photographs: Nos. 1, 2, 14, 28, 40, 42 Free Lance Photographers Guild, Inc., New York. 3, 6 U. S. Navy Photo. 4 Fairey Aviation, Ltd. 5 Chas. E. Brown, England. 7 Bell Aircraft Corp. 8 Verkehrsbüro der Stadt, Ulm. 9 High Commissioner for New Zealand. 12 Joe Clark, Detroit. 13 Radio City Music Hall. 15 Mt. Wilson—Palomar Observatory. 16 National Geographic Assoc. 17, 18, 19 British Museum (Natural History). 20 National Chinchilla Breeders of America. 21 Reproduced by permission of the Controller of Her Britannic Majesty's Stationery Office British Crown Copyright. 23 Chicago Park District. 24 General Electric. 25 Soviet News Bureau. 26 San Jacinto Museum. 27 Ediz. L. Chiovato Vincenza. 29 KWTV. 30 C. G. Grain Co. 32 Ohio Valley Elec. Corp. 33 Jones and Laughlin Steel Corp. 35 ENASA. 36 Mercedes. 37 Royal Danish Ministry for Foreign Affairs. 38 Ingersoll Milling Machine Co. 44 I.B.M. 45 Barrett's Photo Press. 46, 48, 50, 52, 54, 55, 57, 58, 59, 60, 61, 62, 65 Wide World Photos. 47, 51 Planet News. 49 Kenneth R. Gray. 56 Stan Troutman. 63 Dunlop Rubber Co. 64 Sanborn Photo Service.

Part One

THE HUMAN BEING

1. Dimensions

Man's earliest appearance dates from the Tertiary Period of the Cenozoic Era which spans from 60 million to 1 million years B.C. This Tertiary Period is divided into 5 epochs of which the two most recent are the fourth or Miocene (25 to 10 million B.C.), when the Earth was inhabited almost equally by existing and extinct life forms, and the fifth and last or Pliocene (10 to 1 million B.C.), when the Earth was inhabited by a majority of life-forms of present day types.

Though fragmentary remains of apes with possible human links in the thigh bone characteristics have been found in the East African Miocene, earliest "true man" is more acceptably placed in the Pliocene epoch. Man in this period is represented by *Australopithecus, Pleisanthropus, Paranthropus* and *Telanthropus*. Of these Telanthropus is regarded by its discoverers as the earliest form. Fragments of five specimens were found at Swart Kranz, Transvaal, South Africa in January 1953.

There is no evidence of pre-*Homo sapiens* having evolved in the American continent.

The oldest human remains in America are those of a female skull discovered in 1953 near Midland, Texas, dated on geological evidence to be earlier than 10,000 B.C. A fragment of a human skull, known as the Conkling skull, unearthed at El Paso, Texas, in 1929, may be of the same or even earlier period. A skeleton of a young female unearthed at Pelican Rapids, Minnesota, would, from its geological context, appear to date from circa 18,000 B.C.

The oldest dated American material believed to be of human origin is charcoal from an ancient lake-bed deposit near Tule Springs, Nevada, tested by the carbon 14 method and shown to date prior to 21,000 B.C.

The earliest dated artifacts are triangular-shaped blades 10,500 years old (8,500 B.C.) from Gypsum Cave, Nevada. Woven willow basketry 9,000 years old has been recovered from Danger Cave, Utah. Sagebrush-bark rope shoes dating from 7,000 B.C. have been recovered from Fort Rock Cave, Oregon.

EARLIEST MAN

EARLIEST MAN
America

HEIGHT

TALLEST
GIANTS

The only admissible evidence upon the true height of giants is that of recent date made under impartial medical supervision. Biblical claims, such as that for Og, King of Bashan, at 9 Assyrian cubits (16 feet 2½ inches) are probably due to a confusion of units. Extreme mediaeval data from bone measurements refer invariably to mastodons or other non-human remains. Claims of exhibitionists, usually under contract not to be measured, are usually distorted for the financial considerations of promoters. There is an example of a recent "World's Tallest Man" of 9 feet 6 inches being an acromegalic of 7 feet 3½ inches.

Prior to 1872, medical literature tended to accept the claim confirmed by the French anthropometrist Paul Topinard (1830-1912) that the Finn, Kayanus, (Daniel Cajanus, died 1749) was the tallest man who had ever lived at 283 cms. (9 feet 3⅜ inches). His bones, now in Leyden Museum, were however, measured by Langer in 1872 giving a value of 222 cms. (7 feet 3⅜ inches).

Modern opinion now trends to the view that the tallest man of all-time of whom there is irrefutable evidence, was Robert Wadlow, born an 8½ lb. baby in 1918 in Alton, Illinois, and who died on July 15th, 1940, at Manistee, Michigan, weighing 491 lbs. and standing 8 feet 9½ inches (267 cms.) tall.

TALLEST
GIANTESSES

Giantesses are much rarer than giants. The extreme example was Marianne Wehde of Germany (born 1866) who grew to 8 feet 4½ inches (255 cms.).

The tallest present-day giantess is Katja van Dyk of the Netherlands who is reputedly 8 feet 3 inches.

SHORTEST
DWARFS

The strictures which apply to the evidence of the heights of giants apply as fully to dwarfs.

The smallest dwarf in medical literature is one who, at the age of 37, measured only 16 inches in height, recorded by Georges Buffon (1707-1788) in his "Histoire Naturelle." Of better-documented dwarfs, the smallest was the favorite of Queen Henrietta-Maria of England, Geoffrey Hudson (born Oakham, England, 1619) who, in 1649, was only 18 inches tall at the age of 30. He later grew to 3 feet 9 inches and was buried in Westminster, London, in 1682.

Walter Boehning, 48, claiming to be the smallest dwarf in the world died at Delmenhorst, Germany, in February, 1955, at a height of 20½ inches.

WEIGHT

HEAVIEST
HEAVYWEIGHTS

The heaviest man recorded in medical literature is Miles Darden who was born in North Carolina, in 1798. He grew to 7 feet 8 inches in height and attained a weight slightly in excess of 1,000 lbs., dying in 1857 in Henderson County, Tennessee.

The heaviest recorded woman was a negress who died in Baltimore, in 1888, scaling 850 lbs.

The heaviest human in the world today is Robert Earl Hughes, aged 27, of Fish Hook, Illinois, who is 6 feet tall and 946 lbs. He was an 11 lb.

baby and weighed 378 lbs. at the age of 10. He also possesses the greatest recorded girth at 109 inches, (9 feet 1 inch).

The lowest recorded human bodyweight was the 12 lbs. of the Welshman, Hopkin Hopkins, at his death in Glamorganshire, Wales, in March, 1754. At no time in his 17 years of life did he attain a weight of more than the 17 lbs. he was at the age of 14. It is recorded that the biceps measurement of the Frenchman, Claude Seaurat (born 1798) was 4 inches at the age of 26 and that the distance between his back and chest was 3 inches.

2. Longevity

Medical men, who have devoted themselves to the study of old age (gerontologists), do not give credence to reports of people living much beyond 110 years. Few subjects have been so obscured by deceit and falsehood. The most extreme claims are for a man of 185 years (variously 187) named Setrasch Czarten (also Petratsh Zarten) allegedly born near Teneswaer, in Hungary, in 1537, and alive in 1722 and for a woman of 175 years named Louisa Trousco, a South American negress, who died circa 1776.

The claims of such traditional English figures as Henry Jenkins (died at Ellerton-upon-Swale, 1670) allegedly 169 years, and Thomas Parr (died London, 1635) allegedly 152 years, are now regarded as spurious. Parish priests began only to register births and christenings in 1538 and births were not officially registered until 1837. The claim of the Research Institute of Biology of the Gorky University, Kharkov, Russia, made on January 17th, 1955, that there were then 717 centenarians over 110 years living in Russia is not based on the essential evidence of registered birth dates. Mahmud Eivazov in the Azervaijan village of Perassara, allegedly born in 1810, was at 144 the oldest of 4,425 persons cited as of over 100 years of age.

The authenticity of the age of Christian Jacobsen Drakenberg (died October 19th, 1772) who reputedly lived to an age of 145 years 325 days is widely believed in Scandinavia. The evidence that it was he who was born in Denmark on November 8th, 1626, is unacceptable since there is a discontinuity of 15 years in the chronicle of this allegedly single life. A considerable amount of ex post documentation exists upon the age of the illiterate Spanish serving woman, Maria Josefa Nieto Santos, who died in Madrid on December 21st, 1906, at a reputed 125 years and 75 days. A certified baptismal certificate pointing to a birth date on October 7th, 1781, was produced after her death.

The greatest age which has survived official investigation is the 113 years of Pierre Joubert, a French Canadian bootmaker born in Charlesbourg, Canada, on July 15th, 1701, and buried in Quebec on November 18th, 1814. This case was personally investigated in 1870 by Dr. Tache, Official Statistician to the Canadian Government.

The greatest age for a woman for whom there exists acceptable evidence as to the date of birth is the 111 years 328 days of the Hon. Katherine Plunket, eldest daughter of the Rev. Thomas (later 2nd Baron)

Plunket who was born at Kilsaran, County Louth, Ireland, on November 22nd, 1820, and who died at Ballymascanlan House, County Louth, on October 14th, 1932.

In November 1948 the General Register Office for England and Wales in London, filed a Death Certificate for Isabella Shepheard (died November 20th, 1948) showing her age to be 115. She was the last surviving inhabitant of Britain born before compulsory registrations of births but was believed to be born on August 5th, 1833.

OLDEST U.S. CITIZEN

The oldest age contended in the United States is 123 years 42 days for Mrs. Belle Heights Rymes who died in Savannah, Georgia, on April 15th, 1934. She was allegedly born in Dublin, Ireland, on March 4th, 1811, but documents, including one purporting to show evidence of her date of birth, were destroyed in a Pittsburgh fire before her death. The greatest age of a female which is acceptable is 111 years 138 days for Mrs. Louisa K. Thiers, who died on February 17th, 1926, and whose date of birth has been fully attested by the Genealogical Record Office, Washington, D. C., to have been October 2nd, 1814.

OLDEST U.S. MAN

No official records are kept by the Bureau of Census of super-centenarians.

On March 7th, 1956, Colonel Walter W. Williams of Franklin, Texas, a Civil War veteran (born November 14th, 1842), surpassed the hitherto greatest age for any human which has survived official investigation—that of 113 years 124 days set by the Canadian Pierre Joubert (1701-1814) of Canada.

3. *Reproductivity*

MOTHERHOOD

WORLD

The greatest number of children produced by a mother in an independently attested case is that of the wife of the Russian, Fedor Vassilet (died 1872) who in 27 confinements, gave birth to 69 children (16 pairs of twins, 7 sets of triplets and 4 sets of quadruplets).

Mrs. Marie Cyr of Fort Kent, Maine, born 1911, married at 17 has produced a child every year of her first 26 married years (1929-1955) of whom 19 are living. Details of the insupportable case of Margarita Gonçalez, who was alleged in 33 confinements to have produced by two husbands 158 children (144 boys and 14 girls) of whom 99 lived to be baptized, have been reprinted from a report of 1585 by Henrique Cock in the *New York Medical Journal*.

MOST DESCENDANTS

In polygamous countries, the number of a person's descendants soon becomes incalculable, but in monogamous countries perhaps the most impressive of the many tombstone testimonies is that at Markshall Church, Essex, England, to Mrs. Mary Honywood (née Waters) of Lenham, Kent, who died aged 92 on May 16th, 1620. She left 16 children; 114 grandchildren, 228 great-grandchildren and 9 great-great-grandchildren, totalling 367.

MULTIPLE BIRTHS

The celebrated case in 1278 of Countess Margaret, daughter of Florent IV, who is reputed, at the age of 42 to have produced 365 infants (182 males, 182 females and 1 hermaphrodite) may be an exaggerated report of a case of a hydatidiform or multiple molar pregnancy.

Other cases, such as Margaret, Countess Viröboslaus, who, on January 20th, 1296, in Krakow, Poland, is alleged to have produced 36 children at a single birth is similarly explicable. Medical opinion is that reported instances of multiple births in excess of 7 must be looked on with great suspicion. In this apocryphal class are Albucasis's case of 15 at one birth, the Countess of Altdorf's duodecaplets (12) and the English example of Ann Birch who, in 1781, is alleged to have produced decaplets of whom one girl survived to marry.

Recently proved to be in this class also are the Ohio octuplets recorded in the *Boston Medical* and *Surgical Journal* of September 26th, 1872. The 273 lbs. Mrs. Timothy Bradlee (née Eunice Mowery) was reported on August 21st, 1872 to have given birth to 3 boys and 5 girls in Trumbull County, Ohio. The report, a newspaper hoax, remained uncorrected in medical literature for 43 years.

There are two unsubstantiated reports of septuplets. Five girls and two boys were reputedly born at a single birth at Hameln-am-Weser, Germany on January 9th, 1600 but the evidence rests mainly from the raising of a statue in 1818. A less unreliable instance was reported from Ibadan, Nigeria, in 1918, 11 years after its alleged occurrence in 1907.

The highest multiple births which are medically accepted are those of sextuplets in 4 instances in which there were no survivors—none of them within the United States. There are only three examples of quintuplet births with all five surviving, namely Emilie (died August 6th, 1954, aged 20), Yvonne, Cecile, Marie and Annette, born to Mrs. Oliva Dionne, in Callander, Ontario, Canada, on May 28th, 1934 (aggregate weight 13 lbs. 6 ozs.); Franco, Maria Fernanada, Maria Ester, Maria Christian and Carlos Alberto born to Franco and Vallotta de Diligenti in Buenos Aires, Argentina, on July 15th, 1943, and the birth of 5 boys in Turkey in July, 1944.

The highest multiple births in the United States have been quintuplets in 6 instances. The earliest was at Mars Bluff, South Carolina (3 boys, 2 girls in 1776) and the most recent in 1948 in Kentucky (2 boys and 3 girls) but in no case did any survive beyond infancy.

TWINS
Earliest Siamese

The earliest recorded Siamese twins are Mary and Aliza Chalkhurst of Biddenden, Kent, England, born c.1100. They survived to the age of 34.

Longest Delay

The greatest recorded interval between the birth of twins is 137 days in a case reported from Strasbourg in 1846. The first infant was born on April 30th and the second on September 13th. The British record interval is an anonymous case of "about three months", reported in the British Medical Journal in June, 1937. There is also a case of twins in the British peerage, ostensibly born 126 days apart, but this almost is certainly an error of record.

Most Pairs

Apart from the case of Madame Vassilet (see above) the greatest recorded numbers of pairs of twins born by a mother in modern medical history is eleven, a number of whom failed to survive, by a Sicilian woman. The last pair were born in 1947.

BABIES

LARGEST

The largest viable baby of which there is medical record was that of 23¾ lbs. and 30 inches in length born in 1879 to the 7 feet 5½ inches Nova Scotia giantess, Mrs. Anna Bates (born 1847) reported in the *New York Medical Record* of March 22nd, 1879.

SMALLEST

Of full-term viable infants, the smallest on record was Home's case of a 16-oz. baby, 7 to 8 inches in length, born circa 1810 to a camp-follower of the Duke of Wellington's Army, which survived to the age of 9 years.

4. Physiology

LONGEST BONE

The thigh bone or femur is the longest of the 206 bones in the human body. It usually constitutes 27½ per cent of a person's stature—19¾ inches in a 6 ft. man.

SMALLEST BONE

The incus or anvil bone, one of the three auditory ossicles in the middle ear, is the smallest bone in the body.

LARGEST MUSCLE

Muscles normally account for 40 per cent of the body weight and the bulkiest muscle in the human body is the gluteus maximus or buttock muscle which extends the thigh.

SMALLEST MUSCLE

The smallest muscle is the stapedius which controls the auditory ossicle known as the stirrup bone in the middle ear and which is less than 1/20th inch in length.

MOST FINGERS

Researching into polydactylism in 1930, De Linares recorded a case of a Spaniard with twenty-six digits.

LONGEST TRESSES

The longest recorded feminine tresses appear to be those of the 19th century exhibitionist named Miss Owens which were measured at 8 feet 3 inches.

LONGEST BEARD

The longest recorded beard was that of Hans N. Lanoseth, a Norwegian immigrant to North Dakota, in 1912 after 36 years of growth the beard was 11 feet 6 inches long.

LONGEST MOUSTACHE

The longest moustache owned by a member of Britain's "Handlebar Club" is that of Mr. John Roy of Glasgow, Scotland, with a span of 16½ inches.

FASTEST REFLEXES

The results of experiments carried out in 1943 have shown that the fastest messages transmitted by the nervous system travel at 265 m.p.h.

LONGEST COMA

The longest period of human unconsciousness ever recorded was that of Robert Steger, who was severely injured in a factory accident in 1943 and died of deterioration at Bethesda Hospital, Cincinnati, in January 1952 after a coma lasting over 8 years.

BLOOD TRANSFUSION

The record number of donations notified by the Red Cross Blood Transfusion Service is 126 for a man and 91 for a woman.

The greatest recorded transfusion is six gallons in 23 hours received by Douglas H. McLeod, 31, at Brisbane, Australia, on August 4th, 1955.

The preponderance of one blood group varies greatly from one locality to another. On a world basis Group O is the most common but in some areas, for example London, England and Norway, Group A predominates, in the U.S.A., on the A.O.B. system, Group O is the commonest with 46 per cent and AB the rarest with 4 per cent. **BLOOD GROUP**

The earliest recorded successful appendix operation was performed by Claudius Amyand (1680-1740) the Sergeant Surgeon to King George II of England in 1736. **EARLIEST APPENDECTOMY**

The earliest description in medical literature of a duodenal ulcer is by Georg Erhard Hamberger (1679-1755) in 1746. **EARLIEST DUODENAL ULCER**

The earliest description of a prolapsed invertebral cartilage is by George S. Middleton and John H. Teacher of Glasgow, Scotland, in 1911. **EARLIEST SLIPPED DISC**

The earliest recorded operation under general anaesthesia was for the removal of a cyst from the neck of James Venable by Dr. Crawford Long in Jefferson, Georgia, on March 30th, 1842. **EARLIEST ANAESTHESIA**

Vickie Davis, aged two, of Marshalltown, Iowa, was found in a temperature of −24°F during February, 1956. Her body temperature was 60.8°F, 37.6°F below normal. She survived after being thawed out for 2½ hours. **LOWEST TEMPERATURE**

VOICE

The highest musical note ever achieved by the human voice is C in altissimo, sung by Lucrezia Agujari (1743-1783). Mozart heard her sing in Palma in 1770 and recorded the range of her voice. **HIGHEST**
The same note has also been sung by Ellen Beach Yaw, a singer of the early part of this century. C in altissimo is 2,048 (cycles a second).

The lowest musical note ever achieved is a full sounding A by Kaspar Foster (1617-1673) and Norman Allin of England. A "Baso al ottava" is 44 cycles per second. **LOWEST**

The singer with the greatest range of musical value is Miss Yma Sumac of Peru. She is reputed to have a range of five octaves from A♯ to B. **GREATEST RANGE**

The normal range of a human voice on a still day is 150 yards. There is a recorded case, under freak conditions, of a human voice being heard at a distance of ten and a half miles across still water at night. **LOUDEST**

The extreme sensitivity of the fingers is such that a vibration with a movement of .02 of a micron can be detected. **TOUCH SENSITIVITY**

The largest surgical instruments are axis-traction obstetric forceps which measure up to 17½ inches overall. The smallest are Elliot's eye trephine which has a blade 78/1000 inch in diameter. **SURGICAL INSTRUMENTS**

Part Two

THE HUMAN WORLD

---

1. Political and Economic

WORLD

The land area of the Earth is estimated at 58.16 million square miles, 29 per cent of the world's surface area.

LARGEST
POLITICAL
DIVISION

The largest political division in the world is the British Commonwealth of Nations, a free association of eight independent sovereign states together with their dependencies, covers an area of 14,435,060 square miles and has an estimated population of 625 million people.

LARGEST
COUNTRY

The sixteen republics of the U.S.S.R. form the largest nation in the world, comprising 8,598,000 square miles, approximately 17% of the world's total land area.

UNITED STATES

The United States has a land area of 3,022,387 square miles, 5.7% total world land area. It ranks fifth in the world in area behind the U.S.S.R., Canada, China, and Brazil.

SMALLEST
COUNTRY

The smallest political division in the world is the Vatican City with an area of 108.7 acres.

POPULATIONS

The population of the world is now estimated at 2,652 million, giving an average population density of nearly 52 people per square mile.

UNITED STATES

The latest population of the United States is 167,181,000 (March 1, 1956), giving an average population density of nearly 56 to the square mile. The U. S. ranks fourth in a world population table behind China, India and the U.S.S.R.

The country with the largest population in the world is China with 583 million people, 22% of the total world population.

The country with the smallest population is the Vatican City with 970 people.

SMALLEST
TRIBE

The smallest tribe in the world, the phi Thony Luang of Thailand, was reported to have been located in April, 1956. They consist of six men, one boy and a woman whose chances of survival have been regarded as poor.

16

The most densely populated countries are Monaco with 56,979 people per square mile, Macau, a Portuguese colony off the coast of China, with 37,600 people per square mile and Gibraltar with 12,000 people per square mile.

Of countries over 10,000 square miles in area The Netherlands (Holland) is the most densely populated with about 848 people to the square mile.

DENSEST

The least populated continent is Australia with just over three people per square mile.

The least populated territories, apart from Antarctica, are: Greenland 0.03 persons per square mile or one person to every thirty-three and a half square miles, Spitzbergen 0.12 persons per square mile or one person to every eight square miles, and Bechuanaland 1.1 persons per square mile.

SPARSEST

The world's most populous metropolis is London, England, with a population of 8,300,000 in an area of 710 square miles, living at a density of 11,690 to the square mile.

The most populous city in the United States is New York City, with a population of 8,010,000 in an area of 365.4 square miles. The peak population was 8,086,000 in 1952.

The largest city in area in the United States is Los Angeles, which extends over 450.9 square miles.

The largest Standard Metropolitan Area in Continental United States is that of New York-Northeastern New Jersey which takes in the cities of New York, New Jersey and Newark, N. J. It has a latest population figure of 12,900,000 and an area of 4,409.4 square miles, giving a density of 2,925 to the square mile. This official census area extends to an extreme of 136 miles from Columbus Circle (New York City center) in the case of Pine Hill in Ulster County.

LARGEST CITY

The least populous state capital is Carson City, Nevada, with a latest population figure of 4,500. The most populous state capital is Boston, capital of the Commonwealth of Massachusetts, with latest population figures of 801,444 for the city and 2,369,986 for the metropolitan area.

LARGEST AND SMALLEST STATE CAPITALS

The oldest town of European origin in the United States is St. Augustine, St. John's County, Florida (present population 13,600), founded on September 8th, 1565, on the site of Seloy by Pedro Menéndez de Avilés and 1,500 Spanish colonists.

The oldest incorporated city is York, Maine (present population 2,000), which received an English charter in March, 1642, and was incorporated under the name Georgeana.

OLDEST TOWN

More people emigrate from the United Kingdom than any other country. In 1953 emigrants totalled 144,122. The largest number in any one year being 360,000 in 1852.

In 1953 more than 32 per cent of the total United Kingdom emigrants went to Canada, the greatest proportion to any one country.

EMIGRATION

IMMIGRATION   The country receiving the most immigrants during 1954 was the United States with a total of 208,177. The largest number from any one country, 34,873, came from Canada and 19,309 from the United Kingdom.

STATES
Largest   The largest of the 48 States is Texas with an area of 267,339 square miles of which 263,513 square miles is land. It is 222 times larger than Rhode Island.

Smallest   The smallest state is Rhode Island with an area of 1,214 square miles of which 1,058 square miles is land. It has, however, the longest name—The State of Rhode Island and Providence Plantation.

Northernmost   The northernmost point of the Continental United States is Lake of the Woods projection, Minnesota (Lat. 49° 23' 04.5"N.). The northernmost town is Penasse, Minnesota (Lat. 49° 22' N.).

Southernmost   The southernmost point of the Continental United States is Cape Sable, Florida (Lat. 25° 07' N.). The southernmost city is Key West, Florida (Lat. 24° 33' N.) and the southernmost mainland town, Florida City, Florida (Lat. 25° 27' N.).

Easternmost   The easternmost point of the Continental United States is West Quoddy Head, Maine (Long. 66° 57' W.) and the easternmost town Lubec, Maine (Long. 66° 57' W.).

Westernmost   The westernmost point of the Continental United States is Cape Alava, Washington (Long. 124° 44' W.).

Geographic
Center   The geographic center of the Continental United States is Lat. 39° 50' N., Long. 98° 55' W. in Smith County, Kansas. The nearest town is Lebanon.

LONGEST
COASTLINE   Of the 22 states possessing a seaboard totalling 4,840 miles that with the largest general coastline in Florida with 1,197 miles.

COUNTIES
Largest and
Smallest   The largest county of the 3,068 counties in the United States is San Bernardino, California, with an area of 20,131 square miles. The smallest is New York County, New York, with an area of 22 square miles. The state with most counties is Texas with 254 and the state with the least, Delaware with 3.

POPULATION
Most Populous   The latest available population figures (mid-1955) show New York State to be the most populous state with 16,124,000 against California's 13,032,000. This represented 9.8% of the nation's total population of 167,400,000.

Least Populous   The least populous state is Nevada with 225,000 or 0.13% of the nation's population. It is, however, by far the fastest growing with an increase of 40.6% since the 1950 census figure of 160,083. The state which has lost most population since that date is Arkansas with a loss of 6.3%—a decline from 1,909,511 to 1,789,000.

Densest   The most densely populated state is Rhode Island with 845,000 people living in a land area of 1,058 square miles. Its density of 798.67 persons per square mile compares with an average of 55.23 for the whole of the Continental United States.

The most sparsely populated state is Nevada with 225,000 people living in a land area of 109,789 square miles giving a density of 2.05 persons per square mile.

Sparsest

The earliest state to ratify the draft constitution of the United States was Delaware on December 7th, 1789. The state first permanently settled by Europeans was Florida in 1565.

Oldest

The latest and forty-eighth state to enter the Union was Arizona on February 14th, 1912. The latest state to be permanently settled by Europeans was Oklahoma on April 22nd, 1889.

Youngest

The highest crude birth rate in the world is on the Pacific island of Guam with 58 live births per thousand population. The U.S.A. figure over the same period was 24.9 per thousand. Owing to insufficient returns the lowest birth rate figures are difficult to verify but Monaco returns the lowest rate of any country reporting with 14.2.

The highest death rate for any country recorded during 1954 was 33.5 per thousand in Burma. The U.S.A. figure over the same period was 9.2.

The lowest death rate recorded is for Western Samoa with 4.5 per thousand.

BIRTH AND DEATH RATE

The highest birth rate by States in the U. S. is for Utah with 32.9 per thousand. The lowest is in New Jersey with 21.6 per thousand.

The lowest death rate is in Utah with 7.0 per thousand and the highest in New Hampshire with 11.8 per thousand.

BIRTH AND DEATH RATE BY STATES

The largest families are in South Carolina with a figure of 4.19 persons per family.

The smallest are in California with an average 3.29 persons.

LARGEST FAMILIES

Based on deaths before one year of age per 1,000 live births, the lowest infant mortality in the world is in Sweden where only 18.5 deaths are recorded per thousand live births.

The United States rate is 26.6, over the same period.

The highest infant mortality is in Burma where the last available figure shows a rate of 230.5.

INFANT MORTALITY

The state with the highest infant mortality rate is New Mexico with 42.5. Utah has the lowest rate with 20.3.

By States

On figures supplied by the World Health Organization the highest natural increase in the world is recorded for Costa Rica with 35.9 per 1,000 a year. The U. S. average is 1.7%. The world average is 1.3 per 1,000.

NATURAL INCREASE

The country with the longest life expectancy at birth is The Netherlands where males can look forward to 70.6 years of life and females to 72.9 years.

The U.S.A. figures are: white males 66.6 years, white females 72.7 years, other males 59.1 years, other females 63.7 years.

The shortest life expectancy at birth is in India with 32.45 years for males and 31.66 years for women. India and Ceylon are the only

LIFE EXPECTATION

places in the world where the expectation of life for men is greater than that for women.

At the age of 60 the longest life expectancy for males is in Norway with 18.39 years. For females of 60, however, the greatest life expectancy is in Cyprus with 19.5 years. The U. S. equivalents for these figures are: white males 15.9 years, white females 19.0 years, other males 15.0 years, other females 17.4 years.

MARRIAGES

There is no universally accepted definition of marriage for purpose of international comparison of marriage rates. In some countries where the number of so-called "consensual" marriages is high, the apparent marriage rate, based on actual marriages registered, will appear low. Again, in countries and in states in the U. S., where the statistics are based on the number of marriage licenses issued, the apparent rate will be high, since the marriage license is a statement of intent only and usually exceeds the number of marriages actually contracted.

However, during 1954, Hawaii shows the highest average rate of 10.1 new marriages for every 1,000 population. Over the same period the United States figure was 9.2.

Peru showed the lowest rate in the world with only 2.5 marriages per 1,000.

The highest ever marriage rate in the United States since 1900 was the 16.4 per thousand of 1946 during which year there were 2,291,045 marriages. In 1946 the number of divorces was also the highest on record, a total of 610,000 or approximately 4.3 per thousand.

The divorce rate of the United States over the same period was a record 2.5 per 1,000.

By States

The state with the highest number of marriages was New York with 125,863 with a rate equalling 8.3 per thousand.

The state with the highest marriage rate is Nevada with a rate (based on licenses issued) of 251.1, per thousand. The lowest marriage rate in the United States is in Alabama—6.4 per thousand.

The state with the smallest number of divorces is Vermont with 479, a rate of 1.3

The state with the highest divorce rate is Nevada—49.2. The lowest divorce rate in the United States is a distinction shared by New York, New Jersey and North Dakota, all approximately 0.9 per cent.

MOST TOURISTS

Based on the latest available figures for a year, more people visited Italy than any other country, a total in 1954 of 9,327,512. The total visitors to the U.S.A. were 545,433.

Of Italy's visitors, the greatest proportion, 18.6% (1,739,850) came from Switzerland. U. S. visitors totalled 581,248.

Of the United States' 545,433 visitors, the greatest number (apart from visitors from Mexico and Canada) were from the United Kingdom, a total of 94,928 or 17.4% of the visitors.

The country which more Americans visit than any other is Italy, in 1954, 581,248 of Italy's visitors came from the United States.

OLDEST
RULING
HOUSE

Though historians claim to have traced the line of the Japanese Royal family back 124 generations to Jimmu Tenno, who is reputed to have ascended to the throne 2,616 years ago in 660 B.C., there is doubt as to the authenticity of these claims.

The longest continuous reigning line is that of the Royal House of Denmark founded by Gorm the Old in A.D. 811. The present monarch, King Frederik IX (succeeded April 20th, 1947) is the direct descendent of Gorm and the fifty-second in line.

LONGEST
REIGN

The longest recorded reign of any monarch is that of the 6th Dynasty Pharaoh Pepi II. He ascended the Egyptian throne c. 2,566 B.C., aged 6 and reigned for 91 years. The longest reign in European history was that of King Louis XIV of France who ascended aged 5 in 1643 and reigned for 72 years till his death in 1715.

SHORTEST
REIGN

The shortest recorded reign was that of King Jean I of France who succeeded Louis X (died June 5th, 1316) on his posthumous birth on November 5th, 1316 and died 120 hours later.

ENGLISH
MONARCHS

The longest reign of any King of Great Britain was that of George III from October 25th, 1760 to January 29th, 1820 (59 years, 96 days) and the longest of a Queen that of Victoria from June 20th, 1837 to January 22nd, 1901 (63 years, 216 days).

The shortest reign of a King of England was that of Edward V from April 9th, 1483 to June 26th, 1483 (seventy-nine days) and the shortest of a Queen that of Jane from July 6th, 1553 to July 19th, 1553 (fourteen days).

LONGEST AND
SHORTEST
LIVED
PRESIDENTS

The longest lived of the thirty-three presidents was John Adams (the second president) (1797-1801) who was born October 30th, 1735, celebrated his 90th birthday in October 1825 and died on July 4th, 1826. See Photo No. 1, page 37.

The shortest lived president was the twentieth, James Abram Garfield (born November 19th, 1831) who died as a result of gunshot wounds on September 19th, 1881 at the age of 49.

LONGEST AND
SHORTEST
TERMS

The longest term served by any president was the twelve years, one month and eight days by the 32nd president, Franklin Delano Roosevelt, who was first inaugurated on March 4th, 1933 and who remained continuously in office until his death during his fourth term on April 12th, 1945.

The shortest term of office was that of the ninth president, William Henry Harrison (1841-1841), who caught pneumonia during the period of his inauguration on March 4th, 1841 and who died thirty-one days later on April 4th, 1841. See Photo No. 2, page 37.

MOST
EX-PRESIDENTS
LIVING

Between March 4th, 1861 and the death of ex-President Tyler on January 18th, 1862, there were five ex-presidents living: Van Buren, Fillmore, Pierce, Buchanan and Tyler.

The longest period a president has survived office was the 25 years, 4 months by John Adams, from March 4th, 1801 to his death on July 4th, 1826.

The president to die soonest after finishing a term of office was John K. Polk who died on June 15th, 1849, 105 days after the end of his term on March 3rd, 1849.

GREATEST GATHERING OF PRESIDENTS

In the old House Chamber of the Capitol on December 30th, 1834, eight bearers of the supreme office were gathered under one roof: ex-president John Quincy Adams; ex-president Andrew Jackson; Vice-president Martin Van Buren; Senator John Tyler; Senator James Buchanan and Representatives James K. Polk, Millard Fillmore and Franklin Pierce.

OLDEST AND YOUNGEST AT INAUGURATION

The oldest president at inauguration was the ninth, William Henry Harrison (born February 9th, 1773), who succeeded Martin Van Buren on March 4th, 1841 at the age of 68 years.

The youngest president at inauguration was the twenty-sixth, Theodore Roosevelt (born October 27th, 1858), who succeeded William McKinley on September 6th, 1901 at the age of 42 years, 10 months. He was also the youngest president to be elected. On March 4th, 1905 he was aged 47 years and 4 months.

The oldest president in office was the seventh, Andrew Jackson (born March 15th, 1767), who on his last day in office was only 11 days short of his 70th birthday.

MOST CHILDREN

The president with the greatest number of children was the tenth, John Tyler (1841-1845), who had three sons, four daughters and two other children who died in infancy, by his first wife, Letitia Christian (1790-1842), and five sons and two daughters by his second wife, Julia Gardiner (1820-1889), so making a total of sixteen children.

TALLEST AND SHORTEST

The tallest of the thirty-three presidents was the sixteenth, Abraham Lincoln (1809-1865), who stood 6 feet 4½ inches tall and weighed 180 lbs.

The shortest president was the fourth, James Madison (1751-1836), who was 5 feet 4½ inches.

HEAVIEST AND LIGHTEST

The heaviest president was the twenty-seventh, William Howard Taft (1857-1930), who attained a weight of 354 pounds. The lightest president was Madison who was reputed to weigh little more than 100 lbs.

WIVES OF PRESIDENTS

Of all the presidents only the fifteenth, James Buchanan (1857-1861), was a bachelor.

LONGEST AND SHORTEST LIVED

The longest lived of any of the thirty-seven women married to Presidents of the United States was Mary Scott (Lord) Dimmock, second wife of President Benjamin Harrison (1889-1893), who was born in 1857 and who died aged ninety on January 5th, 1948. The longest lived of those married to a president in office was Edith Kermit Carow (1861-1948), second wife of the 26th president, Theodore Roosevelt (1901-1909), who died aged 87.

The shortest lived was Alice Hathaway Lee (1861-1884), first wife of the twenty-sixth president, Theodore Roosevelt, who died aged twenty-four.

The youngest married of the wives of a president was Eliza McCardle (1810-1876), who was married to the seventeenth president, Andrew Johnson (1865-1869) at the age of seventeen on May 17th, 1827.

OLDEST AND YOUNGEST MARRIED

The oldest to marry a president in office was Edith Bolling, Mrs. Galt, the second wife of the 28th president, Woodrow Wilson (1913-1921), married in 1915 at the age of forty-three.

Ex-President Millard Fillmore (1850-1853) married Caroline McIntosh (Mrs. Carmichael) (1813-1881) as his second wife in 1858 when she was forty-five.

The youngest "First Lady" at the White House was Julia Gardiner, second wife of the tenth president, John Tyler (1841-1845), who was married in 1844 at the age of twenty-four.

OLDEST AND YOUNGEST WIVES AT THE WHITE HOUSE

The oldest "First Lady" to occupy the White House was Bess Wallace, wife of the thirty-third president, Harry S. Truman (1945-1953), who was sixty-eight at the time of President Eisenhower's inauguration.

The greatest number of children borne by the wife of a president was the 14 (ten sons and four daughters) born to Anna Symmes (1775-1864), wife of the ninth president, William Henry Harrison (1841-1841).

MOST CHILDREN

VICE PRESIDENTS

The youngest man to become Vice President was John Cabell Breckinridge (born January 21st, 1821), who took office on March 4th, 1857, aged 36 years, 1 month.

YOUNGEST

The oldest man to become Vice President was Alben William Barkley of the second Truman administration (1949-1953). He was born on November 24th, 1877 and took office on January 20th, 1949, aged 71 years and 40 days and served till January 20th, 1953 when he was past 75.

OLDEST

The longest lived vice president was Levi P. Morton of Benjamin Harrison's administration (1889-1893). He was born on May 16th, 1824, and died on his 96th birthday on May 16th, 1920.

LONGEST LIVED

STATE GOVERNORS

The oldest man ever to serve as a governor was Governor Walter S. Goodland of Wisconsin (born December 22nd, 1862). He was 84 years and 2 months old at the time of his death in office on March 11th, 1947. In 1945, he had been elected at the age of 82.

OLDEST

Currently, the oldest governor is Ed C. Johnson, Governor of Colorado (born January 1st, 1884), who will be 73 on the expiration of his term in January, 1957. He was first elected in 1933 and will have served over a 24-year span.

YOUNGEST

The youngest age at which a governor has ever been elected is 25 years in 1836 in the case of Governor Stevens Thomas Mason (born October 27th, 1811), the first Governor of Michigan on its admission into the Union on January 26th, 1837. The youngest governor in the 20th Century has been Harold E. Stassen (born April 13th, 1907), who was elected Governor of Minnesota in November, 1938, aged 31 years, 7 months. Currently, the youngest governor is Frank G. Clement of Tennessee (born June 2nd, 1920), who took office in 1953 at the age of 32 years and 6 months.

HIGHEST AND
LOWEST
SALARIES

Of the 54 United States Governors of the States and Territories, the highest salary is that for the governorship of New York State, currently held by Governor Averell Harriman (term expires January, 1959), at $50,000 with a furnished executive mansion. The lowest salary is that of the Governor of Nevada at $7,600 with the use of the executive mansion and a maintenance and expenses fund.

SPEAKERS

YOUNGEST
AND OLDEST

The youngest of the 46 Speakers of the House of Representatives was Robert Mercer Taliaferro Hunter (born April 21st, 1809) of Virginia, who was chosen Speaker for the 26th Congress in December, 1839, aged 30 years and 7 months. The oldest Speaker is Sam Rayburn of Texas (born January 6th, 1882), who was re-elected for the 84th Congress on January 3rd, 1956, aged 73 years, 11 months so surpassing the record of Henry Thomas Rainey (1860-1934).

YOUNGEST
SENATOR

The youngest senator in the history of Congress was Brigadier General Armistead Thomson Mason (born August 4th, 1787), who was elected Democratic senator for Virginia and began serving on January 3rd, 1816 at the age of 28 years, 5 months. He was killed in a duel with his brother-in-law on February 6th, 1819.

Currently, the youngest senator is Russell B. Long of Florida, son of Huey P. Long, and born November 3rd, 1918. He was elected in 1951 at the age of 32 years, 2 months.

OLDEST
SENATOR

On June 18, 1956, Senator Theodore F. Green (born October 2nd, 1867) of Rhode Island, became the oldest Senator of all-time, surpassing the record of Senator Justin S. Morrill of Vermont who was born April 14th, 1810 and died in office on December 28th, 1898, aged 88 years, 8 months. Senator Green's term expires in 1961 during which year he is due to celebrate his 94th birthday.

The greatest age at which any person has been returned as a senator is 86 years, 10 months in the case of Andrew Jackson Houston (born June 21st, 1854). He was the son of the former President of the Republic of Texas, General Samuel Houston (1793-1863), who had served as a Democratic senator over 118 years earlier in 1823. Senator Andrew Houston entered the Senate on April 21st, 1941, took the oath on June 2nd and died 24 days later, three days after his 87th birthday.

LONGEST
SERVICE

The longest any Senator has ever served is the 37 years of Senator Francis E. Warren (born June 20th, 1844), first Governor of Wyoming and holder of the Congressional Medal of Honor. Elected Republican Senator in November, 1890, he served until his death on November

24th, 1929, apart from a 2-year interval from March, 1893, to March 1895. Currently the Senator with the longest continuous service is Senator Walter F. George of Georgia (born January 29th, 1878) from November 8th, 1922. His present term expires in 1957.

The longest service of any Representative is the 46 years of Representative Joseph G. Cannon (born May 7th, 1836) of Illinois. He was elected as a Republican to the 43rd Congress and the next 8 Congresses (March 4th, 1873—March 3rd, 1891); to the 53rd Congress and the next 9 Congresses (March 4th, 1893—March 3rd, 1913) and to the 64th Congress and the next 3 Congresses (March 4th, 1915—March 3rd, 1923). His span of office covered one day short of 50 years of which 46 years were in office in 23 Congresses from the 43rd to the 67th. He died aged 90 on November 12th, 1926.

The longest service by a Representative currently in office is 22 consecutive terms by Sam Rayburn of Texas (born January 6th, 1882), who entered the House on March 4th, 1913 for the 63rd Congress.

The youngest man who has ever served in the House of Representatives was William Charles Cole Claiborne (born 1775) who, in contravention of the 25 years of age requirement of the Constitution, was elected and served as a Jeffersonian Democrat from August, 1797, at which time he was 22.

YOUNGEST REPRESENTATIVE

The oldest man ever to serve as a Representative was Robert L. Doughton (born November 7th, 1863) of North Carolina who retired on January 3rd, 1953, aged 89 years, 1 month. Currently the oldest Representative is Brent Spence (born December 24th, 1874) of Kentucky, aged 81.

OLDEST REPRESENTATIVE

The first Congresswoman elected to the House of Representatives was Mrs. Jeanette Rankin, Republican from Montana, who served from March 4th, 1917, to March 4th, 1919, and again in 1941-43.

EARLIEST CONGRESS-WOMAN

The first negro to serve in the House of Representatives was Joseph H. Rainey of South Carolina, who took the oath on December 12th, 1870.

EARLIEST NEGRO CONGRESSMAN

The first woman to sit in the Senate was Mrs. Rebecca L. Felton (Democrat) of Georgia, on November 21st, 1922. The earliest occasion on which a woman was elected to Senate was on January 12th, 1932, when Mrs. Hattie Caraway (Democrat) of Arkansas, began her service which lasted till 1945.

EARLIEST WOMEN SENATORS

The first negro senator was Hiram R. Revels of Mississippi, who served from February 25th, 1870, to March 4th, 1871.

EARLIEST NEGRO SENATOR

The first meeting of the Continental Congress was from September 5th to October 20th, 1779, at the Carpenter's Hall, Philadelphia, with 44 delegates. The first Congress opened on March 4th, 1789 in New York, but the first quorum of either the Senate or House of Representatives was not until the meeting of April 6th, 1789.

EARLIEST MEETING

The shortest of the 84 Congresses since the 1st Congress in 1789-90 was the 9th Congress which between December 2nd, 1805 and March 3rd, 1807 comprised two sessions totalling 234 days. The length-

LONGEST AND SHORTEST CONGRESSES

iest was the 80th Congress which between January 3rd, 1947 and December 31st, 1948, comprised two sessions which remained unadjourned for a total of 712 days.

LONGEST AND SHORTEST SESSIONS

The lengthiest session of the 84 Congresses was the Third Session of the 76th Congress which extended over 366 days from January 3rd, 1940 to January 3rd, 1941. The briefest session was the Second Session of the 34th Congress which lasted only 10 days from August 21st to August 30th, 1856.

GREATEST PARTY MAJORITIES

The greatest party majority in the House of Representatives was 242 in the 75th Congress of 1937-38 when the Democrats outnumbered the Republicans 331 to 89.

The greatest Republican majority was 172 in 67th Congress (1921-23) when they outnumbered the Democrats 303 to 131.

The largest party majority in the Senate was 60 during the 75th Congress (1937-38) when the Democratic Senators outnumbered the Republicans 76 to 16.

The greatest Republican Senate majority was 45 in the 41st Congress (1869-71) when Republican Senators outnumbered the Democrats 56 to 11.

NARROWEST PARTY MAJORITIES

The smallest party majority of all-time in the House of Representatives was in the 25th Congress (1837-39) when the Democrats outnumbered the Whigs 108 to 107 for a majority of one.

Since 1867 the only parties to have gained a majority have been the Republicans or Democrats. The smallest majorities have been 6, both in the 65th Congress (1917-1919) with the Democrats leading 216-210, and in the 72nd Congress (1931-1933) when they led by 220-214.

In the Senate the leading parties have twice been at parity. In the 23rd Congress (1833-35) there were 20 Democrats and 20 National Republicans and in the 47th Congress (1881-83) both the Republicans and Democrats had 37 senators.

MOST AND LEAST MEASURES PASSED

The largest number of measures passed by any Congress was 7,024 by the 59th Congress from December 1905 to March 1907. The Congress with the largest number of measures introduced was the 61st from March 1909 to March 1911 with 44,363 of which 884 were passed.

LARGEST AND SMALLEST POPULAR MAJORITIES

Since the introduction of the popular vote in Presidential Elections in 1872 the greatest majority won was 11,072,014 votes in 1936 when President Franklin D. Roosevelt (Democrat) defeated Alfred M. Landon (Republican) with 27,751,597 votes to 16,679,583. The smallest popular majority was 9,464 votes in 1880 when President James A. Garfield (Republican) defeated Winfield S. Hancock with 4,454,416 votes to 4,444,952.

LARGEST POPULAR MINORITY

In the 22 elections since the introduction of the popular vote in 1872 two presidents secured office without a popular majority. Of these, President Hayes in 1876 had the largest minority of 264,292 against the 456 minority of President Harrison in 1888.

The President vetoing most Congressional Bills was Franklin D. Roosevelt (1933-1945) with 371 regular and 260 pocket vetoes. Of this total of 631 the number sustained was 622. The greatest number of bills passed over veto during a presidency was 15 by the 39th and 40th Congress, during the term of President Andrew Johnson (1865-69). The least number of vetoes was by President James Monroe whose single regular veto was sustained.

MOST AND LEAST VETOES

The smallest majorities of all-time in Gubernatorial, Senatorial, Congressional, State and Mayorial elections have never been collated but doubtless occurred in the 19th century during the era of very low electorates. The smallest majorities brought to light in a survey of the last 20 years are:

SMALLEST MAJORITIES

Gubernatorial	430 votes	Kansas	1940	Governor Payne Ratner (Republican) winning by 429,215 to 428,785.
Senatorial	1,102 votes	Connecticut	1950	Senator William Benton (Democrat) winning by 439,551 to 438,449.
Congressional	17 votes	New Hampshire (1st District)	1936	Democrat won by 52,008 to 51,991.
State Legislature	tie	Pennsylvania Philadelphia (2nd Legislative District)	1954	After the disallowing of one Democrat vote (as a result of an appeal) Alphonso Parlante (Democrat) and Abraham Sigman (Republican) tied with 9,824 votes each.
Mayorial	2 votes	New Haven, Conn.	1951	Republican winning over Democrat by 34,848 to 34,846.

The longest speech in the history of the Senate is that of Senator Wayne Morse of Oregon on April 24-25, 1953, when he spoke on the Tideland's Oil Bill for 22 hours, 26 minutes without once being able to resume his seat. The U. S. national record duration for a filibuster is 28 hours, 15 minutes by Texas State Senator Kilmer Corbin of Lubbock at Austin, Texas, on May 17-18, 1955. He was speaking against the financing of water projects by taxation.

LONGEST SPEECHES

WORLD PRODUCTION

The following lists show the principal producing country in the world of various raw materials and foods. Actual production figures (all ton figures are converted to short tons—2,000 lbs.) are shown and also the proportion that they represent of the total world production.

In cases where the principal country is not the United States, the U. S. production has been included for comparison.

The figures in all cases are based on the latest available yearly reports.

When reviewing these figures it should be borne in mind that the United States represents only 6.5 per cent of the world's population, and 5.8 per cent of the world's superficial land area.

Arable land—U.S.S.R. 556 million acres, about 16 per cent of world total. The United States figure is approximately 450 million acres.

AGRICULTURAL

Forest Land—U.S.S.R. 2,270 million acres, about 25 per cent of world total. The United States figure is 623,828,000 acres.

Cattle—India 155 million head, 19 per cent of world total. The United States figure is 94.8 million head.

Horses—U.S.S.R. 16.2 million, 21.4 per cent of world total. The United States figure is 3.4 million.

Sheep—Australia, 26.9 million, 14 per cent of world total. The United States figure is 3.12 million.

Pigs—U.S.A. 48.5 million, 13 per cent of world total.

Cotton—U.S.A. 3.77 million tons, 41 per cent of world total.

Wool—Australia 647,000 tons, 31 per cent of world total. The United States figure is 151,000 tons.

Tobacco—U.S.A. 1.11 million tons, 29 per cent of world total.

FOOD

Wheat—U.S.A. 29.1 million tons, 17.5 per cent of world total.

Maize—U.S.A. 83.1 million tons, 55 per cent of world total.

Oats—U.S.A. 23.9 million tons, 44 per cent of world total.

Barley—U.S.A. 8.9 million tons, 14 per cent of world total.

Rye—Germany 4.5 million tons, 20 per cent of world total.

Rice—China (22 provinces) 54.0 million tons, 29 per cent. The United States figure is 2.9 million tons.

Coffee—Brazil 1.14 million tons, 42 per cent of world total.

Sugar—Cuba 4.99 million tons, 13.2 per cent of world total. The United States figure is 2.48 million tons.

Fish Landings—Japan 4.5 million tons, 26.2 per cent of world total. The United States figure is 2.5 million tons.

Potatoes—Germany 29.5 million tons, 16 per cent of world total. The United States figure is 10.6 million tons.

Meat—U.S.A. 12.6 million tons. The second largest producer in the world is France with 2.6 million tons.

Milk—U.S.A. 61.8 million tons, 25 per cent of world total.

Wine—France 1.33 million U.S. gallons, 27.9 per cent of world total. The United States figure is 219,743 gallons.

Beer—U.S.A. 2.86 million gallons, 37.8 per cent of world total.

Cigarettes—U.S.A. 401,848,000,000, 34.2 per cent of world total.

MINERALS
AND METAL
PRODUCTION

Coal—U.S.A. 416.3 million tons, 25.2 per cent of the world total.

Iron Ore—U.S.A. 44.0 million tons, 38.4 per cent of the world total. (Iron content)

Steel—U.S.A. 88.3 million tons, 36.2 per cent world total.

Copper—U.S.A. 836,000 tons, 30.9 per cent of world total.

Lead—U.S.A. 313,000 tons, 16.5 per cent of world total.

Tin concentrates—Fed. Malay States, 67,983 tons, 34.3 per cent of world total.

Aluminum—U.S.A. 1.4 million tons, 53.8 per cent of world total.

Gold—Union of South Africa 907,689 lbs. (avoirdupois) 51.5 per cent world total. United States figure 127,473 lbs.

Cement—U.S.A. 50.9 million tons, 24.5 per cent of world total.

Shipbuilding—U.K. 1.4 million gross registered tons. The United States figure is 477,000 tons.

Motor vehicles—U.S.A. 6,600,824, 67.6 per cent of total world production.

Petroleum—U.S.A. 156.8 million tons, 72.4 per cent of total world production. (Based on motor spirit.)

Newsprint—Canada 6 million tons, 53.8 per cent of world total. United States figure 1.19 million tons.

Electricity—U.S.A. 544,645 million kw, 40.4 per cent of world total.

INDUSTRIAL PRODUCTION

PROPORTIONS OF TOTAL NATIONAL PRODUCT

It should be mentioned, with regard to these comparisons, that methods for the assessment and classification of these data vary from country to country. The figures, therefore, are approximations only indicating trends rather than quantitative comparisons.

Agriculture and associated industries represent 66 per cent of the domestic economy of Nigeria—more than anywhere else. In the United States, the same industries are only 6 per cent of the total net product. The smallest proportion in the world — 5 per cent is in the United Kingdom.

AGRICULTURE

Manufacturing and mining represent 49 per cent of the economy of Western Germany, the highest proportion anywhere in the world. In Haiti, these industries are only 1 per cent of the total. In the United States the figure for these industries is 32 per cent.

MANUFACTURING

In Northern Rhodesia mining alone accounts for 62 per cent of the total domestic product.

The percentage of the national product absorbed in retail and wholesale distribution is highest in Mexico—31 per cent. The lowest proportion is probably that of 8 per cent in Portugal, while in the United States the figure is 17 per cent of the domestic product.

TRADE

The highest proportion of national income used for administration, defense, judiciary, police, etc., is probably that of Puerto Rico with 27 per cent. The lowest figure recorded under this heading is 3 per cent in Honduras. In the United States this proportion is 12 per cent.

PUBLIC ADMINISTRATION

The country with the greatest value of exports is the United States. During the last year recorded the U.S. exported goods to the value of $14,967 million, approximately 19.6 per cent of the world total.

EXPORTS

The country with the greatest value of imports was again the United States, over the same period the U.S. imported goods to the value of $10,312 million or approximately 13.1 per cent of the world total.

IMPORTS

Of those countries with exports totalling more than $500 million, the country with the greatest excess of exports over imports, or favorable balance of trade, expressed as a percentage, was Venezuela. In 1954 their exports exceeded imports by 88.8 per cent.

BALANCE OF TRADE

Of those countries with exports of more than $500 million, the country with the most unfavorable balance of trade was Norway. In 1954 their imports exceeded exports by 75 per cent.

The country with the greatest excess of exports over imports as an amount was the United States with $4,655 million. This represents an excess by exports of 45 per cent over imports.

INDUSTRIAL
SHARES

Since 1953, the year on which these figures are based (1953 = 100), Austria has shown the greatest rise in the market price of her industrial shares. The rise since 1953 is 53 per cent. The U.S. figure for same sample and covering the same period is a rise of 22 per cent.

The country showing the greatest fall over the same period was Japan whose index fell from 100 to 71.

COST OF
LIVING
Increase

The country with the greatest increase in the cost of living, based on an index figure of 1953 = 100, is Bolivia (the figures being primarily based on the capital La Paz). In 1954 the index had risen to 224. In the ten years 1945-1954 the cost of living in Bolivia had risen to fifteen times above the 1945 level.

The greatest increase over the same ten years, however, is in Paraguay with thirty times.

A rise of 135 times occurred in S. Korea over roughly the same period but owing to the exceptional circumstance of the Korean War the figures are not comparable.

In the U.S. over the same period the cost of living index rose from 67 to 100, a percentage rise of 50 per cent.

Decrease

The greatest decrease in the cost of living index appears in Lebanon, the cost of living is now only 68 per cent of the 1945 level. (The figures are based on Beirut.)

SOCIAL
SECURITY

The United States is the country with the largest old age, invalidity and survivors social security scheme. In 1954, the numbers of participants was 46,600,000.

The country with the greatest number of recipients of old age pensions is the United Kingdom, where there are 4,358,000 old age pensioners. This represents approximately 8.5 per cent of the total population of the United Kingdom, the largest number of pensioners in the world and the highest proportion in the world.

In the United States, 3,519,000 people are in receipt of old age pensions, approximately 2.1 per cent of the total population. The expenditure of the United States on pensions, $3,762,000,000, is the greatest amount in the world.

HOUSING

For these comparisons, dwelling units are defined as structurally separated room or rooms occupied by private households of one or more people and having separate access or a common passage way to the street.

The country with the largest number of dwelling units is the United States with, at the last assessment, 45,983,398. The median number of rooms being 4.6 and the median number of occupants 3.1 per dwelling unit.

The highest density of occupation occurs in the municipality of Singapore where 29 per cent of the dwelling units (mostly one to two room units) contain over five people in each room.

Switzerland has the highest coverage of electricity in the world. One hundred per cent of its urban dwelling units and 95.1 per cent of rural houses have an outside source of electricity. The percentage in the U.S. is 94.3.

ELECTRICITY

In the United Kingdom 93 per cent of all dwelling units have running water available. This is the highest figure of all countries reporting such information. The United States figure is 85.9 per cent.

RUNNING WATER

New Zealand has the highest proportion of baths, approximately 87.5 per cent of their households being equipped with separate bathing accommodation. In the U.S. the percentage is 72.9.

BATHS

TRADE UNIONS

LARGEST

The world's largest trade union is the International Union, United Automobile, Aircraft and Agricultural Implement Workers of America. In 1954, their membership was approximately 1,479,000 of whom 180,-000 were unemployed and 60,000 retired members of the Union. The U.A.W. is affiliated with the C.I.O. (Congress of Industrial Organizations) which has an estimated membership of 5.75 million in thirty-three national unions.

The largest union in the United Kingdom is the Transport and General Workers with a membership of approximately 1,300,000.

The largest labor organization in the world is the A.F.L. (American Federation of Labor) which represents 111 national unions with an estimated 8.5 million members.

The world's longest strike occurred at Dun Laoghaire, County Dublin. The dispute arose after a barman had been dismissed from his position in a public house. The Barmans' Union called the staff out on strike and arranged daily picketing of the premises, the strike commenced on March 6th, 1939, and ended (when a new owner took over) on December 5th, 1953, more than fourteen and a half years later.

LONGEST STRIKE

The country with the most doctors per head of population is Israel where, in 1954, one doctor practiced for every 380 people. At the opposite end of the scale was the Anglo-Egyptian Sudan with, in 1954, one doctor for every 86,000 people.

DOCTORS

The figure for the U. S. is one doctor for every 770 people.

The country with the greatest number of hospital beds per head of population is the Republic of Ireland with one bed for every sixty-seven people.

HOSPITALS

The lowest figure in the world is recorded for China, where available figures show a total of only 3,140 beds maintained by government services. This represents one bed for every 148,000 people.

The figure for the United States is one bed for every 104 people.

CONSUMPTIONS

CEREALS

The largest consumers of cereal products in the world are the people of Southern Rhodesia. They consume 443 lbs. of flour, milled rice, corn, etc., per head per year.

The U.S. per head consumption is 156 lbs. per year.

POTATOES

The greatest eaters of potatoes are the people of the Republic of Ireland. They consume 403 lbs. of potatoes per head per year.

The U.S. consumption figure is 103 lbs. per head per year.

SUGAR

The figures for yearly sugar consumptions recorded since 1950 show the Colombian people to be the heaviest sugar eaters in the world with a consumption of 125 lbs. per head per year.

The U.S. figure is 90 lbs. per head per year.

MEAT

The greatest meat eaters in the world—figures include offal and poultry—are the Uruguayans with a consumption of 264 lbs. per head per year.

The U.S. consumption figure is 174 lbs. per head per year.

MILK

Iceland consumes the greatest quantity of milk. Fresh consumption and that used for dairy products (other than butter) totalled 400 quarts per head per year. The U.S. figure is 243 quarts per head per year.

FATS

Based on fat content, Norway and the Netherlands are the greatest fat eaters. During the last recorded year they consumed 59 lbs. per head. The U.S. figure for a year was 46 lbs. per head.

TOTAL CALORIES

Of all countries in the world, Ireland has the largest total of calories available per capita. Over twelve months the intake averaged 3,545 calories per day. The U.S. figure over the same period was 3,090 calories per day.

TOTAL PROTEIN

Iceland has the highest consumption of protein per capita, a total of 113 grams per day. The U.S. figure is 92 grams per day.

The lowest figures in the world are calories: India with 1,684 calories per day. Protein: India and Ceylon with a daily intake of 46 grams.

ENERGY

To express the various fuels as energy it is usual to convert them all to terms of coal, omitting for the purposes of accuracy vegetable fuels and peat. On this basis the world average is 1.6 tons per head per year. The highest consumption in the world is the United States where it equalled 8.39 tons per year. This is 46.7 per cent of the total world production of energy and equals 1,353,000,000 tons of coal.

To obtain comparisons of the consumption of various fuels it is usual to convert them to coal equivalents. On this basis, omitting for the sake of accuracy peat and vegetable fuels, the average world consumption of coal equivalents is 1.6 tons per head. The highest consumption in the world of energy is in the United States where it averages 8.39 tons of coal equivalents per head per year. This is equivalent to 46.7 per cent of the total world consumption of coal equivalents.

The lowest energy consumption is difficult to verify. The lowest recorded figure is for Haiti where only 87,000 tons of coal equivalents were used. This equals a per head consumption of 44 lbs. a year.

The longest compulsory school attendance in the United States is in the states of Ohio and Utah. All children must attend school through the ages of 6 to 18.

The shortest school attendance period is 8 through 16 in the states of Arizona, California, Connecticut, Montana and Washington.

In the last period for which figures have been issued, Wyoming spent the most money per pupil on education during 1953-4, a total of $445 per pupil.

Mississippi spent the least during the same period, a total of $113 per pupil.

The state with the most farms is Texas with 331,567 with an average acreage of 438.5 acres.

The state with the biggest farms is Arizona with an average of 3,833.7 acres each.

The state with the highest average value per acre is New Jersey with $292.48 per acre. The lowest value per acre in the United States is from New Mexico with an average of $15.01.

Kansas produces more wheat than any other state—18.1 per cent of the U.S. total.

Maine produces more potatoes than any other state—13.7 per cent of the U.S. total.

Texas has more cattle than any other state—8.9 per cent of the U.S. total.

Iowa has more hogs than any other state—21.9 per cent of the U.S. total.

Iowa produces more corn than any other state—18.2 per cent of the U.S. total.

MONETARY AND FINANCE

The United States holds by far the largest gold reserve in the world at $22,100 million (£7,900 million). More than half is stored in the world's greatest treasure house, the United States Bullion Depository at Fort Knox, 30 miles south-west of Louisville, Kentucky. The gold is stored in standard mint bars of 400 troy oz. (6¾ x 3½ x 1¾ inches) each worth $14,000 (£5,000) and number some 900,000. The vault door weighs over 20 tons and no one person knows the whole combination.

The country with the largest National Debt is the United States with a Gross Public Debt of $271,259 million (£96,780 million) or $1,670 (£596) per head.

Paper money is an invention of the Chinese and though the date of 119 B.C. has been put forward, the innovation is believed to date from the T'ang dynasty of the 7th century A.D. The world's earliest bank notes were issued by the Bank of Sweden in 1661. The oldest surviving printed Bank of England note is one of £555 to bearer dated December 19th, 1699 (4½ x 7¾ inches).

LARGEST
BANKING
ORGANIZATIONS

The International Bank for Reconstruction and Development, the United Nations "World Bank," in Washington, has a capital stock of $9,000 million (£3,215 million). The members' quotas to the International Monetary Fund, Washington, stand at $8,850 million (£3,160 million).

WORST
INFLATION

The world's worst inflation occurred in Hungary in June, 1946, when the 1931 gold Pengo was valued at 1.3 nonillion (1.3×10^{30}) paper Pengös.

BIGGEST
CRASH

The biggest individual financial crash in history occurred in 1932 when a group of public utility companies in the United States—Insull Utility Investments—controlled by London-born Samuel Insull, failed to fulfill its obligations.

Samuel Insull, at the time of the crash, was President of eleven companies, Chairman of 65 and on the boards of a total of eighty-five. The group controlled more than 6,000 public utility plants.

The total loss to investors has never been accurately assessed but it has been estimated at more than $518 million. Some estimates even suggest $2,240 million. The group defaulted on its obligations to the amount of $151 million.

Charged with bankruptcy, fraud and embezzlement, Samuel Insull was acquitted and died in France in 1938.

NEW YORK STOCK EXCHANGE

HIGHEST AND
LOWEST PRICE
SEATS

The peak prices ever paid for a New York Stock Exchange seat is $625,000, with rights on February 18th, 1929. The lowest prices ever paid were $4,000 in 1876 and 1878.

OLDEST STOCK

The common stock which has been paying dividends the longest is the Pennsylvania Railroad Co., since 1848.

GREATEST
VOLUME

The highest trading volume was 1,124,800,410 shares reported in 1929, and the lowest 47,431,227 during 1914 in which year the Exchange was closed from July 31st to December 15th. The peak daily figure was 16,410,030 on October 29th, 1929.

OLDEST
MEMBER

The oldest member of the 869 members of the New York Stock Exchange is Mr. Leonard D. White, who was admitted on March 28th, 1889.

INSURANCE

The state with most life insurance in force is Delaware, each family has an average of $9,100 insurance in force. The state with the smallest amount is Mississippi, with a family average of $2,400.

WORLD'S
LARGEST
BUDGET

The greatest annual expenditure of any national economy was that of the United States Government in 1945 when $98,416,219,788 was spent.

The highest revenue was that of 1953 fiscal year with a total figure of $64,825,044,000.

The highest national income figure was in 1953 when it equalled $305,002,000,000.

The United States National Debt attained a peak of $280,616,-132,696 on December 19th, 1955. Piled in dollar bills, this amount would reach a height of over 16,000 miles and would weigh 263,000 tons or—7½ times as much as the world's tallest monument in Texas.

NATIONAL DEBT

The most taxed country in the world is Great Britain where between thirty and forty per cent of the National Income is taken in central and local taxation. In the U.S.—total receipts over gross national product the overall percentage is approximately 20 per cent.

MOST TAXED COUNTRY

The highest average per capita income of the United States was in 1953 with a personal income figure of $1,792.

INCOME

The state with the highest per capita personal income is Nevada with an average $2,414. The state with the lowest per capita income is Mississippi with $873.

MILITARY AND DEFENSE

The longest of history's countless wars was the "Hundred Years War" between England and France which lasted from 1338 to 1453 (115 years) though it may be said that the Holy War, comprising the nine Crusades from the First (1096-1104) to the Ninth (1270-1291), extended over 195 years.

LONGEST

By far the most costly war in terms of human life was World War II (1939-1945) in which, including military personnel and civilians of all countries, the total killed, according to a Vatican estimate, was 22,060,000 with an additional 34,300,000 wounded, making a total of 56,360,000 casualties.

BLOODIEST

In the case of the United States, however, the heaviest casualties arose in the Civil War (1861-1865) with 364,427 (112,414 in battle) dead from the Union Army and 133,785 (74,524 in battle) dead from the Confederate Army making a total of 498,212 killed and died of the 2,638,797 enlisted. Including the 281,894 Union and 100,000 (minimum) Confederate troops wounded the 33.3% proportion of casualties to participants made the Civil War the bloodiest in U. S. history.

MOST CASUALTIES

In World War I there were 4,609,190 engaged. Of these 53,403 were killed in battle and 77,815 died making a total of 130,921 fatalities. The total number of casualties including the 202,261 wounded gave a casualty percentage of 7.3%.

In World War II there was the highest number engaged with 14,903,213. Of these 293,986 were killed in battle and 113,842 died making a total of 407,828 fatalities. The total number of casualties including the 670,846 wounded gave a casualty percentage of 6.7%.

In the Korean War (1950-53) there were 5,720,000 serving personnel involved. Of these 33,629 were killed in battle and 20,617 died making a total of 54,246 fatalities. The total number of casualties including 103,284 wounded gave a casualty percentage of 2.75%.

Though no satisfactory computation has been published, it is certain that the material cost of World War II transcended that of the rest of history's wars put together. The total cost to the United States from December 7th, 1941 to August 14th, 1945, has been computed at

MOST COSTLY

$380,000,000,000. It has been conjectured that the total cost to all nations of the Second World War was of the order of $1,300,000,-000,000.

GREATEST INVASION

The greatest invasion in military history was the Allied "Triphibian" operation against the Normandy coasts of France on D-day, June 6th, 1944. Thirty-eight convoys of 745 ships moved in on the first three days supported by 4,066 landing craft and 347 minesweepers. Within a month, 1,100,000 troops, 200,000 vehicles and 750,000 tons of stores were landed.

GREATEST BATTLE

The greatest land battle in U. S. military history was the Meuse-Argonne offensive in France by the 550,000 strong American First Army in World War I which lasted 47 days from September 26th to victory on November 11th, 1918.

GREATEST NAVAL BATTLE

The biggest naval action ever joined was the Battle of Leyte Gulf, Philippines, from October 22nd to 27th, 1944, with 166 U. S. and 65 Japanese warships engaged of which 32 (26 Japanese and 6 U. S.) were sunk.

WORLD'S LARGEST ARMED FORCES

Numerically, the country with the greatest manpower under arms is the People's Republic of China (Chung-Hua Jen-Min Kung-ho Kuo) with 4,500,000 and an additional home guard militia of perhaps 13,000,000 from her population of 602,000,000. The U.S.S.R.'s regular armed forces have an estimated strength of 4,750,000 against the United States' 3,500,000.

SMALLEST ARMY

Currently the smallest army in the world is that of the Principality of Monaco on the French Riviera with a strength of 65.

OLDEST ARMY

The oldest army in the world is the 83 strong Vatican Swiss Guard with a regular foundation dating back to January 21st, 1506. Its origin, however, extends back before 1400 A.D.

LARGEST NAVY

The largest navy in the world is the U. S. Navy which has a strength greater than that of the combined fleets of the rest of the world. Of the total of 4,420 warships, 1,001 are on the active list. The strength includes 37 Fleet Aircraft Carriers, 66 Escort Carriers, 16 Battleships, 2 Large Cruisers, 29 Heavy and 44 Light Cruisers, 372 Destroyers, 265 Destroyer Escorts, 10 Destroyer-Minelayers and 198 Submarines.

The manpower strength of the Navy as of Mid-1956 was 657,000 and that of the U. S. Marine Corps 193,000.

LARGEST BATTLESHIPS

The 72,200 ton Japanese battleships *Yamato* (sunk by U.S. planes on April 7th, 1945) and *Musashi* (sunk by fifteen bombs and twenty torpedoes on October 24th, 1944) were the largest battleships ever constructed. With an overall length of 863 feet, a beam of 127 feet and a full load draught of 36 feet they mounted nine 18-inch guns in three triple turrets. Each gun weighed 162 tons and was 75 feet in length firing a 3,200 lb. projectile. See Plate 2.

The largest battleships in the U. S. Navy are U.S.S. Iowa (completed February 22nd, 1943) and U.S.S. Missouri (completed June 11th, 1944) each of which has a full load displacement of 57,450 tons and mounts nine 16-inch and twenty 5-inch guns. The U.S.S. New Jersey

1. John Adams, the longest lived President. See p. 21.
2. William Henry Harrison, the President with the shortest ever term of office. See p. 21.
3. The U.S.S. Saratoga, largest warship ever constructed. See p. 38.

4. Lionel Peter Twiss, the pilot of the Fairey Delta 2 (5) holder of the world's official air speed record of 1,132 miles per hour. See p. 39.

5. Fairey Delta.

(57,216 tons full load) is, however, longer than either by 9 inches with an overall length of 888 feet.

LARGEST
AIRCRAFT
CARRIER

The largest warship ever constructed is the aircraft carrier U.S.S. Saratoga which has a full load displacement of 76,000 tons, an overall length of 1,036 feet, a maximum beam of 252 feet (129½ feet on the water-line) and a maximum draught of 37 feet. A shaft horse-power of 260,000 gives her a speed of 35 knots. She was "launched" in her New York Naval Shipyard construction dry-dock at Brooklyn on October 8th, 1955 and joined the fleet on April 14th, 1956. She has a capacity of up to 100 aircraft and carries a complement of 3,826. See Photo No. 3, page 37.

FASTEST
DESTROYER

The fastest destroyer in the U. S. Navy is U.S.S. Timmerman, commissioned in September 1952. She has a full load displacement of 3,540 tons and carries six 5-inch guns. Her engines develop 100,000 shaft horse-power which gave her a speed in excess of 40 knots (46 m.p.h.) on trials.

SUBMARINES

The largest submarines ever constructed were the 1-14, 1-40 and 1-400 of the Imperial Japanese Navy, completed in 1944 at Kawasaki, 400¼ feet in length, carrying three seaplanes, eight 21-inch torpedo tubes, one 5.5-inch gun, with a submerged displacement of 6,560 tons, and a complement of 144.

FASTEST
SUBMARINE

The deepest diving (700 feet), fastest (30 knots submerged) and longest range (25,000 miles) submarine yet constructed is the atomic-powered U.S.S. Seawolf launched on July 21st, 1955. The largest submarine in the U. S. Navy will be the 4,600 ton boat designated type SSNR being built under the 1956 Naval Appropriations at a cost of $95 million.

The largest submarine fleet in the world is that of the U.S.S.R. Navy or Kraszni Flot which numbers 'not less than 400 boats'.

MINES

The earliest use of metal explosive-filled mines was by the Imperial Russian Navy at Kronstadt during the Crimean war in 1854. The largest minefield ever laid was the barrier between Scotland and Iceland in which the Royal Navy, during 1943, laid 92,536 mines.

TORPEDOES

The torpedo was developed from David Bashnell's experiments in 1775 by the American engineer, Robert Fulton (1765-1815), in 1805 but was not perfected as an auto-mobile weapon until 1864 by the Scotsman Robert Whitehead. The largest torpedoes constructed were those of 24-inch calibre used by major vessels of the Royal Navy.

EARLIEST
ARMOR

Scale armor was known in Egypt in the reign of Amenhotep II, 1463-1522 B.C., but was probably an importation from Western Asia where fragments have been recovered from Ras Esh Shamra and Nuzi dating from the second half of the Roman XVth century B.C.

GUIDED
MISSILES

The longest range guided missiles so far being developed are the I.C.B.M.'s (Inter-Continental Ballistic Missiles) under the United States projects Atlas and Titan. These weapons are expected to stand over 80 feet in height and have a gross take-off weight of over 100 tons. With a possible range of upwards of 5,000 miles at 12,000 m.p.h. and a high point of 600-800 miles, they are expected to achieve an accuracy to within 5 miles.

Though it cannot be accepted as proved, the best opinion is that the earliest guns were constructed by the German, Berthold Schwarz, in 1313. The earliest representation of an English gun is contained in an illustrated manuscript dated 1326 at Oxford.

GUNS
Earliest

The remains of the most massive guns ever constructed were found in 1945 near Frankfurt, Germany. They were "Schwerer Gustav" and "Dora" each of which was 31.5 inch calibre with 105 feet long barrels designed to throw a 16,540 lb. projectile 51,000 yards with a 2,500 lb. charge. Each gun with its carriage weighed 1,344 tons.

Largest

The longest range ever achieved by any gun was that of the 20½ ton German 280 mm. (11.02 inch) K.5 with a 70 feet 8 inch long barrel which could send a 300 lb. projectile 93 miles. The 232 mm. (9.14 inch) "Big Berthas" which shelled Paris in 1918 had a range of 70 miles.

Longest Range

The highest range anti-aircraft gun developed is the 30-ton U. S. "Stratosphere" 120 mm. gun developed in 1944 to attain an altitude of 11 miles. The record height for shooting down an aircraft was 36,000 feet (6.8 miles).

Anti-Aircraft

The greatest mortars ever constructed were Mallet's mortar (Woolwich Arsenal, 1857) and the U. S. "Little David". Both were of 36¼ inch (920 mm.) calibre——but neither was ever used in action.

Mortar

The prototype of all tanks was "Little Willie" built by William Foster & Co., Ltd., of Lincoln, England, and first tested in 1915.

TANKS

The heaviest operational tank used by any Army was the German panzerkampfwagen Tiger Model B (Royal Tiger) of 67 tons, mounting an 88 mm. gun and powered with 700 b.h.p. Heavier tanks up to 180 tons and one carrying a 380 mm. (14.97 inches) mortar were discovered in experimental stages in Germany.

The greatest Air Force of all-time was the United States Air Force which, in July, 1944, had 79,908 aircraft and in March, 1944, 2,411,-294 personnel. Currently, it is probable that the U.S.S.R., with a reported annual production of 22,000 'planes, possesses the world's largest air force with 19,500 front line aircraft.

AIR FORCES

The oldest air force in the world is that of the United States which was started in the form of the Aeronautical Division of the Signal Corps with three men on August 1st, 1907.

The world's largest bomber is the American Convair B-36 D which has a wing span of 230 feet, a length of 162 feet, a height of 46 feet 9 inches and is powered by six Pratt and Whitney R-4360 engines and four General Electric J47 turbojets giving a speed of 435 m.p.h. Its gross weight is 179 tons and it has a range, with a bomb load, of 10,000 miles. The GRB-36 version, adapted to carrying an underslung fighter aircraft, has a gross weight in excess of 200 short tons.

LARGEST
BOMBER

The official world's air speed record, under conditions recognized by the Federation Aeronautique Internationale, is 1,132 m.p.h. by the British Fairey Delta 2, powered with a Rolls Royce Avon engine with reheat. The flight was made by Lionel Peter Twiss, 34 (Distinguished Service Cross and bar) between 11:21 and 11:44 a.m. on March 10th, 1956 in level flight at a height of 38,000 ft. (7¼ miles) over a 9-mile course

OFFICIAL
RECORD

between Chichester and Ford, Sussex, England. The speed of the two runs were 1,117 m.p.h. and 1,147 m.p.h. giving an average of 1,132 m.p.h. in a flight lasting 23 minutes. See Photo Nos. 4-5, page 37.

FASTEST
AIRCRAFT

The fastest aircraft was the American Bell Aircraft Corporation X-1A which, on December 12th, 1953, attained a speed of 1,650 m.p.h. over Edwards Air Force Base, California. The aircraft is powered by Reaction Motors Inc. rocket motors of four units using alcohol and liquid oxygen with a fuel duration of 4.2 minutes. Wingspan 28 feet, length 35 feet 7 inches, height 10 feet 8 inches. The pilot was Major Charles E. Yeager (born February 13th, 1923), Silver Star, D.F.C., Bronze Star, Air Medal, U.S.A.F. See Photo No. 7, page 42.

LONGEST
FLIGHT

A U. S. B-47 bomber in December, 1954, stayed airborne 47 hours 35 minutes and covered 21,000 miles.

HIGHEST
FLYING

The Bell X-1A also set the world's highest altitude performance on June 16th, 1954, at a figure in excess of 83,500 feet (probably 90,000 feet) over California. The pilot on this occasion was Major Arthur Murray.

The Soviet bomber Type 37, known as the Bison, has been reported to have a ceiling as high as 85,000 feet.

The 600 miles per hour B-52 eight jet, swept wing, long range heavy bomber has a loaded weight of 175 short tons, a wing span of 185 feet, and a service ceiling of perhaps 55,000 feet.

LARGEST
(NON-RIGID)
AIRSHIP

The U. S. Navy Anti-Submarine airship ZP2N built by Goodyear is the world's largest non-rigid airship with a capacity of 970,000 cubic feet of helium.

LONGEST
DURATION

The duration record for a balloon flight was set by the U. S. Navy 'Blimp' ZPG-2 (Cdr. Marion H. Eppes). Taking off from Lakehurst, N. J., it landed at Boca Chica, Florida, on May 25th, 1955, having been airborne for 8 days, 8 hours, 4 minutes. See Photo No. 6, page 42.

LARGEST
BOMB

The heaviest bomb ever used operationally was the R.A.F. 22,000 lb. "Grand Slam" dropped in 1944 in attacks on concrete U-Boat pens. In 1949, the United States Air Force tested a 42,000 lb. bomb at Muroc Dry Lake, California.

EARLIEST
ATOM BOMBS

The first atom bomb explosion was detonated at Alamogordo, New Mexico at 5:30 a.m. on July 17th, 1945. The first used in warfare was that dropped on Hiroshima, Japan, by the B-29 bomber "EnolaGay" Col. Paul W. Tibbets (Capt.), Major Thomas W. Ferebee (bombardier) on August 6th, 1945.

TRANSPORT

AIRLINES

The country with the busiest airlines system is the United States where the latest available figures show a total of 20,517,582,000 passenger miles, domestic and international services, flown in one year. This equals an annual trip of 122 miles for every one of the 167.2 million inhabitants of the U. S.

The total distance covered by all passenger aircraft was 679,732,-177 miles.

The world's largest mercantile marine is that under the flag of the United States with 4,485 ships of 25,123,434 net register tons with a further 446 ships of 2,506,306 tons plying the Great Lakes.

MERCHANT MARINE

The Merchant Navy of the United Kingdom has the greatest number of ships with 6,036 of 19,122,043 net register tons.

More vessels entered and left United States ports than any other country—a total of 85,762,000 net registered tons entered and 71,-822,000 net registered tons left U. S. ports.

The busiest port in the world is the Port of London on the River Thames, England. In 1955, 54,888 ships arrived and departed involving the loading and unloading of 53,664,831 tons of imports and exports.

WORLD'S BUSIEST PORT

The world's largest port is the Port of New York. In 1954, 23,857 vessels entered and left the harbor, involving the handling of 35,448,-094 tons of foreign trade cargo. Including coastwise, internal and intra-port traffic the total of waterborne cargo handled was 137,353,454 tons. The Port has a navigable waterfront of 460 miles in New York and 295 miles in New Jersey making a total of 755 miles. There are 130 shedded piers and over 70 other piers capable of berthing 400 ships at one time. The total warehousing floor space is 15,000,000 square feet, 235.6 acres.

LARGEST

The country with the greatest length of railway is the U.S.A. with 237,500 miles of track. This equals a density of one mile of railway for every 12.7 square miles. Belgium is the country with the greatest railway density—one mile of track for every 1.43 square miles.

RAILWAY

British Railways carry more people than any other railway system. In 1954, the figure was 991,193,000.

The Japanese State Railway system carries out more passenger miles (one passenger for one mile) than any other system — in 1953 51,950 million.

The United States figure is 29,321 million passenger miles.

The United States railways carry more freight than any other nation's railways, in 1953, 608,964 million freight ton miles.

The United States has the greatest length of road of any country, with 3,366,190 miles of rural and municipal highway.

ROADS

The country with the most motor vehicles is again the United States with 57,876,000 registered private cars, commercial and passenger vehicles.

The country with greatest number of vehicles per mile of road is the United Kingdom. Its 184,000 miles of road carry 5,282,222 vehicles, approximately 29 vehicles for every mile of public road, or one every sixty yards.

In the United States the density is 17 vehicles a mile, or one every 103 yards.

The country with the greatest mileage of road compared on area basis is Belgium with 3.3 miles of road for every square mile area. The United States figure is 1.11 miles per square mile.

Texas has the most mileage of road of any state with 224,937 miles.

6. The U.S. Navy 'Blimp' ZPG-2, holder of the airborne duration record. See p. 40.

7. Major Charles E. Yeager and Major Arthur Murray, the fastest flying and the highest flying pilots ever. See p. 40.

8. Ulm Cathedral, highest church spire in the world. See p. 49.

9. The New Zealand Signpost, with an abbreviated version of the longest place name of the world. See p. 51.

10. Hollywood Freeway, the most heavily traveled facility in the world. See p. 41.

The most heavily traveled facility in the United States and the densest traffic at any point is reputed to be the Hollywood Freeway. During 1955, the average daily volume was 172,000 vehicles a day. In July, 1955, between 7 a.m. and 8 a.m. it reached 13,720 vehicles in an hour. The total for that day was 178,430. See Photo No. 10, page 42.

The country with the greatest length of inland waterways is Finland. The total of navigable lakes and rivers is 31,000 miles.

The United States has a total of 27,480 miles of inland waterway.

The longest navigable inland waterway in the world is the River Amazon, which sea-going vessels can ascend as far as Iquito, Peru, 2,300 miles from the Atlantic seaboard.

INLAND WATERWAYS

The busiest river in the world is the Detroit River between Lake St. Clair and Lake Erie. In 1953, it carried 140.7 million tons of freight.

BUSIEST RIVER

The busiest canal in the world is the St. Marys Falls Canal (Sault Ste. Marie). It connects Lake Superior and Lake Huron and in 1953 carried a total of 128.5 million short tons. The principal commodity carried is iron ore and in 1953, 98.3 million tons were carried.

BUSIEST CANAL

The country with the greatest number of authorized broadcasting stations for commercial or public programs is the United States with a total of 3,909. Also in the United States is the highest total of all types of broadcasting stations, safety, amateur, etc.; in 1954, 1,231,107 were authorized.

COMMUNI-CATIONS

There are more than 260 million radio sets in use throughout the world—approximately 98 for every 1,000 people or roughly one receiver for every ten people in the world.

The United States has more radio receivers in use than the rest of the world put together. Its total of 135,000,000 being 52 per cent of the world total of 260 million.

This figure gives the United States the highest concentration of radio receivers with 807 sets per thousand people.

The country with the greatest number of television sets is again the United States with approximately 40 million sets in use. This figure is equivalent to 239 sets between 1,000 people.

The country with the greatest number of telephones is the U.S.A. with 52,806,476; this provides 32.81 telephones per 100 population which is the highest density in the world.

TELEPHONES

The city with the highest telephone density in the world is Washington, D. C., where there are 61.7 telephones per 100 population.

The metropolitan area with the largest number of telephones in the world is New York with, in 1955, 3,764,790, giving a density of 46.5 per 100 population.

The country with the highest per capita number of telephone conversations is Canada. The average person makes 417.5 calls a year. The U.S.A. figure over the same period was 393.2 calls per capita.

The country with the largest domestic letter mail in the world is the United States, whose population posts 50,384,000,000 letters a year, equivalent to 309 letters per head per year.

POSTAL SERVICES

Of those countries reporting to the International Bureau of the Universal Postal Union, French Somaliland returned the lowest figure for domestic mail with a 6,800 total for 1954.

POSTAGE STAMPS
Earliest

The earliest adhesive postage stamps in the world are the "Penny Blacks" of Great Britain, bearing the head of Queen Victoria, placed on sale on May 1st for use on May 6th, 1840.

The largest postage stamps ever issued were the Express delivery stamps of China in 1913 which measured 9 ¾ inches by 2 ¾ inches.

The smallest stamps ever issued are those of the Colombian State of Bolivar, 1863-1866, at 10 cents and at 1 peso, measuring 5/16ths inch by ⅜ inch.

Denomination

The highest denomination stamp ever issued was the King George V £100 ($280) red and black Kenya stamp of 1925-27. Owing to demonetization it is difficult to determine the claimant for the lowest denomination stamp though this probably is the French ½ centime stamp of 1919-22, then representing 1/12th of a cent.

Rarest

There are a number of stamps of which but a single specimen is known. Of these the most celebrated is the famous British Guiana 1 cent black on magenta of 1856 which was originally bought from a schoolboy for $1.20.

MOST VALUABLE STAMP

The world's most valuable stamp is the British Guiana 1c black on magenta dated 1856 for which it is understood $45,000 has been refused and which has been insured by J. and H. Stolow's of New York for $100,000.

EARLIEST U.S.

The earliest postage stamps of the U. S. Post Office issued for general use throughout the United States were placed on sale in New York City on July 1st, 1847. They were the 5 cent red-brown Benjamin Franklin (3,712,200 issued) for single envelopes to be carried less than 300 miles and the 10 cent black George Washington (891,000) stamps which were withdrawn on June 30th, 1851. The earliest adhesive stamps were those used for local delivery by the City Despatch Post established in New York City on February 15th, 1842.

U.S. LARGEST

The largest U. S. stamps ever issued were the 1865 Newspaper Stamps which measured 3 ¾ inches by 2 inches. Of regular issues, the largest are the 5 cent blue and carmine Air Beacon stamps (issued July 25th, 1928), and the 2 cent black and carmine George Rogers Clark commemorative stamps (issued February 25th, 1929). These measure 1³⁄₃₂ inches by 1¹⁵⁄₃₂ inches.

HIGHEST DENOMINATION

The highest denomination U. S. postage stamps were those for $5. The earliest of these was the $5 black issued on January 2nd, 1893 as part of the first commemorative series for the Columbian quadricentenary.

LOWEST DENOMINATION

The lowest denomination U. S. postage stamps have been for a ½ cent. The earliest of these was the ½ cent sepia Nathan Hale stamp of 1922.

The highest price ever paid for a single stamp at auction in the United States is the $20,000 for the 1851 9 Kreuzer on green paper of Baden, paid on April 23rd, 1956, in New York at the Caspary sale.

The people of the United States send more telegrams than any other country. The latest figure is 144,233,000 in a year. This is equivalent to 88 telegrams per 100 people.

TELEGRAMS

The country with the largest number of different daily newspapers is the United States. Each day 1,760 newspapers issue approximately 55 million copies. This figure is equivalent to 339 copies for every thousand people in the United States.

NEWSPAPERS

The country with the most daily newspapers per head is the United Kingdom with 114 newspapers issuing 29 million copies. The per head figure is 570 for every thousand population.

Many countries and territories do not produce a daily newspaper but the lowest recorded readership figure is for Ethiopia, where one daily newspaper is issued—one copy for every 30,000 inhabitants.

The world's biggest consumer of newsprint is United States who, in 1954, used 5,400,000 tons. This equals a per head consumption of 75 lbs.

2. *Judicial*

CRIME AND PUNISHMENT

Taking figures for the decade (1940-1950) that part of the world with the highest annual average murder rate is the State of Georgia, U.S.A., with 167.3 per million. That with the lowest over the same period is Scotland with 2.7 per million population.

HIGHEST MURDER RATE

The most prolific murderer in crime history was Herman Webster Mudgett (born May 16th, 1860), better known as H. H. Holmes. It has been estimated that he disposed of some 150 young women "paying guests" at his 'Castle' in 63rd Street, Chicago, Ill. After a suspicious fire on November 22nd, 1893, the 'Castle' was investigated and found to contain passages, stairways and a maze of odd rooms, some windowless or padded containing gas inlets and electric indicators. There was also a hoist, two chutes, a furnace, an acid bath, a dissecting table, a selection of surgical instruments and fragmentary human remains. Holmes was hanged on May 7th, 1896, on a charge of murdering his associate, Benjamin F. Pitezal.

MOST PROLIFIC MURDERER

The greatest number of murders ever ascribed to a murderess is 16, together with further 12 possible victims, making a total of 28. This was in the case of Bella Poulsdatter Sorensen Gunness (1859-1908) of La Porte, Indiana. Evidence was obscured by the arson committed upon her farm on April 28th, 1908, when she herself was found by a jury to have committed suicide by strychnine poisoning. Her victims, remains of many of whom were dug from her hog-lot, are believed to comprise 2 husbands, at least 8 and possibly 20 would-be suitors lured by 'Lonely Hearts' advertisements, 3 women and 3 children.

MURDERESS

In 1486 at Tenochtitlan, near Mexico City, 20,000 Aztecs had their hearts cut out in a ritual ceremony.

GREATEST MASS MURDERS

At the S.S. camp at Auschwitz, Silesia, where 4,000,000 people were exterminated in 1943-44, the greatest number killed in a day was 24,000.

SUICIDE

The country with the highest suicide rate (based on latest available figures) is Alaska with 24.8 per 100,000.

EXECUTIONS

MOST CAPITAL
OFFENSES

There are, as of 1956, a total of 31 separate capital offenses throughout the United States. The state with the greatest number is Georgia with 14—arson, burning railway bridges, castration, dueling, dynamiting, foeticide, insurrection, kidnaping, lynching, murder, perjury on capital trial, rape, train-wrecking and treason.

COMMONEST
METHOD

The most commonly used method of execution in the United States is electrocution which is prescribed in 22 states; 8 states employ lethal gas, 7 hanging and Utah is alone giving an option between hanging and shooting.

EARLIEST

The earliest recorded execution among white settlers in the United States was that of John Billington for murder at Plymouth, Mass., on September 30th, 1630. The earliest judicial electrocution was of William Kemmler at Auburn Prison, New York, on August 6th, 1890, for the murder of Matilda Zeigler 495 days before.

MOST AND
LEAST IN
A YEAR

National statistics on executions have only been collated for the 26 years since 1930. The greatest number of executions carried out since that year was 199 in 1935. The lowest total of any year has been 62 in 1953.

MOST AND
LEAST BY
STATES

In the period January 1st, 1930 to January 1st, 1956, there have been 3,409 male and 30 female executions under civil authority. Of the 42 states whose statutes provide for the death penalty the greatest number have been carried out in Georgia with 322 and the least in New Hampshire and South Dakota each with a single execution.

OLDEST AND
YOUNGEST

The ages of executed prisoners have only been collated for the 19 years since 1937. The youngest person to suffer the death penalty since that time was the 14-year-old negro boy murderer, George J. Stinney, Jr., who was sentenced in South Carolina on April 24th, 1944 and electrocuted 83 days later on July 16th, 1944. The oldest person to suffer execution was the murderer James Stephens (born December 6th, 1866) who was sentenced to death on January 5th, 1940 and eventually executed in the State Penitentiary, Canon City, Colorado, by administration of lethal gas 531 days later on June 20th, 1941, when aged 74 years 6 month.

Official records still show the age of the murderer Martin Sullivan, electrocuted in Pennsylvania on March 21st, 1938, to be 74. A subsequent affidavit sworn by his son attests, however, that Sullivan was born on October 16th, 1869 and was hence only 69 years and 5 months at the time of his execution.

The longest recorded prison sentence is one of 300 years awarded on March 21st, 1951 in the Western District Court of the U. S. in Oklahoma to William Edward Cook. The charge was upon 5 counts of kidnaping upon which he received 60 years for each count to run consecutively. After having been received at Alcatraz to commence his 300 year term, Cook was sentenced for murder in the first degree and executed by electrocution at San Quentin State Prison, California, on December 12th, 1952.

LONGEST JAIL TERM

The worst year in the 20th century was 1901 with 130 lynchings (105 negroes, 25 white) and 1952 was the first year with no reported cases.

LYNCHING

The greatest robbery on record was of the German National Gold Reserves in Bavaria by a combine of U. S. military personnel and German civilians in June, 1945. A total of 730 gold bars valued at $9,878,400 together with 6 sacks of bank notes and 25 boxes of platinum bars and precious stones disappeared in transit but none of those responsible have been brought to trial.

BIGGEST ROBBERIES

The biggest "inside job" was that at the National City Bank of New York from which the Assistant Manager, Richard Crowe, removed $883,660. He was arrested on April 11th, 1949.

The greatest robbery in U. S. crime history was that from Brink's Inc., at the North Terminal Garage, Prince St., Boston, Mass., on January 17th, 1950. The total haul was $2,775,395.12 of which $1,218,211.29 was in cash. The robbery was effected by Anthony Pino and 10 confederates who were exposed by an admission made in January, 1956.

LEGAL AND LITIGATION

The longest statute on the Federal Statute Book is the United States Code enacted as law by the 69th Congress on June 30th, 1926, and comprising 2,125 pages in 44 Stat., Part I. There are a number of single sentence statutes. An example of one such, running to less than 30 words, is 69 Stat. 492 or Public Law 228 approved on August 4th, 1955, to increase the mileage allowance of United States marshalls.

LONGEST AND SHORTEST STATUTE

The highest amount ever demanded as bail by any court in the world was the $8,000,000 (£2.85 million) for Seth Ramkrishna Dalmia at New Delhi in 1953, charged with embezzlement of over £2 million of the funds of his own Bharat Insurance Company.

BAIL

It has been recorded that, on trial in Sheffield, England, on December 19th, 1922, Mrs. Theresa Vaughan (or Vaughn), 24, confessed to 61 bigamous marriages in the space of five years. A male record of 72 has been noted.

BIGGEST BIGAMIST

The greatest amount paid to an informer on income tax delinquency is $76,000 paid by the Inland Revenue Service to an undisclosed individual in 1949-50. Payments are limited to 10% of the amount recovered as a direct result of information laid.

HIGHEST REWARD

The record amount ever paid in a divorce settlement is $5,750,000 (£2,053,570) by Winthrop R. Rockefeller to his wife, Barbara Sears

DIVORCE SETTLEMENT

'Bobo' Rockefeller, 37, on June 19th, 1954. The amount was paid in the form of $4 million to a trust, $750,000 in cash and $1 million in trust for the son of the marriage, W. Paul Rockefeller, aged 5.

PRISONS
LARGEST
IN WORLD

The highest capacity prison in the world is Lubianka Jail, Moscow, with an estimated turnover of 80,000 prisoners in a single week. The largest penal camp in the world is the complex of concentration camps at Vorkuta in Northern Russia which was opened in 1943. Recent estimates are that there are 223,000 prisoners working in 40 mines guarded by 12,000 militia.

SMALLEST

The smallest prison in the world is usually cited as that on the Isle of Sark, Channel Islands, which has a capacity of two.

U.S. PRISONS
EARLIEST

The earliest prison built in the U. S. was the Nantucket Prison, Mass., completed in 1676.

OLDEST

The oldest state prison in the U. S. is the Virginia Penitentiary in Richmond, Virginia, opened 1797.

LARGEST

The largest prison in the U. S. is the State Prison of Southern Michigan at Jackson, Michigan, which has a normal capacity for 6,100 prisoners.

3. *Humanities*

RELIGIONS and BELIEFS

LARGEST
RELIGIONS

Religious statistics are necessarily the roughest approximations. The test of adherence to a religion varies widely in rigor, while many individuals, particularly in China, belong to two or more religions.

Christianity is the world's prevailing religion with at least 750 million and probably an additional 250 million Protestants who are not in membership with the Church of their baptism. It would appear that the total of 200 million practicing and 250 million non-practicing Protestants is slightly outnumbered by the 460 million who have received baptism into the Roman Catholic Church. The title of the largest non-Christian religion lies between the Confucians and the Mohammedans, each with over 300 million adherents.

U.S.A.

The largest single religious organization in the United States is the Roman Catholic Church with, in 1956, 32,500,000 members.

The largest Protestant groups are the Methodist Church with 9,151,000 members and the Southern Baptist Convention with 7,883,-000.

The National Council of the Churches of Christ in the United States represents 35,000,000 members of 30 Protestant and Eastern Orthodox church bodies.

SMALLEST SECT

The smallest religion sect in the country is The Society of Primitive Friends with a latest reported strength of nine members.

RICHEST
CHURCH

The richest Christian Church in the United States is the Methodist Church which is organized in 22 groups with a total of 11.7 million members and assets worth $2,700 million.

The largest church in the world is St. Peter's in the Vatican City, Rome. The length of the basilica, measured from the apse, is 611 feet 4 inches. The area is 18,110 square yards. The inner diameter of the famous dome, the largest in the world, is 137 feet 9 inches and its center is 390 feet 5 inches high. The external height is 457 feet 9 inches.

LARGEST CHURCH

The oldest standing Protestant edifice in the United States and the only remaining example of Colonial Gothic Church is St. Luke's Protestant Episcopal Church near Smithfield, Virginia, built in 1632.

OLDEST CHURCH

The highest church spire in the world is that of the Protestant Cathedral of Ulm in Germany. The building is early Gothic and was begun in 1377. The tower, in the center of the west façade, was not finally completed until 1890 and is 528 feet high. See Photo No. 8, page 42.

HIGHEST SPIRE

The shortest interval that has elapsed between the death of a Saint and his canonization was in the case of St. Peter, the Martyr (born in Verona in 1206), who was murdered at Borlasina on April 5th, 1252. Struck on the head by a hatchet, he was unable to speak but dipped his finger in his blood and wrote "Credo in Deum" on the dusty road. He was canonized the following year.

The other extreme is represented by St. Bernard of Thiron, 20 years Prior of St. Sabinus, who died in 1117 and was made a Saint in 1861— 744 years later.

SAINTS MOST and LEAST RAPIDLY CANONIZED

The first U. S. citizen to be canonized was Mother Francis Xavier Cabrini (1850-1917) on July 7th, 1946.

EARLIEST U.S. SAINT

Hagiologists have not yet succeeded in identifying all the Saints but it is established that the commonest of the Saints' names is Mary which is sometimes borne by male Saints.

COMMONEST SAINT'S NAME

Of the four patron Saints of the British Isles the earliest was St. George of England who was martyred at Nicomedia on April 23rd, 303 A.D. He was not adopted as Patron Saint till the reign of Edward III (1327-1377), whereas St. Andrew has been recognized as the Patron Saint of Scotland since the 8th century.

EARLIEST PATRON SAINT

The oldest stained glass in the world is certain figures of the Prophets in a window in the cathedral of Augsburg, Germany, dating from the 11th century.

STAINED GLASS OLDEST

The oldest stained glass window in the U. S. is that at Christ Church, Pelham Manor, N. Y., designed by William Jay Bolton and John Bolton in 1843.

OLDEST IN U.S.

The earliest dated Christian tombstone is a limestone stele showing a *tau* cross (the earliest Christian symbol) at Kutahia (Kutahya), Turkey, erected to Eutyches of Gediz dated 179-180 A.D.

EARLIEST TOMBSTONE

The largest crowd in history was that which assembled at the conference of the rivers Jumna and Ganges for the Hindu festival of Kumbh-Mela at Allahabad on January 31st, 1954. The police estimated the size of the concourse, of whom 400 were trampled to death, at 45 lahks or 4,500,000.

LARGEST CROWD

LARGEST
EVANGELICAL
MEETING

The largest attendance ever recorded at an evangelical meeting is 110,000 at Wembley Stadium, London, England, on May 21st, 1955, at the concluding meeting of Dr. Billy Graham's Greater London Crusade.

PAINTING

EARLIEST

The earliest known painting is probably the Stag's head, painted by finger tip, in the La Pileta Cave at Benaojan, Malaga, Spain, belonging to the Upper Palaeolithic period 30,000 to 15,000 B.C. Ceiling paintings in the Pech-Merle Cave at Lot, France, also belong to this period.

LARGEST

John Banvard's (1815-1891) "Panorama of the Mississippi," completed in 1846, showing the river scene for 1,200 miles in a strip 15,000 feet in length and 12 feet wide is the largest painting in the world with an area of over 4¼ acres. The gigantic canvas, which was housed on rollers, is believed to have been destroyed in a barn fire at Coldspring Harbor, Long Island, New York, in 1896.

The largest flat painting ever executed was the "Panthéon de la Guerre" (just over 400 feet long by over 40 feet high) showing the life-size portraits of 6,000 1914-18 war heroes. The work occupied four years with as many as 130 artists contributing.

The largest Old Master is "Il Paradiso" by Jacopo Robusti (Tintoretto) (1518-1594) and his son Domenico on Wall "E" in the Sala del Maggior Consiglio in the Palazzo Ducale in Venice, Italy. The work was completed between 1587 and 1590 and is 72 feet 2 inches long and 22 feet 11½ inches high.

HIGHEST
PRICED

The highest price ever fetched by a painting in public auction was the $360,000 bid for Gainsborough's "Harvest Wagon" or "Hay Wain" in New York on April 20th, 1928.

The highest price established for a private treaty sale is that for the altar piece "Alba Madonna" by the Italian Raphael (1483-1520), purchased by Andrew W. Mellon, from the Soviet Government in July, 1930.

The exact price has not been disclosed but is known to have been in excess of $1,000,000. The picture was transferred from the former Imperial Gallery, The Hermitage, Leningrad, and is now housed in the National Gallery of Art, Washington, D. C.

The highest price paid for a painting in the life-time of an artist is $70,000 for "Dancers at the Bar" by the French impressionist, Hilaire Degas (1834-1917), just before his death.

LANGUAGE and THE WRITTEN WORD

EARLIEST
LANGUAGE

It is possible that formalized language dates from the Azilian (France) culture of 15,000 B.C. The oldest known formally written language is Sumerian dating from 5,000 B.C.

COMMONEST
LANGUAGE

The language spoken by more people than any other is Chinese, including Mandarin, to an estimated 475 million. Excluding the Indic group of 12 major tongues, the next most commonly spoken language is English in the case of 265 million.

In the British Isles there are eight languages: — English, Scots Gaelic, Welsh, Irish Gaelic, Manx, Romany (Gypsy) and Jersey and Guernsey *patois*. Of these English is, of course, predominant, and Manx has almost followed Cornish (1777) into extinction.

The K'ang-hsi dictionary of Chinese characters has 40,000 entries. Of the eighty-four meanings of the fourth tone of "i" in Chinese the same sound includes "dress," "hiccup" or "licentious." The written language provides 92 different characters of "i⁴" so that the meaning intended identifies itself.

MOST COMPLEX

The longest word in the Oxford English Dictionary is floccinaucinihilipilification (29 letters) meaning estimating as worthless. It was first used in 1741 and later by Sir Walter Scott. The longest regularly formed word is antidisestablishmentarianism (28 letters) coined in 1869 to describe the religious faction in England opposed to the separation of Church and State and used by Prime Minister William Ewart Gladstone. The longest word in Shakespeare is the nonce-word honorificabilitudinitatibus in Love's Labour Lost, Act V, Scene I.

LONGEST WORDS

In a book published late in the 18th century by Dr. Strother, a manufactured word of 53 letters is used to describe the qualities of the spa waters at Bristol, England—Aequeosalinocalcalinocetaceoaluminosocupreovitriolic.

The longest place-name in the world is the 83-letter New Zealand village Taumatawhakatangihangakoauotamateaturipukakapikimaungahoronukupokaiwhenuakitanatahu in the Southern Hawkes' Bay district of the North Island. The name, in Maori, means "the brow of the hill where Tamatea, the man with the big knee who slid, climbed and swallowed mountains, the discoverer of land, played his flute to his loved one." See Photo No. 9, page 42.

PLACE-NAMES

Reputedly the longest place-name in the 48 states is Lake Chargoggugoggmonchauggagoggchaubunagungamaug near Webster, Mass.

The 44 lettered name of this two square mile lake is derived from the Algonquin Indian "You fish on your side, we fish on our side; nobody fish in the middle." The standardized version has been reduced to Lake Chaubunagungamaug by the U. S. board on Geographic Names.

The name Summit is borne by 70 places in the United States, but of these many are merely shipping points and railroad stops and only 11 warrant a post office. Both Franklin and Clinton are listed 27 times.

MOST COMMON

The longest surname in the English-speaking world was the six barrelled one borne by the late Major L. S. D. O. F. Tollemache Tollemache de Orellana Plantagenet Tollemache Tollemache, born 1884, died of wounds in France February 20th, 1917.

LONGEST PERSONAL NAMES

In Burma there is a surname written apostrophe "aitch" or 'H.

The commonest name in the world is Mahommed which can be spelled in many ways. The commonest given name in the English-speaking world is John.

COMMONEST

The commonest surname in the United States is Smith, which is borne by an estimated 1,504,000 persons.

LONGEST
TITLE

The world's longest title is borne by Lieutenant-General His Highness Shri 108 Maharajadhiraj, Raj Rajeshwar Shri Maharja-i-Rajgan Maharaja Sir Yadvindra Singh Mahendra Bahadur, Yadu Vanshavatans Bhatti Kul Bhushan, Rajpramukh of Patiala and East Punjab States Union since its formation in August, 1948. The appellation "Shri 108" indicates that in its fullest form this title contains the word "Shri" 108 times.

OLDEST
TEXTS

The oldest known written text is the cuneiform expression of Sumerian speech of about the 5th millennium B.C. In 1952, some clay tablets of this writing were unearthed from the Sumerian temple of Inanna at Erech (c.3,500 B.C.). The earliest known vellum document is Demosthene's *De Falsa Legatione* of the second century A.D.

BOOKS

OLDEST
PRINTED

The oldest surviving printed book is in the British Museum and is a 16-foot long Buddhist scroll Diamond Sutra of 868 A.D. The earliest known book of folded pages is another Buddhist work dated 949 A.D.

MECHANICALLY
PRINTED

Recent opinion is that the 192-leaved Constance Missal (Missale Speciale Constantiense), from Basle, Switzerland, the first of the three known copies of which was rediscovered in 1880, may have priority over the more generally accepted earliest mechanically printed book— the 42-line Gutenberg Bible of c.1455. The earliest dated printed work is the Psalter completed by Fust and Schoeffer on August 14th, 1457.

SMALLEST

The smallest book in the world is a handwritten one — Poems by Edgar Guest. It was written by Burt Randle in 1942. It is less than 1/8 inch square and is held by a metal clasp.

The smallest printed books in the world were probably those produced by N. V. Lettergietery "Amsterdam"—a firm of Dutch typefounders on the occasion of their 100th year of business. They are approximately 4.1 mm. (5/32 inch) square, leather-bound, stamped in gold, and contain 20 pages. On the first page is a reproduction of the Lord's Prayer.

The smallest book in the world printed from movable type was made by Salmin Brothers of Padua in Italy in 1896—The Galileo a Madama Cristina di Lorena. It has 207 pages and a portrait of Galileo as a frontispiece. The size of the book is 5/8 inch high and 7/16 inch wide.

HIGHEST
PRICED

The highest prices ever paid for printed books are for Gutenberg bibles, a copy of which crossed the Atlantic in 1954 under a private treaty sale for $200,000.

The highest price for a printed book at auction is $151,000 paid in New York on January 28th, 1947, for the Prince-Crowinshield-Stevens-Brinley-Vanderbilt-Whitney copy of the Bay Psalm Book "The Whole Booke of Psalmes," printed by Stephen Day in Cambridge, Mass., in 1640. The book of which some 1,700 copies were originally printed is now in the Yale University library.

The most expensively bound book is the roll of honor for the Seventh Regiment of New York, valued at $42,000. Bound in London, England, by Messrs. Sangorski and Sutcliffe Ltd., 1955, the covers carry the arms of Great Britain, the United States, France and Belgium, fashioned in gold, diamonds, rubies and sapphires. See Photo No. 11, page 59.

MOST
EXPENSIVE
BINDING

The most prolific writer for whom a word count has been published is Grantland Rice (1880-1954). He estimated in his book, "The Tumult and the Shouting," that, as the United States leading sportswriter, he had written over 67,000,000 words.

MOST PROLIFIC
AUTHORS

Of authors, the one with the greatest total of published words is Denise Robins (Mrs. O'Neill Pearson) of London. She has written 110 published novels since 1924, including such best-sellers as "The Long Shadow" and "Strange Meeting," hundreds of novelettes, short stories and articles amounting to 40 million words.

The author whose writings cover the longest period is Douglas Fawcett, whose poem, "The Wrath of Ana," was published when he was 13. He is still writing at the age of 90, a span of 77 years.

LONGEST
LITERARY SPAN

The principal book publishing country in the world is the United Kingdom where, during 1955, 14,192 new titles and 5,770 reprints were produced, a total of 19,962 titles.

PUBLISHING

BIBLE

The oldest known Bible is the Yonan manuscript of the complete New Testament in Syriac-Aramaic of c.350 A.D. presented to the U. S. Library of Congress on March 27th, 1955.

OLDEST

The longest book in the Bible is the Book of Isaiah with 66 chapters and the shortest is the Second Epistle of John with 13 verses.

LONGEST and
SHORTEST
BOOKS

Of the 150 Psalms, the longest is the 119th with 176 verses and the shortest the 117th with two verses. The shortest sentence in the whole Bible is in the Gospel according to St. John, Chapter II, verse 35, consisting of the two words "Jesus wept." The total number of letters in the Bible is 3,566,480 or, with the Apocrypha, 4,291,480.

POETS LAUREATE

The earliest official Poet Laureate was John Dryden (1631-1700) appointed in April, 1668. It is recorded that Henry I (1100-1135) had a King's Versifier named Wale.

EARLIEST

The youngest Poet Laureate was Laurence Eusden (1688-1730) who received the bays on December 24th, 1718 at the age of 30 years and 3 months. The greatest age at which a poet has succeeded is 73, in the case of William Wordsworth (1770-1850) in April, 1843. The longest lived Laureate was Colley Cibber who was born November 6th, 1671 and who died after a laureateship of 27 years on December 12th, 1757, aged 86 years, 1 month. The longest which any poet has worn the laurel is the 41 years 11 months of Lord Tennyson (1809-1892) who succeeded in November, 1850, and who died in office on October 6th, 1892.

YOUNGEST
and OLDEST

MAPS

OLDEST

The oldest map in the world is a cadastral clay tablet of c.2,200 B.C., depicting areas for land taxation, preserved in Istanbul Museum, Turkey. The oldest papyrus map is the Turin Papyrus of an unidentified Egyptian gold mine dated 1,320 B.C.

The earliest representation of Great Britain is that by Ptolemy dated c.150 A.D. The oldest native map of the British Isles is the Anglo-Saxon map from Battle Abbey dated c.980 A.D., now in the British Museum.

Atlas

Creator of the earliest atlas was the Greek Ptolemy (90-168 A.D.) probably c.150 A.D. His work was first printed in Bologna, Italy, in 1477.

The best mapped area in the world is the British Isles in which the Ordnance Survey was founded in 1791 and began to produce maps on the largest scale of 25 inches to the mile in 1853.

BEST
MAPPED

Only 40% of the surface (13 of the 48 states) of Continental United States is mapped by modern methods. The best mapped state is Kentucky, which has been completely mapped to a scale of 2,000 feet to the inch at a cost of $6.36 million.

OLDEST
NATIONAL
FLAG

The oldest national flag is that of Denmark. The Danneborg with its white cross on a red field was adopted c.1218 A.D. after the battle of Lindanissa in Estonia. The American flag was formally approved by Congress on June 14th, 1777 and was first flown from the U.S.S. Ranger in Portsmouth Harbor, N. H., 20 days later on July 4th, 1777.

LARGEST
FLAG

The largest flag in the world is the Stars and Stripes annually displayed on the Woodward side of J. L. Hudson Company's store in Detroit, Michigan. The flag, 104 feet by 235 feet and weighing ¾ ton, was unfurled on June 14th, 1949. The 48 stars are 5½ feet high and each stripe is 8 feet wide. See Photo No. 12, page 59.

OLDEST
FLAG

The oldest Stars and Stripes in existence is that preserved in Bennington Historical Museum in Old Bennington, Vermont, dating from the 18th century.

LIBRARIES

LARGEST

The largest library in the world is the United States Library of Congress, Washington, D. C. It contains 33,152,852 items, including 10,-155,307 volumes and pamphlets, 14,282,594 manuscripts, 2,307,534 maps and views, 2,002,277 volumes and pieces of music and 438,881 gramophone records.

The world's largest medical library is the Surgeon General's Library in Washington, D. C.

NEWSPAPERS

OLDEST

The "Berrow's Worcester Journal," published in Worcester, England, enjoys the distinction of being the oldest continuously produced newspaper in the world. It was founded in 1690 and has appeared weekly since June, 1709. Of daily 'papers, the oldest is "Lloyd's List," the shipping intelligence bulletin of Lloyd's, London, established in 1734.

The earliest newspaper published in the United States was the 8 x 14½ inch broadside "The Present State of the New England Affairs," in Cambridge, Mass., in 1689.

The oldest United States newspaper is the Hartford, Connecticut, Daily Courant (current circulation 94,000), which was established in 1764.

Of the 316 daily morning newspapers in the U. S., Pennsylvania has most with 28, and of the 1,456 daily evening newspapers, also the most with 103.

Of the 541 Sunday newspapers in the United States, Texas has the most with 76 and also the largest overall number of newspapers with 108.

The total circulation of 1,760 English language newspapers is 56.2 million. The highest circulation in the United States is 3,551,000 for the Sunday edition of the New York News, the week-day edition of which also has the record daily circulation of 2,136,000.

The most massive single issue of a newspaper yet published was the 516 page edition of the New York Times of May 6th, 1956.

The largest page size of any newspaper is the 30-inch by 22-inch of the "Nantucket Inquirer and Mirror," published in Rhode Island.

The highest circulation of any newspaper in the world is that of the London Sunday 'paper "News of the World," printed in Bouverie Street, London, which rises to 9,000,000 copies with an estimated readership of over 19,000,000. The 'paper first appeared on October 1st, 1843, and averaged 12,971 copies a week in its first year and surpassed the million mark in 1905. To provide sufficient pulp for the 62,400 five-mile reels, over half a million trees have to be felled each year.

The highest circulation of any daily paper is that of the London "Daily Mirror," founded in 1903, which has attained 4¾ million copies daily. The highest circulation of an evening paper in the world is the London "Evening News," established 1881, which reached an average daily net sale of 1,752,166 in the first six months of 1950.

The largest circulation of any periodical is that of "The Reader's Digest." There are 28 international editions in 12 languages (circulation over 7,000,000) which, added to the U. S. home edition (circulation 10,500,000), make a total monthly circulation of 17½ million.

The highest circulation of any weekly in the world is that of the United Kingdom's "Radio Times." The average print order is 8,223,000 copies a week. The materials used include 885 tons of paper, 9½ tons of ink and 355 miles of stapling wire per issue. The full page advertising rate, facing matter, is $11,200, the highest in the United Kingdom.

The largest index in the world is that maintained by the Social Security Administration of the Department of Health, Education and Welfare, Washington, D. C., known as the National Employee Index. It occupies 27,800 square feet of floor space and contains 155,593,368 names.

MUSIC

OLDEST

The world's oldest surviving musical notation is a Sumerian hymn recorded on a clay tablet dated c.800 B.C. but it has defied interpretation. Musical history is, however, able to be traced back to the 3rd millenium B.C. when in Chinese Temple music the yellow bell (huang chung) had a recognized standard musical tone.

INSTRUMENTS

The harps and flutes of ancient Egypt are known to have dated from at least as early as 4,000 B.C.

LARGEST
ORGAN
World

The largest musical instrument ever constructed is the Atlantic City Auditorium Organ, Atlantic City, New Jersey, U.S.A. Completed in 1930, this heroic instrument has two consoles (one with seven manuals and another movable one with five), 1,225 speaking stops and 33,112 pipes ranging from 3/16th inch to 64 feet in length. It is powered with blower motors of 365 h.p. and cost $500,000 (£178,600).

LOUDEST
STOP

The loudest organ stop in the world is the State Trumpeter stop of the organ in the Cathedral of St. John the Divine, New York City. It is operated by a pressure of 50 lbs. per square inch and has 5 times the volume of the loudest locomotive horns.

LARGEST
ORGAN PIPE

The largest organ pipe in the world is the straight 64 foot pipe in the organ of Sydney Town Hall, Australia. It emits a "note" of 4 cycles per second.

ONE MAN
BAND

The most complex "one-man band" ever constructed was the "Panomonico" built by the Austrian, Karl Waelzel. It incorporated 150 flutes, 150 flageolets, 50 oboes, 18 trumpets, 5 fanfares, 2 timbals and 3 large drums. It was bought by Archduke Charles of Austria (1771-1847) for 100,000 French francs for the express purpose of annoying people at his court.

The largest stringed instrument ever constructed was a pantaleon with 270 strings stretched over 50 square feet used by George Noel in 1767.

LARGEST
DRUM

The largest drum in the world is that owned by the University of Texas Longhorn Band made in Elkhart, Texas. It is 25 feet ¾ inch in circumference and is mounted on wheels and is towed by a tractor.

The most musicians required to operate a single instrument were the six required to play the gigantic orchestrian, known as the Appollonican, built in 1816 and played till 1840.

The largest double bass ever constructed was the 10 foot high octo-bass built by J. B. Vuillaume (1798-1875) in c.1845. The stretch being too great for any musician's finger-span the stopping was effected by foot levers. It was played in London in 1851.

The longest Swiss alpenhorns, which are of wooden construction, attain 14 feet in length and are of pine.

The earliest piano in existence is the Cristofori piano built in Florence in 1721 and now preserved in the Metropolitan Museum of Art, New York.

The vastest orchestra ever assembled was that for the World Peace Jubilee staged in Boston on June 17th, 1872, with 2,000 musicians supported by a choir of 20,000 voices. Johann Strauss conducted this array in a 'rendition' of "The Beautiful Blue Danube."

ORCHESTRA

The extremes of orchestral instruments range between the highest represented by the piccolo or octave flute with 4,752 cycles per second and the lowest with the double bassoon as used in Haydn's "Creation" with 32 cycles a second. The highest note on a standard pianoforte is 4,096 cycles.

HIGHEST and LOWEST NOTES

The limitations of the human ear are generally between 16 cycles and 18,000 cycles such that a note three octaves above the top note of a piano would be inaudible.

The oldest conductor in musical history was Arturo Toscanini (born March 25th, 1867) who conducted the N.B.C. Symphony Orchestra at Carnegie Hall, New York City, for the last time on April 4th, 1954, 10 days after his 87th birthday, so ending a 68 year long career.

CONDUCTORS OLDEST and YOUNGEST

The youngest recorded conductor was Willy Ferrero (1907-1954) of Rome who conducted an orchestra in Paris in 1911 aged 4.

BELLS

The heaviest bell in the world is the Tsar Kolokol cast in 1733 in Moscow. It weighs approximately 193 tons and is 22 feet 8 inches in diameter and about 20 feet high, and its greatest thickness is 24 inches. The bell is cracked and a fragment, weighing about 11 tons, broken from it. The bell now stands on a platform near the Kremlin in Moscow.

HEAVIEST

The heaviest bell ever cast in England and the biggest tuned bell in the world is the bourdon bell of the Laura Spelman Rockefeller Memorial carillon, Riverside Church, New York City, which weighs 18 tons 5 cwts. 1 qr. 18 lb. and is 10 feet 2 inches in diameter.

The oldest bell in the world is reputed to be that found by Layard in the Babylonian Palace of Nimrod and is approximately 3,000 years old.

OLDEST

The biggest carillon in the world is the Laura Spelman Rockefeller Memorial carillon, Riverside Church, New York City, U.S.A. It consists of 72 bells with a total weight of approximately 102 tons.

BIGGEST CARILLON

Eight bells have been rung to their full "extent" (40,320 changes) only once, in 1751, by relays of thirteen bell ringers working continuously for twenty hours. In modern competition rules, set by the Central Council of Church Bell Ringers, relays are forbidden and under these conditions the best that has been done so far is 21,600 changes in 12 hours 56 minutes by a Cheshire team at St. Chad's, Winsford, Cheshire, England, on November 4th, 1950.

BELL RINGING

COMPOSER

The most prolific composer of all-time was Filippo de Monte (c.1521-1603) who composed 1,000 madrigals, of which 600 were published, together with 300 motets and other work.

MOST PROLIFIC

MOST
RAPID

Among composers of the classical period the most prolific was Wolfgang Mozart (1756-1791) who produced 600 operas, operettas, piano and string quartet concertos, violin sonatas, divertimenti, serenades, motets, masses and litanies of which only 70 were published before he died, aged 35. His opera "The Clemency of Titus" (1791) was written in 18 days while three symphonic masterpieces "Symphony in E flat," "Symphony in G minor" and the "Jupiter Symphony in C" were written in the space of 42 days in 1788. His overture "Don Giovanni" was written in full score at one sitting.

OLDEST

The longest lived of any major composer is Jean Sibelius of Finland, writer of *"Finlandia"* and *"Tapiola,"* who was born on December 8th, 1865, and in 1954 surpassed the eighty-eight years of the Italian Guiseppe Verdi (1813-1901).

OPERA

EARLIEST

The earliest real opera, "La Dafne," drama by Ottavia Rinuccini, set to music by Jacopo Peri, was produced in Florence, Italy, in 1597. The earliest comic opera was "Chi Saffre, Speri" by G. Rospigliosi (later Pope Clement IX, 1667-69) and music by Marazzoli and Mazzochi.

LONGEST

The longest of all operas is "Parsifal" by Wilhelm Richard Wagner (1813-1883) first produced in Bayreuth in 1882. Its performance requires 4 hours, 40 minutes. The longest aria is that of Brunhilde in her immolation scene from the "Götterdämmerung" from Wagner's Ring Cycle.

THEATRE

LONGEST
RUNS

The longest run of any show at one theater anywhere in the world is by the play "The Drunkard," written by W. H. Smith and a "Gentleman." First produced, as a moral lesson, by the American showman P. T. Barnum in 1843, it was not used commercially again until the Theatre Mart in Los Angeles, California, revived it on July 6th, 1933. From that date, it ran continuously, one show a night, until September 6th, 1953. Starting on September 7th, 1953, a new musical adaptation of "The Drunkard," called the "Wayward Way," started to play alternate nights with the original version and is still playing. During this time, more than two million people have seen the play at over eight thousand consecutive nightly performances. Two members of the cast, Miss Marie Duvall and Mr. Neely Edwards, are still playing the parts they originated more than twenty years ago.

The longest run on Broadway of any play was the 3,224 performances of "Life with Father."

The longest run of any musical on Broadway was "Oklahoma," with 2,248 performances.

SHORTEST
RUN

There are examples of productions whose first night and last night have clashed. A recent case was "The Starcross Story," by Diana Morgan which had a one day run on Broadway on January 13th, 1954.

LONGEST
CHORUS LINE

The world's longest chorus line are New York Radio City Music Hall's Rockettes. Thirty-six girls dance precision routines across the 144-

11. The Roll of Honor of the Seventh Regiment of New York. See p. 53.
12. The largest flag in the world. See p. 54.
13. The Radio City Rockettes, the longest chorus line in the world. See p. 58.
14. Mt. Lassen, the U. S. only active volcano. See p. 67.
15. The spiral nebula Andromeda, the remotest heavenly body visible to the naked eye. See p. 87.

foot wide stage. The whole troupe, which won the *Grand Prix* in Paris in July, 1937, is forty-six strong but ten girls are always on alternating vacation. See Photo No. 13, page 59.

EDUCATION

ILLITERACY

Literacy is variously defined as "ability to read simple subjects" and "ability to read and write a simple letter." The looseness of definition precludes anything more than approximations but the world percentage of illiteracy has been reliably estimated at between 45 per cent and 55 per cent, roughly 1,250 million people.

The continent with the greatest proportion of illiterates is Africa, where more than 170 million people—approximately 80 per cent of the continent's total can neither read nor write.

Mozambique has the highest illiteracy rate anywhere in the world with 99 per cent of all age groups of its people being unable even to read.

This figure is matched, although measured on a different basis, by the Somaliland Protectorate where only one person in every hundred can read and write.

Of those countries for which figures are available, Sweden records the highest literacy rate. Less than one in a 1,000 is unable to read and write.

UNIVERSITY OLDEST

Probably the oldest educational institution in the world is the Egyptian university of Al-Azhar. According to the Egyptian Education Bureau, Al-Azhar was first established as an academy in 989 A.D. and evidence suggests that such subjects as mathematics, astronomy, medicine and geography were taught there at that time.

The earliest precisely dated foundation of a University is that of the University of Naples which received a charter from Frederick II in 1224.

LARGEST

The largest university building in the world is the Lomonosov University of Moscow on the Lenin hills, which stands 787 feet, has 32 stories and contains 40,000 rooms. It was constructed in 1949-1953.

The tallest U. S. university building is the 535 feet high, 42 stories "Cathedral of Learning" at the University of Pittsburgh, Pennsylvania.

HIGHEST ENROLLMENT

The largest college-grade enrollment in U. S. history was attained in the fall of 1955 at 2,721,000 (1,784,000 men and 937,000 women). It is estimated that at the end of the academic year 1955-56 the total will surpass 3 million for the first time.

LARGEST U.S. UNIVERSITY

The university with the largest 1955 enrollment figure was the University of California, Berkeley, California, founded in 1868. The figure for all campuses was 38,594. The peak enrollment was 43,426 in the fall semester of 1949. The peak for teaching staff reached in 1955 was 5,290.

LARGEST SCHOOL

The largest public secondary day school in the United States is Erasmus Hall High School, Brooklyn, N. Y., with 5,974 pupils. An enrollment of 10,476 was recorded by James Monroe High School, New York, in 1938.

The oldest fraternity is Phi Beta Kappa, founded on December 5th, 1776, at William and Mary College at Williamsburg, Virginia (see below). The oldest fraternity with a continuous existence is the Kappa Alpha Society, founded on November 26th, 1825.

The largest fraternity is Phi Beta Kappa with a current membership of 120,000. It was a secret fraternity with origin dating back to 1776 but after discontinuous activity became in 1883 an honor society. The largest college fraternity is Sigma Alpha Epsilon (founded 1856), with a membership of 81,000.

The oldest sorority is the 40,000 strong Alpha Delta Pi, founded in 1851, with its national headquarters in Atlanta, Georgia.

The largest sorority is the 81,800 strong Beta Sigma Omicron, founded in 1888, with its national headquarters in Chicago, Ill.

Accurate figures as to the total number of people who listened to the British B.B.C. broadcasts or re-broadcasts of the 1953 Coronation are, of course, impossible to obtain, but it is authoritatively estimated that well over 100 million people viewed or listened to the B.B.C. programs, broadcast by the B.B.C. and those re-broadcast by the major United States networks and by over 2,000 stations throughout the world.

Probably the world's most widespread radio program is "The Lutheran Hour." It is sponsored by the Lutheran Laymen's League, a body of approximately eighty thousand who form an agency within the Missouri Synod of the Lutheran Church in the United States. It is transmitted by 1,200 radio stations in sixty-five countries, and the program is broadcast regularly in fifty-six languages.

The Lutheran Church also sponsor a television program which, carried as a public service by 260 television stations, is the most widespread television program in the world.

The largest prize won in any television show is the $100,000 awarded on N.B.C.'s "The Big Surprise." The first successful contestant was Mrs. Ethel Park Richardson, 72, of Los Angeles, who correctly answered questions of American folklore on December 10th, 1955. The 'take home' value after deduction for taxes was about $28,000. The potential for greater amounts exist in C.B.S.'s "$64,000 Challenge" program in which quiz category champions in the "$64,000 Question" may return to win further amounts in defense of their titles. In the General Motors (Frigidaire Division) sponsored program "Do You Trust Your Wife," contestants may win an initial $1,200 and thereafter $100 a week for a year ($5,200 per annum) for as many years as the couple return to win the weekly Trust Fund question.

The youngest television actor ever was Gordon Campbell Kerr, who participated in a 49-station N.B.C. transmission on December 2nd, 1952, when his delivery by Caesarean section from his mother, Mrs. John Kerr, was telecast.

MUSICAL BEST SELLERS

PHONOGRAPH
RECORDS

The greatest seller of any phonograph record to date is Irving Berlin's "White Christmas" which has now sold 18,000,000 copies. This figure includes the total of Bing Crosby's recording of this song which, alone, accounted for more than 9,000,000.

The biggest seller of the pre-electric recording era is "Dardanella," composed by Johnny Black and Felix Bernard which sold more than 6½ million without the present day impetus to sales of radio and motion picture exploitation.

FASTEST
SELLING

The fastest selling record of all time is "The Ballad of Davy Crockett," by Tom Blackburn and George Burns, U.S.A. The record has sold more than seven million copies on twenty different labels in its first six months on the market.

INSTRUMENTAL
WORKS

The greatest selling instrumental work is "The Glow Worm" by Paul Lincke, published in 1902. It has sold over 4,000,000 copies in various arrangements in the ensuing fifty years.

Among non-copyright instrumental works—on which exact figures do not exist—it is generally agreed that "The Blue Danube" waltz by Johann Strauss, is the all-time biggest seller of the world.

BIGGEST
SELLING
SONGS

The title of the biggest selling song is shared by "Till We Meet Again" by Raymond B. Egan and Richard Whiting, published in 1918 and "Let Me Call You Sweetheart" by Beth Slater Whitson and Leo Friedman, published in 1910. Up to 1954, "Till We Meet Again" had sold more than 6,000,000 copies. Precise figures relating to "Let Me Call You Sweetheart" are unknown.

In recent years the biggest selling song is "White Christmas" by Irving Berlin. First published in 1941, by the end of 1947, it had sold over 3,000,000 copies and it still sells at the rate of 300,000 copies a year, particularly at Christmas time, bringing its present total sales to something over 5,000,000.

MUSICAL
COMEDY

The world's most successful musical comedy is "Oklahoma!", created by the Americans Rodgers and Hammerstein, which already 10 million people have paid $35,000,000 to see.

FILM

There is no exact definition of long films throughout the world. Various countries make definition by length but the following data refers to so-called feature films. The biggest producer of feature films in 1954 was Japan with a total of 370, the United States came second in a listing with 303.

The film which has made the most money to date is "Gone With The Wind," which is reputed to have earned $33,500,000.

MOVIE-GOERS

The people of the United Kingdom go to the cinema more often than any other country in the world. Each week on average, half the total population visit a cinema, of which there are a total of 4,527 with a seating capacity of 4,200,000, or one seat for every twelve persons.

In the United States there are 19,101 cinemas and the average attendance equals a visit by every person in the United States once every 22 days.

Australia and New Zealand have more cinema seats per total population than any other country in the world, with one cinema seat for every 7.5 persons.

The earliest sound on motion picture film was demonstrated in New York City on March 13th, 1923, by Dr. Lee de Forest.

EARLIEST TALKIE

The largest screen in current use is that required for the Todd-American Optical process, based on a single 65 mm. projector. With a curve 15 feet deep in the center, the screen has an overall length of 50 feet and is 25 feet high.

LARGEST SCREEN

Walt Disney has won more ''Oscars''—awards of the United States Academy of Motion Picture Arts and Sciences, instituted 1929, than any other person. His total is twenty-four from 1931 to 1955.

OSCARS

The champions for the number of Oscars by 'actors' are the cat and mouse cartoon characters, Tom and Jerry, who have won 7 awards since 1943.

The actor who has appeared in more films than any other is the American Samuel Hinds with a total of 159.

ACTORS

The oldest cinema actor was Cyril Maude (b. 1862) who appeared at the age of 89 years.

Part Three

THE NATURAL WORLD

---

1. Natural Phenomena

METEOR
SHOWER

Meteors are mostly of cometary origin and have been recorded since 644 B.C. The greatest meteor shower on record occurred on the night of November 12-13th, 1833, when the Leonid Meteors were visible from 9 p.m. to 8 a.m. They were seen from the Gulf of Mexico to Halifax, Nova Scotia. At Boston, Mass., the number of meteors in the shower was estimated at 240,000.

METEORITE
CRATER

When a meteor penetrates to the Earth's surface, the remnant is described as a meteorite. The largest meteorite crater is the water-filled Chubb Crater in Northern Ungava, Canada. It was first sighted from a 'plane on June 20th, 1943 and was later found to have a rim 7½ miles round and to be 1,350 deep. See Photo No. 16, page 93.

The largest dry crater is the Coon Butte crater near Canyon Diablo, Winslow, Northern Arizona, which is 4,000 feet in diameter and now about 550 feet deep with a parapet rising 130 to 155 feet above the surrounding plain. It has been estimated that a mass of 25,000 tons travelling at 36,000 m.p.h. would have been required to gouge this crater.

LARGEST
METEORITES

The largest known meteorite is at Hoba West, near Grootfontein in South West Africa. This is a block about 9 feet long by 8 feet broad weighing approximately 60 metric tons (59 long tons). The heaviest meteorite housed by any museum is the "Tent" meteorite on exhibition at the Hayden Planetarium, 81st Street, Central Park West, New York. It weighs 32.5 tons and measures approximately 11 x 7 x 5 feet. It was recovered from Cape York in Greenland (where it was known as Savikase, meaning the "Great Iron") in 1897 by Admiral Peary.

The largest meteorite to hit the earth in historic times fell near Vanovara, Central Siberia, on June 30th, 1908. The lowest estimate of the original mass before disintegration is 200 tons.

The greatest recorded shower of stony meteorites was one of 100,000, varying between 19¾ lbs. and 1/30th of an ounce, at Poltusk, Poland, on January 30th, 1868. There is no recorded instance of a fatality from a meteorite, but on November 30th, 1954, Mrs. Hewlett Hodges of Sylacauga, Alabama, was injured by a glancing blow.

The largest meteorite recovered from the continental United States is the 15½ ton meteorite, discovered in 1902, 3 miles northwest of Oregon City, Oregon. This specimen, known as the Willamette Meteorite, measures 10 feet 3 inches by 6 feet 6 inches by 4 feet 3 inches and originally weighed between 20 and 30 tons before losses due to oxidation. It is now housed in the Hayden Planetarium, New York City. The largest stony meteorite to fall in the continental U.S. was one of 745 lbs, 14 miles southwest of Paragould, Arkansas, on February 17th, 1930.

AURORA

MOST FREQUENT

Polar lights, known as Aurora Borealis or Northern Lights in the northern hemisphere and Aurora Australis in the southern hemisphere, caused by electric solar discharge, occur most frequently in high latitudes. The maximum auroral frequency, of up to 240 displays a year, has occurred in the Hudson Bay area.

MOST SOUTHERLY NORTHERN LIGHTS

The most southerly point in the United States from which Northern Lights have been seen is New Orleans, Louisiana.

ALTITUDE

The extreme height of auroras has been measured at 620 miles while the lowest may descend to 45 miles.

ATMOSPHERE
Lowest Layer

The lowest layer of the atmosphere is the troposphere which extends from the surface of the globe to an altitude of 30,000 feet over the equator and to 15-20,000 feet over the poles. Above this is the stratosphere (extending to 20 miles up), followed by the chemosphere (upper limit 50 miles) and the ionosphere (upper limit 250 miles). At the fusion of the chemo- and iono-spheres there is the coldest layer of atmosphere at $-117°F$.

Highest Layer

The highest layer of the atmosphere is the mesosphere extending from 250 miles, where the temperature has been measured at 4,188°F., to the edge of space variously estimated between 600 and 6,000 miles up.

EARTHQUAKES

WORLD'S GREATEST

Earthquakes are instrumentally measured on the Gutenberg-Richter scale. The highest readings yet obtained are magnitudes of 8.6 on two occasions. The earlier was the Colombian earthquake of January 31st, 1906, with a submarine epicentre Lat. 1°N., Long. 81½°W. and the more recent Assam earthquake of August 15th, 1950, with its epicentre Lat. 28°36'N., Long. 96°30'E. In Sagami Bay, Japan, the sea-bottom in one area sank 1,310 feet after the Kwanto shock of 1923.

WORLD'S WORST

The official total of persons killed and missing after the Kwanto earthquake in Japan on September 1st, 1923, was 142,807 people. The epicentre was in Lat. 24°58'N., Long. 139°21'E. Tokyo and Yokohama were largely destroyed. The damage was estimated at $5,000 million.

UNITED STATES   The earliest dated earthquake in the United States is one which was felt near Providence, Rhode Island, c. 1568 and reported in 1638 to Roger Williams as a 70-year-old recollection by several Indians.

The most extensive earthquakes ever recorded within the continental United States were those centered on New Madrid, Missouri, in 1811-12. The first shock came at 2:05 a.m. on December 15th, 1811, the second on January 23rd, 1812 and the last, and probably the greatest, on February 7th, 1812. The tremors were felt from Canada to New Orleans in an area of at least 2,000,000 square miles. Owing to the sparseness of the population in the area of the epicentres, the loss of life was insignificant.

The most disastrous earthquake in the continental United States from the standpoint of fatalities and material damage was the San Francisco earthquake at 5:13 a.m. April 18th, 1906, which produced a surface rupture 270 miles in length. The best estimates put the number killed at about 700 and the damage caused by the tremors and the ensuing fires at $140,000,000.

The states most free from earthquakes are North Dakota, West Virginia and Wisconsin in which no locally centered earthquakes have been noted.

VOLCANOES

GREATEST
ERUPTION   The total volume of matter discharged in the 1815 eruption from Tambora, the East Indies volcano, on the island of Cumbawa, has been estimated as 36.4 cubic miles. The volcano lost over 4,000 feet in height and a crater 7 miles in diameter was formed. This compares with the 4.3 cubic miles ejected in the Krakatoa eruption. The internal pressure causing this eruption has been estimated at nearly 25,000 tons per square inch.

LOUDEST
EXPLOSION   The greatest explosion in recorded history occurred at 2.56 G.M.T. on August 27th, 1883, with the eruption of Krakatoa, a small island lying in the Sunda Strait between Sumatra and Java in Indonesia. Rocks were projected to a height of 34 miles with dust falling 10 days later at a distance of 3,313 miles. The explosion was recorded 4 hours later on Rodriguez Island 3,000 miles away as the "roar of heavy guns" and was heard over 1/13th part of the surface of the globe. This explosion has been estimated to have had over a hundred times the power of the largest H-bomb test detonation.

HIGHEST
Active   Mount Antofalla (19,921 feet) in the Puna Atacama region of the Andes range in Argentina, South America.

Dormant   Though no eruptions are known, the dormant Andean peak Mount Llullaillaco (21,719 feet) on the borders of Chile and Argentina still occasionally emits gases and volatile substances.

Extinct   Mount Aconcagua (23,036 feet) first climbed in 1897, on the Argentine side of the Chile-Argentina border.

Northernmost   This is Beerenberg (8,349 feet) on Jan Mayen Island in the Greenland Sea, north of the Arctic Circle. The island, probably discovered in 1614, was annexed by Norway in 1929.

The most southerly known active volcano is Mount Erebus (12,762 feet) on Victoria Land in Antarctica.

The highest and only active volcano in the continental United States is Mount Lassen (10,435 feet) in California, which was last active in May, 1915. See Photo No. 14, page 59.

The Waimangu geyser, New Zealand, in 1909 erupted to a height in excess of 1,000 feet but is now quiescent. Currently the world's largest active geyser is the "Giant" in the Yellowstone National Park, Wyoming, U.S.A., which erupts at intervals varying from 7 days to 3 months, throwing a spire 200 feet high at a rate of 700,000 gallons an hour. The "Great Geyser" in Iceland, from which all others have been named, spurts, on occasions, to 180 feet.

2. Weather

The meteorological records printed below necessarily relate largely to 19th and 20th Centuries, since data before that time are both sparse and unreliable.

The world average temperature is 59°F (15°C).

On September 13th, 1922, at Azizia in North Western Libya, 25 miles south of Tripoli, a shade reading of 58.0°C (136.4°F) was obtained under standard conditions.

A temperature of 63°C (145.4°F) has been recorded recently at the Dalol Sulphur Mines in the Danakil Desert in Northeastern Abyssinia. Other readings of 158°F and even one of "nearly 170°F" have been recorded from this area but none can be accepted as official because of the lack of details upon the accuracy and exposure of the thermometers employed. The hottest place in the world considered over the year is generally allowed to be the Red Sea port of Massawa in Eritrea where the annual average (day and night) is 86°F (30°C).

The highest temperature ever recorded within the United States and for the American continent is 134°F, recorded at Greenland Ranch near Death Valley, Inyo County, California, on July 10th, 1913.

The U.S. weather station with the highest mean annual temperature is Key West, Florida, with 76.6°F. The highest summer average is at Cow Creek, California, with 98.8°F and the highest winter average at Key West with 71.4°F.

The highest midnight temperature recorded in New York City has been 87°F (48.8°C) most recently on August 31st, 1953. The highest ever in the city was 102°F.

The lowest acceptable temperature ever recorded is −68°C (−90.2°F) at Oimekon in Siberia in February, 1933. Another reading of −78°C (−108°F) from this station was reported in 1938 but cannot be accepted as official until its confirmation is accompanied by further essential details.

TEMPERATURE RECORDS IN THE 48 STATES
All-Time Highest Readings

State, Station and County	Date	Highest
ALABAMA—Centerville, Bibb	September 5, 1925	112°
ARIZONA—Parker, Yuma	July 7, 1905*	127°
ARKANSAS—Ozark, Franklin	August 10, 1936	120°
CALIFORNIA—Greenland Ranch, Inyo	July 10, 1913	134°
COLORADO—Bennett, Adams	July 11, 1888	118°
CONNECTICUT—Waterbury, New Haven	July 22, 1926	105°
DELAWARE—Millsboro, Sussex	July 21, 1930	110°
FLORIDA—Monticello, Jefferson	June 29, 1931	109°
GEORGIA—Louisville, Jefferson	July 24, 1952	112°
IDAHO—Orofino, Clearwater	July 28, 1934	118°
ILLINOIS—E. St. Louis, St. Clair	July 14, 1954	117°
INDIANA—Collegeville, Jasper	July 14, 1936	116°
IOWA—Keokuk, Lee	July 20, 1934	118°
KANSAS—Alton (near), Osborne	July 24, 1936*	121°
KENTUCKY—Greensburg, Green	July 28, 1930	114°
LOUISIANA—Plain Dealing, Bossier	August 10, 1936	114°
MAINE—North Bridgton, Cumberland	July 10, 1911*	105°
MARYLAND—Cumberland, Allegheny (also Frederick, Frederick)	July 10, 1936*	109°
MASSACHUSETTS—Lawrence, Essex	July 4, 1911*	106°
MICHIGAN—Mio, Oscoda	July 13, 1936	112°
MINNESOTA—Moorhead, Clay	July 6, 1936*	114°
MISSISSIPPI—Holly Springs, Marshall	July 29, 1930	115°
MISSOURI—Warsaw, Benton	July 14, 1954*	118°
MONTANA—Medicine Lake, Sheridan	July 5, 1937*	117°
NEBRASKA—Minden, Kearney	July 24, 1936*	118°
NEVADA—Overton, Clark	June 23, 1954*	122°
NEW HAMPSHIRE—Nashua, Hillsboro	July 4, 1911	106°
NEW JERSEY—Runyon, Middlesex	July 10, 1936	110°
NEW MEXICO—Orogrande, Otero	July 14, 1934*	116°
NEW YORK—Troy, Rensselaer	July 22, 1926	108°
NORTH CAROLINA—Weldon, Halifax	September 7, 1954*	109°
NORTH DAKOTA—Steele, Kidder	July 6, 1936	121°
OHIO—Gallipolis (near), Gallia	July 21, 1934*	113°
OKLAHOMA—Tishomingo, Johnston	July 26, 1943*	120°
OREGON—Pendleton, Umatilla	August 10, 1898*	119°
PENNSYLVANIA—Phoenixville, Chester	July 10, 1936*	111°
RHODE ISLAND—Greenville, Providence	July 30, 1949*	102°
SOUTH CAROLINA—Camden, Kershaw	June 28, 1954*	111°
SOUTH DAKOTA—Gannvalley, Buffalo	July 5, 1936	120°
TENNESSEE—Perryville, Decatur	August 9, 1930*	113°
TEXAS—Seymour, Baylor	August 12, 1936	120°
UTAH—Saint George, Washington	June 28, 1892	116°
VERMONT—Cornwall, Addison	August 21, 1916*	104°
VIRGINIA—Balcony Falls, Rockbridge	July 15, 1954*	110°
WASHINGTON—Wahluke, Grant	July 24, 1928	118°
WEST VIRGINIA—Martinsburg, Berkeley	July 10, 1936*	112°
WISCONSIN—Wisconsin Dells, Columbia	July 13, 1936	114°
WYOMING—Basin, Big Horn	June 12, 1900	114°
DISTRICT OF COLUMBIA—Washington, Dist. of Columbia	July 20, 1930*	106°

*This same record temperature was also recorded within the state at an earlier date.

TEMPERATURE RECORDS IN THE 48 STATES
All-Time Lowest Readings

State, Station and County	Date	Lowest
ALABAMA—Valley Head, De Kalb	February 14, 1905	—18°
ARIZONA—Maverick, Apache	January 4, 1949*	—33°
ARKANSAS—Pond (P.O.: Gravette), Benton	February 13, 1905	—29°
CALIFORNIA—Boca, Nevada	January 20, 1937	—45°
COLORADO—Taylor Park, Gunnison	February 1, 1951	—60°
CONNECTICUT—Falls Village, Litchfield	February 16, 1943	—32°
DELAWARE—Millsboro, Sussex	January 17, 1893	—17°
FLORIDA—Tallahassee, Leon	February 13, 1899	— 2°
GEORGIA—CCC Camp F-16, Floyd (near Lafayette)	January 27, 1940	—17°
IDAHO—Island Park Dam, Fremont	January 18, 1943	—60°
ILLINOIS—Mount Carroll, Carroll	January 22, 1930	—35°
INDIANA—Greensburg, Decatur	February 2, 1951	—35°
IOWA—Washta, Cherokee	January 12, 1912	—47°
KANSAS—Lebanon, Smith (P.O.: Bellaire)	February 13, 1905	—40°
KENTUCKY—Sandyhook, Elliott	February 11, 1899	—33°
LOUISIANA—Minden, Webster	February 13, 1899	—16°
MAINE—Van Buren, Aroostoock	January 19, 1925	—48°
MARYLAND—Oakland, Garrett	January 13, 1912	—40°
MASSACHUSETTS—Turners Falls, Franklin	February 16, 1943	—30°
(also W. Cunnington, Hampshire)		
MICHIGAN—Vanderbilt, Otsego	February 9, 1934	—51°
MINNESOTA—Pokegama Falls, Itasca	February 16, 1903*	—59°
MISSISSIPPI—Batesville, Panola	February 2, 1951*	—16°
MISSOURI—Warsaw, Benton	February 13, 1905	—40°
MONTANA—Rogers Pass	January 20, 1954	—70°
NEBRASKA—Camp Clarke, Cheyenne	February 12, 1899	—47°
NEVADA—San Jacinto, Elko	January 8, 1937	—50°
NEW HAMPSHIRE—Pittsburg, Coos	January 28, 1925	—46°
NEW JERSEY—River Vale, Bergen	January 5, 1904	—34°
NEW MEXICO—Gavilan, Rio Arriba	February 1, 1951	—50°
NEW YORK—Stillwater Reservoir, Herkimer	February 9, 1934	—52°
NORTH CAROLINA—Mt. Mitchell, Mitchell	November 30, 1929*	—21°
NORTH DAKOTA—Parshall, Mountrail	February 15, 1936	—60°
OHIO—Milligan, Perry	February 10, 1899	—39°
OKLAHOMA—Watts, Adair	January 18, 1930*	—27°
OREGON—Seneca, Grant	February 10, 1933*	—54°
PENNSYLVANIA—Smithport, McKean	January 5, 1904	—42°
RHODE ISLAND—Kingston, Washington	January 11, 1942	—23°
SOUTH CAROLINA—Longcreek (near), Oconee	January 26, 1940	—13°
(P.O.: Mountain Rest)		
SOUTH DAKOTA—McIntosh, Corson	February 17, 1936	—58°
TENNESSEE—Mountain City, Johnson	December 30, 1917	—32°
TEXAS—Seminole, Gaines	February 8, 1933*	—23°
UTAH—Strawberry Tunnel E., Wasatch	January 5, 1913*	—50°
VERMONT—Bloomfield, Essex	December 30, 1933	—50°
VIRGINIA—Monterey, Highland	February 10, 1899	—29°
WASHINGTON—Deer Park (near), Spokane	January 20, 1937	—42°
WEST VIRGINIA—Lewisburg, Greenbrier	December 30, 1917	—37°
WISCONSIN—Danbury, Burnett	January 24, 1922	—54°
WYOMING—Moran, Teton	February 9, 1933	—63°
DISTRICT OF COLUMBIA—Washington, D. C.	February 11, 1899	—15°

*This same record temperature was also recorded within the state at an earlier date.

A spot temperature of −89°F was recorded on December 6th, 1949 on the Central Greenland Ice-cap which suggests that the world's lowest temperatures may in fact be located in this region (elevation 9,820 feet).

The coldest place in the world considered over a year is most probably the South Pole (elevation 9,075 feet) where it has been estimated that the mean annual temperature must be at most −22°F (−30.0°C).

U.S. LOWEST

The U.S. weather station with the lowest mean annual temperature is Mount Washington, New Hampshire (elevation 6,262 feet) with 26.9°F or over 5 degrees below freezing. The mean annual temperature at Barrow, Alaska, is 10.1°F or nearly 22 degrees below freezing.

The lowest temperature ever recorded in the U.S. is −70°F at Rogers Pass, Montana, on January 20th, 1954.

Excluding mountain peaks, the record is held by Fraser, Colorado, at 32.9°F. The lowest winter average is 3.8°F at Hannah, North Dakota, and the lowest summer average is 51.8°F at Lake Moraine, Colorado.

The lowest temperature recorded on the North American continent is −81°F at Snag Air Station in the Yukon on February 3, 1947.

LONGEST FREEZE

The longest unremitting freeze known in the United States was one of 119 days at Lakeview, Montana, between November 4th, 1948 and March 1st, 1949.

GREATEST RANGE

In the Siberian settlement of Yakutsk, a daily range of 181.4°F (100.7°C) has been recorded.

The greatest temperature range of any United States station is the 175°F (97.2°C) recorded at Medicine Lake, Montana, which during the years 1921-1956 has experienced differences of from 117°F to −58°F.

The greatest temperature variation recorded in a day in the United States is 100°F (a fall from 44° to −56°) at Browning, Montana, on January 23-24, 1916. The most freakish rise was 49°F in 2 minutes at Spearfish, South Dakota, from −4° at 7:30 a.m. to 45° at 7:32 a.m. on January 22nd, 1943.

RAINFALL

The world average is 28.5 inches per year.

GREATEST

The rain gauges of the world provide such a minute target that the chances of the heaviest rainfalls ever being measured are extremely remote.

Minute

The world's most intense authenticated rainfall is 0.69 inch in a period of one minute at Jefferson, Iowa, on July 10th, 1955.

Day

During a typhoon at Baguio on the island of Luzon, Philippines, 45.99 inches of rain fell in the 24 hours on July 14-15, 1911. This deluge represented 4,645 tons of water per acre.

The highest recorded rainfall in twenty-four hours in the U.S. is 26.12 inches at Hoegees Camp, California, on January 22-23, 1943. However, 38.2 inches in twenty-four hours was unofficially observed at Thrall, Texas, on September 9-10, 1951.

During the July 1861 monsoon, 366.14 inches were reported from Cherrapunji in the Khasi Hills of Assam, North East India.

The U.S. record for a calendar month is 71.54 inches at Helen Mine, Calif., during January 1909.

Month

The highest recorded figure for any given year was 1,041.78 inches at Cherrapunji, between August 1st, 1860 and July 31st, 1861.

The highest figure for a calendar year is 905.12 inches at the same station in 1861.

The U.S. record for a calendar year is 167.97 inches at Glenora, Oregon, in 1896.

Year

The annual average for Cherrapunji since 1882 is 450 inches and is thus surpassed by Mount Waialeale on the Island of Kauai, Hawaiian Islands, which has averaged 471 inches since 1912.

ANNUAL AVERAGE

The wettest state is Louisiana, which has an annual average rainfall of 55.6 inches this century compared with the United States average of 29 inches. The figure for the state in 1905 was 75.57 inches.

WETTEST STATE

The greatest number of consecutive days with measurable rain at any station in the United States is 58 days for Tatoosh Island, Washington.

LONGEST RAIN SPELL

Based on the number of days with rain in a year the rainiest station in the world is Bahia Felix in Southern Chile with an average of 325 rainy days a year with an extreme of 348 days in 1916.

RAINIEST

There is evidence that there has been no significant rainfall in parts of the Atacama Desert in Chile for the last four centuries. In nearby Arica, the annual average during the last 43 years has been 0.02 inches, the lowest recorded.

The lowest annual rainfall recorded in the U.S. is 1.66 inches (since 1910) at Greenland Ranch, Calif.

WORLD'S LOWEST RAINFALL

The longest absolute drought (no measurable rain) recorded in the U.S. is one of 767 days from October 3rd, 1912 to November 8th, 1914 at Bagdad, California.

LONGEST DROUGHT

The driest state in the United States is Nevada, averaging 8.61 inches annually this century, compared with the United States overall average of 29 inches. The figure for the state in 1928 was 4.87 inches.

UNITED STATES DRIEST STATE

SNOWFALL

The ratio of inches of snow to equivalent inches of rain vary between extremes from 5 to 1 (granular) to 50 to 1 (very loose). A common value is 10 inches of snow to 1 inch of rain.

The greatest recorded seasonal snowfall is 884 inches (more than 73 feet) at Tamarack, California, during the winter of 1906-07.

The greatest annual average is 575.1 inches at Paradise Ranger Station in the Rainier Park, Washington.

GREATEST

The greatest recorded depth on the ground was here on March 9th, 1911 with 37 feet, 10 inches (454 inches).

The most intense snowfall on record is 87 inches in the space of 27½ hours at Silver Lake, Colorado, on April 14-15, 1921. At Giant Forest, California, 60 inches was once recorded in 24 hours.

The New York City record is 26 inches in 24 hours on December 26-27, 1947. It was estimated that 100,000,000 tons descended over the city, immobilizing 10,000 automobiles and incurring an expense of $8,000,000 in clearance.

The heaviest snowfall recorded for Washington, D. C., was 28 inches in 24 hours on January 27-28, 1922. The death roll was over 100, mostly from a single incident when the roof of a theater collapsed, killing 96 persons.

The record for fatalities, however, occurred during the New York blizzard of March 12-13, 1888, when over 400 deaths were reported.

MOST SOUTHERLY

The most southerly snowfall recorded in the United States has been at Brownsville, Texas, and Fort Meyers, Florida. Snow has never been recorded at Key West, Florida.

LATEST

The latest date to which snow has been delayed in any season is in the winter of 1927-28 when no measurable snow fell before January 22nd, 1928. The latest date in spring on which measurable snow has fallen is April 18th in 1887 when 2.1 inches fell. Traces of snow have been observed in the month of May.

SUNSHINE

In polar latitudes higher than 66°, the sun does not sink below the horizon during the summers.

At the Canadian-United States Weather Station, Alert, Dum Bell Bay, Ellesmere Island, above 82° North, the sun does not set over a period of 147 days.

Observations in Antarctica showed conditions of cloudiness, permitting continuous sunshine for over 59 hours during December 9-12, 1911.

The sunniest station in the United States is at Yuma, Arizona, where observed duration of sunshine has attained 100 per cent of that possible for its latitude of 32°40'N for periods of over a month, and 96 per cent of that possible over the whole year in 1924.

HIGHEST SUN ANGLE

The highest altitude attained by the sun in the continental United States is 88° or within two degrees of the zenith (90°) in southernmost Florida. The highest mid-summer angle in New York City is 69° 40' but owing to refraction the sun appears to be slightly above 70 degrees.

WORLD'S MINIMUM

In polar winters, there are periods of months when the sun does not appear above the horizon.

At Alert (see above), there is an annual period of sunlessness, lasting 145 days.

U. S.

At Tatoosh Island, Washington, there have been periods of complete sunlessness of over a week, and an instance of a monthly sunshine figure of only 2 per cent of that possible for the latitude.

The world's average sea-level barometric pressure is 1,013 millibars—29.92 inches.

The highest barometric pressure ever recorded was at Irkursk, Siberia, on January 14th, 1893, when there was a reading of 31.75 inches (1,075 millibars).

The lowest recorded barometric pressure is the 26.185 inches in a typhoon in the Luzon Sea aboard the Dutch vessel "Sapoeroea" on August 18th, 1927.

The highest sea-level barometric pressure ever recorded in the United States is 31.29 inches at Lander, Wyoming, on December 20th, 1924.

The lowest recorded and authenticated sea level barometric pressure is 26.35 inches (829 millibars) during a hurricane at Long Key, Florida, on September 2nd, 1935. The lowest recorded on the mainland is 27.61 inches, also in a hurricane, on September 18th, 1926, at Miami, Florida.

The most thundery weather station in the world is Buitenzorg in Java, where thunderstorms are recorded on an average of 322 days a year.

The most thundery weather station in the United States is Lakeland, Florida, which has an annual average of 101 days on which thunderstorms are heard. The station most free from thunderstorms is Santa Maria, California, averaging less than a single instance each two years.

It has been calculated from the destructive effects produced that wind speed attained during tornadoes surpasses 500 m.p.h. Calculations have given values of 682 m.p.h. during the tornado at Mayfield, Ohio, February 4th, 1842, and 558 m.p.h. at St. Louis, Missouri, May 27th, 1896. Doubts, however, have been cast on these estimated figures. The highest instrumental reading obtained is 231 m.p.h. at 1:21 p.m. on April 24th, 1934, by Salvador Tagluica at Mount Washington Research Station, New Hampshire (altitude 6,248 feet). It is known that in the upper atmosphere 'jet streams' attain speeds of over 300 knots (345 m.p.h.).

The highest average annual wind speed in the U.S. is 36.9 m.p.h. at Mt. Washington, New Hampshire. The highest coastal average is 16.6 m.p.h. and the lowest average is 4.3 m.p.h. at Roseburg, Oregon.

A condition of fog exists when the visibility is less than 1,100 yards.

The foggiest area of the Earth is recognized to be the Grand Banks of Newfoundland which are highly subject to advection sea fogs.

The foggiest sea-level station in the U.S. is the Libby Island off the coast of Maine with an annual average of 1,554 hours. The record number of hours of fog in a year is 2,734 reported from Sequin Light Station, Maine, during 1907.

The foggiest weather station in the United States is Mount Washington, New Hampshire, with an annual average of heavy fog on 302 days per year. Some stations in Arizona, California, Florida and Nevada recorded less than a single foggy day each two years.

Marginal headings:

BAROMETRIC PRESSURE WORLD EXTREMES Highest

Lowest

U.S. Extremes

THUNDER

MOST AND LEAST THUNDERY

WIND EXTREMES

FOG World

U.S.

MOST AND LEAST FOG

CLOUD

The highest standard cloud form is the cirrus averaging 27,000 feet and above but the rare nacreous or mother-of-pearl formation sometimes reaching nearly 80,000 feet. The lowest is stratus, below 3,500 feet. The cloud form with the greatest vertical range is cumulo-nimbus which sometimes towers to 30,000 feet. Noctilucent 'clouds' a famous manifestation of which was observed from Dvobak, Norway, on July 27th, 1909, are believed to pass at a height of over 60 miles.

MOST AND
LEAST CLOUDY

The cloudiest weather station in the United States is Mount Washington, New Hampshire, with an annual average of 236 cloudy and 77 partly cloudy days. The station with the greatest number of clear days is Yuma, Arizona, with an average of only 20 cloudy days a year.

HUMIDITY

Humidity of 100 per cent is not infrequently recorded.

The station with the highest relative winter humidity is Eugene, Oregon, at an average of 94 per cent for January morning readings and that with the highest summer humidity is Tatoosh, Washington, with 94 per cent for July morning readings. The lowest average summer reading is 15 per cent at Bishop, California, for July evenings.

WORLD'S
LARGEST
HAILSTONES

The largest authenticated hailstones recorded were those weighed and measured, dissected and photographed at Potter, Nebraska, July 6th, 1928. One weighed 1½ lbs. and was 17 inches in circumference. There is an older and less well established record of 4½ lbs. at Cazorla, Spain, on June 15th, 1829, but this may have been coalesced stones.

3. Structure and Dimensions

LARGEST
DIAMETER

The Earth is not a true sphere. The polar diameter of the Earth (7,899.98 miles) is 26.7 miles less than the equatorial diameter (7,926.68 miles). As well as this spheroid departure from a true sphere, the Earth also has a slight ellipticity of the equator which shows it is a geoid form with a long axis (about longitude 0°) approximately 174 yards greater than the short axis. The greatest circumference of the Earth, at the Equator, is 24,901.96 miles.

SURFACE
RANGE

The surface of the Earth, although broken by mountains, which rise to 29,160 feet and fissures which descend to 35,640 feet above and below sea level, has in relation to its size a very smooth surface. The total difference between the highest and lowest points being 64,800 feet or (estimating on the equatorial diameter of the Earth) a surface accuracy of 0.1545 per cent. On the basis of a billiard ball 2.1 inches in diameter, this would be represented by a scratch .00315 inch.

EARTH'S
STRUCTURE

The Earth weighs 5,887,613,230,000,000,000,000,000 long tons and has a density of 5.522. Modern theory is that the earth has an outer shell or lithopshere about 25 miles thick, then an outer and inner rock layer extending 1,800 miles deep after which there is a molten iron-nickel core at a temperature of perhaps 8,000°F and at a pressure of 20,750 tons to the square inch. If the iron-nickel core theory is correct iron must be by far the most abundant element in the Earth. If calculations are confined to the Earth's crust, the most abundant element is oxygen particularly in the form of silica (silicon dioxide SiO_2) constituting 59 per cent of the crust and alumina (Al_2O_3) 15 per cent of the crust.

The most abundant metal in the Earth's crust is aluminium at 7.85 per cent. Gold accounts for perhaps 0.0000005 per cent while it has been contended that the existence in nature of masurium and illinium has not yet been established.

The age of the Earth must of necessity be only an approximation but modern theory suggests 5,000,000,000.

Rocks estimated stratigraphically (by the study of their formation and structure) have been found in Africa and Canada which are regarded as the oldest outcrops in the world, being probably in excess of 3,000 million years old.

One of the modern methods of estimating age in geological formation is by measurement of the disintegration of radio-active substances in the sample.

The oldest reliably dated mineral is a monazite from ebonite tantalum claims in the Bikita District of Southern Rhodesia at a minimum of 2,600 million and a maximum of 2,680 million years. There is a less well founded claim for a 2,820 million year old lepidolite from Popes Claim near Salisbury, S. Rhodesia and a 3,300 million year old granite pebble from the same area.

The oldest rock in the continental United States are gneisses in Minnesota estimated by the Larsen-Zircon method to be 1,530 million years old.

The area of the Earth covered by the sea is approximately 139,-573,699 square miles, 70.92 per cent of the world's surface.

The largest ocean in the world is the Pacific. Including adjacent seas, it represents 47.31 per cent of the world's oceans and is 66,030,-124 square miles in area.

The deepest ocean sounding in the world was made by the British Navy Survey Ship "Challenger" on June 14th, 1951. In the Western Pacific Ocean near the Mariana Islands, 200 miles south-west of Guam, the depth of the Mariana Trench was established at 35,640 feet. A metal object, say a pound ball of steel, dropped into the water above this deep would take approximately 62 minutes to fall to the sea-bed 6 ¾ miles below. The average depth of the Pacific Ocean is 13,215 feet.

The deepest sounding in the Atlantic Ocean is in the Puerto Rican trench at 28,200 feet deep.

The deepest sounding in the Indian Ocean is the Sundar Trench at 17,850 feet deep. The average depth of the Indian Ocean is 12,750 feet.

The most common elements by weight in sea-water are chlorine, approximately 1.9 lbs., and sodium, approximately 1.05 lbs. in every 100 lbs. of sea water.

Although the proportions of the salts in the sea remain very much the same all over the world, salinity does vary. It is saltiest in the Red Sea where evaporation is high and the total salts may exceed 41 parts in a thousand.

In the Arctic and Antarctic regions, snow and melting ice tend to dilute the oceans and the total salts are approximately 3.2 lbs. per 100 lbs.

TEMPERATURE

The temperature of the water at the surface of the sea varies from approximately 28.5°F in the Polar regions to 90°F in the Equatorial zones such as the Persian Gulf.

HIGHEST WAVE

The greatest possible height of a wave at sea is usually cited at 60 feet. However, the highest recorded sea-wave was measured from U.S.S. Ramapo proceeding from Manila to San Diego on the night of February 6-7, 1933, during a 68-knot (78.3 m.p.h.) gale. The wave measured 112 feet from trough to crest.

Another maximum recorded was 80 feet by the British White Star liner "Majestic" (56,621 tons gross) in the North Atlantic on December 22nd, 1922.

The highest seismic sea wave, or tsunami, recorded is that produced by the Krakatoa earthquake of 1883 (q.v.) at 135 feet. This type of wave has been observed to travel across oceans at over 460 m.p.h.

STRONGEST CURRENT

The world's strongest currents are those of the Saltfjord, off the coast of Norway, which reach a speed of 16 knots.

The strongest current on the East coast of the United States is 5.3 knots off Blackwells Island in the East River, New York.

The strongest current on the West coast of the United States is 8.3 knots at Deception Pass Narrows, Washington.

WATERSPOUTS

The highest reliably measured waterspout recorded was the 3,600 feet of the Cottage City 'spout measured off the Massachusetts coast on August 19th, 1896.

An estimated height of 5,000 feet has been recorded off the New South Wales coast, Australia, in 1894.

ICEBERG

The largest iceberg on record is one approaching 10,000 square miles in extent (100m x 10m) and 130 feet high, reported in the Antarctic off Clarence Island in the Scotia Sea, in January 1927.

The dimensions of the iceberg sighted off South Georgia by the U.S.S. Atka, on February 25th, 1955, are the largest accurately recorded at 42.5 miles by 10 miles.

MOST SOUTHERLY

The most southerly Arctic iceberg was sighted in 30°50' North 45°06' West on June 2nd, 1934.

The most northerly Antarctic was a remnant sighted in 26°30' South 25°40' West on April 30th, 1894.

TIDES— WORLD'S GREATEST

The greatest tides in the world are found in the Bay of Fundy which separates Nova Scotia from the United States' north-easternmost state of Maine and the Canadian province of New Brunswick. Burncoat Head in the Minas Basin, Nova Scotia, has the largest mean spring range with 47.5 feet. Extreme ranges up to 53.0 feet have been recorded, for example, at Moncton on the Petitcodiac River, New Brunswick, in 1869.

The highest tide in the United States is at Calais, Maine, with a mean range of 20 feet and a spring range of 22.8 feet.

The lowest listed tide in the United States is 0.2 feet at Barnes Sound on the Florida Keys.

The highest tide on the West coast is 11 feet at Burns Point, Totten Inlet, Washington.

The lowest listed tide on the West coast is the 0.4 feet at Warrendale on the Columbia River, Oregon.

Only 29 per cent of the Earth's surface is land. The Eurasian land mass is the largest with an area of 20,750,000 square miles.

LARGEST AND SMALLEST CONTINENT

The smallest is the Australian mainland with an area of 2,974,581 square miles, which together with New Zealand and the Pacific Islands is included in Oceania.

Discounting Australia, which is usually regarded as a continental land mass, the largest island in the world is commonly cited as Greenland, with an area of 827,300 square miles. Recent exploration of its ice-cap suggests, however, that it may in fact consist of three islands. If this proves to be the case, New Guinea, with an area of 316,861 square miles, would be recognized as the world's largest island.

LARGEST ISLANDS

The largest atoll in the world is Bikini in the Pacific, which encloses a lagoon of 280 square miles. Christmas Island, however, though its lagoon is only 89 square miles, has a coral area of 184 square miles.

ATOLLS

The largest reef in the world is the Great Barrier Reef off Queensland, North East Australia, which is 1,260 geographical miles in length.

REEFS

The northernmost land in the world is Cape Morris Jesup, 440 miles from the North Pole, in Lat 83°0'39".

NORTHERNMOST LAND

The world's greatest mountain range above sea level is the Himalayas which include eleven of the world's seventeen peaks above 26,000 feet. The greatest mountain range, however, is the submarine mid-Atlantic range which is 10,000 miles long by 500 miles wide, the highest peak is Mount Pico in the Azores, which rises 27,500 feet of which 7,613 feet are above sea level.

MOUNTAIN RANGE

MOUNTAINS

HIGHEST

The Eastern Himalayan peak on the Tibet-Nepal border named Kang Chamolung (variously Cho-Mo-Lung-Ma) of 29,160 feet was discovered to be the world's highest mountain in 1852 by Radhanath Sikdar, Chief Computer to the Survey Department of the Government of India, from theodolite readings taken three years before. In 1860 its height was computed to be 29,002 feet. The 5½-mile high peak was renamed Mount Everest in 1856 after Sir George Everest, former Surveyor General of India. After a total of eleven lives since the first attempt in 1921, Everest was finally conquered at 11:30 a.m. on May 29th, 1953, by Edmund P. Hillary of New Zealand, 33, and the Sherpa, Tensing Norkay, 39. The successful expedition was commanded by Col. H. C. J. Hunt.

The highest point in the South American continent is disputed between the Andean peaks Ojos del Salado and Mount Aconcagua

ALTITUDE RECORDS IN THE 48 STATES
Highest Points

State, Location and County	Elevation Highest
ALABAMA—Cheaha Mountain, Clay-Talladega	2,407
ARIZONA—Humphreys Peak, Coconino	12,670
ARKANSAS—{Blue Mountain, Polk-Scott	2,830
ARKANSAS—{Magazine Mountain, Logan	2,830
CALIFORNIA—Mount Whitney, Inyo-Tulare	14,495
COLORADO—Mount Elbert, Lake	14,431
CONNECTICUT—Mount Frissell, Litchfield	2,380
DELAWARE—Centerville, New Castle	440
DISTRICT OF COLUMBIA—Tenleytown, N. W. Part	420
FLORIDA—West boundary, Walton	345
GEORGIA—Brasstown Bald, Towns-Union	4,784
IDAHO—Borah Peak, Custer	12,655
ILLINOIS—Charles Mound, Jo Daviess	1,241
INDIANA—Greensfork Top, Randolph	1,240
IOWA—North boundary, Osceola	1,675
KANSAS—West boundary, Wallace	4,135
Kentucky—Big Black Mountain, Harlan	4,150
LOUISIANA—Driskill Mountain, Bienville	535
MAINE—Mount Katahdin, Piscataquis	5,268
MARYLAND—Backbone Mountain, Garrett	3,360
MASSACHUSETTS—Mount Greylock, Berkshire	3,491
MICHIGAN—Porcupine Mountains, Ontonagon	2,023
MINNESOTA—Misquah Hills, Cook	2,230
MISSISSIPPI—Woodall Mountain, Tishomingo	806
MISSOURI—Taum Sauk Mt., Iron	1,772
MONTANA—Granite Peak, Park	12,850
NEBRASKA—S. W. part of County, Banner	5,340
NEVADA—Boundary Peak, Esmeralda	13,145
NEW HAMPSHIRE—Mt. Washington, Coos	6,288
NEW JERSEY—High Point, Sussex	1,801
NEW MEXICO—Wheeler Peak, Taos	13,160
NEW YORK—Mount Marcy, Essex	5,344
NORTH CAROLINA—Mount Mitchell, Yancey	6,684
NORTH DAKOTA—Black Butte, Slope	3,468
OHIO—Campbell Hill, Logan	1,550
OKLAHOMA—Black Mesa, Cimarron	4,978
OREGON—Mount Hood, Clackamas-H. R.	11,245
PENNSYLVANIA—Mt. Davis, Somerset	3,213
RHODE ISLAND—Jerimoth Hill, Providence	812
SOUTH CAROLINA—Sassafras Mountain, Pickeens	3,560
SOUTH DAKOTA—Harney Peak, Pennington	7,242
TENNESSEE—Clingmans Dome, Sevier	6,642
TEXAS—Guadalupe Peak, Culberson	8,751
UTAH—Kings Peak, Duchesne	13,498
VERMONT—Mount Mansfield, Lamoille	4,393
VIRGINIA—Mount Rogers, Grayson-Smyth	5,720
WASHINGTON—Mount Rainier, Pierce	14,408
WEST VIRGINIA—Spruce Knob, Pendleton	4,860
WISCONSIN—Sugarbush, Forest County	1,951
WYOMING—Gannett Peak, Fremont	13,785

Lowest Points

State, Location and County	Elevation Lowest
ALABAMA—Gulf of Mexico	Sea Level
ARIZONA—Colorado River, Yuma	100
ARKANSAS—Ouachita River, Ashley-Union	55
CALIFORNIA—Death Valley, Inyo	—282
COLORADO—Arkansas River, Prowers	3,350
CONNECTICUT—Long Island Sound	Sea Level
DELAWARE—Atlantic Ocean	Sea Level
DISTRICT OF COLUMBIA—Potomac River	Sea Level
FLORIDA—Atlantic Ocean	Sea Level
GEORGIA—Atlantic Ocean	Sea Level
IDAHO—Snake River, Nez Perce	720
ILLINOIS—Mississippi River, Alexander	279
INDIANA—Ohio River, Vanderberg	320
IOWA—Mississippi River, Lee	480
KANSAS—Verdigris River, Montgomery	700
KENTUCKY—Mississippi River, Fulton	257
LOUISIANA—New Orleans, Orleans	—5
MAINE—Atlantic Ocean	Sea Level
MARYLAND—Atlantic Ocean	Sea Level
MASSACHUSETTS—Atlantic Ocean	Sea Level
MICHIGAN—Lake Erie	573
MINNESOTA—Lake Superior	602
MISSISSIPPI—Gulf of Mexico	Sea Level
MISSOURI—St. Francis River, Dunklin	230
MONTANA—Kootenai River, Lincoln	1,800
NEBRASKA—S. E. cor. of State, Richardson	840
NEVADA—Colorado River, Clark	470
NEW HAMPSHIRE—Atlantic Ocean	Sea Level
NEW JERSEY—Atlantic Ocean	Sea Level
NEW MEXICO—Red Bluff Reservoir, Eddy	2,817
NEW YORK—Atlantic Ocean	Sea Level
NORTH CAROLINA—Atlantic Ocean	Sea Level
NORTH DAKOTA—Red River, Pembina	750
OHIO—Ohio River, Hamilton	433
OKLAHOMA—Red River, McCurtain	300
OREGON—Pacific Ocean	Sea Level
PENNSYLVANIA—Delaware River	Sea Level
RHODE ISLAND—Atlantic Ocean	Sea Level
SOUTH CAROLINA—Atlantic Ocean	Sea Level
SOUTH DAKOTA—Big Stone Lake, Roberts	962
TENNESSEE—Mississippi River, Shelby	182
TEXAS—Gulf of Mexico	Sea Level
UTAH—Beaverdam Creek, Washington	2,000
VERMONT—Lake Champlain, Franklin	95
VIRGINIA—Atlantic Ocean	Sea Level
WASHINGTON—Pacific Ocean	Sea Level
WEST VIRGINIA—Potomac River, Jefferson	240
WISCONSIN—Lake Michigan	582
WYOMING—B. Fourche River, Crook	3,100

(23,096 feet) in the Chile-Argentine border region. In February 1956 a Chilean claim was made that the summit of Ojos del Salado reached an altitude of 23,293 feet.

U. S.

The highest point in the North American continent is Mount McKinley (20,300 feet) in Alaska, first climbed in 1911. The highest mountain in continental United States and the 24th highest in North America is Mount Whitney (14,495 feet) in Inyo County, California, first climbed in 1872. The lowest point in the North American continent is only 85 miles distant in Death Valley, also in Inyo County, California, where there is a depression 282 feet below sea level. The highest mountain in Eastern United States is Mount Mitchell in North Carolina at 6,684 feet, while the highest mountain east of the Rockies is Harney Peak (7,242 feet) in the Black Hills of South Dakota.

The state with the highest mean elevation is Colorado with an estimated 6,800 feet. The state has 49 peaks over 14,000 feet.

The state with the lowest mean elevation is Delaware with an estimated 60 feet.

HIGHEST
UNCLIMBED
MOUNTAIN

The highest unclimbed mountain in the world is the 26,811 feet Dhaulagiri (Dhavala-giri = White Mountain) in the Central Nepal Himalaya. The mountain, which is believed by some to be very nearly 27,000 feet, is the sixth highest mountain and the 9th highest summit in the world. On June 20th, 1954, an Argentine expedition got to within 700 feet of the top in an attempt in which their leader, Francisco Ibañez, died after frostbite amputations. No useable photographs of the mountain were known before 1949.

On May 7th, 1949, the Clark Expedition claimed an unacceptable altitude of 29,661 feet for a peak in the Amyni-Machin group in Western China. The marking out of the 1,000 metre base line, the elevation of which was only estimated, did not conform to accepted standards of accuracy.

LARGEST

The world's tallest mountain measured from base to peak is Mount Kea in the Hawaiian Island at 30,750 feet of which 13,784 feet is above sea level. Another mountain whose dimensions exceed those of Everest is the Hawaiian peak, Mauna Loa of 13,680 feet. The greater and lesser diameter of its elliptical base, 15,000 feet below sea level, have been estimated at 74 miles and 53 miles.

MOST RECENTLY
DISCOVERED

It was announced on February 16th, 1955, that Soviet surveyors had discovered a peak in N.E. Siberia 24,664 feet high. This mountain, higher than any in Africa, America, or Europe, was named Stalin Peak.

DEEPEST
DEPRESSION

The deepest depression on the land surface of the Earth is the shores surrounding the Dead Sea, 1,286 feet below sea level.

A depression of 1,200 feet discovered beneath the Central Greenland ice cap by L'expeditions Polaires Francaises, suggests a still lower land surface.

REMOTEST
ISLAND

The remotest island in the world is the island of Tristan da Cunha (population 294) in the South Atlantic, discovered by the Portuguese in 1516. It has an area of 12 square miles and was annexed by Great

Britain in 1816. The nearest inhabited land is the island of St. Helena, 1,320 miles to the north-eastward. The nearest continent, South Africa, is 1,700 miles away.

RIVERS

LONGEST

The longest river in the world, according to the latest published survey of the National Geographic Society, is the River Nile which runs from the Victoria Nyanza to the Mediterranean. Its length of 4,145 miles compares with the 3,900 miles listed for the Amazon and the 3,892 of the Mississippi-Missouri-Red Rock, the longest river in the United States.

RIVER BASIN

The largest river basin in the world is that drained by the 3,900 mile River Amazon. It covers an area of 2,053,000 square miles.

GREATEST FLOW

The greatest flow of any river in the world is that of the River Amazon, which discharges up to 3.5 million cubic feet of water per second into the Atlantic Ocean.

    U.S.A.—Mississippi—700,000 cu. ft. per second.

    Canada—St. Lawrence—400,000 cu. ft. per second.

WORLD'S GREATEST RIVER BORE

The bore on the Tsientang-kiang (Hang-chow-fe) in Eastern China is the most remarkable in the world. At spring tides, the wave attains a height of up to 25 feet and a speed of 13 knots. It is heard advancing at a range of 14 miles. The bore on the Hooghly branch of the Ganges travels for 70 miles at over 15 knots.

RIVER BORE

The greatest river bore in the North American continent is that in Turnagain Arm near Anchorage, Alaska. At the time of spring tides, this bore sometimes attains a height of six feet and travels at six knots.

On the east coast the greatest bore is on the Petitcodiac River in The Bay of Fundy, New Brunswick, Canada. On some spring tides, its height exceeds five feet.

There are no bores within the limits of the continental United States.

WATERFALLS

The highest waterfall in the world is the Angel Falls, in Venezuela, on a tributary of the River Caroni, with a total drop of 3,312 feet—the longest single drop is about 2,650 feet. (See Frontispiece)

GREATEST WATERFALLS

On the basis of the average annual flow, probably the greatest waterfall in the world is the Guayra in Brazil, sometimes known as the Sete Quedas on the Alto Parana. Although only attaining an average height of about 110 feet, its estimated annual average flow over the 5,300 yard wide lip is 470,000 cubic feet per second, more than twice the average annual flow of Niagara.

During monsoon periods the Cauvery Falls in India attain an unsurpassed 650,000 cubic feet per second.

HIGHEST WATERFALLS

The highest waterfall in the United States is the Ribbon Fall at Yosemite, California, which has a drop of 1,430 feet. This forms part of the Yosemite Falls which continues with a 675 foot cascade followed by the lower Yosemite Falls of 320 feet, making a total drop of 2,425 feet.

LAKES AND
INLAND SEAS

The largest inland sea or lake in the world is the Caspian Sea. It is approximately 795 miles long and its total area is approximately 169,-500 square miles. Its maximum depth is 3,100 feet.

LARGEST
LAKE—
NORTH
AMERICA

The largest lake in the North American continent is Lake Superior, which is 31,820 square miles in extent, 350 miles long, 160 miles broad, and 1,302 feet deep at its deepest point. Lake Superior is partly in the United States (20,710 square miles) and partly in Canada (11,110 square miles).

The largest lake wholly within the geographical limits of the United States is Lake Michigan, with a water surface of 22,400 square miles. It is 307 miles long, 118 miles in breadth and has a deepest sounding of 923 feet.

DEEPEST
LAKE

The deepest lake in the world is Lake Baikal, Central Siberia. It is approximately 250 miles long and between 20 and 45 miles wide. It reaches depths of 5,650 feet.

The deepest lake in the United States is Crater Lake in Oregon. It is approximately 2,000 feet in depth.

HIGHEST
LAKE

The highest lake in the United States is Tulainyo in California, which is at an elevation of 12,865 feet.

LARGEST
GLACIER

The world's largest glacier undoubtedly exists somewhere in the six million square miles of Antarctica which contains 87 per cent of the world's glaciated surface. Comparative topography of the continent is not sufficiently developed to be more explicit. The largest glacier of the northern hemisphere is usually allowed to be the Muir Glacier in South East Alaska (59°N., 136°W.) which has an area of 350 square miles.

The Malaspina Glacier, on the Gulf of Alaska, between Juneau and Cordova, which results from the junction of several "expanded foot" glaciers, covers an area of 1,400 square miles. It has been estimated that, if returned to the sea, the 11 million cubic miles of the world's ice-sheets would raise the sea-level by 160 feet.

LARGEST U.S.

The largest glacier in the United States is the Emmons Glacier on Mount Rainier, Washington. It is six miles long and 11 square miles in area.

LONGEST
GLACIER

The greatest measured valley glacier is the Fedtschenko Glacier in the Alai Pamirs of central Asia. It is 48 miles long. Some unsurveyed glaciers of Greenland and Antarctica may, however, exceed 100 miles in length.

WORLD'S
LARGEST
AVALANCHES

These probably occur in the remotest parts of the Himalayas, in Antarctica and Alaska, but few are observed in such unpopulated wastes and are thus less disastrous than many lesser avalanches in the European Alps where over 9,000 recognized avalanche paths have been charted.

In the great Glarnisch avalanche of 1890 (44° slope) the speed of snow was estimated at 217 m.p.h.

DEEPEST ICE
BORING

The deepest ice boring ever made is one of 496 feet bored by the *L'expéditions Polaires Française* in the Greenland ice cap in June 1950. The thickness of the Greenland ice cap reaches a maximum of 11,000 feet.

The Sahara Desert in North Africa is the largest in the world. At its greatest length, it is approximately 3,200 miles from east to west, from north to south it varies between 800 and 1,400 miles. The area covered by the desert is more than 3½ million square miles. The land level varies from below sea level to the mountain Emi Koussi (11,204 feet). The diurnal temperature range in the West Sahara may be more than 80°F. (45°C.) in 24 hours.

The largest desert in the United States is part of the Sonoran Desert which, including that part in Mexico, has an area of 120,000 square miles. The largest desert wholly within the United States is the Mohave (Mojave) Desert, California, which extends over 15,000 square miles.

LARGEST DESERT

The largest gorge in the world is the Grand Canyon on the Colorado River in North Central Arizona, U.S.A. It extends from Marble Gorge to the Grand Wash Cliffs, a distance of approximately 280 miles. It varies in width from 5 to 15 miles and, in parts, is more than one mile in depth (see Photo Plate 1).

The Colorado River has, in the course of about a million and a half years, exposed rock beds ranging in age from the Pre-Cambrian era (more than 1,500 million years ago) to the Triassic period (about 160 million years ago).

LARGEST GORGE

The deepest cave in the world is the Puits Berger, near Grenoble, 2,959 feet deep. In July 1955, its floor was reached by six French speleologists.

But in 1956, there was a report of a penetration to 3,050 feet in the same locality.

Recent tests carried out in the Gouffre Gachtiaggia Bella system in the French-Italian Maritime Alps suggest that there may be a cave system over 4,300 feet deep.

The deepest cave which has been explored by speleologists in the United States is one of 780 feet deep in an undisclosed location in Tennessee.

The biggest known underground chamber in the world is the Big Room of the Carlsbad Caverns in New Mexico. It is 4,000 feet long, 300 feet high and reaches 625 feet in width.

The most extensive labyrinth (cave system) is believed to be the Floyd Collins Crystal caves near Cave City, Kentucky. They have a proven length of 32 miles and a surmised length of 60 miles.

DEEPEST CAVE

The longest natural bridge in the world is the Landscape Arch in Utah's Arches National Monument. This natural sandstone arch spans 291 feet and is set about 100 feet above the canyon floor. In one place erosion has narrowed its section to six feet.

NATURAL BRIDGE

The highest sea cliffs in the United States are at Cape Flattery, Washington, and Cape Mendocino in California, both 700 feet high. The highest on the east coast are at Somerset Sound, Mount Desert Island, Maine, and are 640 feet high.

SEA CLIFFS

4. Flora

WORLD'S LARGEST FOREST

The largest afforestated areas of the globe are the vast coniferous forests of Northern U.S.S.R. lying mainly between 55°N and the Arctic Circle. The total wooded areas amount to 2,275,000,000 acres.

WORLD'S LARGEST LIVING THING

The 272 feet, 4 inches tall Californian redwood (*Sequoia gigantea*) tree named "General Sherman" in the Sequoia National Park, California, U.S.A., is the most massive living thing on Earth. It has a base circumference of 101 feet, 7 inches and requires 17 men to encircle it with outstretched arms. Its mean base diameter is 32 feet, 3 inches with a maximum of 34 feet, sufficient to provide 600,120 board feet of timber, enough for 35 five-room bungalows. The tree has blue-green foliage with red-brown tan bark up to 24 inches thick.

WORLD'S TALLEST TREE

Of trees now standing, the tallest is the Californian redwood (*Sequoia sempervirens*) named the Founder's Tree in the Humboldt State Park, Dyerville, California. Measurements taken in 1947 showed it to be 364 feet high.

A Douglas fir (*Pseudotsuga taxifolia*) felled by George Carey in Lynn Valley, North Vancouver, Canada, in 1895, stood 417 feet and was possibly the tallest tree of all time. The tree had a base circumference of 75 feet and was an estimated 1,800 years old. A redwood with a reported height of 367 feet, 8 inches and a basal circumference of 45 feet was felled near Guerneville, California, in 1873.

GREATEST GIRTH IN THE WORLD

The Santa Maria del Tule tree, in the State of Oazaca, in Mexico, which is a Montezuma cypress (*Taxodium mucronatum*) has a base circumference of 160 feet and would require twenty-seven men with outstretched arms to encircle it.

WORLD'S OLDEST TREE

The ages of standing trees cannot be determined, but some of the Californian redwoods are thought to be 4,000 to 5,000 years old. The "General Sherman" tree (see above) has been cited as the "oldest living thing." But these estimates are based on inconclusive data and may be considerably in error. The earliest definitely dated tree-ring grew in 1305 B.C. It is located on the 3,300-year-old sequoia stump D.21 in the Sequoia National Forest a mile to the northwest of the General Grant tree.

WORLD'S FASTEST GROWING TREE

Discounting bamboo, which is not botanically classified as a tree, the fastest growing tree is the *Eucalyptus saligna* which in Uganda, Central Africa, has been measured to grow 45 feet in 2 years.

Bamboo (*Dendrocalamus giganteus*) has been observed, in Ceylon, to grow as much as 16 inches in a day on its way to a maximum height of 120 feet.

SLOWEST GROWING

The speed of growth of trees depends largely upon the conditions which surround it, some trees such as bow and yew are always slow growing. The extreme is represented by the Sitka Spruce (*Picia sitchensis*) an example of which, growing under conditions of extreme rigor, took 98 years to grow eleven inches with a diameter of less than one inch.

The heaviest of all woods is Black Ironwood *(Krugiodendron ferreum)* with a specific gravity of up to 1.49 and a weight of up to 93 lbs. per cubic foot. This timber, though still the heaviest, does not attain quite such extreme density within the United States, where the hardest wood is Osage Orange *(Maclura pomifera)*.

The lightest wood is *Aeschynomene hispida* found in Cuba which has a specific gravity of 0.044 and a weight of only 2 ¾ lbs. per cubic foot. The lightest U.S. species is *Nyssa sp.* of the Tupelo gum genus with a specific gravity of 0.124 and a weight of 7 ¾ lbs. per cubic foot.

The largest leaves of any plant belong to the Royal Water Lily *(Victoria Regia)* found in the back waters of the River Amazon in South America. They are circular up to 21 feet in circumference with an upturned rim two inches high. The white blooms measure up to 15 inches across.

The mottled orange-brown and white *Rafflesia arnoldi* has parasitic blooms which attach themselves to the Cissus vines of the Malaysian jungle and measure up to 3 feet across and attain a weight of 15 lbs. See Photo No. 17, page 93.

The largest native United States wildflower bloom is that of the rose-mallow *(Hibiscus grandiflorus)*. It has a white and rose bloom measuring up to 12 inches across. 'Flowers' produced by sunflowers are classed as inflorescences, being in fact groups of very small flowers closely aggregated.

The 50-year-old "Lady Banksia" rose tree at Tombstone, Arizona, U.S.A., has a trunk 40 inches thick, stands 9 feet high and has arms spreading over 2,000 square feet supported by 32 posts so enabling 150 people to be seated under the arbor.

The largest of all cacti is the Saguaro *(Carnegiea gigantea)* found in Arizona, California, U.S.A., and Sonora, Mexico. The green fluted column is surmounted by candelabra-like branches rising, in some instances, to 70 feet. They have waxy white blooms which are followed by edible crimson fruit.

The largest fungus ever found—a Giant Puff Ball *(Calvatia gigantea)* was discovered in New York State in 1884. It was 5 feet, 3 inches long, 4 feet, 5 inches wide, and 9 ½ inches thick.

The yellowish-olive death cap *(Amanita phalloides)* is regarded as the world's most poisonous of all fungi. It is also found in England. Six to fifteen hours after tasting, the effects are vomiting, delirium, collapse and death. Among its victims was Pope Clement VII (1478-1534).

The largest of all ferns are the Costa Rican specimens of the tree ferns of the family *Cyatheaceae*. They attain heights of over 25 feet and possess leaves over ten feet in length.

Of the U. S. species, those with the longest fronds are *Acrosticham aureum* which have reached a length of over 13 feet.

The smallest of all ferns are the Central American *Hecistopteris pumila,* and the *Azolia Caroliniana* which is native to the United States.

LONGEST
SEAWEED

Claims made that seaweed off Tierra del Fuego, South America, grows to 600 and even 1,000 feet in length have gained currency. More recent and more reliable records indicate that the largest species of seaweed is *macrocyctis pyrifera* which does not exceed 195 feet in length.

NORTHERNMOST
PLANT LIFE

The seaweed *cryophilia* grows on the sea-ice in polar regions hundreds of miles north of the Arctic Circle.

RAREST
ORCHID

In nature there are a number of orchids of which only single occurrences have been reported. The rarest of all in the hands of orchid growers is the rosepink and vermilion. *Disa grandiflora,* native to the Cape of Good Hope, the exportation of which was prohibited by the South African Government in 1890. The highest price ever paid for an orchid is $2,600 in 1953 at Santa Barbara, California, for a single 3 bulbed plant of *Cymbidium Rosanna,* variety Pinkie.

LARGEST SEED

The largest seeds in the world are those of the double coconut *(Lodoicea sechellarum)* the single seeded fruit of which may weigh up to 40 lbs.

SMALLEST SEED

The smallest seeds in the world are those of the Epiphytic orchids at 35,000,000 to the ounce.

MOST DURABLE
SEED

The most durable of all seeds are those of the lotus *Nelumbium speciosum.* Tests on specimens from Manchurian peat, conducted at the Washington, D. C., Park Conservatory, U.S.A., showed that one which flowered on June 29th, 1952, had germinated from a seed at least a thousand years old. Suggestions that lotus seeds retain their viability for 50,000 years are unconfirmed.

Part Four

THE UNIVERSE

The universe is the entirety of space and matter. The remotest known heavenly bodies are extra-galactic nebulæ at a distance of some 1,000 million light years or nearly 6,000,000,000,000,000,000,000 miles. There is reason to believe that even remoter nebulæ exist but, since it is possible that they are receding faster than the speed of light (670,455,000 m.p.h.) they would be beyond man's "observable horizon."

REMOTEST KNOWN BODIES

The highest measured speed of recession is 14,400,000 miles per hour.

The largest nebulæ range up to 200,000 light years (1,200,000,-000,000,000,000 miles) in diameter and have a luminosity up to 6,000 million times that of the sun.

LARGEST NEBULÆ

The nearest heavenly body outside our own lens-shaped galaxy is the Greater Magellanic Cloud at a distance of 86,000 light years (505,-000,000,000,000,000 miles). This is easily visible in our southern hemisphere. The nearest nebula is that of Andromeda (diameter 840,000,-000,000,000,000 miles) visible in the northern hemisphere at a distance of 1,500,000 light years (9,000,000,000,000,000,000 miles).

NEAREST NEBULA

Andromeda, a spiral nebula, is also the remotest heavenly body visible to the naked eye. See Photo No. 15, page 59.

Sirius (*Alpha Canis Majoris*), also known as the Dog Star, is the brightest star in the heavens with a magnitude of −1.6. It is in the constellation Canis Major and is visible in the winter months of the northern hemisphere, being due south at midnight on the last day of the year. Sirius is over 50 billion miles distant and has a luminosity twenty-six times greater than the sun. It has a diameter of 1,500,000 miles and a mass of 45,800,000,000,000,000,000,000,000 tons.

BRIGHTEST STAR

The brightest star visible only in the southern hemisphere is Canopus (magnitude −0.9), and the brightest visible only in the northern hemisphere is Vega (magnitude 0.1).

If all stars could be viewed at the same distance, the most luminous would be the faint Sigma Dodarus which is 300,000 times brighter than the sun.

NEAREST STAR

Excepting the special case of our own sun, the nearest star is the very faint Proxima Centauri which is 4.3 light years (25,757,000,000,-000 miles). Travelling in space, a 5,000 m.p.h. rocket would take 576,-600 years or over 23,000 generations to reach it. The nearest star visible to the naked eye is the southern hemisphere star Alpha Centauri (4.33 light years).

LARGEST STAR

Of those measured, the star with the greatest diameter is Epsilon Aurigae at 2,500 million miles. So vast is this star that our own solar system of the sun and the six planets out as far as Saturn could be accommodated inside it.

The Alpha Herculis aggregation, consisting of a main star and a double star companion, is enveloped in a cold gas. This system, visible to the naked eye, has a diameter of 170,000,000,000 miles.

FASTEST STAR

The star with the largest proper motion is the tenth magnitude Munich 15040 (Barnard's Star). As viewed from the Earth, this star would move through an angle equivalent to the moon's diameter in less than 200 years.

HOTTEST STAR

The temperature of stars refers to their surface temperature, and not to their interior temperature, which is estimated to reach 20 million degrees Centigrade. Two 0-type stars of the Wolf-Rayet class have an estimated surface temperature of 70,000° C.

DENSEST STAR

The densest stars are the 'white dwarfs'. The invisible companion to Sirius (see above) is 70,000 times as dense as water but there seems to be scarcely any limit to the density of this category of star. The limitation is at the neutron state, that is, when the atomic particles exist in a state in which there is no space between them.

SMALLEST STAR

The smallest star is L886-6, halfway between Sirius and Procyon, at a distance of 30 light years, with a diameter of 3,000 miles. It was discovered by two American astronomers in 1952.

REMOTEST PLANET

Planets are bodies (including the Earth) which belong to the solar system and which revolve round the sun in definite orbits. The remotest of these, as measured from the sun, is Pluto (discovered by Tombaugh in 1930). Its mean distance from the sun is 3,675,300,000 miles and its period of revolution is 248.4 years.

It has recently been suggested that Pluto may in fact be an "escaped" satellite of Neptune.

NEAREST PLANET

The planet whose orbit is closest to the sun is Mercury, which revolves at a mean distance of 36 million miles. The fellow planet closest to Earth is Venus which at times is less than 25¾ million miles distant inside our orbit as opposed to Mars's closest approach of just over 34 million miles.

BRIGHTEST PLANET

Viewed from the Earth, by far the brightest of the five planets visible to the naked eye (Uranus at Magnitude 5.7 is only marginally visible) is Venus (with a maximum magnitude of —4.4). The faintest is Pluto with a magnitude of 14.

Jupiter, with an equatorial diameter of 88,700 miles and a polar diameter of 82,790 miles, is the largest of the nine major planets with a mass 318 times that of the Earth. It also has the fastest period of rotation on its own axis at only 9 hours 50 minutes.

LARGEST PLANET

Over 2,000 minor planets have been charted since 1800 but they are, for the most part, too small to yield to diameter measurement. Of the major planets, Mercury, whose period of revolution round the sun is only 87.97 days, is the smallest with a diameter of 3,010 miles and a mass only one-twentieth part that of the Earth, that is 300 trillion tons. Mercury also has the fastest velocity in orbit at 108,000 m.p.h. compared with the Earth's 66,600 m.p.h. Neither the density nor the period of rotation of the most recently discovered planet, Pluto (Tombaugh 1930) has yet been determined.

SMALLEST PLANET

The hottest of the planets is Mercury, which has a surface temperature of 670°F. on its hot side, but one of nearly −450°F. on its cold side. Mercury's hot side temperature depends to an extent upon its distance from the Sun (surface temperature 10,000°F.) which varies between 28,566,000 miles and 43,455,000 miles. The planets with a surface temperature closest to Earth's 59°F. are Mars with 28°F. (maximum 50°F.) and Venus with 68°F.

HOTTEST PLANET

The coldest planet is not unnaturally that which is farthest from the Sun, namely Pluto, which has an estimated surface temperature of −380°F.

COLDEST PLANET

Of the nine major planets, all but Mercury, Venus and Pluto have satellites. The planet with most is Jupiter with four large and eight small moons. Earth is the only planet with a single satellite. The distance of the solar system's thirty-one known satellites from their parent planets varies between the 5,830 miles of Phobos from Mars and the 14,700,000 miles of Satellite IX from Jupiter.

MOST SATELLITES

In the belt which lies between Mars and Jupiter, there are some 50,000 minor planets, or asteroids, which are for the most part too small to yield to diameter measurement. The largest of these is Ceres, with a diameter of 421 miles. The closest measured approach to the Earth by an asteroid was 400,000 miles, in the case of Hermes in 1937.

LARGEST ASTEROID

THE SUN

Earth's orbit around the sun is elliptical, hence our distance from the sun varies. The average distance of the sun is 93,003,000 miles. The closest approach (perihelion) is 91,342,000 miles and the farthest departure (aphelion) is 94,452,000 miles.

EARTH'S NEAREST APPROACH

To be visible to the protected naked eye, a sun-spot must cover about one two-thousandth part of the sun's hemisphere and thus have an area of 500 million square miles. The largest recorded sun-spot occurred on April 8th, 1947, in the sun's southern hemisphere. Its area was 7,000 million square miles with an extreme longitude of 187,000 miles and an extreme latitude of 90,000 miles. Sun-spots appear darker because they are over 2,000°C. cooler than the rest of the sun's surface.

LARGEST SUN-SPOT

ECLIPSES

EARLIEST RECORDED

The earliest date of an identifiable eclipse accurately recorded is one in Assyria in the year 911 B.C. but records exist from three centuries earlier.

The next total solar eclipse visible from continental United States will be seen from the southern part of New England on October 2nd, 1959. The next such eclipse visible from New York City will not be until April 8th, 2024.

LONGEST DURATION

The maximum possible duration of an eclipse of the sun is 7 minutes 40 seconds. This could only occur at the Equator, but the longest actually occurring since 717 A.D. was on June 20th, 1955 (7 minutes 8 seconds), visible from the Philippine Islands.

The longest period of totality of a solar eclipse visible from Continental United States was 3 minutes 30 seconds on September 10th, 1923, in California.

The longest totality of a lunar eclipse is 104 minutes. This has occurred on many occasions.

FREQUENCY

Seven is the greatest number of eclipses possible in a year, for example as in 1935 when there were five solar and two lunar eclipses, or four solar and three lunar eclipses as will occur in 1982. The least possible number in a year is two, both of which must be solar as in 1944.

COMETS

EARLIEST RECORDED

The earliest records of comets date from the 7th century B.C.

The successive appearances of Halley's Comet have been traced to 240 B.C. The first prediction of its return by Halley proved true on Christmas Day 1758, sixteen years after his death. Its next appearance will be in 1986.

CLOSEST APPROACH

On July 1st, 1770, Lexell's Comet, travelling at a speed of 23.9 miles per second (relative to the sun) came within 1,500,000 miles of the Earth. In May, 1910 however, the Earth is believed to have passed through the tail of Halley's Comet.

SHORTEST PERIOD

Of all the recorded periodic comets (these are members of the solar system), the one which most frequently returns is Encke's Comet, first identified in 1786. Its period is 3.3 years and not a single return has been missed by astronomers. The very faint comets, Schwassmann-Wachmann I (also designated 1925—II), and Oterma, travel in nearly circular orbits, and are known as the two annual comets. At the other extreme is the comet 1910a, whose path was not accurately determined, but which is not expected to return for perhaps four million years.

LARGEST COMET

Comets are so tenuous that it has been estimated that even their heads contain no mass in excess of 20 miles in diameter and that 10,000 cubic miles of tail contain less matter than a cubic inch of air. These tails, as in the case of the Great Comet of 1843, may trail out to 200,000,000 miles.

The moon, Earth's closest neighbor and only satellite, is at a mean distance of 238,857 miles. Its closest approach (perigee) is 221,463 miles and its extreme distance away (apogee) is 252,710 miles. The moon was first hit by radar on January 10th, 1946.

Only 59 per cent of the moon's surface is visible from the Earth. The largest known crater is the walled plain Bailly towards the South Pole which is 183 miles across and with walls rising to 14,000 feet. The nearby Newton crater is the deepest crater with a floor 29,000 feet below its rim.

It has been conjectured that these craters have been gouged by meteors travelling at 112,000 m.p.h.

There being no water on the moon, the heights of mountains can only be measured in relation to lower-lying terrain near their bases. The highest of all the lunar mountains are the Leibnitz near the South Pole which rise to nearly 35,000 feet.

When the sun is overhead, the temperature on the lunar equator reaches 230°F. (above the boiling point of water). By sunset the temperature is 58°F. but after nightfall the temperature sinks to nearly −300°F.

LIGHT YEAR—is that distance travelled by light (speed 186,239 miles per second) in one year and is 5,873,185,800,000 miles.

MAGNITUDE—is a measure of stellar brightness such that the light of a star of any magnitude bears a ratio of 2.512 to that of a star of the next magnitude. Thus a sixth magnitude star is 2.512 times less bright than a fifth magnitude star, while one of the first magnitude is exactly one hundred or $(2.512)^5$ times brighter. In the case of such exceptionally bright bodies as Sirius, Jupiter or the Moon, the magnitude is expressed as a minus quantity.

PROPER MOTION—that component of a star's motion in space, which, at right angles to the line of sight, constitutes an apparent change of position of the star in the celestial sphere.

Part Five

THE ANIMAL KINGDOM

1. Mammalia

MAMMALS
LARGEST and
HEAVIEST

The Blue Whale (Balaenoptera musculus) is the largest animal which has ever inhabited the Earth. Specimens have been recorded up to a length of 108 feet and a weight of 131¼ tons. They inhabit the colder seas and can swim at 14 knots. The young can be 25 feet long at birth and weigh up to 7.14 tons.

Specimens of up to an estimated 95 feet in length have been recorded off the Western seaboard of North America.

LARGEST
LAND ANIMAL

The largest bull African elephants (Loxodonta africana) stand 11 feet at the shoulder and may exceed 7 tons in weight.

The largest wild land animal in U. S. fauna is the 'buffalo' (Bison americanus) measuring up to 11 feet 6 inches in length and weighing 2,000 lbs.

LARGEST
RODENTS

The largest of all rodents is the tropical South American Capybara (Hydrochoerus capybara) which measures up to 4 feet in length and weighs up to 150 lbs. The largest rodent in U. S. fauna is the beaver (Castor canadensis) weighing up to 60 lbs.

TALLEST
LAND ANIMAL

The giraffe (Giraffa camelopardalis) with neck erect measures up to 18 feet 5 inches in height. These are now found only in Africa, south of the Sahara.

The tallest wild animal in U. S. fauna is the bull Alaska moose (Alces gigas) which stand up to 7 feet at the shoulder, weigh 1,600 lbs. and have antlers which spread up to a record 6 feet 5⅝ inches, the greatest of any deer.

SMALLEST

The species of shrew (Suncus truscus) found along the coasts of the northern Mediterranean has a body length of only 1½ inches.

The smallest mammal in U. S. fauna is the Pygmy Shrew (Microsorex hoyi) species of which measure only 3¼ inches overall and weigh only 2.3 grams.

The slightly heavier Little Short-tailed Shrew (Cryptotis parva) is the shortest mammal with some specimens measuring only 2.8 inches overall.

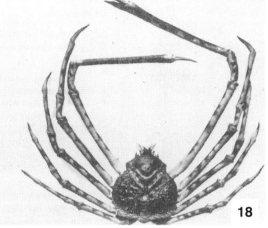

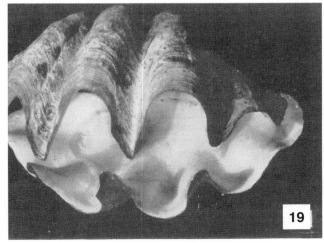

16. The Chubb Crater, the largest meteorite crater in the world. See p. 64.
17. Raffelasia arnoldi, the largest bloom in the world. See p. 85.
18. The Japanese Spider Crab, capable of spanning 11 feet between claw-tips. See p. 102.
19. Tridacna gigas, the largest of all shells. See p. 101.
20. The Chinchilla with the most expensive fur. See p. 96.

SMALLEST
HOOFED
ANIMAL

The Mouse Deer or Cheurotain *(Tragulus Kanchil)* of the East Indies and West Africa is the smallest of all Ungulates or hoofed animals and also of all ruminants measuring only 12 inches high at the shoulder.

FASTEST
LAND ANIMAL

Over very short distances the fastest of land animals is the cheetah *(Aciconyx jubatus)* at 84 m.p.h. Average specimens weigh 100 lbs. They are found chiefly in Central India where they are trained for hunting. Tests in London, England, in 1939, showed that on an oval track over 500 yards, the cheetah's average speed was 44 m.p.h.

LONGEST
LIVED

No mammal can match the extreme proven age of 115 years attained by man *(Homo sapiens)* (see page 11). It is probable that the elephant makes the closest approach with about 70 years.

RAREST

The Tasmanian wolf *(Thylacinus cynocephalus),* the largest of the carnivorous marsupials, is now confined to the wildest parts of Tasmania. So close is it to extinction that recent expeditions failed to find any specimens though there was evidence of their continued existence.

HIGHEST

The highest altitude to which any animal has travelled is 80 miles by the Rhesus monkey "Mike" in an experimental Aerobee rocket in 1954.

GREATEST
TUSKS

The longest recorded elephant tusks came from Kenya and are in the American National Collection. They are 11 feet 5½ inches and 11 feet in length, 18½ inches in circumference and weigh 293 lbs. together. The world's heaviest, also from Kenya (10 feet 5½ inches), weigh 214 lbs. and 226½ lbs., or together 440½ lbs.

The longest walrus tusks on record are 37½ inches in length, 10¾ inches in circumference, weighing 10 pounds 13 ounces. The longest mammoth tusks on record are 13 feet long, weighing 200 lbs.

LONGEST and
SHORTEST
GESTATION
PERIODS

The longest of all mammalian gestation periods is that of the Indian elephant *(Elephas maximus)* with an average of 620 days and a maximum of 760 days (2 years and 30 days)—over 2½ times longer than a human. The gestation period of the young opossum *(Didelphis marsupialis),* which are born in a very immature stage of development, may be as little as 8 days though normally 12 days.

DOMESTICATED ANIMALS

HORSES
Age

The oldest recorded age for a horse is the 62 years credited to "Old Billy", an English barge horse from the River Mersey believed to be a cross between a Cleveland and Eastern blood, which died in 1822. No reliable evidence confirms this claim and forty-five years more probably represents the extreme in the case of an Orkney mare which died at Fintray, Aberdeenshire, Scotland, in 1936.

Largest

The heaviest horse on record was the Shire mare Erfyl Lady Grey, London show champion 1924-26. She weighed 25 cwt. The tallest horse on record is a Clydesdale of 21 hands.

The largest mane on record was one of 13 feet—a Percheron—measured in Dee in 1891. The horse also had a 10 foot long tail.

A carefully conducted test carried out in Liverpool, England, in 1924 showed that two Shire geldings were able to pull an 18½ ton load.

Strength

Dogs over 18 are very rare but some live to a little over 20 and even 34 years has been accepted by some authorities. The oldest dog recently reported in the British Isles is a cross-bred terrier "Toss" of Studfold Farm, Horton-in-Ribblesdale, Yorkshire, England, which was 22 in 1955.

DOGS
Age

The largest litter of puppies on record is the twenty-one thrown by the St. Bernard bitch, "Lady Millard", owned by a Mr. Thorp of North-wold, Norfolk, England, on February 9th, 1895.

Largest
Litter

The longest dog team ever harnessed is the seventy-three dog team led by the Siberian husky "Waka" used in U. S. Army tests at the Chinook Kennels, Wonalancet, New Hampshire, in 1941, to pull a 10-ton Army truck.

Longest
Team

The highest price bid for a dog is £10,500 ($29,400) offered in January, 1956, by an agent in Montreal, Canada, to Miss Mary de Pledge of Bracknell, England, for the 3-year-old golden pekingese, Champion Caversham Ku-Ku of Yam.

Highest
Price

The most successful breed in the leading national dog show, that of the Westminster Kennel Club (instituted 1877) is the wire-haired fox terrier with 9 "Best-in-Show" titles in 1917, 1920, 1926, 1928, 1930-31, 1934, 1937 and 1946. The only 3 time winner was Winthrop Rutherford's Champion Warren Remedy, a smooth-haired fox terrier in 1907-09. The record entry was 3,146 in the 1937 show.

Most
Successful
Breed

Though 21 years is normally regarded as the limit for long lived cats, there is a well authenticated case of a female tabby "Ma" owned by Mrs. Alice St. George Moore of "Newton Barton", Drewsteignton, Devon, England, attaining 33 years in 1956.

CAT
Oldest

The talking bird with the greatest vocabulary in the world is "Sandy Paul", a yellow brown-beaked budgerigar owned by Mrs. Irene Pauls of Staines, Middlesex, England. This bird, hatched in 1952, believed to be a female, knows twelve nursery rhymes straight through and has a total vocabulary of over 300 words. This compares with the 845 words devised by C. K. Ogden in 1930 for a Basic English vocabulary.

BIRDS

For auction prices, milk yield and prolificacy records for cattle, sheep and pigs, see under Agriculture.

FURS

In 1913, a pair of silver foxes for breeding purposes changed hands for the all-time record figure of $35,000. The highest price quoted in modern times is $10,000 for an 18 oz. albino chinchilla exhibited in Toronto, Canada, on February 12th, 1956 and thus worth 16 times its weight in gold. See Photo No. 20, page 93.

MOST
VALUABLE

Fur prices have been subject to violent market fluctuation ever since Richard Dalton established the earliest farm to raise black foxes on Prince Edward Island, Canada, in 1887. The highest price ever paid for a single skin is $2,627.00 for one silver fox pelt sold in 1910. Of more recent times the highest priced single skins have been those of the sapphire mutation mink (Lutreola lutra). At the first open auction of these in January 1951 a bundle of hand-picked male skins brought $350.00 each.

The average top prices of mink mutations at $95.00 a skin is, however, below that of the Siberian sable (Mustela zibellina) which consistently brings over $140.00 a skin. It is probable that the protected and hence only illegally killed sea otter (Latax lutris) would surpass all other furs in value, though the extremely rare solid white and solid black chinchilla mutations have not yet been marketed. Sea otter pelts have been valued at $2,500.00.

FURCOAT

A coat made from 120 to 150 ranch-raised casualty pelts of chinchilla (Lanigera chinchillaidae), the bluish-gray South American rodent, is reputed to have been bought for $35,000.00 in the United States before the war. At the first regular sale of chinchillas in June 1954, the average price per skin was $36.77 and the peak $175, thus giving a top material cost of $26,250.00 per 150 skin coat.

The most valuable fur coat of all-time was a unique azure blue mink coat purchased in Paris for the late Mme. Eva Peron (died June 1952) at an undisclosed price.

2. Fishes

LARGEST (Sea)

Though not comparable in size with the larger species of whales (mammals), the whale-shark (Rhinedon typus), first discovered off Cape Town in 1828, has been measured up to 45 feet in length. Specimens are credibly reported to reach lengths of 60 feet or even more, weighing up to 67 tons. The whale-shark, blackish with white dots, is harmless unless attacked and lives in the warmer areas of the Atlantic, Pacific, and Indian Oceans.

The largest fish in U. S. waters is the comparatively rare man-eating White Shark (Carcharodon carcharodon). A specimen off the Californian coast in excess of 20 feet long has been recorded.

LARGEST (Freshwater)

The giant Russian sturgeon (Acipenser) found in the Volga river, has been measured to attain 26 feet in length and a specimen has been weighed at 3,221 lbs. (1.44 tons).

SMALLEST (Sea)

The fully grown male guppy fish (Lebistes reticulatus) is smaller than a queen bee. These tropical fish come from the waters around the Southern Caribbean and Venezuela.

SMALLEST (Freshwater)

The freshwater fish Pandaka pygmaea of the goby group found in the lakes of the Philippine Islands measure only fractionally over ⅜ inch (9-11 mm.).

FASTEST

The swordfish, which include marlins (Makaira mitsukurii), are regarded as unrivalled for speed though the practical difficulties of measurement makes data extremely hard to secure. A maximum of 50 knots (57.5 m.p.h.) has been quoted, but 30 to 35 knots is the most that will be conceded by some experts.

Aquaria are of too recent origin to be able to establish which species of fish can fairly lay claim to the title of the longest lived. Early indications are that it is the European pike at 60 to 70 years. An 81 inch long, 215 lb., sturgeon caught on July 15th, 1953, in the Lake of the Woods, Kenora, Ontario, Canada, was believed to be 150 years old based on a growth ring *(annuli)* count in the spiny ray of its pectoral fin.

The greatest depth from which living organisms have been recovered is 34,120 feet by the Danish Research vessel "Galathea" in the Pacific Ocean in 1950.

Periodically specimens of fish never before identified are recovered. Such specimens, of which only a single known example exists, occur particularly among abyssal fauna.

The ocean sun-fish *(Mola mola)* weighing up to ½ ton and 8 feet in length produces up to 300,000,000 eggs 1/10th inch long and 1/20th inch in diameter. The estimated increase in weight between young and adult is 60 million-fold (human increase 22 fold).

The highest measured charge delivered by an electric eel is 1 amp. at 700 volts.

3. *Reptiles and Amphibians*

(Crocodiles, snakes, turtles, tortoises and lizards)

The salt-water or estuarine crocodile *(Crocodilus porosus)* of South-East Asia may attain a length of 30 feet. Strictly carnivorous, they live in tidal waters and have been sighted far out at sea. They will devour anything they can overcome and will eat human corpses.

The longest reptile in U. S. fauna is the Mississippi alligator *(Alligator mississippiensis)* found in Southeastern states. Older specimens lose their yellow cross-bars and are dark grey when dry. They may attain a length of 19 feet or nearly 5 feet more than the American Crocodile *(Crocodylus acutus)* found in Florida in 1875.

The leatherback turtle *(Dermochelys coriacea)* found rarely on Oceanic islands has been known to weigh up to 1,902 lbs. and attain 9 feet in overall length.

The rich yellow, brown and black reticulated python *(Python reticulatus)* is the longest of all snakes. It is found in Malaya, Burma and Indo-China and has been known to attain an extreme length of 33 feet.

The longest snake in U. S. fauna is the Boa constrictor measuring up to 13 feet.

The longest poisonous snake in the world is the King Cobra *(Hamadryad)* a specimen of which killed in Siam was measured at 18 feet 4 inches. The longest poisonous snake in U. S. fauna is the Eastern diamond-backed rattler *(Crotalus)* measuring up to 8 feet.

The shortest of all snakes is the worm-snake of the family *Leptotyphopide* found in the southwestern states of the U. S. and measuring only 4 inches overall.

MOST POISONOUS

The toxicity of the venom of the Australian tiger snake (*Notechis scutatus*) is unmatched by any other serpent. These snakes, tawny with dark bands, commonly grow to 4 or 5 feet in length.

The most poisonous snake in U. S. fauna is the Western diamond-backed rattlesnake (*Crotalus cinereous*) but the greatest number of deaths are caused by the more widespread Copperhead (*Agkisrodon laticinctus*).

FASTEST MOVING SNAKE

The fastest measured speed for a snake is that of the Black Mamba (*Dendroaspis polylepis*) which, on a favorable surface, can attain nearly 7 m.p.h.

The fastest-moving snake in the United States is the Red Racer (*Coluber flagellum*) which has been timed at 3.6 m.p.h.

SLOWEST MOVING REPTILE

Tests on a giant tortoise (*Testudo gigantea*) in Mauritius show that even when hungry and enticed by a cabbage it cannot exceed 5 yards in a minute (0.17 m.p.h.). Over longer distances its speed is greatly reduced.

LARGEST LIZARD

The largest of all lizards is the Komodo Monitor (*Varanus Komodoensis*) first discovered on the Indonesian island of Komodo in 1914. This dragon-like creature may attain a length of nearly 12 feet and a weight of 250 lbs.

LONGEST LIVED

The Royal Tongan tortoise ''Tui Malila'' is reputed to have been presented to Queen Salote's antecedent by Captain Cook in 1773, 1774 or 1777, thus indicating an age of 180 or more years.

The greatest proven age of a continuously observed tortoise is the 116 years of a Mediterranean spur-thighed tortoise (*Testudo graeca*) in Paignton Zoological Gardens, Devon, England.

The longest lived — and the heaviest — snake is the Anaconda which has been known to live 28 years (Washington, D. C. Zoo) and weigh over 335 lbs.

AMPHIBIANS

(Salamanders, toads, frogs, newts, etc.).

LARGEST

The giant salamander (*Megolobatrachus maximus*) found in Japan grows to over 5 feet in length and weighs up to 90 lbs.

The largest frog is the rare goliath frog (*Rana goliath*) first found in 1906 in West Africa, which measures nearly 12 inches in length.

LONGEST LIVED

A toad in captivity in Copenhagen has reached the age of 54 years but there is evidence of giant salamanders attaining 60 years.

LONGEST FROG JUMP

The greatest distance achieved by a frog in an official contest is 16 feet 10 inches (aggregate of 3 jumps) by a frog named ''Lucky'', owned by Roy Weimer, on May 24th, 1954 at Angels Camp, Calif. At the same stadium in May 1955 an African frog made an unofficial single leap of over 15 feet when being retrieved for placement in his container.

4. Birds

Of living species, by far the largest is the ostrich *(Struthio camelus)* of Africa. Male examples of this flightless bird reach 300 lbs. in weight and stand 8 feet tall. Ostriches are able to run at a speed in excess of 30 m.p.h.

LARGEST

The wandering albatross *(Diomedea exulans)* of the southern oceans measures up to 11 feet 4 inches in wingspan. There is reason to believe that some unmeasured specimens may be in excess of 12 feet.

LARGEST WINGSPAN

The largest wild bird of the United States is the trumpeter swan *(Cygnus buccinator)* of which the cob (male) averages 27.9 lbs. in weight.

The largest U. S. land bird and bird of prey is the Californian condor *(Gymnogyps californianus)* now rarely found in the canyon country of South California. It is sooty black with a naked yellowish-red head and a pure white underwing with a length of up to 55 inches and wingspan of up to 10 feet 6 inches.

The smallest bird in the world is the male bee hummingbird *(Mellisuga helenae)* of Cuba known locally as the Zunzuncito. It has a fiery red throat and a bluish and greyish white body and measures only 2.3 inches overall. The smallest bird in the United States is the male Calliope hummingbird *(Stellula calliope)* measuring barely 3 inches overall. It has red rays on its white throat and is found in the Western mountains from Washington State to Southern California.

SMALLEST

Claimant for this title is the North American ivory-billed woodpecker *(Campephilus principalis)* which may even be extinct. It is believed, however, that less than a dozen still exist in the Florida area.

RAREST

The most abundant of all birds are the Wilson's petrels. They range as far south as Antarctica.

MOST ABUNDANT

Of those birds about which information is available the carrion crow is the only proven centenarian with the cockatoo second at 95 years.

LONGEST LIVED

The spine-tailed swift are alleged to have been timed to fly 2 miles in 36 seconds in India (200.0 m.p.h.) but experiments have shown that a bird of this size would be invisible even through binoculars at such a distance. The highest reliable ground speed recorded for any bird is the 93.55 m.p.h. average by a racing pigeon over an 80-mile course in Northern Ireland in 1914. Wood pigeons are reported to have attained an air speed of 150 m.p.h. (40 m.p.h. into a 110 m.p.h. wind) in Scotland in January, 1953.

FASTEST FLYING

The most reliable observation of a U.S. bird in level flight was of a Golden Plover *(Charadrius dominicus),* timed from a railroad train to do 62 m.p.h.

The most extensive migration of any bird is that of the Arctic tern *(Sterna paradisaea)* which breeds in the Arctic within 8° of the North Pole and is found on the Antarctic coast in the northern winter after a flight of 11,000 miles.

LONGEST MIGRATION

HIGHEST
FLYING

The celebrated example of a skein of 17 geese photographed crossing the sun from Dehra Dun, India, on September 17th, 1919, at a height variously estimated up to 58,000 feet has been discredited by experts. The highest acceptable altitudes are 24,000 to 25,000 feet by a lammergeier (Gypaetus barbatus) on Everest in 1922 and a chough (Phyrrhocorax) at approximately 26,000 feet in 1953.

LARGEST
EGG

Of living birds, that producing the largest egg is the ostrich. These are found 6 to 7 inches in length and 4 to 6 inches in diameter. They require about 40 minutes for boiling.

SMALLEST
EGG

The smallest egg is laid by the green and greyish white Vervain hummingbird of Jamaica (Mellisuga minima) known as the Little Doctor Bird. The egg looks like a large pearl with an overall length of only ½ inch.

5. Insects

LARGEST

The bulkiest of all insects is the beetle (Macrodontia cervicornis) which measures up to 5.85 inches (150 mm.) in length. Some tropical stick-insects (Plasmidae) have a body length up to 13 inches (330 mm.) while the Indian atlas moth (Attacus) has a wing span of fully 12 inches (305 mm.).

SMALLEST

Several hundred new species of insect are discovered yearly, but of those known the smallest are minute beetles (Coleoptera trichopterygidae) and the Hymenoptera mymaridae known as the "battledore-wing fairy fly", both of which are only 1/128 of an inch (0.2 mm.) in length. These could crawl through the eye of a needle with ease.

FASTEST
FLYING

Experiments have proved that widely published statements that the female deer bot-fly could attain 800 m.p.h. are wildly exaggerated. The highest ground speed instrumentally measured is the 55-60 m.p.h. of the dragonfly Austrophlebia, but modern experiments have established that the highest maintainable air-speed of any insect is 27 m.p.h. rising to a maximum of 35 m.p.h. in short bursts.

LONGEST
LIVED

Little data have been published but a Cicada septemdecim has been known to live 17 years of which 16 were in the larval stage.

FASTEST
WING BEAT

The fastest wing beat of any insect is 57,000 per minute by the midge Forcipomyia. In experiments at a temperature of 98.6°F. with truncated wings the rate attained 133,080 beats per minute. The muscular contraction—expansion cycle in 0.00045 or 1/2,218th of a second represents the fastest muscle movement ever measured.

**BUTTERFLIES
and Moths**

LARGEST

Butterflies and moths form the order Lepidoptera of which there are 140,000 species.

The largest moths are the Indian atlas moths (Attacus) with a wing span of fully 12 inches (305 mm.). The world's largest butterfly is the

New Guinea birdwing *(Troides Alexandrae)*, the female of which has a span of 12 inches.

The largest moth in North America is the Noctuid moth *(Thysania agrippina)* with a wing span of 10 ½ inches. The moth in U. S. fauna with the largest wing span is the Imperial Moth *(Basilona imperialis)* which is matched in wing area by the great *Rothschildia orizaba*.

The largest U. S. butterflies are the large western swallowtail *(Papilio Multicaudata)*, the orange-dog swallowtail of the South *(Papilio cresphontes)* and the southern tiger swallowtail *(Papilio glawcus australis)* all of which have a wing span of 4 ½ inches.

The smallest *Lepidoptera* is the *Nepticula microtheviella* with a wing span of less than ⅛ th of an inch (3 mm.).

SMALLEST

The smallest of all North American butterflies is the Pygmy Blue *(Brephidium excilis)*. It has a wing expanse of from ½ to ⅝ inch (13-17 mm.) and is found in the Gulf States and Southern California.

It has been successfully established that the male wax moth can detect the smell of a female at a range of one mile.

SENSE OF SMELL

SPIDERS

The world's largest spider is the *(Theraphosa blondi)* from the Guianas which is 3 ½ inches (9 cm.) in body length.

LARGEST

The smallest spiders in the world are the *Orchestina* and the *Cepheia longiseta* which have a body length of less than 1/30th of an inch (0.8 mm.).

SMALLEST

Spiders are the highest permanent inhabitants of the Earth. Jumping spiders *(Salticidae)* have been collected at 22,000 feet on Everest. Spiders also live deep down in coalmines and caves.

HIGHEST

The South American black widow spider *(Latrodectus mactans)* has a bite capable of killing a human being, but lethal results occur in less than one in ten instances.

MOST POISONOUS

(Squids, octopods, snails, shells, etc.).

MOLLUSKS

The giant squid *(Architeuthis)* found on the Newfoundland Banks may have a body length of 8 feet and measure up to 40 feet overall. The largest snail is the *Achatina achatina* measuring 7 inches in length.

LARGEST

The largest of all shells is the marine bivalve *(Tridacna gigas)* found on the Indo-Pacific coral reef. A specimen in the American Museum of Natural History, New York, measuring 43 inches by 29 inches, weighs 579 lbs. (over ¼ of a ton). See Photo No. 19, page 93.

The largest mollusk native in the United States is the rosy-lipped Queen Conch shell *(Strombus gigas)* which weighs 5 lbs. and has a horny exterior measuring over 12 inches overall. The slenderer Horse Conch *(Pleuroploca gigantea)* found on the Atlantic seaboard measures up to 24 inches overall. The largest shell on the Pacific seaboard is the ear-shaped mother of pearl Red Abalone *(Haliotis rufescens)* measuring up to 12 inches overall.

SMALLEST

The minute marine gastropod *Homalogyra atomus* from the Atlantic is only 1/30th inch in diameter, the smallest of all shells.

PEARLS

Pearls are protective secretionary bodies produced by mollusks. Gem pearls come chiefly from the western Pacific (*genus Pinctada*) and the fresh water mussel (*genus Quadrula*).

The largest in the world is the Hope Pearl of 1,800 grains or nearly 3 ozs. It is fractionally over 3 inches in length and has a circumference at its globular end of 4 ½ inches. The largest known pearl of regular shape was known as "La Pellegrina" and weighed 111 ½ grains.

CRUSTACEA

(Crabs, lobsters, shrimps, woodlice, etc.).

LARGEST

The scarlet Giant Japanese Spider crab (*Macrocheiva*), possessing a body a foot across and legs capable of spanning 11 feet claw-tip to claw-tip, is the largest of all Crustacea. See Photo No. 18, page 93.

SMALLEST

The water-flea (*Alonella*) has an overall length of 1/100th of an inch.

MOST LEGGED

The creatures with greatest number of legs are millipedes which are distinguished from centipedes by having two instead of one pair of legs on most segments of the body. The extreme case among millipedes is a species with 784 legs while one species of centipede has only 16 legs.

6. *Microbes*

SMALLEST VISIBLE

The smallest object visible to the unaided human eye under the best possible conditions measures approximately 3.4 microns in diameter, roughly 1/7,500th of an inch. A micron is a thousandth part of a millimetre.

LARGEST BACTERIA

The largest of the bacteria is *Bacillus megatarium* which measures 1.5 x 4 microns, about 60 millionths by 160 millionths of an inch.

SMALLEST BACTERIA

The line between the smallest bacteria and the largest viruses is extremely difficult to draw since many of the organisms in this size group, 250-300 mμ (a mμ — or millimicron — is a millionth part of a millimetre) share various distinguishing characteristics. The rickettsiae, which causes typhus and similar fevers, are an example of what appears to be bacteria but also exhibit traits of viruses. They have in fact been variously classified as the largest virus and the smallest bacteria. The rickettsiae causing Psittacosis or parrot fever measure 275 mμ and are probably the largest virus-type particle.

SMALLEST VIRUS

The smallest virus is that of foot and mouth disease, approximately 10 mμ in diameter, 1/4,000,000th of an inch.

The smallest plant virus is the mosaic disease of alfalfa which is approximately 16 mμ in diameter.

SMALLEST MICROSCOPICALLY VISIBLE

The limit of resolution which can be obtained by the use of the normal optical system microscope and seen with the human eye is a particle about 250 mμ, the limiting factor being the wavelength of visible light which lies between about 7,500A and 4,000A (1 Angstrom = 10^{-7}

mm. or a tenth of a mμ). By using light of a shorter wave length than that visible to the human eye, e.g. ultra violet, and a specially equipped microscope, it is possible to obtain photographs of particles down to 100 mμ.

The development of the electron microscope, which uses a focusable beam of electrons with a wave length (dependent on the electron beam voltage) up to 100,000 times shorter than that of visible light, enables a resolution to be obtained down to 5 mμ. This is smaller than any virus yet discovered and is approximately the size of a hemoglobin molecule.

The most primitive of all animals was for a long time thought to be the amoeba but this title is now accorded protozoa (first life) of the class Flagellata. Of these the most rudimentary appears to be the *Monosiga Gracilis*.	MOST PRIMITIVE

EXTINCT ANIMALS

The giant dinosaur or thunder-lizard (*Diplodocus*) which roamed the swamps of North America 160 million years ago measured up to 87½ feet in length. These semi-aquatic reptiles weighed over 40 tons. The heaviest of prehistoric animals was the swamp-dwelling *Brachiosaurus* which is believed to have weighed 50 tons.	LAND ANIMALS LARGEST
The *Baluchitherium*, a type of extinct rhinoceros, unearthed in Mongolia was found to measure 17 feet 9 inches to the shoulder and probably stood nearly 25 feet tall to the crown of its head.	LARGEST MAMMAL
The largest of any carnivorous prehistoric animal was the *Tyrannosaurus rex* remains of which were found in Montana in 1908. This fiercest looking of all monsters stood 18½ feet high and was 47 feet in length.	LARGEST FLESH-EATER
The largest tusk of any prehistoric mastodon is the specimen from an *Archidiskodon Imperator* found at Port, Texas, and now housed at the American Museum of Natural History, New York, measured slightly in excess of 16 feet in length.	LARGEST TUSK
The *Gigantophis*, inhabiting Egypt 60 million years ago, is estimated to have attained a length of 50 feet.	LONGEST SNAKE
The *Aepyornis titan* of Southern Madagascar which may have survived into the 18th century was a large flightless bird standing 10 feet in height. Its eggs were also the largest of any bird, being 13 inches in length with a diameter of 9½ inches and a capacity of 2 gallons — six times that of an ostrich egg. The extinct flightless bird from New Zealand, the moa, was probably taller, attaining a height of over 11 feet.	LARGEST BIRD
The extinct winged lizard (*Pteramodon*) had an overall wing span of 27 feet.	LARGEST FLYING CREATURE
The earliest known of birds was the *Archaeopteryx* belonging to the era of 150 million years ago, remains of which were first discovered at Solenhofen in Bavaria in 1861. It has recently been suggested that the *Archaeopteryx* was only a 'glider'.	EARLIEST BIRD

Part Six

THE SCIENTIFIC WORLD

ELEMENTS

All matter in the Solar System is made up of 92 natural chemical elements comprising 2 liquids, 11 gases and 79 solids.

GASES
Lightest

Hydrogen, a colorless gas discovered by H. Cavendish (British) in 1766, is less than 1/14th the weight of air, weighing only 0.005611 lb. per cubic foot or 0.08988 grams per liter.

Heaviest

Radon, a colorless gas discovered by F. E. Dorn (Germany) in 1900, is 111.5 times heavier than hydrogen. It is also known at Niton and is an emanation from radium salts.

Lowest and
Highest
Melting and
Boiling
Points

Of all substances, helium has the lowest boiling point (−268.94°C). This element, which is at normal temperatures a colorless gas, was discovered in 1868 by Sir Joseph Lockyer (British) and Pierre Jannsen (French) working independently. Helium was first liquefied by the Dutch physicist, Kammerlingh Onnes, in 1908. Liquid helium, which exists in two forms, can only be solidified under pressure.

Of the elements that are gases at normal temperatures, chlorine has the highest melting point (−101.6°C) and the highest boiling point (−34°C). This yellow-green gas was discovered by the Swede, C. W. Scheele, in 1774.

Commonest

The Earth's atmosphere has been computed to weigh 5,000,000,-000,000,000 tons of which nitrogen constitutes 78.09 per cent by volume in dry air. Hydrogen, however, constitutes some 90 per cent of all the matter in the universe.

Rarest

By far the rarest of the eleven elemental gases, which constitute the atmosphere is radon (see above), which probably accounts for only .0000000000000006 per cent of the atmosphere.

METALS
Lightest

Lithium (Li), a silvery white metal discovered by the Swede, J. A. Arfvedson, in 1817, is the lightest of all metals with a specific gravity of 0.534 grams per milliliter (c.c.) or a density of 33.32 lb. per cubic foot. It is over 42 times lighter than osmium.

Densest

Osmium (Os), a grey-blue metal of the platinum group, discovered by S. Tennent (British) in 1804, is the densest of all metals with a specific gravity of 22.48 grams per milliliter (c.c.) or a density of 1,403 lb. per cubic foot or 250,000 times denser than hydrogen. A cubic foot of uranium would weigh only 1,164 lbs.

Excluding mercury, which is liquid at normal temperatures, caesium (Cs), a silvery-white metal discovered by the Germans, R. W. von Bunsen and G. R. Kirchoff in 1860, melts at 28°C (82.4°F).

Tungsten or wolfram (W), a grey metal discovered by the Spaniard, D. F. de Elhuyar, in 1784, melts at 3,370°C.

Excluding mercury as above, the metal which vaporizes at the lowest temperature is caesium at 670°C.

Tungsten has to be heated to 5,900°C (2,530°C above its melting point) before it vaporizes.

Lowest and Highest Melting and Boiling Points

The highest linear thermal expansion of any metal is that of caesium which, at about 20°C., is 97×10^{-6} in. per inch per one degree C°.

The lowest linear expansion is that of the alloy Invar, containing 36.1 per cent nickel, the remainder being iron: the linear thermal expansion of this being a maximum of 2×10^{-6} in. per inch per one degree C° at ordinary temperatures.

Expansion

The most malleable, or ductile, of metals is gold; either pure or in the form of an alloy containing 97 per cent gold, the remainder being copper and silver, can be beaten down without annealing from 1/1000 inch thickness to about 1/250,000 inch thickness. One ounce of gold (avoirdupois) can be drawn in the form of a continuous wire thread to a length of fifty-one miles.

Ductility

Of the natural elemental metals, a number of the 15 described as the Rare Earths have only recently separated into metallic purity. Doubt has been expressed even as to the existence in nature of element 43 named masurium and element 61 named illinium.

The rarest form of matter on earth was the 17 atoms of mendelevium (Element 101, Symbol Mv) synthesized in the University of California's Cyclotron at Berkeley, California, by Dr. Glenn T. Seaborg early in 1955. This transuranic element, which has properties similar to thallium, was found to have a half-life not much more than thirty minutes.

Rarest

Though ranking behind oxygen (47.33%) and silicon (27.74%) in abundance, aluminium is the commonest of all metals, constituting 7.85 per cent of the Earth's crust.

Commonest

Beginning in 1940 with neptunium (Element 93) artificial transuranic elements have been created by cyclotron bombardments as follows:— plutonium (Element 94) 1940, americium (Element 95) 1944, curium (Element 96) 1944, berkelium (Element 97) 1949 and californium (Element 32) 1950. Reports in 1954 indicated the achievement of einsteinium (Element 99) and Fermium (Element 100), and in 1955, mendelevium (Element 101) see above.

Newest

Diamond, a crystalline form of carbon (Element 6) is the hardest of all known substances. The hardest of man-made compounds is tungsten carbide. (See also p. 108.)

HARDEST SUBSTANCE

The strength of acids and alkalis is measured on the pH scale. The pH of a solution is the logarithm to the base 10 of the reciprocal of the hydrogen-ion concentration in gram molecules per liter. True neutrality,

STRONGEST ACID

pH 7, occurs in pure water at 22°C. The strongest acid is hydrochloric acid (HCl) (an aqueous solution of hydrogen chloride gas discovered by B. Valentine in 1644).

STRONGEST ALKALI

The strength of alkalis is expressed by pH values rising above the neutral 7.0. The strongest are caustic soda or sodium hydroxide (Na OH) and caustic potash or potassium hydroxide (KOH).

SMELLIEST SUBSTANCE

The most powerfully smelling substance is ethyl mercaptan (C_2H_5SH). This can be detected in a concentration of 4 by 10^{-8} milligrams per liter of air and smells of rotting cabbage, garlic, onions and sewer gas. Thus 4 mg. completely volatilized would still be detectable in an enclosed space with a floor the size of a full-sized football pitch and a roof 45 feet high.

SWEETEST SUBSTANCE

The sweetest compound yet prepared is 1-propoxy-2-amino-4-nitrobenzene which is 5,000 times sweeter than a 1% solution of sucrose.

MOST EXPENSIVE PERFUME

The costliest perfume in the world is Jean Patou's "Joy" from Paris. It is based on the finest rose oils, rosa damascena and jasmin oil blended with over one hundred other flower essences. It retails at $45 an ounce. The biggest and most expensive listed bottle of perfume is the one liter (1.05 quarts) size of Chanel No. 5. Made in France, it retails in the United States at $300 a bottle.

FOOD

HIGHEST CALORIFIC VALUE

The highest calorific value of any standard foodstuff is that of margarine at 720 calories per 100 grams, 4 more than for butter.

The food with the lowest calorific value is raw cucumber which rates only 12 calories per 100 grams.

HIGHEST PROTEIN

The highest protein values of standard foods is 28.0 grams per 100 grams of cooked salmon and cooked shoulder of veal. Granular sugar contains no protein.

CARBO-HYDRATES

The highest amount of carbohydrates in any food is 99.5 grams per 100 grams in the case of granulated sugar. Pork, veal, swordfish and tuna contain no carbohydrates.

FAT

The fattiest of standard foodstuffs is butter and margarine at 81.0 grams per 100 grams, while granulated sugar and 4% beer contain no fat.

CALCIUM

The most calciferous of standard foods is cheddar cheese at 725 mg. per 100 grams.

Granulated sugar and salmon contain perhaps some traces of calcium.

PHOSPHORUS

Baker's yeast contains more phosphorus than any other foodstuff, with 605 mg. per 100 grams, while granulated sugar contains none.

VITAMIN A

The foodstuff richest in Vitamin A $(C_{20}H_{29}OH)$ is cooked beef liver at 53,500 international units per 100 grams. Vitamin A is not present in bread, cucumbers, lemons or peanuts.

The food richest in Vitamin B_1 or thiamine ($C_{12}H_{17}Cl\ N_4OS$) is pork at 0.83 mg. per 100 grams. A deficiency of this causes beriberi.

VITAMIN B_1

The food richest in Vitamin B_2 or riboflavin ($C_{17}H_{20}N_4O_6$) is beef liver at 3.96 mg. A deficiency causes inflammation of oral mucous membranes.

VITAMIN B_2

The food richest in niacin ($C_6H_5NO_2$), another of the B_2 vitamins, is baker's yeast at 28.2 mg. per 100 grams. A deficiency causes pellagra.

The food richest in Vitamin C or ascorbic acid ($C_6H_8O_6$) is common raw parsley with 193 mg. per 100 grams. A deficiency causes scurvy.

VITAMIN C

Meats, bread and eggs do not contain any ascorbic acid.

DRINK

The strength of spirituous liquor is gauged by degrees proof. Proof spirit is that mixture of alcohol (C_2H_5OH) and water which at 51°F. weighs 12/13ths of an equal measure of distilled water. Such spirit in fact contains 57.06 per cent alcohol by volume so that pure or absolute alcohol is 74.5° over proof (O.P.).

MOST ALCOHOLIC

The strongest drink was Royal Navy issue rum which prior to 1948 was 40° O.P. or 79.8 per cent alcohol. Since that time it has been reduced to 4½° U.P. or 54.5 per cent alcohol. The most potent standard drink now obtainable is Swiss absinthe, an aromatized spirit flavored with wormwood (*artemisia absinthium*), angelica root, fennel and hyssop, which contains up to 75 per cent alcohol.

Largest bottle used in the wine and spirits trade is called the Nebuchadnezzar. It holds three and a third gallons. (Equivalent of twenty normal bottles.)

LARGEST BOTTLE

The weakest liquid ever marketed as beer was the sweet ersatz beer with an original gravity of 1000.96. Brewed by Sunner, Colne-Kalk in Germany in 1918, it had a strength one thirtieth of the weakest beer now obtainable in the United States.

WEAKEST BEER

The state with the highest consumption of beer in 1955 was Wisconsin with 208 pints per head while that with the lowest was North Carolina with 36 pints per head.

U.S. BEER CONSUMPTION

The most expensive cigarettes obtainable in the U. S. are a pastel colored imported brand of Egyptian manufacture named "Special Brand." They measure, including a filter, 5½ inches overall and retail at 75 cents for ten, or sixfold the price of the standard brands.

MOST EXPENSIVE CIGARETTES

The most expensive and also the largest cigar in the world is the Cuban Partagas Visible Immensas, 9¾ inches in length and sold individually for $7.50. Longer cigars have been made which are merely rolls of chewing tobacco wrapped in cigar leaf and are not in fact able to be smoked. The most expense regular cigar is the La Meridiana Kohinoor from Havana which now retail for $1.50 each.

MOST EXPENSIVE CIGARS

The most rapidly acting method of administering poison is by intra cardiac injection. The large dosage of the barbiturate thiopentone, given in this way will cause the permanent cessation of respiration within 1 to 2 seconds of injection.

QUICKEST KILLING POISON

MOST POISONOUS SUBSTANCE

The most poisonous substance known is the toxin of *Clostridium botulinum*. The fatal dose for an adult male, calculated on the basis of animal experience is 0.01 milligram so that one ounce would provide a lethal dose for over 3,100,000 people. Six gallons would be sufficient to wipe out the entire population of the world.

GEMS

Most Precious

A flawless emerald of good color is carat for carat the most precious gem and may cost in excess of $2,800 per carat. A carat = 3 grains.

Rarest

Only two stones are known of the pale mauve gem Taaffeite first discovered in a cut state in Dublin, Ireland, in November 1945. The bigger of the two examples is of 0.84 carat.

Hardest

Hardest of all gems and the hardest known substance is diamond which chemically is pure carbon. Diamond is 90 times harder than the next hardest gem corundum (Al_2O_3).

On the corrected Mohr scale the South American brown bort diamond has a hardness of 42.4 against the 19.4 of boron carbide.

Densest

The densest of all gems is Cassiterite or tinstone (SnO_2), a colorless to yellow stone found in Australia, Bolivia, Malaya, Mexico and in Cornwall, England. It has a specific gravity of 6.90 rising to 7.1 in opaque mass.

Highest Refractive Index

Rutile, the reddish titanium oxide TiO_2, has a refractive index of 2.903 compared with the 2.421 of a diamond.

Largest

The largest gem ever found was a 520,000 carat aquamarine near Marambaia, Brazil, in 1910, which yielded over 200,000 carats of gem quality stones.

DIAMONDS

The largest white diamond ever discovered was a 3106 metric carat (over 1¼ lb.) stone by Captain M. F. Wells, in the Premier Mine, Pretoria, South Africa, on January 26th, 1905. It was named after Sir Thomas Cullinan, D.S.O., Chairman of the mining company, and was presented to King Edward VII. The Star of Africa (Cullinan No. 1) in the Royal Sceptre, cut from it, is the largest cut diamond in the world at 530.2 metric carats with 74 facets. See Photo No. 21, page 117. The largest colored diamond known is the 44.4 metric carat vivid blue Hope diamond found in the Killur mines, Golconda and purchased by Jean Baptiste Tavernier in 1642.

EMERALDS

Emerald is green beryl. Hexagonal prisms up to 15¾ inches long and 9¾ inches in diameter have been recorded from the Ural mines. The largest cut green beryl crystal is the Austrian Government's 2,680 carat unguent jar carved by Dionysio Miseroni in the 17th century. Of gem quality emeralds, the largest known is the Devonshire stone of 1,350 carats from Muso, Columbia.

SAPPHIRES

Sapphire is blue corundum (Al_2O_3). Vague reports exist of a 1,988 carat sapphire found in a mine in Burma but the largest identified stone was a 951 carat specimen housed in the King of Ava's treasury in Burma in 1827.

The largest cut sapphire in existence is the 563.55 carat "Star of

India" from Ceylon, now in the American Museum of Natural History in New York City. The largest uncut sapphire is a white stone of 1,200 carats found at Anakie, Queensland, Australia, in May, 1956.

Ruby is red corundum (Al_2O_3). Though there have been reports of a semi-transparent 2,000 carat Tibetan ruby, the largest gem stone known was a 1,184 carat stone of Burman origin.   RUBIES

Pearls are protective secretinary bodies produced by mollusks. Gem pearls come chiefly from the western Pacific genus Pinctada and the fresh water mussel genus Quadrula.   PEARL

The largest known opal is one of 2,975 carats found in the Czerwenitza mines of Hungary (now Cervenica, Czechoslovakia) in 1770 and now in the Imperial Museum, Vienna. The rarest variety of opal is the Ilouiznandos.   OPAL

The largest known topaz is a 596 lb. crystal from Minas Geraes, Brazil. The largest known aquamarine is a 134½ lbs. crystal valued at $400,000 found near Governador Valladores, Brazil, in December, 1955.   CRYSTAL
The largest crystal ball is the Warner 106-pound sphere of Burman quartz in the U. S. National Museum in Washington, D. C.

The largest gold nugget ever found was the 7,560 oz. Holtermann Nugget taken from Hill End, New South Wales, Australia, in 1872.   NUGGET
The largest silver nugget ever recorded was one of 2,750 lbs. troy, found in Sonora, Mexico. The largest found within the United States is one of 1,840 lbs. troy, found in the Smuggler Mine, Aspen, Colorado, in 1884.

TELESCOPES

Although there is evidence that the early Arabian scientists understood something of the magnifying power of lenses, their first use to form a telescope has been attributed to Roger Bacon (c.1214-92) in England. The prototype of modern refracting telescopes was that completed by Hans Lippersheim for the Dutch government on October 2nd, 1608.   EARLIEST

The largest refracting (i.e. magnification by lenses) telescope in the world is the 62 feet long, 40-inch Yerkes telescope located at Williams Bay, Wisconsin, and belonging to the University of Chicago, U.S.A. The largest in the British Isles is the 28-inch at the Royal Greenwich Observatory, completed in 1894.   LARGEST
The largest reflector telescope in the world is the 200-inch Hale Telescope of the California Institute of Technology on Palomar Mountain, 66 miles north of San Diego, California, U.S.A. The project took 20 years to complete, the telescope being dedicated on July 3rd, 1948. The essential reflecting surface consists of an ounce of aluminium spread on a polished parabolic pyrex-type glass lens of over 15½ tons operated in a 450 ton steel frame-work. Stars can be photographed, the brightness of which is no greater than that of a candle flame at a range of 40,000 miles. Its astronomical range is 1,000 million light-years and stars of magnitude 23.5 can be located.

PHOTOGRAPHY

EARLIEST

The earliest photograph was taken by the French scientist, Nicephore Niepce, in 1826. It probably took something like eight hours to expose, and was taken on a sensitized polished pewter plate and showed the courtyard of his home.

The world's earliest aerial photograph was taken by "Nadar" from a captive balloon over the Arc de Triomphe, Paris, in 1858.

FASTEST CAMERAS

The world's fastest cine camera is at the Los Alamos Scientific Laboratory in the United States. It exposes at the rate of 14.4 million frames a second—ninety-six exposures on 36 mm. film in 1/150,000 seconds. It contains a mirror rotating at 23,000 revolutions a second.

LARGEST PHOTOGRAPHS

The largest color transparency in the world is at Grand Central Station, New York. An advertising photograph, it is 18 feet high and 60 feet long with rear illumination by a 61,000 watt bank of lights.

The world's largest radiograph was made at the University of Rochester, New York. The subject was a jeep, and the size of the complete X-ray was 12 feet long, 4 feet 9 inches high.

HIGHEST PHOTOGRAPHS

The highest photographs ever taken on earth were the Kodachrome 35 mm. transparencies exposed by Sir Edmund Hillary on the summit of Everest in 1953 and by the 1956 Swiss Expedition.

The highest photograph ever taken by man was exposed from the balloon Explorer II of the National Geographical Society by Capt. A. W. Stevens in 1935. From a height of 72,395 feet over South Dakota, the photograph shows the horizon 330 miles away and includes an area larger than the state of Indiana (36,291 square miles).

LARGEST LAMP

The largest artificial light source in the world is the 75,000 watt incandescent lamp bulb made by General Electric in Cleveland, Ohio, in December, 1955. It is 42 inches in height and 20 inches in diameter and weighs 50 lbs. The filament weighs 2.7 pounds and the lamp produces 2,400,000 lumens. See Photo No. 24, page 117.

BRIGHTEST LAMP

The brightest lamp in the world is the Mazda Type F.A.5 Flash Tube, produced by British Thomson-Houston. The lamp, which contains xenon in a cylindrical arc tube of hard glass, has an electrode sealed into each end of the tube to give an arc gap of only a few millimeters. The tube gives a top brightness intensity of 1,000,000 candles per square inch for periods of 1/25 of a second. This compares with the brightness of the sun which is about 800,000 candles per square inch.

LARGEST SCIENTIFIC INSTRUMENT

The world's largest scientific instrument is the Radio Telescope of the Manchester University Experimental Station, Jodrell Bank, Cheshire, England. Work began in September, 1952. The sheet steel skeletal bowl and 180 foot high supports weigh 1,500 tons and is fully steerable. Its cost is in excess of $1,960,000.

RADIO TELESCOPE

The largest radio telescope in the United States is that at Harvard University, Cambridge, Mass., dedicated on April 28th, 1956. It is mounted on a 50 foot tower and has a bowl-shaped antenna with a diameter of 60 feet.

The largest electronic brain in the world is that installed at the Institute of Precision Mechanics and Calculating Technology in Moscow, Russia, in 1952. The unit which is 100 feet long, 25 feet wide and 10 feet high, contained over 5,000 electronic tubes and required 700 man-years work to construct.

LARGEST ELECTRONIC BRAIN

The most powerful radio transmitter in the world is the U. S. Navy's installation in Jim Creek Valley, Arlington, Washington, opened in November, 1953. It has a power output in excess of one million watts necessary to combat sunspot interference.

MOST POWERFUL RADIO TRANSMITTER

METROLOGY

In metrology the following prefixes have these meanings:—

Mega	=	×	1,000,000	1 million.
Kilo	=	×	1,000	1 thousand.
Centi	=	×	0.01	1 hundredth.
Milli	=	×	0.001	1 thousandth.
Micro	=	×	0.000001	1 millionth.

In dealing with large numbers scientists use the notation of 10 raised to various powers to eliminate a profusion of noughts, for example, 19,160,000,000,000 miles would be written 19.16×10^{12} miles. Similarly a very small number of .0000154324 grain would be written 15.4324×10^{-6} grain.

The earliest measures were measures of length based on the proportions of human limbs. The cubit (elbow point to tip of middle finger) is believed to have been in use as a timber measure as early as 7,000 B.C.

EARLIEST MEASURES

The longest linear measure is an astronomical unit used in measuring stellar distances known as the parsec, which is the distance at which the semi-major axis of the Earth's orbit would subtend one second of arc, that is 19,160,000,000,000 miles.

LONGEST MEASURE

The shortest linear measure used for visible objects is normally the millimeter (1/1000th of a meter = 0.0393701 inch). The micromillimeter or micron is hence a millionth of a meter or 1/25,490th part of an inch. For microscopy, the unit of a millimicron ($M\mu$) is used, being 1/1,000th part of a micron. In work on light waves, however, the Angstrom unit (1/10th of a millimicron) is employed which represents 1/254,900,000th of an inch.

SHORTEST MEASURE

If the parsec is accepted as the largest linear measure, then it follows that the cubic parsec must be the greatest measure of capacity. Similarly the cubic millimicron is the smallest measure of capacity.

CUBIC MEASURE

The heaviest measure of weight is the long ton (2,240 lbs.). The Spanish ton, however, is 31.64 lbs. heavier while the Chilean cajon is 2.90 tons or 6,496 lbs. The metric ton or tonne is 2,204.622 lbs., hence the megatonne is 984,206 tons.

HEAVIEST WEIGHT

The lightest unit for measuring weight is the grain which is 0.323995 of a metric carat, 15.4324 to the gram and 437½ to the ounce avoirdupois. The microgram one millionth of a gram (μg or γ) is, however, 0.0000154324 of a grain.

LIGHTEST

In sub-atomic physics the smallest constant is the mass of an electron (at rest) which is $(9.1066 \pm 0.0032) \times 10^{-28}$ gram which equals nine thousand-septillionths of a gram.

SMALLEST TIME
MEASURE

The fundamental unit of time is provided by the Earth's daily axial rotation. The smallest standard subdivision of the day is the second which is 1/24th part (hour) divided into 1/60th part (minute) and further subdivided by sixty.

For scientific purposes, the micro-second (a millionth part of a second) is employed.

LONGEST TIME
MEASURE

The terms such as an age, epoch or aeon used to express time are all indeterminate. The term millennium, however, expresses 10 centuries or 1,000 years. The most fundamental year is the sidereal year of 365.2563604 days.

SHORTEST
YEAR

The year 1752 lasted only 271 instead of 365 days. Prior to 1752 the year was reckoned to begin on March 25th. Owing also to discrepancies between the old style (Julian) and the new style (Gregorian) calendar, September 2nd was followed by September 14th. A legacy of the old style remains in the income tax year in which April 5th is a new style version of the old March 25th date for the beginning of a new year.

HIGHEST
PRIME
NUMBER

The highest known prime number is $2^{2281}-1$ or

446,087,557,183,758,429,571,151,706,402,101,809,886,208,632,
412,859,901,111,991,219,963,404,685,792,820,473,369,112,545,
269,003,989,026,153,245,931,124,316,702,395,758,705,693,679,
364,790,903,497,461,147,071,065,254,193,353,938,124,978,226,
307,947,312,410,798,874,869,040,070,279,328,428,810,311,754,
844,108,094,878,252,494,866,760,969,586,998,128,982,645,877,
596,028,979,171,536,962,503,068,429,617,331,702,184,750,324,
583,009,171,832,104,916,050,157,628,886,606,372,145,501,702,
225,925,125,224,076,829,605,427,173,573,964,812,995,250,569,
412,480,720,738,476,855,293,681,666,712,844,831,190,877,620,
606,786,663,862,190,240,118,570,736,831,901,886,479,225,810,
414,714,078,935,386,562,497,968,178,729,127,629,594,924,411,
960,961,386,713,946,279,899,275,006,954,917,139,758,796,061,
223,803,393,537,381,034,666,494,402,951,052,059,047,968,693,
255,388,647,930,440,925,104,186,817,009,640,171,764,133,172,
418,132,836,351

The 687 digit number was discovered by Professor D. H. Lehmer on the S.W.A.C. computer in October, 1952, and evaluated in decimal form by Professor Horace S. Uhler of Yale.

CALENDAR

EARLIEST
EASTER

The earliest date upon which Easter can fall is March 22nd. This last occurred in 1818 and will not occur during the 20th century.

LATEST
EASTER

The latest date upon which Easter can fall is April 25th. This last occurred in 1943 and will not recur during the 20th century.

PHYSICAL EXTREMES

HIGHEST TEMPERATURE

The highest man-made temperatures yet attained are those produced in the center of the thermonuclear fusion bomb which are of the order of 50,000,000°C. The highest reported laboratory temperature produced is 15,000°F in a shoch tube (see Highest Velocity) at Avco Manufacturing Co., Everett, Mass., in March, 1956.

LOWEST TEMPERATURE

The lowest temperature reached is 0.0015°K or within 1/1,500th of a degree of absolute zero (−273.16°C) by Dr. Kurti at the Clarendon Laboratory, Oxford, announced on October 25th, 1954. There is evidence that sub-absolute temperatures are possible since spin energy still remains undissipated at absolute zero.

HIGHEST ENERGY

The highest energy ever artificially given to atomic nuclei is about 5 GeV (five thousand million volts). This was achieved with the bevatron of the University of California's Radiation Laboratory at Berkeley.

Two machines to give higher energies are at present in the design stage, the proton synchrotron at Brookhaven, U.S.A., and the one for the European Council for Nuclear Research (C.E.R.N.) at Geneva. Both of these have design energies of 20-30 GeV.

LARGEST MAGNET

The largest magnet in the world is the 10 GeV synchro-phasotron at the Soviet Academy of Sciences. Its external diameter is 200 feet and it weighs 36,000 tons. See Photo No. 25, page 117.

HIGHEST PRESSURE

The highest static maintained pressure ever measured under laboratory conditions is the 6.25 million pounds per square inch achieved by Prof. P. W. Bridgeman of the Lyman Laboratory of Physics, Harvard University, Massachusetts.

HIGHEST VACUUM

The highest vacuums obtained in scientific research are of the order of 10×10^{-9} atmospheres. This compares with an estimated pressure in inter-stellar space of 10×10^{-19} atmospheres.

WIND TUNNELS

The world's largest wind tunnel is the low-speed tunnel with an 80 ft. wide test section at Ames Aeronautical Laboratory, Iowa. The most powerful is the 216,000 h.p. installation at the Arnold Engineering Test Center at Tullahoma, Tennessee. The highest Mach number attained with air is Mach 13 (9,880 m.p.h.), but Mach 15 was reached at Princeton, U.S.A., with helium early in 1954. For periods of micro-seconds, shock Mach numbers of the order of 30 have been attained in impulse tubes at Cornell University, New York, U.S.A.

PUREST METAL

The purest material ever made by man are crystals of the metal germanium to a purity of 99.9999999% or to one part in a billion produced by the electronic zone-melting process at the laboratories of the Western Electric Co.

HIGHEST VELOCITY

The highest imparted velocity attained by man is 18,000 m.p.h. in the case of shock waves produced by exploding highly compressed air at 2,000 p.s.i. into high vacua in impulse tubes. This velocity was recorded in March, 1956, in the Avco Manufacturing Co. Laboratories at Everett, Mass.

PUREST SOUND

The purest sounds that can be heard are those made in the "Dead Room" of the Bell Telephone Laboratory at Murray Hill, New Jersey, completed in July, 1947. In this 35 ft. by 28 ft. chamber, 99.98 per cent of reflected sound is eliminated.

Part Seven

THE WORLD'S STRUCTURES

1. Buildings for Working

TALLEST BUILDING

The tallest building in the world is the Empire State Building, New York. Standing on approximately two acres of ground, it is 1,472 feet high to the top of the television tower, which was added to the existing 1,250 feet building in 1950.

In its 102 stories, 950 firms employ approximately 20,000 people. About 1,000 people are constantly employed in day to day maintenance in the operation of the building, including the cleaning of the 6,500 windows. There are 63 elevators, or, if you prefer to walk, 1,860 steps from top to bottom. Completed on May 1st, 1931, it cost nearly $42,000,000 and occupied 7,000,000 man hours.

Greatest Sway

The maximum recorded sway on the Empire State Building occurred on March 22nd, 1936, during a 102 m.p.h. gale and was 2.97 inches. No readings were taken during the even higher winds recorded on September 21st, 1938, but no action was perceptible since the vibration period of 8.25 seconds is too slow to be felt.

Record Climb

The record for climbing the stairs in the building was set on February 16th, 1932, by 5 members of the 1932 Polish Olympic Skiing Team, Bronislaw Czech, Andrzej and Stanislaw Marusarz, Zdislaw Motyka and Stanislaw Skupien who negotiated the stairs from the 5th to the 102nd floor in 21 minutes.

HIGHEST BUILDING

The highest inhabited building in the world is the Chacaltaya High Altitude Laboratory. Maintained by the Laboratorio de Física Cósmica for Cosmic Ray Research, it stands at a height of 17,180 feet above sea level. It is situated in the Andes about 22 miles from the Bolivian city of La Paz. The laboratory can accommodate about 20 people. Usually four or five are maintained constantly at the laboratory, each person staying only for five to seven days.

NORTHERNMOST & SOUTHERNMOST HABITATION

The most northerly habitation in the world is the Danish Scientific Station set up in 1952 in Pearyland, Northern Greenland, over 900 miles north of the Arctic Circle.

The most southerly permanent human habitation is the Australian Antarctic research base at Mawson at 67°30'S.

The largest office building in the world is the Pentagon, Washington, D. C. Built to house the U. S. Government's war offices, it was completed in January, 1943, and cost approximately $83,000,000. Each of the outermost sides of the Pentagon is 921 feet long and the perimeter of the building is approximately ⅞ mile. The five stories of the building enclose a floor area of approximately 6½ million square feet. During the day 28,500 people work in the building. The telephone system of the building has over 44,000 telephones connected by 160,000 miles of cable and its 220 staff handle 280,000 calls a day. Two restaurants, six cafeterias and ten snackbars and a staff of 675 form the catering departments of the building.

LARGEST OFFICE BUILDING

The British European Airways servicing bays at London Airport are the largest pre-stressed concrete buildings in the world. The two hangar buildings each measure 900 feet by 110 feet. The long side of each hangar building contains five doors each with a clear opening 150 feet wide x 30 feet high which gives access to a concrete apron 900 feet long x 300 feet wide. The total installation covers an area of 4½ acres and approximately 2,000 engineers and maintenance men are employed there.

LARGEST PRE-STRESSED CONCRETE BUILDING

The world's largest exhibition hall is the New York Coliseum, completed in 1956, with an area of 9 acres on four floors. The second floor can be converted into an auditorium with seating space for 10,000 people.

LARGEST EXHIBITION HALL

The world's largest carpet consists of 88,000 square feet (just over two acres) of maroon carpeting at the Coliseum exhibition building, Columbus Circle, New York. This was first used for the International Automobile show on April 28th, 1956.

LARGEST CARPET

The world's largest warehouse is that of the Port of New York Authority owned by the Pennsylvania Railroad Co., known as the Harborside Warehouse in Jersey City, New Jersey, U.S.A., which has a total floor space of 43½ acres.

LARGEST WAREHOUSE

The largest garage in the world is beneath Grant Park, Chicago, and has a capacity of 2,359 cars. It was opened in September, 1953, at a cost of $8,300,000.

LARGEST GARAGE

The largest hangar is the Britannia Assembly Hall at the Bristol Aeroplane Company's works at Filton, England. Originally intended for the construction of a flight testing base for the Bristol Brabazon, it now houses the construction of the Britannia airliner. The overall width of the Hall is 1,054 feet and the overall depth of the center bay is 420 feet. It encloses a floor area of 7½ acres. The cubic capacity of the Hall is 33 million cubic feet. The building was begun in April, 1946, and completed by September, 1949.

LARGEST HANGAR

The largest sewerage works in the world is the West and South-West Plant in Chicago, U.S.A., opened in 1940. It serves an area containing 3,250,000 people.

LARGEST SEWERAGE WORKS

The largest general hospital in the United States and in the world is the King's County Hospital, Brooklyn, N. Y., with 3,451 beds.

LARGEST HOSPITALS

The largest mental hospital in the United States and in the world is the Pilgrim State Hospital, Long Island, N. Y., with 14,201 beds.

The largest maternity hospital in the world is the Obstetrical Department of Cook County Hospital, Chicago, Illinois, with 236 beds. In 1955, 14,400 babies were delivered with a peak of 1,374 in the month of September.

The largest medical center in the world is the District Medical Center in Chicago, Ilinois, which covers 478 acres, and contains among its institutions five hospitals, with a total of 5,600 beds, and eight professional schools with 3,166 students.

The Center, which has over 12,000 persons employed by or affiliated to it, was created by Act of Legislature in 1941 by the State of Illinois in order to advance the scope and usefulness of medical science. Out-patient visits amounted to more than 430,000 in 1955.

2. Buildings for Living

EARLIEST
CASTLES

Castles in the sense of unfortified manor houses existed in all the great early civilizations including that of Ancient Egypt prior to 3,000 B.C. Fortified castles in the more accepted sense only existed much later. The oldest in the world is that at Gomdan in the Kingdom of Yemen in Arabia which originally had twenty stories and dates from prior to 100 A.D.

The oldest stone castle in the British Isles is Richmond Castle, Yorkshire, built c.1075 A.D.

OLDEST
HOUSE

The oldest dwelling in the country is a 12th century adobe or unburnt brick Indian structure in Santa Fe, New Mexico, dated before 1190.

The oldest wooden frame house in the United States is Fairbanks House at Eastern Avenue and East Street, Dedham, Mass. It was built by Jonathan Fayrebanke in 1636 and still stands in its original form.

LARGEST
CASTLES

The largest castle in the world is that at Aleppo in Syria which is oval in shape and was built with a surrounding wall 1,230 feet long and 777 feet wide. It dates, in its present form, from the Hamanid dynasty of the tenth century A.D.

The most massive keep in the world is that in the thirteenth century Chateau-fort de Coucy, in the Department of l'Aisne, France. It is 177 feet high, 318 feet in circumference and has walls over twenty-two and a half feet in thickness.

The largest castle in the British Isles is the Royal residence of Windsor Castle which is primarily of twelfth century construction and is in the form of a parallelogram, 1,890 feet on its longest side by 540 feet. The overall dimensions of Carisbrooke Castle (450 feet by 360 feet), Isle of Wight, if its earthworks are included, are 1,350 feet by 825 feet.

LARGEST
PALACE

The largest palace in the world is the Vatican Palace, Vatican City, in Rome. Covering an area of 13½ acres, it has 1,400 rooms, chapels and halls of which the oldest date from the 15th century. The Papal Library has approximately 700,000 printed books and 70,000 manuscripts.

21. The Royal Sceptre with the Star of Africa, largest cut diamond in the world. See p. 108.
22. Manhattan House, N. Y. C., the largest apartment house in the U. S. See p. 118.
23. Soldiers Field, scene of the greatest recorded stadium crowd. See p. 118.
24. The largest artificial light source in the world of 75,000 watts. See p. 110.
25. The largest magnet in the world weighing 36,000 tons. See p. 113.

LARGEST
HOTELS

The largest hotel in the world based on number of rooms is the Conrad Hilton in Chicago. Its twenty-five floors contain 3,000 guest rooms. It would thus take more than eight years to spend one night in each room in the hotel. The hotel employs about 2,000 people of which more than 70 are telephone operators and supervisors and 72 elevator operators. The laundry of the hotel, with nearly 200 employees, handles 530 tons of flat work each month as well as some 30,000 shirts, and 18,000 pairs of socks.

The largest hotel in the world on the basis of cubic footage is the Waldorf-Astoria, Park Avenue, New York. It occupies a complete block just under two acres in extent and reaches a maximum height of 625 feet 7 inches. The Waldorf-Astoria has 47 stories and about 2,200 guest rooms and maintains the largest hotel radio receiving system in the world. Any house or overseas program that the visitor wishes to hear can be transmitted to his suite, as well as speeches and music from the public rooms of the hotel.

LARGEST
APARTMENT
HOUSES

The largest apartment houses in the United States are Manhattan House in East 66th Street, New York City with 2,511 rooms forming 581 dwelling units, and 11 Riverside Drive with 2,273 rooms forming 644 dwelling units. See Photo No. 22, page 117.

HOLIDAY
CAMP

The largest holiday camp in the world is Butlin's Filey Holiday Camp, England. Every year more than 150,000 people spend a holiday there, and, in 1955, 9,000 holidaymakers were accommodated during the peak weeks. The camp covers 498 acres including 2,574 guest chalets with hot and cold water. On the camp are two theaters, two ballrooms, each able to hold 3,000 dancers, boating lake, swimming pool, tennis courts, putting and bowling green, Church of England and Roman Catholic churches. The total staff is approximately 1,000.

LARGEST
HOUSE

The largest house in the United Kingdom is Wentworth Wood-house, near Rotherham, Yorkshire, formerly the seat of the Earls Fitz-william. The main part of Wentworth Woodhouse, built over 300 years ago, has more than 240 rooms with over 1,000 windows, and its principal façade is 600 feet long.

3. Buildings for Entertainment

LARGEST
STADIUMS

The world's largest stadium is the Strahov Stadium, Prague, completed in 1934 to accommodate 240,000 spectators of mass displays of up to 40,600 gymnasts.

The largest football stadium in the world is the Maracaña Stadium in Rio de Janeiro, Brazil, which has a normal capacity of 150,000. On July 1st, 1950, Brazil v. Yugoslavia, a crowd of 200,000 was accommodated. A nine foot moat protects players from spectators.

The stadium with the greatest rated capacity in the United States is the Municipal Stadium, Philadelphia, which seats 105,000. The greatest recorded stadium crowd was that for the Eucharistic Congress at the still uncompleted Soldier Field, Chicago, Illinois, on June 21st, 1926, when over 200,000 were gathered. See Photo No. 23, page 117.

The world's largest auditorium is the Atlantic City, New Jersey, municipal auditorium and convention hall. The Auditorium seats 41,000 people and covers seven acres. The Main Hall is 488 feet long and 288 feet wide and 137 feet high. The total floor space available for exhibitions is 300,000 square feet and each stand is independently equipped with water, gas, electricity, steam, compressed air and sewerage. A regulation football field (360 feet x 160 feet) can be laid out in the Main Hall and still leave room for 12,000 seats.

AUDITORIUM

The indoor theater with the greatest seating in the world is the Blanquita Theater, Havana, Cuba (completed 1949), with a 6,500 capacity.

LARGEST
THEATERS

The largest indoor theater in the world is the Radio City Music Hall, Rockefeller Center, New York. It seats more than 6,200 persons and the average annual attendance is more than 8,000,000 people.

The stage is 144 feet wide and 66 feet 6 inches deep, equipped with a revolving turntable 43 feet in diameter and three 70 feet long elevator sections. It is one of the most modern and mechanized in the world. The orchestra lift—large enough to house 75 musicians—rises from sub-basement level 27 feet below the stage to form an extension to the main stage and it can then travel 60 feet backstage under its own power. The theater is equipped with dressing rooms to accommodate 600 persons. Usually 600 staff are employed in the theater, including artists, management, electricians and stage hands.

The largest open-air theater in the world is at Mendoza in Argentina. It can seat 40,000 people.

The greatest number of tiers in any theater is six in Teatro Della Scala (La Scala), Milan, Italy, completed in 1778 and the Bolshoi Theater, Moscow, Russia.

The largest opera house in the world is the La Scala with a capacity of 3,600 compared with the 3,418 of the Metropolitan Opera House, New York.

The oldest theater in the world is the Teatro Olimpico in Vicenza, Italy. Designed by Palladio in the Roman Style, it was finished after his death by his pupil Scamozzi in 1582. It is preserved today in its original form. See Photo No. 27, page 124.

OLDEST
THEATER

The largest open-air cinema in the world is in Berlin in the British Sector. Converted from the Olympic Stadium Amphitheater, it seats 22,000 people.

LARGEST OPEN-
AIR THEATER

The biggest pleasure beach in the world is Coney Island, New York. As well as its five mile beach it features more than 350 business and amusement places, side-shows, "rides" and penny arcades. During the season it is conservatively estimated that 50,000,000 people visit Coney Island and each of them spends about $1.25.

PLEASURE
BEACH

The longest pleasure pier in the world is Southend Pier, England, 1 1/3 miles in length. It is decorated with more than 75,000 lamps.

The largest "pub" in the world is the Downham Tavern, near Bromley, Kent, England. Built in 1930, it has two large bars with a counter

LARGEST
"PUB"

length of 45 feet, each able to hold about a thousand people. At holiday weekends about 130,000 bottles of beer are served.

WINE CELLARS

The largest wine cellars in the world are at Paarl near Cape Town, in the center of the wine-growing district of the Union of South Africa. They have a capacity of 20 million gallons.

LONGEST BAR

The longest bar in the world is that built in 1938 at the Working Men's Club, Mildura, Victoria, Australia, which has a counter 285 feet in length, served by 32 taps.

4. Specialized Structures

WORLD'S TALLEST STRUCTURE

The tallest structure in the world is the 1,572 foot television transmitting tower of station KWTV in Oklahoma City, U.S.A.

The tower is triangular in cross section, 12 feet a side, to the 1,420 feet level. Above that point the tower tapers to the two antennas which it carries. One is a 79-foot RCA fourteen-layer supergain and the other a 73-foot RCA twelve-bay superturnstile, with a total effective radiated power of 316,000 watts.

The tower, which weighs 1,323,000 pounds (approximately 590 tons) rests on a set of porcelain insulators designed to withstand a crushing load of 11,200,000 pounds (5,000 tons). The tower is guyed by twenty-four stranded steel cables which vary in diameter from 1 1/2 to 2 inches and radiate 950 feet from the base. An electric lift runs to the 1,340 foot level and the tower carries nine 1,000 watt flashing beacons and eighteen obstruction lights. From the top of the tower the line of sight to the horizon is over 50 miles. See Photo No. 29, page 124.

The pre-stressed concrete Brussels Telecommunication Tower, due to be completed for the 1958 Exhibition, has been planned to reach a height of 1,935 feet 5 inches and will be the highest structure in the world.

OLDEST WOODEN BUILDING

The oldest wooden building in the world is the Horyuji Temple at Kyoto in Japan. It is reputed to be 1,349 years old.

LARGEST CATHEDRAL

The largest cathedral in the United States and in the world is the Cathedral Church of the Diocese of New York, St. John The Divine with a floor area of 121,000 square feet and a size of 16,822,000 cubic feet. The cornerstone was laid on December 27th, 1892, and the cathedral is still uncompleted after 66 years. The nave, the longest in the world, is 601 feet in length with a vaulting 124 feet in height.

The cathedral with the greatest floor area is the Cathedral of Seville in Spain, dedicated to Santa Maria de la Sede. It was built in the Spanish Gothic style between 1402 and 1519 and is 414 feet long and 271 feet wide.

OLDEST PROTESTANT CHURCH

The oldest Protestant Church in the U. S. is St. Luke's Protestant Episcopal Church in the Tidewater section of Virginia. It was built in 1632 in Colonial Gothic style.

OLDEST SYNAGOGUE

The oldest synagogue in the United States is the Touro Synagogue in Newport, Rhode Island, which was dedicated on December 2nd, 1763.

The largest synagogue in the United States and the world is the Temple Emanu-El, Fifth Avenue at 65th Street, New York City. The internal dimensions are 100 feet by 200 feet and it has a seating capacity of over 2,000.

The smallest synagogue in the United States is that of the 30 strong Beth Israel Congregation, founded in 1849 at Honesdale, Pennsylvania.

LARGEST SYNAGOGUE

The world's biggest concrete dam, and the biggest concrete structure in the world, is the Grand Coulee Dam on the Columbia River, Washington State. 4,173 feet long and 550 feet high, it contains 10,585,000 cubic yards of concrete, and weighs about 21,600,000 tons.

Measured by volume, the Fort Peck Dam, across the Missouri River in Montana, is the largest in the world. It contains 128 million cubic yards of earth and rock fill, and is 21,026 feet long. It maintains a reservoir containing 19.4 million acre feet.

CONCRETE DAMS

The highest dam in the world is the Grand Dixence in Switzerland. It is 932 feet from base to rim and the total volume of concrete in the dam is 520,000 cubic yards.

The highest dam in the United States and the second highest in the world is the Hoover (Boulder) dam, of the Colorado River. It is 726 feet high, 1,244 feet long and contains 4,400,000 million cubic yards of concrete. See Photo No. 28, page 124.

HIGHEST DAM

When the Owen Falls scheme is completed, Lake Victoria, Uganda, will be the biggest reservoir in the world, both in area, approximately 27,000 square miles, and in volume. The dam at Jinja is 2,500 feet long and has a maximum height of 100 feet and contains 230,000 cubic yards of concrete. Eventually ten turbines will be installed producing 50,000 kilowatts.

At the present moment, the reservoir with the largest capacity is Lake Mead, formed by the Hoover Dam (Boulder) of the Colorado River. It is 245 square miles in area, and has a capacity of 31,142,000 acre feet or 10,150,000,000,000 gallons.

BIGGEST RESERVOIR

The largest monument ever constructed is the Pyramid of Cheops (Khufu) at Gizeh near Cairo, built in the 4th Egyptian Dynasty, c.2800 B.C. Its original height was 481 feet (now 451 feet) with a base covering 12½ acres. It has been estimated that it required 100,000 slaves 20 years to maneuver the 2½ ton stone blocks, totalling nearly 7 million tons, into position.

LARGEST MONUMENT

The Pyramids of Egypt, of which the earliest is the step pyramid at Saqqara, were reckoned among the Seven Wonders of the World. Of these ancient wonders only fragments remain of the Temple of Diana of the Ephesians built c.500 B.C. at Ephesus (destroyed 262 A.D.) and of the Tomb of Mausolus built at Halicarnassus c.325 B.C. No trace remains of the Hanging Gardens of Babylon (c.600 B.C.), the Statue of Zeus, the Colossus of Rhodes (destroyed by earthquake 224 B.C.), or the Pharos Lighthouse (destroyed by earthquake in 1375 A.D.).

SEVEN 'WONDERS'

The tallest monument in the United States and the world is the San Jacinto monument near Houston, Texas. It stands on the site of the Battle

TALLEST MONUMENT

of San Jacinto of April 21st, 1836, where General Sam Houston killed 630 Mexicans for the loss of only 9 Texans.

Constructed in 1936-39 at a cost of $1,500,000, the memorial rises to a height of 570 feet. The column, which tapers from 47 feet square at its base to 30 feet square at its observation tower, is surmounted by a 220 ton star. It is built of concrete faced with buff limestone and weighs 35,150 tons. See Photo No. 26, page 124.

LARGEST
WAR
MEMORIALS

The largest of the memorials raised to America's war dead overseas is that at Fort McKinley, 4 miles southeast of Manila, Philippines, which when completed will cover 1½ acres. Besides the names of 36,274 missing which will be recorded there, the cemetery contains 17,370 graves, making it the largest of any on overseas soil.

The largest cemetery in Europe from World War I is the Meuse-Argonne Cemetery near Romagne, France, with 14,245 graves. The largest from World War II is the Lorraine Cemetery near St. Avold, France, from which region the remains of 15,300 have been returned home and 10,489 remain buried.

LARGEST
SCULPTURES

The world's largest sculptures are the Mount Rushmore National Memorial, South Dakota. Known as the Shrine of Democracy, these sculptures, in granite, take the form of the busts of Presidents Washington, Jefferson, Theodore Roosevelt and Lincoln. The busts are proportionate to men 465 feet high, and the distance between the top of Washington's head to his chin is 60 feet.

LARGEST
STATUE

When completed, the world's largest statue will be that of the Sioux Indian chief, Crazy Horse, begun in 1939 near Mount Rushmore, South Dakota. A projected 561 feet high and 641 feet long, it will require the removal of 6 million tons of stone.

TALLEST
STATUE

The tallest statue in the world is the standing idol of Buddha, 173 feet high, 2 miles east of Barmian in Afghanistan to which there are references as early as 630 A.D. Nearby there are the remains of the recumbent Sakya Buddha built on plastered rubble which was "about 1,000 feet in length."

LONGEST
INLAND
WATERWAY

The longest inland waterway in the United States is the Missouri River. It is navigable from Fort Benton in Chouteau County in Montana to the mouth, a distance of 2,203 miles.

LARGEST
CANALS

The world's longest big ship canal is the Suez, 101 miles in length.

The world's biggest canal, measured in cross section area, is the Panama which varies from 22,000 to 45,000 square feet.

The world's deepest lock is the Donzère-Mondragon lock on the River Rhône at 86 feet. It takes 8 minutes to fill.

BRIDGES

Modern bridges fall into three main groups: arch, cantilever, and suspension.

LONGEST
SPAN
SUSPENSION

The longest single span bridge in the world is the Golden Gate Bridge in California. It spans the entrance to San Francisco Bay joining San Francisco to Marin County in the north. A suspension bridge, it is

4,200 feet between uprights. The two towers of the bridge are 746 feet high and it carries six lanes of roadway and two footways on a deck 90 feet wide, 220 feet above the water level. It was opened to traffic in May 1937 at a cost of approximately $35,000,000.

The longest steel arch bridge in the world is the Bayonne Bridge (completed November, 1931), which connects Bayonne, N. J., to Staten Island. Its span is 1,652 feet—two feet longer than the Sydney Harbour Bridge.

LONGEST SPAN STEEL ARCH

The largest steel arch bridge in the world is the Sydney Harbour Bridge. Its main span is 1,650 feet wide and it carries four railway tracks, six lanes of roadway, two footways, 172 feet above the waters of Sydney Harbour. It took seven years to build and was completed in March, 1932, and cost approximately $18 million.

The highest suspension bridge in the world is the bridge over the Royal Gorge of the Arkansas River, 1,053 feet above the water level. It has a main span of 880 feet.

HIGHEST

The Quebec Bridge over the St. Lawrence river in Canada has the longest cantilever span of any in the world—1,800 feet. It carries two railway tracks. Begun in 1904, it was completed in 1918.

LONGEST SPAN CANTILEVER

The longest reinforced concrete span is that of the Sandö Bridge of the Angerman River, Sweden. It is a hingeless, hollow-box section arch and spans 866 feet 5 inches. The bridge carries a motor road 132 feet above the river.

LONGEST CONCRETE ARCH

The longest brick built span in the world is the Maidenhead railway bridge in England, spanning the River Thames. Completed in 1839 to a design of I. K. Brunel, it includes two 128 feet brick spans with a rise of only 24½ feet.

LONGEST BRICK SPAN

Man's deepest penetration into the Earth's crust is at the No. 1-L test oil well in Plaquemines Parish (State Lease 2414), Louisiana, 35 miles south of New Orleans. Boring for 256 days from February 26th, 1955, at a cost of $1.9 million, the Richardson and Bass drilling crew surpassed the previous record of 21,482 feet at 7 a.m. on November 9th, 1955. By January, 1956, a depth of 22,570 feet (4 miles, 1,450 feet) had been attained when a bottom hole temperature of 350°F was reported. See Photo No. 33, page 132.

BORINGS

The most prolific wildcat recorded is Lucas No. 1 at Spindletop, 3 miles north of Beaumont, Texas, on January 10th, 1901. The gusher was heard over a mile away and yielded 700,000 barrels during the 10 days it was uncapped. The surrounding ground yielded 340,000 barrels an acre.

GREATEST GUSHER

The deepest water well in the United States is that drilled in 1942 at Ellsworth Air Force Base, Rapid City, South Dakota, to a depth of 4,645 feet.

DEEPEST WATER WELL

The deepest well in the world is the 7,009 feet deep Springleigh No. 3 near Blackall, Queensland, Australia, completed 1921.

The longest aqueduct in the world in the modern sense of a water conduit, is the Colorado Aqueduct, completed in 1939. Its total length, comprising siphons, canal conduits and tunnels is 242 miles.

LONGEST AQUEDUCT

26. The San Jacinto Monument, tallest monument in the U. S. See p. 121.
27. Teatro Olimpico, oldest roofed-in theater in the world. See p 119.
28. The Hoover Dam, highest in the U. S. See p. 121.
29. The station KWTV, tallest structure in the world. See p. 120.
30. The C-G Grain Company's elevator, largest in the world. See p. 126.

The world's deepest mine is the Ooregum section of the Champion Reef gold mine in the Kolar Gold Field, Mysore State, India, where the Auxiliary Main Winze is 9,811 feet below the surface.

Note.—Owing to the oblateness of the Earth, the Ooregum miners cannot claim to have set the record for the closeness to the Earth's center. This distinction was achieved on April 6th, 1909, by the polar explorers Robert E. Peary, Matthew Henson, and the Eskimos Ooqueah, Ootah, Egingwah and Seegloo when they reached the North Pole which *is 70,488 feet nearer the Earth's center* than sea-level points on the equator and is nearly 9,000 feet nearer than the South Pole which is on the Antarctic plateau.

MINES

The largest gold mining area in the world is the Witwatersrand gold field extending 30 miles east and west of Johannesburg, South Africa. Gold was discovered there in 1886 and by 1944 over 45% of the world's gold was mined there by 320,000 Bantu and 44,000 Europeans.

The largest gold mine in area is the East Rand Proprietary Mines Ltd. whose 8,785 claims covered, on January 1st, 1956, 13,177 ½ acres. The gold mine with the most active shafts (55), and in 1955 with the greatest milled tonnage (3,588,000 tons), is Crown Mines Ltd. The mine with the richest yield in 1955 was Blyvooruitzicht Gold Mining Company Ltd. with a total of 719,367 ounces of fine gold.

LARGEST GOLD MINE

The world's largest excavation and the largest open-pit iron mine in the world is the Hull-Rust-Mahoning pit at Hibbing, Minnesota. The pit was started in 1895 and now extends over 1,535 acres to a maximum depth of 490 feet. The length of the pit is 3 ¼ miles with a width varying from ½ to one mile. The floor is traversed by 33 miles of railway line. The total tonnage of material excavated in the 60 years of operation is 982 million tons.

The longest and heaviest railway loads ever made are those from the iron ore mines at Hibbing, Minnesota. They are limited by law to 180 cars of 70 tons each, giving a rolling weight of over 13,000 tons.

LARGEST EXCAVATION

The deepest operating anthracite mine in the United States is the Askan shaft of the Glen Alden Coal Co. near Nanticoke, Pennsylvania, at 2,140 feet. The deepest bituminous mine shaft was the 1,004 feet deep shaft of the Assumption mine, 10 miles north of Pana, Illinois.

DEEPEST COAL MINES

The largest coal field is District No. 8 which embraces southwest West Virginia, southern Virginia, eastern Kentucky, northeast Tennessee and part of North Carolina.

LARGEST COAL FIELD

The world's longest continuous tunnel is the London Transport Executive underground railway line from Morden to East Finchley, via Bank in London, England. It is 17 miles 528 yards long and the diameter of the tunnel is 12 feet and the station tunnels 21 feet 2 ½ inches.

The world's longest main-line tunnel is the Simplon Tunnel, completed after eleven years' work in 1906. Linking Switzerland and Italy under the Alps, it is 12 miles 559 yards long.

The longest road tunnel in the world is the Mersey Tunnel, joining Liverpool and Birkenhead—2.13 miles long, including branch tunnels 2.87 miles. Work was begun in December, 1925, and it was opened by King George V in July, 1934. The total cost was $21.7 million. The 36 feet wide roadway carries nearly 7 ½ million vehicles a year.

WORLD'S LONGEST TUNNELS

LARGEST
TUNNEL

The largest diameter tunnel in the world is that blasted through Yerba Buena Island, San Francisco. It is 76 feet wide, 58 feet high and 540 feet long. In 1955, 33,332,837 vehicles passed through on its two decks.

GRAIN
ELEVATOR

The world's largest single-unit grain elevator is that operated by the C-G Grain Company at Wichita, Kansas, and built by Chalmers and Borton of Hutchinson, Kansas. Consisting of a triple bank of storage tanks, 123 on each side of the central head house, the unit is 2,717 feet long and 100 feet wide, each tank being 120 feet high and 30 feet inside diameter. The total storage capacity of this unit is 20 million bushels. The grain is carried to the separate tanks by two conveyor belts each over 2,000 feet in length. See Photo No. 30, page 124.

WORLD'S
HIGHEST
STACKS

The highest smokestacks in the United States and the world are the three 628 feet high reinforced concrete structures at the Clifty Creek Plant. These were completed in 1954 for the Ohio Electric Corporation at Madison, Indiana. See Photo No. 32, page 132.

LIGHTHOUSES

The most powerful lighthouses in the world are Belle Ile (Anse de Goulphar) and Gatteville (Pointe de Barfleur) lighthouses on the French coast. Each has an intensity of 20 million candlepower.

The brightest lighthouse in the United States is the Hillsboro Inlet Lighthouse, Florida, with a candlepower of 5.5 million.

EARLIEST
LIGHTHOUSE

The earliest lighthouse in the United States was the Little Brewster Island light at the entrance to Boston harbor. It was first lit on September 14th, 1716.

AQUARIA

LARGEST

The world's largest aquarium is the John G. Shedd Aquarium, 12th Street in Grant Park, Lake Michigan, completed in November, 1929, at a cost of $3 ¼ million. The total capacity of its display tanks is 450,000 gallons with reservoir tanks holding 2,000,000 gallons. 10,000 specimens of 250 species are housed. Salt water is brought in rail tankers from Key West, Florida. Record attendances are 78,658 in a day on May 21st, 1931, and 4,689,730 visitors in the single year of 1931.

OCEANARIA

EARLIEST

The world's first oceanarium is the Marine Studios, eighteen miles south of St. Augustine, Florida, opened in 1938. Up to seven million gallons of seawater is pumped daily through two major tanks, one rectangular (100 feet long by 40 feet wide by 18 feet deep) containing 450,000 gallons and one circular (233 feet in circumference and 12 feet deep) containing 400,000 gallons. The tanks are seascaped, including a seven-ton coral reef and even a ship-wreck.

LARGEST

The largest salt water tank in the world is that at the Marineland of the Pacific, Palos Verdes, Los Angeles, California. It is 251 ½ feet in circumference and 22 feet deep with a capacity of 640,000 gallons. The total capacity of the whole oceanarium is 1,190,000 gallons.

ZOO

EARLIEST

Egyptian tomb inscriptions indicate that animals, other than domestic animals, were kept in captivity as early as 2000 B.C. but the earliest zoo of which there is definite evidence is one in China dated c.1100 B.C.

The earliest zoo in the United States was the Philadelphia Zoo of the Zoological Society of Philadelphia. It was opened to the public on July 1st, 1874.

The world's largest zoo is the Whipsnade Zoo, Bedfordshire, England, which extends over 600 acres. This open air reserve houses part of the collection of the Zoological Society of London which is the oldest privately owned zoo in the world, having been founded in 1828. The Society who also own the 36 acre Regent's Park Zoo in central London (record attendance over 3 million in 1950), have the most comprehensive collection of any zoo with 3,372 mammals, birds and reptiles and an aquarium housing 2,782 fish.

LARGEST

The largest zoo in the United States is the New York Zoological Park, known as the Bronx Zoo, which extends over 252 acres. It also has the most comprehensive collection with 186 species of mammals, 572 of birds and 235 of reptiles, a total of 992 as at January 1st, 1956.

The world's largest park is the Kafue National Park in Northern Rhodesia which has an area of 5,536,000 acres. The largest park in the United States is the Yellowstone National Park of 2,213,207 acres.

PARKS

The longest fence in the world will be the dingo-proof fence enclosing the main sheep areas of Queensland, Australia. The wire netting fence, to be completed in about two years, will be six feet high and stretch for 3,437 miles.

LONGEST FENCE

Because of the difficulty of definition there does not appear to be a world record for doors, our researches, however, indicate the following as being the two largest in the world.

LARGEST DOOR

The largest doors in the United States are those made for the U. S. Navy dirigible hangar, Lakehurst, N. J., 250 feet wide and 120 feet high.

The largest doors in the United Kingdom are those to the Britannia Assembly Hall at Filton, Bristol. The doors are 1,045 feet in length and 67 feet high, divided into three bays of 345 feet long.

The largest tent in the world is one made by Piggott Brothers in 1951 and used by the Royal Horticultural Society at their annual show in the grounds of the Royal Hospital, Chelsea, London. The tent is 310 feet long x 480 feet wide, and consists of 18 ¾ miles of 36 inch wide canvas.

LARGEST TENT

The world's largest curtain is that covering Jan Styka's painting, "The Crucifixion," at Forest Lawn Memorial-Park, Glendale, Calif. It is of velvet, 195 feet wide, 45 feet long and weighs 1.56 tons.

LARGEST CURTAIN

The largest chandeliers in the world are those in the central Lecture Hall of the University of Moscow. Each of the eight has six tiers of lights and weighs 2 ½ tons. They were hung in 1953.

LARGEST CHANDELIERS

The world's highest fountain is the Jet d'Eau de La Rade, Geneva, Switzerland. The 1,360 h.p. pump, installed in 1951, can throw the column in calm weather to a height of 426 feet. See Photo No. 34, page 132.

HIGHEST FOUNTAINS

The highest fountain in the United States is "Old Faithful," installed in October, 1931, at the Du Pont estate of Longwood Gardens near Kennett Square, Pennsylvania. The spire attains a height slightly in excess of 140 feet.

LARGEST WINDOWS

The largest plate glass window ever made was one 50 feet long by 8 feet high exhibited at the Festival of Britain, South Bank, London, in 1951. This was made by Pilkington Bros. Ltd. at St. Helens, Lancashire, but was later cut up.

The largest windows installed in any building in the United States are the ½ inch thick sheets 22 feet high by 10 feet wide in the Fifth Avenue frontage of the Manufacturers Trust Company building in New York City, completed in September, 1954.

TALLEST FLAGSTAFF

The tallest flagstaff ever erected was that at the Oregon Building at the Panama-Pacific International Exhibition, at San Francisco in 1915.

It was a single trimmed Douglas fir and stood 299 feet 7 inches in height.

Currently the world's tallest flagstaff is the eighteen and a half-ton, 214 feet high Canadian Douglas fir flagstaff at Kew, London. It was towed down the Thames and erected on October 18th, 1919.

LARGEST DRY DOCKS

The world's largest and longest graving dock is the Sturrock Dock at Capetown, South Africa, completed in 1945. It is 1,212½ feet in length, 148 feet wide and 45¾ feet in depth. The widest of all graving docks is that completed in 1932 at St. Nazaire, France, with a width of 164 feet and the deepest is the 52½ feet deep Le Havre Dock.

The largest floating dry docks ever constructed are the U. S. Navy's Battleship Size A.B.S.D.'s (Advanced Base Sectional Docks). These consist of 10 sectional units which give an effective keel block length of 827 feet, a clear width of 140 feet and a lifting capacity of 80,000 tons.

LARGEST EXPOSITION

The greatest exposition ever staged was the New York World's Fair, opened in May, 1939. The fair, staged in Flushing Meadow Park, Queen's Borough, Long Island, N. Y., extended over 1,216½ acres and, despite the outbreak of World War II in September, 1939, attracted an attendance of 25,817,265.

LARGEST FERRIS WHEEL

The largest Ferris wheel ever constructed was the original construction for the 1893 Chicago Exposition by George W. G. Ferris (1859-1896), erected at Midway, Chicago. Standing 263 feet in height and weighing 4,300 tons overall, the 250 feet diameter wheel had a circumference of 785 feet upon which 36 cars with a total capacity of 1,440 was suspended. After 11 years, the great wheel, which had cost $300,000, was disassembled to be moved to the 1904 St. Louis Exposition. It was eventually sold for scrap for $1,800.

LARGEST FLOATS

The largest recorded parade float is the 1,375 feet long dragon paraded in Saigon by the Chinese Community to commemorate the first anniversary of the South Vietnam national police force in May, 1956.

Part Eight

THE MECHANICAL WORLD

1. Road Vehicles

OLDEST

The oldest "horseless carriage" in the world still in running order is the Grenville Steam Carriage, designed by R. Neville Grenville of Glastonbury, and built in 1875. The three-wheeled carriage, which weighs about 45 cwt., is powered by a two-cylinder, slide-valve steam engine, bore and stroke 5 inches x 6 inches. The steam was supplied by a coal-fired upright boiler working at a pressure of 100 lbs., placed between the rear wheels. See Photo No. 3, page 132.

Two bench-type seats were fitted across the machine, each seating three people, the steersman sat front and center with the brakesman on his right. One man at the rear would stoke the boiler and change gear.

The top speed of the machine was said to be 15 m.p.h. The carriage was used by its designer until well into the 1890's as a conveyance. It was then used as a stationary engine driving a cider mill in Glastonbury, England, until the 1940's, and is now in the Bristol Museum.

OLDEST
I.-C. CAR

The oldest internal-combustion engined car still in running order is the Danish "Hammel." Designed by Albert Hammel, who took out the original patents in 1886, it was completed in 1887.

The engine is a twin-cylinder, horizontal water-cooled four-stroke with a capacity of 2,720 cc., bore and stroke 104.5 x 160 mm. and a compression ratio of 3.5 : 1. The inlet valve gear is automatic, exhaust by push-rod. The carburetor is of the surface type and the ignition by tube burner. The engine is governed by a valve on the induction manifold and recently, on a test bed, it produced 3.5 b.h.p. at 500 r.p.m.

The transmission is by chain and sprockets, forward gear from the crankshaft and the reverse from the camshaft. No differential was fitted, a differential effect being achieved by cone clutches allowing rear wheel slip. In 1953, it completed the London-to-Brighton run in England in 12½ hours, a distance of 52 miles.

EARLIEST
U.S. CAR

The earliest automobile in the United States was the steam automobile invented by Henry and James House in Bridgeport, Conn., in 1866. The earliest automobile patent was filed on May 8th, 1879, by George B. Selden of Rochester, New York, for a road vehicle driven by internal combustion. A gasoline tractor was completed by September, 1892, by John Froelick at Froelick, Iowa. The earliest gasoline driven passenger automobile was built by the brothers Charles and Frank Duryea at their shop at 47 Taylor Street, Springfield, Mass. Construction began in August, 1891, and the first run has been variously claimed for April 19th, 1892 and September 21st, 1893. The original patent was granted to Charles Duryea on June 11th, 1895.

FASTEST SEDAN

The fastest "closed" car in the world is the Mercedes Benz 300 SL Sports Coupé produced by Daimler Benz A.G. of Stuttgart, Germany.

The 300 SL is powered by a six-cylinder engine of 2,996 cc. capacity with bore and stroke 85 x 88 mm., compression ratio of 8.55 : 1, which develops 240 b.h.p. at 6,000 r.p.m. The 300 SL has no carburetors but utilizes a system of direct petrol injection into the cylinders by means of a special Bosch pump which ensures extremely accurate metering of fuel.

The transmission is effected through a single dry plate clutch to a 4-speed synchromesh box and maximum speed in top is c. 165 m.p.h. The all-round independent suspension is by helical springs, unequal wishbones at front and swing axles at rear.

MOST POWERFUL CAR

The most powerful standard car in the world is the Ferrari 375 Millemiglia produced by Ferrari of Modena, Italy.

An open two-seater, with an all-up weight of 2,000 lbs., the Millemiglia is equipped with a twelve cylinder 4,522 cc. engine arranged as a 60° V-12.

The bore and stroke ratio is oversquare (84 x 68 mm.), and the compression ratio 9 : 1, the carburetion is by three quadruple choke Weber carburetors, and the transmission is through a multiple plate clutch to a 4-speed synchromesh gearbox. The maximum b.h.p. of the Millemiglia is c. 340 at 7,000 r.p.m. which indicates a power weight ratio around 5.9 and maximum speeds with 3.4 back axle ratio and without modifications of 1st gear 74 m.p.h., 2nd 104 m.p.h., 3rd 144 m.p.h., top gear c. 180 m.p.h.

MOST POWERFUL SEDAN

The most powerful sedan car in the world is the Chrysler 300, manufactured by the Chrysler Corporation, Detroit, U.S.A.

The two-door, 4-5 seater hardtop is powered by a 300 h.p. Firepower V-8 engine of 5,432 cc. capacity, bore and stroke 96.7 x 92.2 mm. and a compression ratio of 8.5 : 1. The engine, which develops peak horsepower at 5,200 r.p.m., is fitted with two four-choke carburetors.

Automatic gearbox and power assisted steering are standard equipment. The "300" has been timed in the U. S. Stock Car Speed Trials Championships at 127.58 m.p.h.

MOST EXPENSIVE

The most expensive standard cars in the world are the Pegasos, manufactured in Spain by the Empresa Nacional de Autocamiones, S.A. The Pegaso, for which a wide variety of body styles is offered, is powered by a 3.2 or 2.8 liter engine. The 90° V-8 engine has twin overhead camshafts on each bank of cylinders, an oversquare bore-stroke ratio, and such refinements as sodium-cooled valves. The power developed is about 250 b.h.p. at 6,500 r.p.m.

From the single dry plate clutch the propeller shaft transmits the drive to the 5-speed constant mesh box mounted behind the rear axle. The drive then passes forward to the ZF limited slip differential. The rear axle is a modified De Dion set forward of the gearbox and differential housing. The suspension is by torsion bars throughout.

The type Thrill Berlinetta, 2 door aerodynamic sedan, has sold for $27,440. See Photo No. 35, page 132.

The least expensive car in the world in volume production is the Ford "Popular." The four-seater, two-door Popular sedan is powered by a 4-cylinder side valve engine of 1,172 cc. bore and stroke 63.5 x 92.5 mm. with a compression ratio of 6.16 : 1. The transmission is by single dry-plate clutch through a 3-speed gearbox with synchromesh on 2nd and top. The engine develops maximum horsepower, 30.1, at 4,000 r.p.m. and the car has a maximum speed of 60 m.p.h. The car retails in the United Kingdom at a basic price of £275 ($770 without taxes).

The Russian Zis has the largest engine capacity of any standard car in the world. A design closely based on the pre-war American Packard, it has a capacity of 5,998 cc. The engine is a straight-eight with a compression ratio of 6.85 : 1 and it develops 138 b.h.p. at 3,600 r.p.m. and has a maximum speed of 87 m.p.h.

The most powerful dumper truck in the world is the Euclid LLD 50-tonner. The LLD is powered by two 12.2 liter, 300 h.p. Cummins diesels, the total horsepower developed is 600 at 2,100 r.p.m. The transmission is by two 3-speed and reverse automatic Allison torque converters each driving one of the tandem rear axles. The net weight empty is 46 tons and maximum speed 36 m.p.h. The truck is 36 feet 5 inches long and is mounted on ten 5 feet 9 inches diameter wheels. The maximum payload is 45 tons, bringing the gross weight of vehicle and maximum load to about 92 tons, with a top laden speed of 32 m.p.h.

The fastest truck in the world is the open-bodied transporter used by Daimler Benz to transport their racing cars. It is fitted with a Mercedes 300 SL sports engine and, fully laden with a car on the back, has been timed at 106 m.p.h. Its cab will hold three people. See Photo No. 36, page 132.

The heaviest 1956 U. S. built stock car is the Continental Mark II with a shipping weight of 4,920 lbs.

The longest 1956 U. S. built stock car is the Imperial C-73, V-8 with a length of 230 inches.

The lightest 1956 U. S. built stock car is the Studebaker Champion 6 with a shipping weight of 2,915 lbs.

The 1956 U. S. built stock car with the highest compression ratio is the Packard 400 with a compression ratio of 10 : 1.

The lowest compression ratio is that of the Nash Statesman with 7.4 : 1.

The 1956 U. S. built car with greatest displacement is the 8-cylinder Packard 400. It has a piston displacement of 374 cubic inches.

The 1956 U. S. built car with the greatest claimed horsepower is the 1956 Chrysler 300. It has a maximum of approximately 340 h.p.

31. Grenville Steam Carriage, oldest "horseless carriage" in the world. See p. 129.
32. The Clifty Creek smoke stacks, highest in the world. See p. 126.
33. The No. 1-L Test Oil Well, deepest boring in the world. See p. 123.
34. The Jet d'Eau de La Rade, the world's highest fountain. See p. 127.
35. The Pegaso, most expensive standard car in the world. See p. 130.
36. The Mercedes-Benz racing car transporter, fastest truck in the world. See p. 131.

The longest bicycle ever made was the ten-man "Oriten" tandem made in Walton, Massachusetts, about 1898. It was twenty-three feet long, weighed 305 lbs. and had a reputed speed of over 40 miles per hour. See Photo No. 39, page 136.

LONGEST
BICYCLE

2. Railways

The world rail speed record is held jointly by two French Railway electric locomotives, the CC7107 and the BB9004. On March 29th and 30th, 1955, hauling three carriages of a total weight of 100 tons, they both achieved a speed of 205.6 m.p.h. The runs took place on the 1,500 volt D.C. Bordeaux-Dax line, and the top speed was maintained for nearly 1 ¼ miles.

FASTEST

Both locomotives were selected from those running under ordinary service conditions but the transmission system of both was modified to raise the gear ratio to allow for higher than normal speeds.

The CC7107 weighs 106 tons and has a continuous rating at 1,500 volts of 4,300 h.p.

The BB9004 weighs 81 tons and has a continuous rating of 4,000 h.p.

The fastest train in the U. S. is the "Pennsylvania Special," now the "Broadway Limited" of the Pennsylvania Railroad. It ran three miles near Ada, Ohio, in 85 seconds, achieving a speed of 127.06 miles per hour.

The world's speed record for steam locomotives is held by the British 4-6-2 Mallard, which, hauling seven coaches weighing 240 tons gross, achieved a speed of 126 m.p.h. on July 3rd, 1938.

Steam

The fastest transcontinental run ever made was the streamlined Union Pacific Diesel "City of Portland," on an experimental run from Los Angeles to New York in October, 1934. The "City of Portland" covered the 3,258 miles in 56 hours 55 minutes, an average of 57.24 miles per hour.

FASTEST TRANS-
CONTINENTAL

The fastest regular run is the "Twin Zephyrs" diesel traction train which runs from East Dubuque to Prairie du Chien, U.S.A., at an average speed of 86.2 m.p.h. over the 54.6 mile journey.

FASTEST
REGULAR
RUNS

Fastest electric traction run is the French National Railways' "Mistral" from Paris to Lyons, a distance of 317.4 miles at an average speed of 76.2 m.p.h.

Fastest steam traction run is the Union Pacific "Overland Limited" between North Platte and Kearney, Nebraska, covering the 95 miles in 79 minutes—72.1 m.p.h.

The longest daily non-stop run in the world is the "Elizabethan" from King's Cross, London, to Edinburgh. It covers the 392.75 miles in 390 minutes at 60.5 m.p.h. average speed, hauling a 400-ton train of eleven coaches.

LONGEST
NON-STOP

The world's most powerful steam locomotives, reckoned on tractive effort, are the Class M4- 2-8-8-4 loco's built by the Baldwin Locomotive Works, U.S.A., for the Duluth, Missabe & Iron Range Railroad in 1941-1943. They have a tractive force of 140,000 lbs.

MOST
POWERFUL

PERMANENT
WAY

For lengths by country and square mile, see Page 41.

The longest straight in the world is over the Nullabor Plain, Southern and Western Australia, 328 miles dead straight although not level.

The longest straight track in U. S. is 78.86 miles on Seaboard Air Line Railroad, between Wilmington and Hamlet, North Carolina.

The longest length of unbroken four-lane track in the world is between Castleton and Dunkirk, New York, in the United States, and is 342½ miles in length.

WIDEST
GAUGE

Widest gauge in standard use is 5 feet 6 inches. This width is used in India, Pakistan, Ceylon, Spain, Portugal, Argentina and Chile.

HIGHEST
ALTITUDE

The highest altitude standard track in the world is on the Peruvian Central Railways at La Cima, where the track rises to 15,806 feet.

The altitude record for non-standard track is also in South America at Montt, on the Collahausi branch of the Antofagasta and Bolivian Railway. It reaches a height of 15,809 feet.

The highest of any track in U. S. is the cog track at Pike's Peak, Colorado, on the Manitou and Pike's Peak Railway, climbing to an altitude of 14,110 feet above sea level.

The highest standard adhesion track in U. S. is at Climax, Colorado, on the Colorado and Southern road, at 11,319 feet above sea level.

LOWEST
ALTITUDE

The lowest track in U. S. is at milepost 635.4 near Salton, Calif., in the Salton ''sink,'' at 199.2 feet below sea level, on the Southern Pacific Railroad.

STEEPEST
GRADIENTS

The world's steepest standard gauge gradient by adhesion is 1 : 11. This figure is achieved by the Guatemalan State Electric Railway—between River Samala Bridge and Zunil.

This gradient is matched by the 1 meter gauge Chamonix line of the South-East Region of French National Railways between Chedde and Servoz.

The steepest grade of any main line is 4.7 per cent on the Southern Railway at Saluda Hill, North Carolina.

The steepest of any line-haul is operated by special type locos on the Pennsylvania Railroad at Madison, Indiana. The grade is 7,012 feet long and climbs 413 feet, giving 5.89 per cent.

The steepest rack and pinion railway in the world is the 50 per cent grade on the Pilatus Mountain Railway, Switzerland.

The steepest funicular (cable drawn by stationary engine) railway in the world is between Piotta and Piora, Lake Ritom, Switzerland, with a maximum gradient of 1 : 1 ⅛ or 88 per cent.

BUSIEST
JUNCTION

The world's busiest railway junction is Clapham Junction in London, England, on the Southern Region of British Railways. More than 2,500 trains pass through every 24 hours.

LONGEST
VIADUCT
BRIDGE

The longest railway viaduct or bridge in the world is largely a matter of definition. The following are the longest in their various types.

The Great Salt Lake Viaduct is a pile trestle bridge nearly twelve miles long. It carries the tracks of the Southern Pacific Railroad across the Great Salt Lake in Utah.

The Huey P. Long bridge, Louisiana, 23,235 feet long (4.4 miles) including approach roads, has spans each 262 feet 6 inches in length.

The highest standard gauge viaduct in the world is at Fades, in the Puy de Dome, between Clermont-Ferrand and Mont Lucon, France. It is a 472 feet span, 435 feet above the river.

The longest main line railway tunnel in the world is the Simplon between Switzerland and Italy—12 miles 559 yards long.   TUNNELS

The longest railroad tunnel in the Western Hemisphere is the Cascade Tunnel on the Great Northern road, 41,152 feet (7.79 miles) long, through the Cascade Mountains, Washington.

Said to be the only natural tunnel in the world used by a railroad, the Natural Tunnel, Virginia, is 100 feet high, 100 feet wide, and 1,557 feet long.

The longest tunnel in the world in an underground railway system is on the Northern Line of the London Transport Executive between Morden and East Finchley—a total length of 17 miles 528 yards.

The world's biggest railway station is the Grand Central Terminal, New York. It covers 48 acres on two levels with 41 tracks on the upper level and 26 on the lower.   STATIONS

The highest station in the world on standard gauge railways is Ticlio, at 15,610 feet, on the Peruvian National Railways.

The longest platform in the world is at Sonepur on the North-Eastern Railway of India and is 2,415 feet long.   PLATFORM

The most extensive and oldest (opened 1863) underground railway system in the world is that of the London Transport Executive with 253 miles of route, of which 67 miles is bored tunnel and 23 miles is "cut and cover." The whole Tube system is operated by a staff of 20,000 serving 277 stations. The 478 trains, comprising 3,300 cars, carry 671,400,000 passengers in a year. The greatest depth is 192 feet at Hampstead.   UNDERGROUND RAILWAYS

The busiest subway in the world is the New York City Transit Authority (opened on October 27th, 1904) which embraces the I.R.T. (Interboro Rapid Transit), the B.M.T. and some Independent lines with a total of 228 miles of track. The stations are closer set and total 475 while the 1955 total of passengers carried was 1,378,149,559, having dropped from a peak of 2,051,400,973 in 1947.

3. Ships

The earliest known references to sea-going vessels are dated approximately 2000-3500 B.C. and are of Egyptian origin. Propelled by oars and a square-rigged sail, they were used for trading in the Mediterranean. Parts of a vessel dating from c.3200 B.C. have been found at Sakkara, Egypt.   EARLIEST

Generally accepted as the earliest mechanically propelled vessel was a boat designed by James Rumsey in the United States in 1786.   EARLIEST POWER

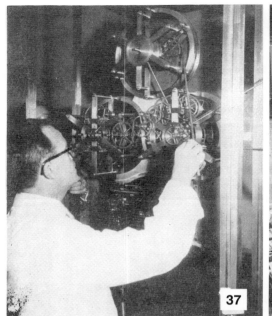

37. The Olsen Clock, most accurate and complicated clock in the world. See p. 145.
38. The Ingersoll Milling Machine, largest of its type in the world. See p. 143.
39. The Oriten bicycle, longest bicycle ever made. See p. 133.
40. Capt. Edward V. Rickenbacker, top scoring U. S. air ace in World War I. See p. 164.
41. The world's largest excavator and the largest mobile land machine. See p. 143.

Working on a jet principle driven by a pump, it reached about four miles an hour.

The "Charlotte Dundas" was the first really successful power-driven vessel. She was a paddle-steamer built by Symington in Scotland in 1801-2.

The earliest regular steam run is reputed to be by the "Phoenix," which maintained a service from New Jersey to Philadelphia in 1809.

EARLIEST TURBINE

The first turbine ship was the "Turbinia," built in 1894 to the design of the Hon. Charles Parsons. The "Turbinia" was 100 feet long and of 44½ tons displacement with machinery consisting of three steam turbines totalling about 2,000 shaft horsepower. At the first demonstration of the vessel, she reached a speed of over 32 knots.

OLDEST REGISTERED

The oldest vessel on Lloyd's register is the "Galicia," built by T. & W. Smith in 1853 at Newcastle-on-Tyne. Of 279 tons gross, the steam-powered "Galicia" is 137 feet overall, 21 feet breadth, and she sails under the Spanish flag.

ATLANTIC CROSSINGS

The first crossing of the Atlantic by a power vessel as opposed to an auxiliary engined sailing ship was in the year 1827. The ship was the "Curacao," built in Dover in 1826 and purchased by the Dutch Government for the West Indian mail service. She was a paddle boat of 438 register tons and of wooden construction.

ATLANTIC CROSSINGS FASTEST

The fastest Atlantic crossings were made by the "United States," flagship of the United States Lines Company. On her maiden voyage in July, 1952, from New York to Southampton, measured on a 2,949 mile route from the Ambrose Light Vessel to the Bishop Rock, she averaged 35.59 knots, about 41 m.p.h., for 3 days 10 hours 40 minutes.

During this run, on July 6th, she steamed the greatest distance ever covered by any ship in a day's run (24 hours)—868 nautical miles, hence averaging 36.17 knots.

NORTHERNMOST

The farthest north ever reached by a ship is 83° 11′ N. at 49° 3′ E. by the Russian ice-breaker "Feodo Litke" on September 12th, 1955.

SOUTHERNMOST

The most southerly point reached by ship is 78° S., 39° W. achieved by the Argentine ice-breaker "General San Martin" on Jan. 3rd, 1955 while establishing a base in the Weddell Sea.

PASSENGER LINER LARGEST

The "Queen Elizabeth," of the Cunard fleet, is the largest passenger vessel in the world and also has the largest displacement of any ship in the world, with a gross tonnage of 83,673. She has an overall length of 1,031 feet, and is 118 feet 7 inches in breadth. She is powered by steam turbines which develop about 200,000 h.p. The "Queen Elizabeth's" normal sea speed is about 28½ knots. Her lowest day's run was 252 miles in gales in March, 1947.

The largest room in any ship is the main restaurant of the R.M.S. "Queen Mary," which extends over 18,720 square feet (160 feet long and 118 feet wide), accommodating 815 passengers.

LARGEST TANKER

The largest tanker in the world is the S.S. "Spyros Niarchos" of 31,000 gross tonnage. The tanker, launched in England in 1955 entered service June 1956. She is 757 feet long with a moulded beam of 97′ 2″ draws 37′ 9″, and is a single screw steam turbine vessel with a shaft horse power of 20,000 tons.

LARGEST
CABLE SHIP

The world's largest cable-laying ship is Her Majesty's Telegraph Ship "Monarch," of 8,056 tons gross. Launched in 1945, she can carry between 5,000 and 6,000 tons of cable in her holds, with full oil bunkers. With a crew of 130, she can stay at sea for 100 days.

MOST
FUNNELS

The ship with the greatest number of funnels was the "Leviathan," built in New York in the 19th century. The "Leviathan" had a cigar-shaped hull 700 feet in length and was equipped with sixteen engines and thirty-two funnels. Designed to exceed 30 knots, it only reached 4 on trials and the project was eventually abandoned.

LARGEST
ANCHOR

The largest anchors in the world are those designed for the 57,000 ton U. S. aircraft carriers of the "Forrestal" class. The anchors, which are of the stockless type, are approximately 14 feet overall and weigh 30 tons each.

HEAVY
LOADS

Heaviest single items ever carried by sea were probably a consignment of three large lighters shipped from Rotterdam to India in 1931. Each lighter weighed 190 tons and the three were carried as deck cargo by the M.S. "Belpareil," a vessel in the Belships fleet.

LOUDEST
SIREN

The loudest ship's siren in the world is that on the R.M.S. "Queen Elizabeth." Keyed to lower bass 'A,' the sirens can be heard over 10 miles away and can be detected at a range of 100 miles.

SAILING SHIPS
LARGEST

The largest sailing vessel ever built was the "France II," launched at Bordeaux in 1911. The "France II" was a steel-hulled, five-masted barque (square-rigged on four masts and fore and aft rigged on the aftermost mast). She had a tonnage of 5,806 gross and her hull measured 368 feet overall. Although principally designed as a sailing vessel with a stump topgallant rig, she was also fitted with two steam engines.

The largest "fully rigged" sailing ship (square-rigged on all masts) ever built was the steel-hulled German "Preussen," launched at Geestemund in 1902. She was 408 feet in length and of 5,081 tons gross.

On each of her five masts, she carried six yards and could set 47 sails with a total area of about 50,000 square feet. She had more than 19 miles of running rigging and about 6½ miles of standing rigging.

The largest schooner (fore and aft rigged on all masts) ever designed was the "Thomas W. Lawson," built in 1902 in Massachusetts, U.S.A. She was 385 feet overall and 5,218 tons gross and constructed of steel. Her rig was unique; she was the only vessel ever to have seven masts and set seven similar fore and aft sails.

The greatest distance ever covered by a sailing ship in one day was the 465 mile run of the clipper "Champion of the Seas." Commanded by Capt. Newlands, she was on her maiden voyage from Liverpool to Melbourne and made her record run in the South Indian ocean on December 12th, 1854.

4. Aircraft

LARGEST

The largest aircraft ever constructed was the Hughes "Hercules" flying boat, which was raised a few feet into the air in a test run in Los Angeles Harbor, Calif., U.S.A., in November, 1947. The eight-engined, 190 ton aircraft has a wing span of 320 feet, and a length of 219 feet. It has never again flown.

The first controlled power-driven flight occurred at 10:30 a.m. on December 17th, 1903, near Kill Devil Sand Hill, North Carolina, when Orville Wright (1871-1948) flew the 12 h.p. chain-driven "Flyer" at an airspeed of 30-35 m.p.h. at an altitude of 8-12 feet for 12 seconds, watched by his brother Wilbur (1867-1912) and a crowd of five. The earliest cross-English Channel flight was achieved from 4:35 a.m. from Barraques, France, to 5:12 a.m. near Dover Castle, England, when Louis Blériot flew his "Blériot XI," powered by a 23 h.p. Anzani engine, across in 37 minutes on July 25th, 1909.

A flight of 1½ miles has been claimed for Gustave Whitehead near Bridgeport, Conn., as early as August 14th, 1901.

EARLIEST FLIGHTS

The earliest transcontinental flight was achieved by Calbraith P. Rogers on November 5th, 1911, when he arrived at Pasadena, Calif., in his Burgess-Wright biplane 49 days after leaving Sheepshead Bay, New York. The first non-stop coast-to-coast flight was by a U. S. Navy Fokker T.2 in 27 hours on May 2-3, 1923.

EARLIEST COAST-TO-COAST FLIGHT

The earliest transatlantic flight was achieved from 5:13 p.m. on June 14th, 1919, from St. John's, Newfoundland, to a bay near Clifden, County Galway, Ireland, at 9:25 a.m., June 15th, when Capt. John Alcock, D.S.C., and Lt. Arthur Whitten Brown flew across in a Vicker "Vimy," powered by two Rolls-Royce "Eagle" engines, at times only 10 feet above the waves.

The first true jet flight was achieved in Germany on August 27th, 1939, when the Heinkel 178 was flown a short distance.

The first British jet flight occurred on April 7th, 1941, at Gloster's aerodrome, when P. E. G. Sayer, O.B.E., flew the Gloster E28/39 (wing span 29 feet, length 25 feet 3 inches, height 9 feet 3 inches).

The earliest flight of a jet aircraft built in the United States was that of the Bell XP59, using 2 Whittle designed engines, in secret at Muroc, California, on October 1st, 1942.

EARLIEST U.S. JET AIRCRAFT

The first aircraft fatality in the U. S. was the death of Thomas E. Selfridge, U. S. Army, on September 17th, 1908, at Fort Myer, Virginia.

EARLIEST ACCIDENT

The largest international airport in the world is London Airport, Hounslow, Middlesex. It covers an area of 2,874 acres (roughly 2½ miles by 2 miles). Its longest runway is 9,504 feet (1.79 miles) long.

AIRPORT

Twenty-eight airline companies use London Airport and during 1954 there were a total number of 79,649 aircraft movements, handled by the estimated 14,000 staff employed by the various companies and the Ministry of Transport and Civil Aviation. The total number of passengers, both incoming and outgoing during 1954 was 1,724,139.

The longest commercial runway in the world is that of the Logan International Airport, East Boston. It is 10,022 feet long. When extended thru to Rosamund Ivy Lake the Edwards Air Base runway, at Muroc, Calif. will be 22 miles in length.

AIRPORT RUNWAY

The busiest airport in the world is Chicago Midway Airport, opened in 1927. Eighteen scheduled airlines operate from the airport which, during 1955, handled 401,500 aircraft and 9,135,120 passengers.

AIRPORT BUSIEST

LARGEST
AIRLINE

The largest airline in the United States and the world is American Airlines, Inc. In 1955, they carried a record 7,300,000 passengers.

LARGEST
AIRLINER

The largest turbo-prop airliner in production in the world is the "Britannia", built by The Bristol Aeroplane Company Limited. The full passenger version, series 300, accommodates 99 passengers and 910 cubic feet of cargo and has an all-up weight of 155,000 lbs. (over 69 tons). Powered by four Bristol "Proteus" 755 engines, each of 4,120 equivalent horsepower, it has a maximum range of 5,368 miles with a payload of 25,000 lbs. and an economical cruising speed of 346 m.p.h.

LARGEST
TRANSPORT

The world's largest cargo plane is the Convair XC-99, which was developed as a U. S. Air Force version of the B-36. With a wing span of 230 feet and a maximum weight of over 142 tons, the XC-99 can carry up to 400 troops or 44½ tons of freight. Its six 3,000 h.p. Pratt & Whitney R4360-41 piston engines would give it a maximum range of 8,100 miles with a 5 ton payload.

MOST POWERFUL
JET ENGINE

The performances of a number of the world's most advanced jet engines are secret. Though security regulations do not permit of a published figure above 12,000 lbs. thrust for the British 'Olympus' 6, it has been published in the United States without denial that this engine has yielded 16,000 lbs. on a test stand and that its development program calls for a power of 21,000 lbs. by 1958.

The highest published type-approved maximum sea-level static thrust rating for any straight turbo-jet engine is the 15,000 lbs. thrust of the de Havilland Gyron (diameter 46.25 inches, length 12 feet 10 inches). The most powerful by-pass turbo-jet in the world is the Rolls-Royce Conway (diameter 41 inches, length 10 feet 8¾ inches) officially rated at 13,000 lbs. thrust.

Estimates varying between 14,000 and 18,000 lbs. have been ascribed to the Russian Mikulin M.109 jet engine.

HEAVIEST
LOAD

The heaviest single piece of freight ever handled by air was an automatic mesh welder weighing 6,500 kilos (14,300 pounds), transported from Zurich, Switzerland, to London Airport. The equipment measured 15 feet 6 inches x 5 feet 6 inches x 4 feet 8 inches and was flown in a chartered Airwork DC 4 Skymaster in May, 1955.

HELICOPTER
ALTITUDE

The greatest height attained by a helicopter is 26,932 feet by Jean Boulet in a Sud-Est S.E. 3130 Alouette over Buc, near Paris, France, on June 6th, 1955.

SPEED

The fastest speed attained by a helicopter is 156 m.p.h. by W/O. B. I. Wester at Windsor Lake, Connecticut, on August 26th, 1954.

LARGEST
HELICOPTER

The greatest weight ever raised by a helicopter is 7,800 pounds (3.9 tons) by Howard Hughes' "Whirlybird" at Culver City, California, on December 21st, 1955.

SMALLEST
AIRCRAFT

The smallest aircraft in the world is the U.S.N. Hiller Flying Platform which is only six feet in diameter and had its first free flight test on February 4th, 1955.

LONGEST
TICKET

The longest air-line ticket ever issued was one measuring 15 feet 8 inches long, weighing 3 lbs. 5 ozs. The ticket was issued at the Algiers office of Air France to Mr. Georges Kurtz in October, 1955, and covered a seven-month journey across Africa in 47 laps, terminating at Madagascar, a distance of 25,000 miles.

Kites were used for meteorological purposes before balloons came into general use. A record altitude of 23,385 feet was attained by flying ten kites in tandem on a fine steel wire 8½ miles in length.

HIGHEST
KITES

5. Power Producers

The earliest recorded use of wind power was for grinding corn in Persia about the 7th century A.D.

WINDMILLS

In the United States the largest windmill ever designed was a "depression" type erected in Vermont in 1941. It was built to produce 1,250 kilowatts but a mechanical failure occurred on test and the project was abandoned.

The biggest single boiler ever designed in the world is at present under construction by Babcock and Wilcox at the River Rouge plant of the Detroit Edison Company in U.S.A.

BIGGEST
BOILER

More than 150 feet high, it will have an evaporative capacity of 1,720,000 pounds of steam per hour and deliver steam to the turbine at 2,000 pounds per square inch.

The main pressure drum of the boiler is 82 feet long and the thickness of its steel walls is nearly 6 inches. Of welded construction, it weighs 193 tons.

The boiler will supply steam to a turbine producing 273,000 kw.

The largest power house at present operating is the T.V.A. plant at Kingston, Tennessee. It has an output of 1.6 million kilowatts, and uses four million tons of coal a year.

POWER PLANT
LARGEST

The largest generator in the world is being built by Allis-Chalmers Manufacturing Co. for the River Rouge plant of the Detroit Edison Co.

GENERATOR
LARGEST

The unit will have a capacity of 300,000 kw. (400,000 h.p.) and is designed to be the most economical ever built. It will produce a kilowatt hour of electricity (one unit) for less than three-quarters of a pound of coal.

The cross-compound turbine is designed for an initial pressure of 2,400 pounds per square inch and an exhaust pressure of 1 in. Hg. absolute. The initial temperature is 1,050°F and reheat temperature 1,000°F and both high and intermediate pressure turbines are on the 3,600 r.p.m. shaft.

The world's largest reversible pump turbine is being made by Allis-Chalmers for the extension to the Tennessee Valley Authority's Hiawassee Dam in North Carolina, U.S.A.

LARGEST
PUMP
TURBINE

The single unit is intended to operate in one direction as a pump and in the reverse direction as a turbine. A directly connected electrical machine serves as a motor for pump operation and as a generator for turbine operation. As a turbine, it will have a maximum rating of 120,000 h.p., and when used as a pump will have a rated pumping capacity of 3,900 cubic feet per second against a 205 feet head, or 3,300 million gallons a day.

LARGEST
ELECTRIC
MOTOR

This same electrical unit, when used as a motor, is the world's largest, rated at 102,000 h.p. at 106 revolutions per minute. As a generator it is rated at 70,000 kw., 13,800 volts.

In a normal cycle of operations, the water from the Hiawassee reservoir will drive the turbine to provide power during peak demand periods. During off-peak periods when surplus power is available from other plants, the unit will operate as a pump to lift water back to the reservoir. The operation of the unit is economically practicable because the off-peak power for pumping will cost less than the value of that produced during peak demand periods, and will also improve the load factor on the local system.

LARGEST
GAS WORKS

The largest gas works in the world is the Beckton plant of the North Thames Gas Board, London, England. The Beckton Works, which covers 300 acres and employs 3,500 people, contains over seventy miles of standard gauge railway line on which there are fifty locomotives and 1,100 wagons. The maximum gas-making capacity is 164 million cubic feet a day from about six thousand tons of coal.

LARGEST
ATOMIC
PLANT

The largest atomic plant in the world is the Savannah River Project, South Carolina, extending 27 miles along the river and over a total area of 315 square miles. The plant, comprising 280 permanent buildings, cost $1,400 million. Construction was started in February, 1951, and by September, 1952, the labor force had reached 38,500. The present operating strength is 8,500.

6. Engineering

LARGEST
MACHINE
TOOLS

The largest machine tool in operation in the world is the 50,000 ton closed die forging press at the Wyman-Gordon plant in Worcester, Massachusetts.

The press, which weighs 10,605 tons, is used mainly for producing aircraft components in die forged aluminum.

It stands 48 feet above the work floor and extends 60 feet below, six columns, 108 feet high, guide the crossheads. The moving parts of the press, which has platens 32 feet by 12 feet, and a stroke of 6 feet, weigh 6,450 tons.

The press is hydraulically operated by water pressure delivered at 4,500 pounds per square inch and during press operations pressures up to 6,000 lbs. per square inch are reached. To withstand these pressures, the water lines are of forged steel with walls five inches thick.

LARGEST
BORING MILL

The largest boring mill in the world was made by Craven Brothers of Manchester, England, for a Canadian firm in 1953.

The mill, which weighs a total of approximately 650 tons, can accept work up to 42 feet 6 inches in diameter and up to 13 feet 4 inches in height and up to 140 tons in weight.

The main work table is 41 feet in diameter and weighs approximately 170 tons. It is driven by two 150 h.p. variable speed motors, which give it, in conjunction with a three-speed gearbox, a speed range of 0.15 to 3.5 r.p.m.

The machine is operated by 28 separate motors and generators and the electrical system includes special interlocking devices to ensure the maximum degree of safety.

The largest milling machine in the world was constructed by the Ingersoll Milling Machine Company for the Schenectady Works of General Electric Company. The machine, which can accept work 18 x 16.5 x 50 feet, weighs 1.25 million pounds and is 120 feet overall. The main purpose of the machine will be to work turbine and generator parts. It cost approximately $1,250,000. See Photo No. 38, page 136.

BIGGEST
MILLING
MACHINE

The world's largest testing machine is that built for the Fritz Engineering Laboratory of the Lehigh University. It can exert a pressure of 5,000,000 pounds and is large enough to accept for test vertical specimens 40 feet high and beams, girders, etc., up to 100 feet long.

LARGEST
TESTING
MACHINE

The largest machine shop in the world is the Large Steam Turbine Generator Department of the General Electric Company's works at Schenectady, N. Y. It covers 22 acres of ground and cost approximately $30,000,000. The main manufacturing bays, of which there are nine, are 1,400 feet long, and house 4,600 employees who make turbine and generator parts which range in size from a fraction of an ounce to over 200 tons. The plant has a total of 54 overhead traveling cranes which range in capacity from 2 to 200 tons.

LARGEST
MACHINE
SHOP

The plant produces turbine-generators capable of adding approximately seven million kilowatts a year to the nation's electrical capacity.

The largest stripping shovel (mechanical excavator) in the world is now being built for an American coal mining company for open cast working, by Marion Power Shovel Co. of the U.S.A.

EXCAVATOR
SHOVEL

The machine has been designed to remove approximately a 90 feet depth of overburden, and the bucket size is 60 cubic yards in capacity. On the machine's normal operating cycle it will be removing 100 tons of earth every 50 seconds.

The excavator, which weighs approximately 2,200 tons, is carried on eight caterpillar tracks mounted in pairs, each 8 feet high, 22 feet long and having a 54 inch tread width.

It is powered by sixteen electric motors having an available total of 4,500 h.p.

The largest dragline excavator in the world is that designed and made by Ransomes & Rapier Ltd. for Stewart & Lloyds' opencast ironstone workings at Corby, Northamptonshire. The excavator has a bucket size of 20 cubic yards with a capacity reach of 260 feet. The tubular steel boom has a length of 282 feet and the overall height is 175 feet. It is powered by two generator sets of 1,500 h.p. each and its working weight is 1,650 tons.

DRAGLINE

The two walking shoes set on eccentrically mounted legs are 48 feet long and 9 feet 6 inches wide and weigh 56 tons each; they have a "stride" of 6 feet 10 ½ inches.

The world's largest excavator of any type, and the largest mobile land machine, is the bucket wheel excavator, built by Orenstein-Koppel und Lubecker Maschinenbau, operating on opencast workings at Auenheim, Rhineland, Germany. The material dug is carried by belt conveyors

EXCAVATOR
BUCKET
WHEEL

to the loading plant at the rear end, where it is loaded into rail trucks.

The bucket wheel is 52 feet in diameter, carries twelve buckets, each of 4.7 cubic yards capacity, and can be raised or lowered on its boom to dig anywhere from ground level to a height of 164 feet.

Complete with loading plant, and mounted on 18 caterpillar tracks, the whole unit is 216 feet high, 656 feet long, and weighs 6,270 tons. With a crew of 5-6 men, it can cut and load at the rate of over 14,220 tons (x 2,000 lbs.) an hour. Power is supplied by 120 electric motors totaling over 4,000 h.p. See Photo No. 41, page 136.

LARGEST CRUSHER

The world's largest gyratory crusher is a 56 ton Allis-Chalmers unit, crushing taconite in Minnesota. Powered by two 500 h.p. electric motors the crusher can accept pieces of rock up to 5 feet in one dimension and crush them to a maximum of nine inches in any one dimension. The rock can be handled at the rate of 3,500 tons an hour.

WEIGHING MACHINE

Construction of the world's largest weighing machine, 52 feet 9 inches high with a capacity of 669 tons per hour, was begun in The Hague in July, 1955, for shipment to Australia. Britain's largest scale is one with a capacity of 300 tons per hour at Tate & Lyle's London sugar refinery.

LONGEST PIPES

The longest crude oil pipe line in the world is the Interprovincial Pipe Line Company's installation from Redwater, Alberta to Sarnia, Ontario, a distance of 1,775 miles. Along the length of the pipe, thirteen pumping stations maintain the flow of oil. Just after a pumping station the pressure in the pipe is between 900 and 1,000 pounds per square inch but this high pressure falls to 50 pounds per square inch before it reaches the next pump. Approximately 6.9 million gallons of oil a day are pumped along the line.

The longest natural gas pipe line in the world is the 30-inch line from Rio Grande, S. Texas 1,840 miles to New York.

LARGEST VALVE

The largest straight-flow valves in the world are those made by the English Electric Co., Ltd., for the Castelo-do-Bode and Gabril Hydro-electric power stations in Portugal. They have a bore of 11 feet.

SMALLEST TUBING

The smallest tubing in the world is made by Accles & Pollock of Birmingham, England. Produced in anticipation of an industrial demand, it is .0017 inch—seventeen ten-thousands of an inch outside diameter and the bore is five ten-thousandths of an inch in diameter. The average human hair measures twenty to thirty ten-thousandths of an inch in diameter. The tubing, which is stainless, has been used for the artificial insemination of queen bees and "feeding" nerves.

DIE CASTING

The largest die casting ever produced is a 6-cylinder automobile engine block in aluminum weighing 43 pounds. It was made by the Doehler-Jarvis Division of National Lead Co. in Toledo in March, 1955. The block was cast on a 72 inch machine with a locking pressure of 2,000 tons. It is capable of producing castings up to 70 pounds in weight and with a maximum surface area of 1,500 square inches. It is the largest die casting machine in the world.

HIGHEST ROPEWAY

The highest and longest aerial ropeway in the world links Chamonix and Aiguille du Midi on the French side of Mont Blanc. The ropeway is in two sections, intermediate and upper. From the intermediate station, the rope to the upper mountain station is 3,170 yards long and the negotiated height of the upper section is 4,840 feet.

The fastest elevators in the world are those fitted in the R.C.A. Building, Rockefeller Plaza, New York City. They rise a total of 795 feet at a speed of 1,400 feet per minute, or 15.9 miles per hour.

FASTEST
PASSENGER
ELEVATORS

The longest wire rope ever spun is that manufactured by Jacob Holm & Sonne, Copenhagen, in 1950, for the Danish ocean survey vessel "Galathea." The rope tapers from a diameter of 0.22 to 0.55 inch and is 7.45 miles in length.

LONGEST
ROPE

The longest conveyor belt in the world is that installed at the U. S. Steel's Fairless works, Morrisville, Pennsylvania, for carrying coke to blast furnaces over a mile distant. The belt is 11,000 feet long, 4 feet in width and was made by Goodyear.

LONGEST
CONVEYOR
BELT

CLOCKS

The world's biggest clock is on the Colgate-Palmolive plant in Jersey City, U.S.A. The dial is 50 feet in diameter and covers an area of 1,963 square feet. The minute hand is 27 feet 3 inches and the hour hand 19 feet 6 inches. It was started at noon, December 1st, 1924.

WORLD'S
LARGEST

The most accurate and complicated clock in the world is the Jens Olsen clock installed in Copenhagen Town Hall, Denmark. The clock, which has more than 14,000 units, took ten years to make and the mechanism of the clock functions in 570,000 ways. The celestial pole motion of the clock will take 25,700 years to complete circle, the slowest piece of moving mechanism in the world. The clock was set in motion in December, 1955, and has a maximum deviation of 0.4 second each 300 years. See Photo No. 37, page 136.

MOST
ACCURATE

The oldest working clock in the world is that dating from at least 1386 at Salisbury Cathedral, England, which was restored in 1956. The Dijon clock in France is perhaps slightly older (1382) but only the iron frame is original.

OLDEST
CLOCK

The most accurate mechanism for the measurement of short periods of time has been developed by Dr. C. H. Townes of Columbia University, New York, U.S.A.

TIME
MEASURER

Using a new principle, the design permits direct amplification of high frequency microwaves without the use of vacuum tubes. Using, for instance, the energy of the ammonia molecules, the clock can produce microwaves with frequencies to the order of 24,000,000,000 cycles per second.

The oldest watch (portable clock-work time keeper) is that made of iron by P. Hele in Nürnberg, Germany, c.1504, now in the Memorial Hall, Philadelphia, U.S.A.

OLDEST
WATCH

Part Nine

THE BUSINESS WORLD

1. Commerce

LARGEST
MANU-
FACTURING
CONCERNS

The largest manufacturing company in the world is General Motors Corporation of Detroit, Michigan. During 1955, they sold 12,443,277,-420 dollars worth of products. Their unit sales of cars and trucks equalled 5,031,000 of which 4,477,000 were produced in the United States. Their total assets are $6,344,772,161. Their shareholders total 565,408. Their products include Chevrolet, Oldsmobile, Buick, Cadillac and Pontiac cars and in America include heavy off-the-road vehicles, household appliances and air conditioning plants, refrigerators, diesel engine locomotives, aluminum castings, turbo-jet and turbo-prop aircraft engines.

They are the parent company of Vauxhall in England, Opel in Germany and Holden's in Australia.

Their average employment figure during 1955 was 624,011.

In the United States alone they employed 410,022 hourly rate employees at an average rate of $2.41 per hour; the average for the U. S. in the manufacturing industries was $1.88. They earned an average weekly pay of $102.41 for 42.5 hours of work.

On November 23rd, 1954, General Motors produced its fifty millionth United States built car since 1908.

GREATEST
ASSETS

The business with the greatest amount in physical assets in the world is the Bell Telephone System which comprises the American Telephone and Telegraph Company and its principal Telephone Subsidiaries. The consolidated balance sheet assets figure as at January 1st, 1956, was $14,479,641,983. The plant involved included 46,218,233 telephones, 197,145,000 miles of wire (enough to girdle the earth 7,896 times).

LARGEST
PARTNERSHIP

The largest partnership in the world and also the world's largest investment house is Merrill, Lynch, Pierce, Fenner and Beane of 70 Pine Street, New York. The title of the firm took its current form on August 18th, 1941. It has 106 partners, 5,700 employees, 116 offices and 263,000 customers for whom $4 billion are held. The firm is referred to in stock exchange circles as "We" or "We, the people."

Assessed by total deposits, the Bank of America, San Francisco, is the largest in the U. S. with, on December 31st, 1954, a total of $8,270,534,751 in deposits.

Assessed by capital funds, the National City Bank of New York is the largest with $552,663,000 in capital stock, surplus and undivided profits.

The largest mutual savings bank is the Bowery Savings Bank of New York with $1,190,029,708 in deposits.

BANKS

The richest man in the United States is Haroldson Lafayette Hunt, owner of the Hunt Oil Company in Texas. He is reputed to have an income approaching $50 million per annum and, aided by the operation of the 27½ % Federal depletion allowance, a capital of some $2,000 million.

RICHEST MAN

The top paid executive in the U. S. is Harlow H. Curtice, president of the General Motors Corporation who, in 1955, earned $201,400 in salaries and fees, $77,713 in stock and $497,287 in cash bonuses, totalling $776,400. Of this total, $655,072 (84.35%) was deducted in Federal income taxes, leaving a balance of $121,328.

HIGHEST PAID EXECUTIVE

The largest steel works in the world are the U. S. Steel's Gary Plant at Gary, Indiana, which produce over 7,000,000 tons of steel per annum.

LARGEST STEEL WORKS

The largest grocery chain in the world is The Great Atlantic and Pacific Tea Company in the U.S.A., with over 4,000 stores, including some 400 supermarkets. They operate thirty-nine bakeries, two laundries for the uniforms of their 120,000 employees.

GROCERY CHAINS

The largest department store chain in the world is J. C. Penney Co., Inc., originally founded in Wyoming in 1902; in 1955, they operated 1,666 stores in every one of the forty-eight states, ranging from one in Rhode Island to 149 in California. In 1955, their turnover was $1,220,085,325.06.

DEPARTMENT STORE CHAINS

The largest mail order house in the world is the Sears, Roebuck Company of Chicago, Illinois. In 1955, the Company sold $3,306,826,181 worth of goods. They have 707 stores in the United States alone. The Company issues seven different catalogues annually with a total circulation of over fifty million copies, listing 103,000 items.

MAIL ORDER

The store with the largest number of sales in the world is the Gosudarstvenny Universalny Magazin (G.U.M.—State Universal Shop) in Red Square, Moscow. It was opened in 1922 and remodeled in 1953. It can accommodate 25,000 customers simultaneously and 150,000 a day with ease. Selling everything "required for stomach, body or mind," the store served thirty million customers in the last six months of 1954 who made fifty million purchases worth $500 million. The store has a sales area of 11½ acres and 1½ miles of counters.

DEPARTMENT STORE

The largest shoe store in the world is Lilley & Skinner, Ltd., 356-360 Oxford Street, London, England. The shop has a floor area of

SHOE STORE

70,000 square feet spread over four floors. With a total staff of more than two hundred and fifty people, it offers, in ten departments, a choice of some 200,000 pairs of shoes. Every week, on average, 24,000 people visit this store.

BOOK SHOP

The world's biggest book shop is that of Messrs. W. & G. Foyle of London, England. First established in 1904 in a small shop in Islington, Foyle's now maintain a stock of four million books on approximately thirty miles of shelving in their Charing Cross Road premises. The total staff is approximately six hundred people and they handle about nine million letters a year, more than four thousand every working hour. Foyle's sell more than five million books every year.

LARGEST PASSENGER LINE

The largest passenger shipping line in the world is the Cunard Steamship Co. of Great Britain. On the transatlantic run they operate 13 liners from 7 U. S. and 6 Canadian ports which, in 1955, carried a total of 259,000 passengers.

LARGEST PRINTERS

The largest printers in the United States and the world is the U. S. Government Printing Office in Washington, D. C., founded in March, 1861. It now operates 160 presses and 378 typesetting and casting machines with which a daily average of nine million 'ems' are type set. The Office operates on 32½ acres of floor space, employing 6,750 people on a 24 hour production schedule worth $77,000,000 per annum.

The largest commercial printers in the United States and the world are R. R. Donnelly's of Chicago, Ill.

LARGEST PUBLISHERS

The largest publishers in the world are the U. S. Government Printing Office in Washington, D. C. The Superintendent of Documents Division, in 1955, dispatched 150,800,000 items. The annual list of new titles and annuals is about 6,000 per year.

LARGEST BREWERY

The largest output of any brewery in the United States and the world is the Jos. Schlitz Brewing Co. who, in 1955, sold 5,780,000 31-gallon barrels from their 3 plants in Milwaukee, Los Angeles and New York. The largest single brewing plant in the world is that of Anheuser-Busch, Inc., at St. Louis, which extends over 66 acres. In 1953, Anheuser set an all-time record of 6,711,000 barrels.

The largest stout brewery in the world and the largest brewery in Europe is the St. James's Gate Brewery, Dublin, Ireland, of Arthur Guinness Son & Co., Ltd. (founded 1759) which extends over 64 acres.

MOST BEER EXPORTS

The largest exporters of beer, ale and stout in the world are Arthur Guinness Son & Co., Ltd., of Dublin, Ireland. Exports of Guinness Stout from the Republic of Ireland in the calendar year 1955 reached 1,642,000 barrels or 1,857,000 ½ pint glasses per day.

BRICKWORKS

The largest brickworks in the world is the London Brick Company plant at Stewartby, Bedford. The works, established in 1898, now cover 160 acres and produce over twelve million bricks every week.

ROPEWORKS

Established in 1876, the Belfast Ropework Company, Ltd., has grown to be the biggest ropeworks in the world. It now covers an area of forty acres and employs some 2,000 people. Between two hundred and three hundred tons of finished products are produced each week at their Connswater, Belfast, factory.

The longest ropewalk in the factory is 1,000 feet long and they have produced rope up to thirty-six inches in circumference.

The largest advertising agency in the United States and the world is J. Walter Thompson of New York City, with an estimated world total annual billing of $220,000,000 in 1955.

ADVERTISING AGENTS

The largest advertising sign ever erected is that at Port Tampa, Florida, 387½ feet long and 76 feet high, weighing 175 tons and containing 5 miles of red neon tubing.

ADVERTISING SIGNS LARGEST

The sign, completed in 1953, carries the 6 word message, "Atlantic Coast Line Port Tampa Terminal" in letters 19½ feet high and 13 feet wide. A larger sign was painted in yellow letters 50 feet high on the surface of Michigan Avenue, Jackson, Michigan, in July, 1954. This spelled out the words "Freedom Festival" to a length of 1,551 feet, comprising an area of 77,550 square feet (1.78 acres) in connection with the city's double celebration of the Republican Parties centennial on July 6th, 1854 and the 125th anniversary of the founding of the city in 1829.

The most elevated sign in the world is the R.C.A. sign atop the 70 story, 850 foot high Radio Corporation of America Building in Rockefeller Plaza, New York City.

HIGHEST

The largest capital expansion program ever undertaken by a single company is the 1956 $2,100,000,000 scheme by the American Telephone and Telegraph Company to expand its total of telephones from 47 to 50 million by 1957. The company is the world's largest public utility.

GREATEST INVESTMENT

The largest check in the history of banking was one for $642,600,-000 drawn by the Ford Motor Company of Detroit in favor of the Ford Foundation on January 26th, 1956, from the proceeds of the public sale of the Company's common stock.

LARGEST CHECK

The greatest pay-out in insurance history for personal injury was $400,000 by Lloyd's of London to Dr. Hugh G. Hamilton for the loss of a foot in 1951.

INSURANCE

2. Agriculture

Agriculture and associated industries represent 57 per cent of the domestic economy of Siam (Thailand) and Turkey—the highest proportion of any country. In the United Kingdom the same industries provide only 5 per cent of the total national net product—the lowest of any country in the world. Over 13 per cent of the land surface of the United Kingdom is urbanized.

MOST AND LEAST AGRICULTURAL COUNTRIES

The largest farms in the world are collective farms in Russia upon which there are no data available.

FARMS

The world's largest single wheat field is probably that sown in 1951 near Lethbridge, Canada, extending over 35,000 acres.

LARGEST RANCHES

The world's largest ranch is the Gang Ranch, British Columbia, which is over 3,900,000 acres.

The largest ranch in the United States is the King Ranch in south central Texas, south of San Antonio, owned by the Kleberg family, covering 1,250,000 acres in 5 counties with headquarters in Santa Gertrudis.

HOP FIELDS

The largest hop field in the world is one of 710 acres at Toppenish, Washington, U.S.A., owned by John I. Haas, Inc. John I. Haas, Inc., are the world's largest hop growers with hop farms in British Columbia, Canada, California, Idaho, Oregon and Washington, with a total net area of 3,065 acres.

GRAIN ELEVATOR

The world's largest single unit grain elevator is that operated by the C-G Grain Company at Wichita, Kansas, and built by Chalmers and Borton of Hutchinson. It consists of a triple row of storage tanks 120 feet high, 100 feet wide overall and 2,717 feet long. Its total capacity is 20,000,000 bushels of wheat, or 544,200 tons.

CROP YIELDS Wheat

Crop yields for highly tended small areas are of little significance. The world record wheat yield is 70½ cwt. per acre on an 8.96 acre field in 1952 at Wiggenhall St. Mary, Norfolk, by Turrell Bros. This compares with the average United Kingdom yield of 20½ cwt. per acre—double that which obtains in North America.

FOOT AND MOUTH DISEASE

The worst recorded pandemic of foot and mouth disease, a febrile virus infection, was that centered in South Germany in 1920 where there were 181,067 affected premises and a further 37,000 in France. The earliest positive outbreak in the British Isles occurred in 1839.

WORLD RECORDS MILK YIELD

The highest life-time milk yield of any cow is that given by the British Friesian "Manningford Faith Jan Graceful" owned by R. and H. Jenkinson of Oxfordshire, England. Before her death in November, 1955, aged 17½ years, she gave 326,453 lbs. (163.27 tons.)

The world record for one lactation (365 days) is 45,081 lbs. (20.13 tons) by R. A. Pierson's British Friesian "Bridge Birch" in England in 1947.

The world record for milk yield in a day is 198 lbs. by R. A. Pierson's British Friesian "Garsdon Minnie."

BUTTER FAT

The world record butter fat yield for a life-time was set in the United States at 10,936 lbs. by the Jersey cow "Silken Lady's Ruby of F" in its twenty-one years of life.

The world's record butter fat yield in a lactation is 1,799 lbs. (33,184 lbs. milk at 5.42 per cent) by A. Drexler's "Zenda Bountiful" at Manor Farm, Kidlington, Oxfordshire, England, for the year ended March 3rd, 1953, sufficient to produce 2,116 lbs. of butter.

The record for butter fat in one day is 6.44 lbs. (57 lbs. milk at 11.30 per cent) by the Hon. Mrs. W. P. A. Bradshaw's Guernsey cow "Fillette 3rd of Les Videclins" in October, 1953.

WORLD BREED RECORDS

Milking frequencies and special feeds may influence abnormal milk and butter fat output, hence uniform comparisons are unobtainable. The data below represent extreme recorded yields. W = World Record.

	AYRSHIRE	BRITISH FRIESIAN	DAIRY SHORTHORN	GUERNSEY	HOLSTEIN	JERSEY
MILK LIFETIME YIELD	206,410 lbs. "Cowgrove Nora" to 1947 (James Gibson) U.K.	W (see above)	223,917 lbs. "Winton Gentle 2nd" (J. R. Burge & Son) U.K.	W 194,276 lbs. "Caumsett Ida," U.S.A.	W 281,193 lbs. "Pansco Hazel" to 1953 of Whittier, Cal., U.S.A. (F. F. Pellisser)	W 196,457 lbs. "Silken Lady's Ruby of F" of California, U.S.A.
LACTATION YIELD (Limit 365 days)	30,910 lbs. "Nether Craig Janet," 1936 (Alexander Cochrane) U.K.	W 45,081 lbs. (see above)	41,644 lbs. "Cherry" in 1939 (Wort and Way) U.K.	26,672 lbs. "Welcome in Forward's Clara," U.S.A.	W 42,805 lbs. "Green Meadow Lily Pabst" in 1951, Michigan, U.S.A. (Merle H. Green)	W 25,680 lbs. "Stranges Musical" in 1956 (J. R. Proctor) U.K.
YIELD in 24 HOURS	103½ lbs. (two milkings) "Faulkners Rosebud," May 1953 (James Alexander) U.K.	W 198 lbs. (see above)	129½ lbs. "Eva" in 1930 (Mrs. Kate Hollas) U.K.	98½ lbs. "Hazelby Sea Fancy," 1949 (Capt. Cosmo Douglas) U.K.	W 165.1 lbs. "Ravensworth Skylark Johanna," 1948, Virginia, U.S.A. (Smith and Janney)	120¾ lbs. "Moors Pacified Diana," Feb., 1950 (Prof. R. W. Wheldon) U.K.
BUTTER FAT LACTATION YIELD (Limit 365 days)	—	W 1,799 lbs. (see above)	W 1,614 lbs. "Melba 15th of Darbalara," 1923, Australia	W 1,383.9 lbs. "Fascination 3rd of the Pastures," 1954 (Sir Robert Black) U.K.	W 1,511.8 lbs. "Carnation Homestead Daisy Madcap," 1953 Carnation, Wash., U.S.A.	W 1,475.65 lbs. (305 days) 24,676 lbs. milk at 5.98%. "Baring's Flower," 1953 (Mr. & Mrs. K. MacDonald)
YIELD in 24 HOURS	—	—	—	W 6.44 lbs. from 57 lbs. milk at 11.30% (see above)	—	4.12 lbs. from 71.8 lbs. milk at 5.73% "Lady Spotted Pearl," 1930 (R. G. W. Berkeley) U.K.

LIVESTOCK RECORDS

CATTLE
Bull

The highest price ever fetched by a bull is the $100,000 (£35,714) paid by Dr. Hammer at the International Chicago Agricultural Show in November, 1950, for a Black Aberdeen, Prince Eric of Sunbeam. This price was also paid in May, 1954, at Fair Oaks Ranch, Boerne, Texas, for Hillcrest Larry 25th. However, the same figure of $100,000 was paid in February, 1955, by J. Danciger for a one-third share in the Black Angus bull "Prince 105 SAF" owned by J. V. Hampton and Simon of Decatur, Texas.

Cow

The world record price for a cow is the $40,600 (£14,500) paid by R. Pavin Davies of England, for a Shorthorn "8th Duchess of Geneva" at the 1873 New York Mills auction.

DIMENSIONS
Cattle

Reputedly the largest ox now living is the 9 year old Hereford-Friesian "Big Bill Campbell" at Major C. H. Still's Hall Farm, Upton, Northamptonshire, England, weighing 35 cwt. (4,920 lbs.), standing over 6 feet in height and 12 feet 6 inches from nose to tail.

Reputedly the smallest cow in the world "Sally," a Dexter breed, standing only 34 inches, is on the same farm.

The highest recorded birthweight for a calf is 172 lbs. (12 stone 4 lb.) from a South Devon cow owned by J. H. Pears & Sons of Berry Pomeroy, Devon, in September, 1952.

Horses

The highest price ever paid for a farm horse is $27,930 for the Clydesdale stallion "Baron of Buchlyvie" paid by W. Dunlop in Scotland in December, 1911.

Pigs

The world's record price for a pig is $10,200 paid in 1953 for a Hampshire boar "Great Western" for a farm at Byron, U.S.A.

Sheep

The world record for any breed of sheep is $16,170 for a Kent ram at Fielding, New Zealand, in January 1951.

EGG LAYING

The greatest authenticated egg-laying record is 355 eggs in 365 days by a black Australorp at the Glen Agricultural College laying test, South Africa, in 1944-1945.

CHEESE

The largest cheese recorded was one of 13 feet in circumference, weighing 1,474 lbs. (13 cwts. 18 lbs.), made by James Elgar of Peterborough, Northants, in 1849.

RATTING

All rat-killing records are held by Mr. J. Shaw's "Jacko" which, in killing 1,000 rats in under 1 hour 40 minutes in London, England on May 1st, 1862, accounted for the first 100 in 5 minutes 28 seconds.

Part Ten

ACCIDENTS AND DISASTERS

The greatest human disaster of all time was the Black Death which raged from 1347 to 1351 and caused about 25 million deaths in Europe including over 45 per cent of the population of Britain. Some authorities state that including the Orient the total number of fatalities was of the order of 75 million.

GREATEST HUMAN CATASTROPHE

In recent times the greatest loss of life was in the Influenza Pandemic of September-November, 1918, with a total loss estimated at 21,640,000 deaths.

The greatest recorded flood disaster was that in the Honan province of China in 1887, when the Hwang Ho river overflowed with 900,000 perishing. (For worst U.S. floods see under Hurricanes.)

FLOODS

The worst earthquake was the Chinese shock of January 23rd, 1556, when over 830,000 were killed in the Shensi Province from all causes.

EARTHQUAKES

The worst recorded group of tornadoes were those of March 18th, 1925, which raged through the 6 states of Missouri, Illinois, Indiana, Kentucky, Tennessee and Alabama. The death roll was 792 and the estimated damage $17,800,000. The most damaging group of tornadoes reported were a group of 12 in Michigan, Ohio and New England which, on June 7-9, 1953, caused $93 million worth of damage in addition to killing 234 people.

TORNADOES

The worst recorded toll of human life from a circular storm was that at Haiphong, Indo-China, in 1881, when a typhoon caused 300,000 deaths. The worst hurricane in the United States was that which inundated Galveston, Texas, on September 8th, 1900. The 120 m.p.h. wind gathered a storm wave which rose to a level 15 feet above mean high water, causing $20 million damage and drowned an estimated 6,000 people. The most damaging hurricane recorded was 'Diane,' August 17-19, 1955, which caused "over $1,000 million of damage" in North Carolina and the New England states. There are an average of 10 hurricanes a year but these range between the extremes of 1890, when there was only 1 and 1933 when there were 21.

TYPHOONS AND HURRICANES

LANDSLIDE

The greatest recorded loss of life in a landslide occurred in Central Java on April 17th, 1955, when 405 people were killed and many cattle were buried. Some bamboo houses were swept more than ¼ of a mile.

AVALANCHE

The worst avalanche disaster in the United States occurred on March 1st, 1910, at Wellington, Washington, when 3 snowbound Great Northern R.R. trains were swept by a single avalanche to the bottom of the Stevens Pass canyon, resulting in 96 passenger and 22 other fatalities.

FIRES

The greatest number of people killed in a single building was the 2,500 who were burned to death in the Church of La Compañía, Santiago, Chile, on December 8th, 1863.

Apart from fires consequent upon earthquakes, the most destructive fire was the Chicago Fire of October 8th, 1871, which destroyed over 17,400 buildings in 2,124 acres and caused $168,000,000 of damage and 250 deaths.

The fire which followed the Kwanto earthquake killed about 60,000 people and the total damage, including the results of the tremors, was $2,800 million.

FOREST FIRES

The worst recorded forest fire was the Peshtigo Fire, Wisconsin, in October, 1871, which destroyed 1,280,000 acres of forest and resulted in 1,152 deaths. In acreage, however, this fire was surpassed by some in Russia in 1921 and 1932 in which years over 5,000,000 acres were burned down and the forest fire in Miramichi, Maine, and New Brunswick, which razed 3,000,000 acres. This started on October 7, 1825, and advanced 80 miles in 6 hours, killing 160 people.

MINING

The world's worst mining disaster occurred in the Honkeiko Colliery in Manchuria on April 26th, 1942, when 1,549 miners were killed.

The worst U.S. disaster was at Monongah, W. Va. on Dec. 6, 1907 when 367 miners lost their lives.

MOUNTAIN-
EERING

The worst mountaineering accident in the continental United States was on the west side of Mount Baker on July 24th, 1939, when 6 of a party of 25 climbers were lost in a wet snow avalanche. Four of the bodies have never been found.

MARINE

The worst marine disaster of all time occurred on February 18th, 1945, when the 25,000 ton German merchantman "Wilhelm Gustloff" was torpedoed off Danzig and sank within a few minutes. The ship was carrying 5,000 refugees and 3,700 U-Boat personnel, a total of 8,700 of whom over 7,000 were drowned.

The greatest number of persons lost on a single warship was the 3,033 Japanese lost when the 72,200 ton battleship "Yamato" was sunk off Kyushu Island on April 7th, 1945.

The greatest toll taken in a marine accident in time of peace was when 1,517 were drowned on April 14th-15th, 1912, when the White Star Liner "Titanic" struck an iceberg steaming at 22½ knots in the Western Atlantic. On June 17th, 1940, 2,500 were drowned in the bombing of the British trooper 'Lancastria" off St. Nazaire, France.

The worst lifeboat disaster in the history of the Coast Guard (prior to January 28th, 1915, the U. S. Life Saving Service) was to the surf boat of the Monomoy Point Life-Saving Station, Nantucket Sound, on March 17th, 1902, when Captain M. N. Eldredge and 6 men were lost together with the 5 of the crew of the barge *Wadena* who they were attempting to save.

The most celebrated of all lifesavers was Joshua James (1826-1902), one-time Keeper of Point Allerton Station, Boston harbor, who assisted in the saving of over 140 lives during his 61-year career.

WORST LIFEBOAT DISASTER

The worst single submarine disaster in history was the loss of the British H.M.S. "Thetis" in Liverpool Bay on June 1st, 1939, when 99 passengers and crew were entombed.

SUBMARINE

The worst disaster in world railway history occurred on December 12th, 1917, at Modane, France, when an overloaded leave train left the rails and crashed, killing 543 persons.

RAILWAYS
World

The world's worst air accident occurred on June 18th, 1953, when a U. S. Air Force C-124 (Globemaster) crashed near Tokyo, Japan, killing 129 persons, including the crew of seven.

AIR
World

The worst air accident in the United States and the worst ever civilian air crash occurred on June 30th, 1956, at Grand Canyon, Arizona. Two air liners, a Super Constellation and a DC-7, crashed in the Canyon with a total loss of 128 lives.

Since records were kept for domestic air carriers, the year with the highest number of accidents was 1930, with 28.2 fatalities every 100 million passenger-miles.

The highest speed at which a bale out has been survived is 777 m.p.h. by George F. Smith from a F 100A Super Sabre on the California coast on February 26th, 1955. The 215 lb., 30-year-old test pilot survived an air blast of 1,240 lbs. per square foot compared with Colonel Stapp's previous record of 1,108 lbs. per square foot.

FASTEST
BALE OUT

The worst airship disaster was that of April 4th, 1933, when the U. S. dirigible Akron crashed into the sea off the New Jersey coast, killing 73 personnel.

AIRSHIP

The world's earliest fatal motor accident occurred on September 13th, 1895, when a Mr. W. H. Bliss was knocked down and killed in New York, U.S.A. Since that time in the U.S.A. there have been 1,115,-000 killed (up to 1955) with 1937 being the worst year with a toll of 39,643 (over 108 a day) killed.

ROAD

The worst single car accident on record occurred near Whitesburg, Kentucky, U.S.A., when on July 31st, 1954, a car ran into a cliff and burned out, killing 11 and injuring 1. Though there are no collated world statistics, it is believed that the worst road accident of any kind occurred outside Guatemala City, Guatemala, on July 27th, 1954, when 47 were killed and 27 injured when a bus crashed over a cliff edge. On January 26th, 1952, 49 were killed in a bus crash at Pueblo, Mexico.

The worst disaster in sporting history occurred at Le Mans, France, in the annual 24-hour motor race on June 11th, 1955, when a Mercedes

SPORTS
DISASTER

300 SLR driven by the Frenchan, Pierre Levegh, collided with another car when traveling at 160 m.p.h. and leaped the barrier and exploded among the crowd, killing 82.

AIR ATTACK
Raids

The greatest number of civilian casualties caused in any single raid was the estimated 20,000 killed and 60,000 wounded in the Royal Air Force's 827 bomber "saturation" attack on Hamburg, Germany, on the night of July 26th-27th, 1943.

The worst raid in Britain was on London, England (1,224 alerts), on the night of May 10th-11th, 1941, when 1,436 were killed and 1,792 injured.

The worst raid in World War I was that of September 3rd, 1917, in which a single bomb on a Chatham drill hall killed 107 and wounded 86.

The most sustained attack was 57 consecutive nights (September 7th to November 2nd, 1940) on London, England.

Flying Bomb

The worst V.1 incident occurred at Korte van Ruysbroeckstraat, Antwerp, at 8:19 p.m. on January 21st, 1945, when 76 were killed and 57 wounded.

Rockets

The worst V.2 incident occurred at the Cinema Rex, Avenue de Keyser, Antwerp, at 3:23 p.m. on December 16th, 1944, when 567 persons were killed and 291 wounded.

The worst of the 1,050 V.2 incidents during the 199-day assault on Southern England occurred at the premises of F. W. Woolworth & Co., Ltd., 279-281 New Cross Road, South London, on November 25th, 1944, when 164 were killed.

Atom Bombs

Of the two atom bombs dropped during World War II, that causing the greater casualties was the one dropped from the U. S. B-29 bomber "Enola Gay," piloted by Col. Paul W. Tibbets, Jr., over the Japanese town of Hiroshima (pop. 343,000), at 9:15 a.m. on August 6th, 1945, which caused 91,233 deaths.

Part Eleven

HUMAN ACHIEVEMENTS

---

1. Honors, Decorations and Awards

The prototype of the princely Orders of Chivalry is the Most Noble Order of the Garter founded in c.1348 by King Edward III of England. The earliest campaign medals were those issued by Queen Elizabeth to senior officers engaged in the defeat of the Spanish Armada in 1588 but these were, in fact, in the nature of decorations.

No statistics of the number of repeat awards to U. S. decorations are officially kept. The following information has been derived with official assistance.

MOST CLUSTERS
& GOLD STARS

Navy Cross	4 gold stars	Brig. Gen. Lewis B. Puller, U.S.M.C.
		Cdr. Ray M. Davenport, U.S.N.
Distinguished Service Cross	9 clusters	Capt. Edward Rickenbacker (see p. 136)
Silver Star	6 clusters	Gen. of the Army Douglas MacArthur
	2 gold stars	Lt. Col. Raymond L. Murray, U.S.M.C.
		Cdr. Richard H. O'Kane, U.S.N.
Distinguished Flying Cross	8 clusters	Col. David C. Schilling
	8 gold stars	Capt. Howard J. Finn, U.S.M.C.
Distinguished Service Medal (Army)	4 clusters	Gen. of the Army Douglas MacArthur (also one Naval award)
Distinguished Service Medal (Navy)	3 gold stars	Fleet Admiral William F. Halsey
Legion of Merit	3 gold stars	Maj. Gen. Field Harris, U.S.M.C.
Air Medal	18 clusters	Col. David C. Schilling
	26 gold stars	Major Howard E. Cook, U.S.M.C.

**MOST
DECORATED
SOLDIER**

The most decorated officer or enlisted man in the U. S. Armed Forces is General of the Army Douglas MacArthur who has been awarded the:

	Official Army List Abbreviation
Congressional Medal of Honor	M.H.
Distinguished Service Cross and 2 oak leaf clusters	D.S.C. (2 o.l.c.)
Distinguished Service Medal (Army) and 4 oak leaf clusters	D.S.C. (4 o.l.c.)
Distinguished Service Medal (Navy)	D.S.M. (Navy)
Silver Star Medal and 6 oak leaf clusters	S.S. (6 o.l.c.)
Distinguished Flying Cross	D.F.C.
Bronze Star Medal	B.S.M.
Purple Heart and oak leaf cluster	P.H. (o.l.c.)
Air Medal	A.M.
Distinguished Unit Citation (4 times)	

**MOST
DECORATED
SOLDIER
World War II**

In World War II, Lt. Audie L. Murphy of Farmersville, Texas, was awarded the Congressional Medal of Honor (for bravery near Holtzwihr, France, on January 26th, 1945), the D.S.C., the Silver Star with oak leaf cluster, the Legion of Merit, the Bronze Star Medal with cluster, the Purple Heart with 2 clusters, the European Theater Medal with 7 battle participation stars, the French Legion d'Honneur and the Croix de Guerre. See Photo No. 42, page 159.

**MEDALS OF
HONOR**

The following officers and men have received multiple awards:

1. 2nd Lt. (later Col.) Thomas W. Custer (Co. B, 6th Michigan Cavalry) 1863 and 1865.
2. Coxswain John Cooper, U.S.N.—USS BROOKLYN, August, 1864 and at Mobile, Alabama, April, 1865.
3. Boatswain's Mate Patrick Mullen, U.S.N. — USS DON (Mattox Creek) March, 1865 and May, 1865.
4. Sgt. William Wilson (Co. I, 4th U.S. Cavalry)—March, 1872 and and September, 1872.
5. Capt. (later Maj.-Gen.) Frank D. Baldwain (Co. D, 19th Michigan Inf.) 1864 and 1874.
6. Capt. of the Mizen Top Albert Weisbogel, U.S.N.—USS BENICA, June, 1874; USS PLYMOUTH, April, 1876.
7. Sgt. Patrick Leonard (Co. C, 2nd U.S. Cav.) 1870 and (Corporal, Co. A, 23rd U.S. Inf.) 1876.
8. First Sgt. Henry Hogan (Co. G, 5th U.S. Inf.) 1876-77 and 1877.
9. Ord. Seaman Robert Sweeney, U.S.N.—USS KEARSARGE, October, 1881; USS JAMESTOWN, December, 1883.
10. Capt. of the Hold, Louis Williams, U.S.N.—USS LACKAWANNA, March, 1883 and June, 1884.
11. Chief Watertender John King, U.S.N.—USS VICKSBERG, May, 1901; USS SALEM, September, 1909.
12. Chief Boatswain (later Lt.) John McCloy, Navy Cross U.S.N.—CHINA, June, 1900; VERA CRUZ, April, 1914.

42

43

URS
16
GOAL
48

46

44

45

42. Lt. Audie Murphy, the most decorated soldier of World War II. See p. 158.

43. The Seven Little Sisters, the raft of William Willis. See p. 169.

44. Miss Stella Pajunas, the world's fastest typist. See p. 166.

45. Donald Campbell, holder of the world water speed record. See p. 165.

46. Rev. Clinton Locy delivering the longest sermon on record. See p. 169.

13. Sgt. Daniel Joseph Daly, Navy Cross, D.S.C., Purple Heart — U.S.M.C.—CHINA, August, 1900; HAITI, October, 1915.
14. Maj. (later Maj. Gen.) Smedley Darlington Butler, D.S.M., U.S.M.C.—1914 and Haiti, November, 1915.

The following MARINES received both the Army and the Navy Medals of Honor:

Gunnery Sgt. Ernest August Jenson (nom de guerre Charles Hoffman) U.S.M.C.—June, 1918.
Sgt. Louis Cukela, U.S.M.C.—FRANCE, July, 1918.
Sgt. Matej Kocak, U.S.M.C.—FRANCE, July, 1918.
Pfc. John Joseph Kelly, U.S.M.C.—FRANCE, October, 1918.
Cpl. John Henry Pruitt, U.S.M.C.—FRANCE, October, 1918.

NOBEL PRIZE

The Nobel Prize Fund was set up under a $9,000,000 section of the will of Alfred B. Nobel, the Swedish inventor of dynamite, who died on December 10th, 1896. The highest cash value of the award in each of the five fields of Physics, Chemistry, Medicine, Literature and Peace was the 1955 figure of $36,720.

MOST AWARDS

The United States has won the greatest number of awards with a total of 56. This compares with the 48 of Germany and the 46 of Great Britain.

The U. S. total is made up of 17 for Medicine, 12 for Physics, 12 for Peace, 10 for Chemistry and 5 for Literature. By classes, Germany holds the record for Chemistry with 20, Great Britain for Physics with 15 and France for Literature 8.

Individually the only person to have won two Prizes is the Polish born Frenchwoman, Madame Marie Curie, who shared the 1903 Physics Prize with her husband, Pierre Curie, and H. A. Becquerel and in 1911 won the Chemistry Prize. The Peace Prize has been awarded twice to the International Committee of the Red Cross in 1917 and again in 1944.

OLDEST

The oldest laureate was Ferdinand Buisson (France), who shared the 1927 Peace Prize with Ludwig Quidd (Germany) at the age of 86. The oldest of all U. S. winners was Emily G. Balch, who shared the 1946 Peace Prize with John P. Mott (U.S.A.) at the age of 79. The oldest male U. S. winner was Cordell Hull, who was awarded the 1945 Peace Prize at the age of 74.

YOUNGEST

The youngest laureate has been Professor Sir William Lawrence Bragg, O.B.E., M.C., F.R.S., who shared the 1915 Physics Prize with his father, Sir William H. Bragg, for work on X-rays and crystal structures, aged 25. The youngest U. S. winner has been Carl David Anderson, winner of the 1936 Physics Prize, aged 31.

ENGLISH PEERAGE

MOST
ANCIENT
CREATION

The year 1223 A.D. has been ascribed to the Premier Irish barony of Kingsale (formerly of Courcy) though on the Order of Precedence the date is listed as 1397. The premier English barony De Ros, at present held by a Baroness in her own right and 26th in her line, dates from 1264.

MOST
TITLED PEER

The peer with the greatest number of titles is the Duke of Atholl who is also the Marquess of Atholl, Marquess of Tullibardine, Earl of

MISS AMERICAS

The Miss America Pageant of Atlantic City, New Jersey, was inaugurated in 1921. It is open to contestants from the United States, Canada, Hawaii and Puerto Rico. The annual scholarship fund totals over $100,000, the winner receiving a $5,000 scholarship.

Extreme data on the 28 winners—1921 through 1956:

Tallest	5 ft. 10 in.	Bess Myerson, hazel-eyed brunette	Miss New York 1945
	5 ft. 10 in.	Colleen Kay Hutchins, blue-eyed blonde	Miss Utah 1952
Shortest	5 ft. 1 in.	Margaret Gorman, blue-eyed blonde	1921 Winner
Heaviest	143 lbs.	Colleen Kay Hutchins, blue-eyed blonde	Miss Utah 1952
Lightest	106 lbs.	Jacque Mercer, brown-eyed brunette	Miss Arizona 1949
Oldest	25 years	Colleen Kay Hutchins, blue-eyed blonde	Miss Utah 1952
Youngest	16 years	Margaret Gorman, blue-eyed blonde	1921 Winner
		Mary Campbell, blue-eyed brunette	1922-23 Winner
		Marion Bergeron, blue-eyed blonde	Miss Connecticut 1933
Biggest Bust	37 inches	BeBe Shopp, hazel-eyed brunette	Miss Minnesota 1948
		Evelyn Margaret Ay, green-eyed blonde	Miss Pennsylvania 1954
Smallest Bust	30 inches	Margaret Gorman, blue-eyed blonde	1921 Winner
Largest Waist	27 inches	BeBe Shopp, hazel-eyed brunette	Miss Minnesota 1948
Slimmest Waist	22 inches	Jo-Carroll Dennison, brown-eyed brunette	Miss Texas 1942
		Jacque Mercer, brown-eyed brunette	Miss Arizona 1949
		Lee Ann Meriwether, blue-eyed brunette	Miss California 1955
Widest Hips	37½ inches	Marion Bergeron, blue-eyed blonde	Miss Connecticut 1933
		Venus Ramey, blue-eyed redhead	Miss Washington, D. C. 1944
Slenderest Hips	32 inches	Margaret Gorman, blue-eyed blonde	1921 Winner
Most Winners (State)	5 by California		1925, 1941, 1943, 1946, 1955
	5 by Pennsylvania		1929, 1935, 1936, 1940, 1954

Atholl, Earl of Tullibardine, Earl of Strathtay and Strathardle, Earl Strange, Glenalmond, and Glenlyon, Viscount of Balquhidder, Lord Murray, Balvenie, and Gask, Baron Strange, Baron Percy, Baron Murray of Stanley, Lord Murray of Tullibardine and Baron Glenlyon—nineteen titles in all.

OLDEST

Collated records do not exist but the greatest age established for any peer is the 98 years 99 days of the 1st Earl Halsbury (born September 3rd, 1823, died December 11th, 1921). The oldest age at which any person has been raised to the peerage is 94, in the case of William Francis Kyffin Taylor, G.B.E., K.C. (born July 9th, 1854) who was created Baron Maenan of Ellesmere, County Salop, in 1948.

The oldest living peer is the Marquess of Winchester, Premier Marquess of England, who was 93 on October 30th, 1955.

HIGHEST NUMBERING CREATIONS

The highest succession number borne by any peer is that of the present 34th Baron of Kingsale.

The largest number of new peerages created in any year was the fifty-four in 1296. The greatest number of extinctions in a year was the sixteen in 1923 and the greatest number of deaths forty-four in 1935.

2. *Endurance and Endeavor*

CIRCUM-NAVIGATION

Man's earliest circumnavigation of the world was achieved by Sebastian del Cano and 31 other survivors in the Spanish ship *Vittorio* on September 6th, 1522. Del Cano was a navigator to the Portuguese-born explorer, Ferninand Magalhães (Magellen) (c.1470-1521) who, having sailed westward from the estuary of the Guadalquivir, Spain, on September 20th, 1519, with five ships, was killed on April 27th, 1521, on Mactan Island in the Philippines.

EARLIEST SIGHTINGS

The earliest sightings of the North American continent are conjectural and rest on unverified sagas about voyages from a Viking Settlement of Southwestern Greenland. The earliest claims are for Bjarni Herjulfson in 986 A.D. and Leif Ericson in 1000 (Karlsevni Saga) or 1002 (Greenland Saga).

The new world was rediscovered by Christopher Columbus (Cristóbal Colón) (1451-1506) on October 12th, 1492, when he sighted Guanahini, probably the Watling Islands in the Bahamas, 70 days out from Palos, Spain. The man to sight land at 2 a.m. was Rodrigo de Triana, one of the 18 crew aboard the 50 ton *Pinta*.

Pre-Columbian claims have been made by Portugal. They are based on the publication (1954) by Prof. Armando Cortesão of the University of Coimbra, Portugal, of the Nautical Chart of 1424, from the Sir Thomas Phillipps manuscript collection, showing land to the far westward of the Atlantic; the Venetian map of 1448 by Andrea Biancho showing *Ixola Otinticha* the Authentic Island (suggested as South America), and the voyages of Diogo de Teive and Pedro Vasquez in 1452.

John Cabot (from about 1455) rediscovered the North American continental mainland on June 24th, 1497 when, having sailed from Bristol, England, on May 21 with a crew of 18, he sighted land in the vicinity of Cape Breton and took possession of the area in the name of King Henry VII of England.

The name 'America' was coined by the geographer Martin Wald-seemüller in his world map in his *Cosmographiae Introductio,* published at St. Dié, France, in April, 1507, in honor of Amerigio Vespucci (born March, 1454), who had written an account of an exploration of the Venezuelan coast in 1499. Columbus had discovered the South American continent when he sighted Punta Bombeador, Venezuela, on his third voyage on August 1st, 1498.

EARLIEST USE OF 'AMERICA'

The smallest boat ever to cross the Atlantic from West to East was the *Sapolio*—a canvas covered folding boat, 14 feet 6 inches by 5 feet 5 inches by 3 feet. W. A. Andrews left Atlantic City, New Jersey, in the *Sapolio* on July 2nd, 1892, and landed at Fuzetta, South Portugal, 2,845 miles away, on September 24th, 1892—eighty-four days later.

The only two men to have rowed the Atlantic were George Haroo and Frank Samuelson, who left New York on June 6th, 1897, and covered 3,075 miles in fifty-five days, landing at St. Mary's, Scilly Isles. Their boat was 18 feet, 5 feet beam, clinker built double ender, and had no mast or sails in its equipment. They stowed five pairs of oars.

ATLANTIC CROSSINGS

The conquest of the North Pole was first achieved on April 6th, 1909, by Cdr. Robert E. Peary (1856-1920), accompanied by Matthew Henson and four Eskimos. Peary's party stayed at the Pole for thirty-six hours.

The conquest of the South Pole was first achieved on December 14th, 1911, by the Norwegian Roald Amundsen (1872-1928) in a fifty-three-day southward march from the Bay of Whales which he had reached in the *Fram.*

POLAR

The conquest of the highest point on Earth, Mount Everest (29,160 feet), was first achieved at 11:30 a.m. on May 29th, 1953, by Sir Edmund P. Hillary, and the Sherpa, Tensing Norkay.

MOUNTAIN-EERING

A number of mountains in Continental U. S. have not yet been climbed. Among the first ascents of 1955 was that of Mount Buckindy (7,311 ft.) in Washington on August 28th. The hitherto highest unclimbed peak in North America, University Peak (15,030 feet), on the Alaska-Yukon border, was conquered on July 4th, 1955.

The highest human settlement of which there is evidence is the remains of a South American Indian settlement one hundred feet below the summit of the dormant volcano Llullaillaco (21,719 feet) on the borders of Chile and Argentina.

MOUNTAINS

The deepest penetration yet made into the ocean's depths is the 13,287 feet (2.52 miles) 160 miles S.W. of Dakar, French West Africa, in the bathyscaphe *F.N.R.S. 3,* manned by Lt.-Cdr. Georges S. Houet and Lt. Pierre Henri Willm on February 14th, 1954. The vessel dived at 10:08 a.m. and touched the bottom at 1:30 p.m. where the water pressure was 5,900 lbs. (2.63 tons) per square inch. After thirty-six minutes on the bottom it ascended to break the surface at 3:21 p.m.

OCEAN DEPTH

The greatest descent made in a flexible diving suit is 535 feet by Petty Officer William Bolland, Royal Navy, at Loch Fyne, Scotland, August 28th, 1948.

DIVING

The deepest salvage operation ever is that by the British Admiralty salvage ship "Reclaim" in Oslofjord. On June 28th, 1956 Boatswain G. M. Wookey descended to 1,060 feet.

MINING
DEPTH

Man's deepest penetration made into the ground is at the Kolar Gold Field, Mysore State, South India, where in the Champion Reef mine a working depth of 9,811 feet (1.86 miles) below the surface has been attained.

ALTITUDE

The highest altitude yet obtained by man in the stratosphere is subject to U. S. Air Force security regulations but is believed to be 90,000 feet (17.04 miles) by Major Arthur Murray in the Bell X-1A over California during June 16th, 1954.

The record altitude achieved by a manned balloon is 72,394 feet (13.17 miles) by "Explorer II" over South Dakota, U.S.A., at 11:40 a.m. on November 11th, 1935, manned by Capt. Albert Stevens and Capt. Orvil Anderson.

The greatest known altitude attained by a large unmanned balloon is 22 miles (116,160 feet) by the 3.2 million cubic feet Super Skyhook, released from the University of Minnesota, in August, 1954. Smaller meteorological balloons may have attained 130,000 feet before bursting.

The greatest published altitude for any rocket is 250 miles achieved by a two-stage 5,000 m.p.h. V2/WAC Corporal rocket, separating at twenty miles, over White Sands, New Mexico, on February 24th, 1949. A temperature of 1,898°F was recorded at the high point. The highest published figure for a one-stage rocket is 163 miles by a U.S. Navy Aerobee-Hi in June, 1956.

TOP AIR
ACES

The top score of any fighter pilot in the 1914-1918 war was 80 kills by the German, Manfred von Richthofen. Major Erich Hartman of the Luftwaffe, released from Russia in 1955, is reputed to have shot down 352 allied aircraft in the 1939-45 war.

The highest score credited to a British fighter pilot is 73 enemy aircraft destroyed, also in the 1914-18 war, by Major E. Mannock, V.C. The top score in the 1939-45 war was 38 'planes by Group-Capt. J. E. Johnson. The greatest success against flying bombs was achieved by Squad/Ldr. Berry, who brought down 60 in 1944-1945.

U. S.

The top scoring U. S. air ace in World War I was Capt. Edward V. Rickenbacker, who shot down 21 enemy planes and destroyed 4 balloons in the brief period from April, 1918, to the armistice in November, 1918. He was awarded the Congressional Medal of Honor and the D.S.C. with 9 oak leaf clusters. See Photo No. 40, page 136.

The top scoring U. S. air ace in World War II was the late Major Richard I. Bong, with an official score of 36 kills in the Pacific Theater. He was also awarded the Congressional Medal of Honor and the D.S.C.

ANTI-SUBMARINE
SUCCESSES

The highest number of U-Boat kills attributed to one ship in the 1939-45 war was 13 to H.M.S. *Starling* (Capt. F. J. Walker, R.N.). Capt. Walker was in overall command at the sinking of a total 25 U-Boats between 1941 and the time of his death in 1944.

For details of world air speed record, see page 39. The highest speed ever achieved by a woman pilot is the 708.362 m.p.h. by Jacqueline Auriol, 37, in a Mystère jet near Paris on July 1st, 1955.

SPEED AIR

The fastest speed ever achieved on land is the 632 m.p.h. by Lt.-Col. John L. Stapp in an experimental rocket sled at the Air Development Center, Alamogordo. Running on rails and impelled by nine rockets with a total thrust of 40,000 lbs., the top speed is reached within five seconds. An un-manned rocket attained 1,292 m.p.h. at Edwards Field, Calif., in September, 1955.

SPEED LAND

The fastest speed ever achieved by a wheeled vehicle is the 403.135 m.p.h. by the Englishman John Cobb's Railton Special, in one direction, on the Bonneville Salt Beds, on September 16th, 1947. The mean for two runs in opposite directions and the official World Land Speed Record, is 394.196 m.p.h. The timing mile was covered in 9.1325 seconds. The car was powered by two, 12-cylinder Napier-Lion engines of 478,728 c.c., developing 2,860 h.p.

The fastest speed ever achieved on water was the 215.08 m.p.h. by Donald Campbell (Great Britain) on July 23rd, 1955, in his first run. His mean speed over two runs, and the world's water speed record is 202.32 m.p.h., in the turbo-jet engined "Bluebird" K7 on Ullswater, England. See Photo No. 45, page 159.

WATER

The world record for cutting six "shoes" to ascend and sever the top of a 12-inch diameter log is the 1 minute 46 seconds set by the Tasmanian axeman, Ray Youd, at the Sandfly Sports, Tasmania, on March 12th, 1955.

WOOD-CUTTING

The world record for sawing through (hand-bucking) a 32-inch log is 1 minute 26.4 seconds by Paul M. Searls, 46, in Seattle, Washington, on November 5th, 1953. The 18-inch long double-handed record is 10.3 seconds by W. Donnelly and E. Hogg of New Zealand, at Rivertown, South Island, in December, 1955.

The world record for brick-laying was established by Joseph Raglon of East St. Louis, Illinois, in 1937 who, supported by assistants, laid 3,472 bricks in 60 minutes—at a rate of nearly 58 a minute.

BRICK-LAYING

The greatest number of barrels jumped on ice is fifteen (total length 28 feet 7 inches) in January, 1955, at Grossinger, New York, by Leo Lebel, 24. The women's world record was set at the same competition by Lebel's sister, Aldrina, 23, who cleared eight barrels (18 feet 3 inches).

BARREL-JUMPING

The only juggler in history able to juggle—as opposed to "shower" —ten balls or eight plates was the Italian Enrico Rastelli, who was born in Samara, Russia, on December 19th, 1896, and died on December 13th, 1931, in Bergamo, Italy.

JUGGLING

The greatest distance which a standard U. S. Army grenade has been thrown is 284 feet 6½ inches by Lt. Alfred C. Blozis at Fort Benning, Georgia, in 1944.

GRENADE THROWING

The greatest tightrope walker of all-time was the Frenchman, Jean François Gravelet ("Blondin") (1824-1897) who made the earliest cross-

TIGHTROPE WALKING

ing of the Niagara on a 1,100-foot long 3-inch rope, 160 feet above the Falls on June 30th, 1859. He also made a crossing with an assistant, Harry Colcord, pick-a-back.

The world tightrope endurance record is 113 hours by Willi Pischler, 23, ending on July 12th, 1955.

The highest high-wire act was that of the Germans Alfred and Henry Traber on a 520-feet rope stretched from the Zugspitze (9,750 feet) to the Western Peak, Bavaria, during July and August, 1953.

BULLFIGHTING

The highest paid bullfighter in history is Luis Miguel Domínguín who retired in 1953, having killed 2,000 bulls and made a fortune of $2,000,000. In March, 1956, after a comeback at Maracay Plaza, Venezuela, he received a record of $30,000 for a single *corrida*.

TRAPEZE ARTISTRY

The greatest aerialist of all time was the Mexican, Alfredo Codona, who, in 1920, became the first man ever to perfect a triple somersault.

STILT-WALKING

The highest stilts ever successfully mastered were 22 feet, from the ankle to the ground, by Harry Yelding ("Harry Sloan") of Great Yarmouth, Norfolk, England.

LION-TAMING

The greatest number of lions mastered and fed in a cage by an unaided lion-tamer was forty by "Captain" Alfred Schneider in 1925.

BALL PUNCHING

The Australian Ron Reunalf equalled his own world duration ball punching record of 125 hours 20 minutes at 10:20 p.m. on December 31st, 1955, at the Esplanade, Southport, Australia.

HANDSHAKING

The world record for handshaking was set on New Year's Day, 1907, by President Theodore Roosevelt (1858-1919) who shook hands with 8,513 people.

MORSE

The highest speed at which anyone has received Morse code is 75.2 words per minute—over seventeen symbols per second. This was achieved by Ted R. McElroy in a tournament at Asheville, North Carolina, on July 2nd, 1939.

TYPEWRITING

International competitions in typewriting have occurred between only 1906 and 1946.

The highest speeds attained with a ten-word penalty per error on a manual machine are:—

One Minute: 170 words, Margaret Owen (U.S.A.) (Underwood Standard) New York, October 21st, 1918.

One Hour: 147 words (net rate per minute), Albert Tangora (U.S.A.) (Underwood Standard), October 22nd, 1923.

The official hour record on an electric machine is 9,316 words (forty errors) giving a net rate of 149 words per minute by Margaret Hamma (U.S.A.) in Brooklyn, New York, on June 20th, 1941, on an I.B.M. machine. Since then, in unofficial tests, Miss Stella Pajunas has attained 216 words per minute on an I.B.M. machine. See Photo No. 44, page 159.

SHORTHAND

The earliest record of shorthand dates from 63 B.C. as used by Marcus Tullius Tiro in recording the speeches of Caesar and Cicero in Rome. The Tironian system was in fact only a highly abbreviated form of longhand. Shorthand proper dates from a treatise by Dr. Timothy Bright in 1588.

The highest speeds ever attained under championship conditions are:—

300 w.p.m. (99.64 per cent accuracy) for five minutes and 350 w.p.m. (99.72 per cent accuracy, that is, two insignificant errors) for two minutes by Nathan Behrin (U.S.A.) in New York in December, 1922. Behrin (born 1887) used the Pitman system invented in 1837.

Mrs. Beverly Nina O'Malley, 45, a Los Angeles barmaid, set a world record in May, 1955, by obtaining her thirteenth divorce to marry Gabriel Avery, her fourteenth husband.

MOST
MARRIAGES

The greatest number of marriages contracted by a man in the monogamous world is 9 by Tommy Manville (born 1894).

MOST MARRIED
MAN

Transcending all other personal fortunes is that of Dr. J. T. Williamson, the Canadian geologist, who discovered and staked in 1934 the Mwadui diamond mine near Shinyanga, Tanganyika, East Africa.

GREATEST
MONEY MAKERS

Turning from largely unexploited but wholly owned capital assets to income, the highest ever attained is that of $2,800,000 every ten days ($102,200,000 per annum) stemming from oil-rights which accrued to His Late Majesty Abdul Aziz Ibn Abdul Raham al Faisal Al Saud, King of Saudi Arabia, Lord of Arabia and Guardian of the Holy City of Mecca.

The largest estate ever left by a woman financier was the $95 million by Mrs. Hetty Green Wilks, 80, in March, 1952. She had a balance of over $31,400,000 in one bank alone. Her will was found in a tin box with four pieces of soap.

RICHEST
WOMAN

The richest man in the world, income-wise, is His Highness Sir Abdullah al-Subah, the Ruler of Kuwait. His weekly income from oil royalties is currently running at $5,100,000 or $265 million per annum.

RICHEST
MAN

The wealthiest man in the British Isles is usually allowed to be Sir John Reeves Ellerman, the shipowner, whose father left the largest ever proved will in the United Kingdom of over $102,717,983 in 1933.

BIGGEST WILLS

The greatest will proved in Ireland was that of the 1st Earl of Iveagh who died in 1927, leaving $37,776,120.

The greatest number of millionaires in one family is probably the eighty-three members, each worth over $5,500,000, of the Lykes family of Florida. This represents over 1 per cent of all America's 8,000 dollar millionaires.

RICHEST
FAMILIES

The largest number of millionaires in one family in the British Isles is that of the Wills family of the Imperial Tobacco Company, of whom thirteen members have left estates in excess of $2,800,000 since 1910.

The greatest bequests in a life-time of a millionaire were those of the late Andrew Carnegie (1835-1919), who left only $12,400,000. His major bequests totaled $309,940,000. The greatest benefactions of a living British millionaire are those of Viscount Nuffield which, in an era of very much higher taxation, total some $75.6 million to date.

GREATEST
BEQUESTS

The largest single bequest made in the history of philanthropy was the $500,000,000 gift to 4,157 educational and other institutions by the $2,500 million Ford Foundation (established 1936) announced on December 12th, 1955.

It has been calculated that the Rockefeller Family mainly through the agency of the Rockefeller Foundation (established 1913) at the General Education Board (established 1902) has disbursed $2,500 million.

LARGEST FOUNDATION

The largest philanthropic foundation in the world is the Ford Foundation, established in 1936. With assets estimated at $2,500 million, it has donated a total of $650 million.

MOST FLYING HOURS

The record for flying hours is 29,100, held by the Russian-born Capt. Ivan Vasilivitz Smirnoff (born January 30th, 1895), formerly of K.L.M., accumulated during the period 1915-1948. His total of 4 million miles was surpassed by Capt. O. P. Jones, C.V.O., O.B.E., who retired from the B.O.A.C. in May, 1955, with 4,300,000 miles flown in 21,600 hours.

GASTRONOMIC RECORDS

Records for eating and drinking by trenchermen do not match those suffering from the rare disease of bulimia (morbid desire to eat) and polydipsia (pathological thirst). Some bulimia patients have to spend fifteen hours a day eating, with an extreme consumption of 384 lbs. of food in six days in Mortimer's Case of 1743. Some polydipsomaniacs are unsatisfied by less than ninety-six pints of liquid a day.

Specific records have been claimed as follows:—

Raw Eggs

24 in 14 minutes, by Glen Johns (Canada) in Ontario, Canada, on March 14th, 1955.

Boiled Eggs

44 boiled eggs in 30 minutes by Georges Grogniet of Belgium on May 31st, 1956.

Hamburgers

77 at a sitting, by Philip Yazdzik (U.S.A.) in Chicago, Illinois, on April 25th, 1955.

Oysters

480 in 60 minutes, by Joe Garcia (Australia) in Melbourne on February 5th, 1955.

Meat

One whole roast ox in 42 days by Johann Ketzler of Germany in 1880.

Sausages

17 in 90 seconds, by Sepp Poelzleitner of Nurnberg, East Germany, in April, 1956.

Beer

28.8 pints in 52 minutes by Auguste Maffrey of France.

'Chuggalugging'

3 ⅛ pints in 12.0 secs. by R. Hawk (Oxford Univ.), 1955.

ENDURANCE Running

The greatest non-stop run recorded is the 127 miles 275 yards by J. Saunders round a track in New York in a "Go as You Please" race on February 21st-22nd, 1882. Saunders covered this distance in 22 hours 49 minutes.

The greatest distance covered in twenty-four hours is the 100 miles 562 yards of W. H. Hayward (South Africa) at Motspur Park, Surrey, England, from 11 a.m., November 20th, to 11 a.m., November 21st, 1953. He consumed 2 lbs. of sugar and 16 eggs during the trial but lost 7 lbs. in weight. The distance comprised 2 miles 12 yards more than six marathons and entailed over 637 laps of the track.

The greatest distance covered in six days is 623 miles 1,320 yards between November 25th and December 1st, 1888, by George Littlewood of England on a track in New York.

The longest officially recorded walking race was that of 3,415 miles from New York to San Francisco, U.S.A., from May 3rd to July 24th, 1926, by A. L. Monteverde, 60, occupying 79 days 10 hours 10 minutes.

Walking

The longest recorded survival alone on a raft is 133 days (4½ months) by Second Steward Poon Lim of the British Merchant Navy whose ship was torpedoed in the Atlantic. He was picked up by a fishing boat and was awarded the B.E.M. in July, 1943.

The longest intentional single-handed voyage on a raft was that of William Willis, aged 61, who set out from Callao, Peru, and sailed 6,700 miles across the Pacific Ocean. He arrived at Pago Pago, Samoa, on October 15th, 1954, after a voyage of 115 days. See Photo No. 43, page 159.

Longest on a Raft

The longest duration swim ever recorded is the 292 miles of John V. Sigmund (U.S.A.) who swam down the Mississippi River, U.S.A., from St. Louis to Caruthersville in 89 hours 48 minutes, ending on July 29th, 1940.

The longest duration swim by a woman was 87 hours 27 minutes in a pool by Mrs. Myrtle Huddleston of New York in 1931.

Swimming

The world record for staying underwater was set at San Rafael, California, by Dr. Robert Keast, 34, on March 18th, 1956, with 10 minutes, 58.9 seconds.

The longest submergence in a frogman's suit is the 25 hours 6 seconds at the Salon du Sportsmen, Montreal, Canada, by Guy Cadieux, 27, who entered the water (88-92°F.) at 9:49 a.m. on March 28th, 1955, and emerged at 10:49 a.m. on March 29th.

Underwater

The duration record for cycling on a track is 125 hours by Anandrao Halyalkar, 22, at Shivaji Park, Bombay, from 1 p.m. on April 14th to 6 p.m., April 19th, 1955. The monocycle duration record is 11 hours 21 minutes (83.4 miles) by Raymond Le Grand at Maubeug, France, on September 12th, 1955.

Cycling

The world record for non-stop talking was set at Church Hall, Dartford, England, by Kevin Sheenhan of Limerick, Ireland, with 133 hours (5 days 13 hours) from 10 a.m., Monday, November 28th, to 11 p.m., Saturday, December 3rd, 1955.

The longest running commentary was one of 27 hours 15 minutes by Pierre Chouinard of CKAC Station, Montreal, Canada, when reporting a piano-playing marathon starting at 7:30 p.m. on February 25th, 1955.

Talking

The longest sermon on record was delivered by Clinton Locy of West Richland, Washington, in February, 1955. It lasted 48 hours 18 minutes and ranged through texts from every book in the Bible. See Photo No. 46, page 159.

Sermon

Marathon dancing must be distinguished from dancing mania which is a pathological condition. The worst outbreak of dancing mania was at Aachen, Germany, in July, 1374, when hordes of men and

Dancing

women broke into a frenzied dance in the streets which lasted for hours till injury or complete exhaustion ensued.

The Charleston duration record is 22½ hours set at the Roseland Ballroom, Broadway, New York City, in 1926 by John Giola, 23.

Ballet

Among the world's greatest ballet dancers, the Russian-born Pole, Vaslav Nijinsky (1890-1950), was alone in being able to execute the *entrechat dix*—crossing and uncrossing the feet ten times in a single elevation.

The greatest number of spins called for in classical ballet choreography is the thirty-two *fouettés en tournants* in Swan Lake. Miss Rowena Jackson of New Zealand has achieved 121 such turns in class in Melbourne in 1940.

Rocking-Chair

The longest recorded duration of a "Rockathon" is 92 hours by two Canadians ending on March 27th, 1955, in Hawkesbury, Canada.

Piano-playing

On May 1st, 1955, in Berlin, Heinz Arntz set a world record by playing the piano non-stop, except for refreshment intervals, for 423 hours (17 days 15 hours).

Drumming

The world's duration non-stop drumming record was set by Jim Rogers at Columbus, Ohio with a break of 80 hrs., 35 mins., 14 secs., ending on March 2nd, 1956.

Pole-Squatting

There being no international rules, the "standards of living" atop poles vary widely. The record squat for men is 196 days by William L. Howard, 34, at Portland, Oregon., ending on December 25th, 1952. The women's record is 152 days by Miss Erma Leach, 25, at San Francisco on a 51-foot pole ending on January 1st, 1951.

Modern records do not, however, compare with that of the Syrian monk, Simeon the Stylite, in the fifth century A.D., who spent over thirty years on a 50-foot high stone pollar at Qualat-Seman, near Aleppo, Syria.

Corn Husking

The record number of bushels husked (net) in 80 minutes in a U. S. corn husking championship is 46.58 by Irvin Bauman of Woodford County, Ill., in 1940. The only 4 time winner was Fred Stanek of Webster County, Ia., in 1924, 1926-27 and 1930. The attendance at the 1940 championship was 150,000 in Scott County, Iowa.

Pipe-Smoking

The world record for keeping a pipe alight (3.3 grams of tobacco and two matches) is 1 hour 55 minutes 11 seconds by Paul Lauderback of Los Angeles, U.S.A., in an international contest in March, 1954.

Log-Rolling

The most protracted log-rolling on record was in Chequamegon Bay, Wisc. in 1900, when Allan Stewart dislodged from 24" diameter log Joe Oliver after 3 hours, 15 minutes birling.

Fasting

Most humans experience considerable pain after an abstinence from food for even twelve hours. Records set free from unremitting medical surveillance are of little value.

The world "record" is claimed by Mrs. Cornelia Foster, 61, of Kew Township, Johannesburg, South Africa, who claims to have lived 102 days on nothing but water and soda water. An earlier claim of 210 days had been made for a seventeen-year-old Indian girl Dhanalakshim of Mercara in South India in November, 1952.

The longest recorded hunger-strike is that of the Irish playwright, Terence MacSweeney, in Brixton Prison, London, which lasted seventy-four days before death ensued on October 25th, 1920.

Hunger Strike

The most extreme case of survival without sleep is that of the Italian Ugo Dell'aringa, a bank clerk from Lucca, who has only been observed to have one hour's sleep in the thirty-eight years since 1917, when privations in an Austrian Prisoner of War Camp affected his centers of sleep.

Sleeplessness

The earliest demonstration of a parachute was by the Frenchman Sebastien Lenormand from the tower of Montpellier Observatory, France, in 1783. Ten years later, in 1793, J. P. Blanchard made a descent from a balloon but broke a leg. The first successful parachute jump from a balloon was by Jacques Garnerin (1769-1823) from 2,230 feet over Monceau Park, Paris, on October 22nd, 1797. The earliest descent from an airplane was that of Captain Berry, U.S. Army, over St. Louis, Missouri, in 1912.

PARACHUTING
Earliest Descent

Captain Edward Sperry and First-Lt. Henry P. Nielsen of the U. S. Army in ejection tests from a B-47 jet bomber over the Gulf of Mexico in the summer of 1954, parachuted from a height of 45,200 feet.

Highest

The lowest recorded voluntary jump is the 154-foot jump by John Tranum (G.B.) from Pasadena Bridge, California, U.S.A., in October, 1927.

Lowest

In August, 1945, Lt.-Col. Vasily Romanuk of Russia jumped from 43,005 feet and fell 39,833 feet (7.54 miles) before his 'chute was opened at 3,172 feet. The time taken for such a fall at a terminal velocity of 120 m.p.h. would be 3¾ minutes. In the seventeen years from 1934 to September 4th, 1951, when he made his two-thousandth jump, Romanuk logged 150 parachuting hours. The feminine record for a free fall is 26,230 feet from a height of 27,430 feet by Mlle. Odette Rousseau, near Paris on August 24th, 1955.

Longest
Delayed Drop

Sgt. Bonvizotto made fifty jumps in 4 hours 41 minutes (one every 5 minutes 37.2 seconds) in a specially staged Argentine army test near Buenos Aires on April 6th, 1954.

Frequency

The greatest load ever dropped by parachute is 5.35 tons of lead and cement from 2,300 feet at El Centro, California, in a U. S. army test in June, 1952. The nylon parachute with an area of three-quarters of an acre was the largest ever used.

Heaviest Load

Part Twelve

SPORT

ANGLING

LARGEST CATCHES

The largest fish ever caught on a rod is the 2,536 lb., 16 feet 9 inches long man-eating White Shark (*Carcharodon carcharias*) by A. Dean at Denial Bay, near Ceduna, Australia, on April 12th, 1955. The largest fish ever caught by a woman was the 1,230 lb. Black Marlin by Mrs. David Bartlett (U.S.A.) off Cabo Blanco on April 5th, 1955.

The largest fish ever taken underwater was a 804 lb. Giant Black Grouper by Don Pinder of Miami Triton Club in 1955.

The world surf casting record is 705 feet 4 inches made at San Mateo, Calif., in 1949 with a nine-foot bamboo rod by Prima Livernais.

WORLD RECORDS (SEA) (as ratified by the International Game Fish Assoc.)

NAME	WEIGHT Lbs.	Ozs.	LENGTH Ft.	Ins.	GIRTH Inches	DATE	LOCATION AND ANGLER	LINE Lbs.
Albacore	66	4				1912	Catalina, Calif.—F. Kelly	30
Amberjack	119	8	5	3½	46½	1/13/52	Rio de Janeiro, Bra.—C. de Mello Cunha	80
Barracuda	103	4	5	6	31¼	1932	West End, Bahamas—C. E. Benet	80
Bass (Calif. White Sea)	83	12	5	5½	34	3/31/53	San Felipe, Mex.—L. Baumgardner	30
Bass (Channel)	83		4	4	29	8/ 5/49	Cape Charles, Va.—Zack Waters, Jr.	50
Bass (Giant Sea Jewfish)	551		8	4		6/29/37	Galveston Bay, Tex.—G. Pangarakis	80
Bass (Giant Black Sea— Cal. Black Sea)	483		7	3	73	5/22/51	Coronados Is., Mex.—R. E. DeGroff	80
Bass (Sea)	8		1	10	19	5/13/51	Nantucket Sound, Mass.—H. R. Rider	50
Bass (Striped)	73		5		30½	8/17/13	Vineyard Sound, Mass.—C. B. Church	50
Black Drum	90		5		39	5/17/55	Wildwood Highlands, N. J.—J. W. Douglas	50
Blackfish or Tautog	21	6	2	7½	23½	6/12/54	Cape May, N. J.—R. N. Sheafer	30
Bluefish	24	3	3	5	22	8/27/53	San Miguel, Azores—da Silva Beloso	12
Bonefish	18	2	3	5½	18	10/14/54	Mana, Kauai, T.H.—Wm. Badua	80
Bonito (Oceanic)	39	15	3	3	28	1/21/52	Walker Cay, Bahamas—F. Drowley	50
Cobia	102		5	10	34	7/ 3/38	Cape Charles, Va.—J. E. Stansbury	130
Cod	57	8	4	8		12/24/49	Ambrose Lightship, N. Y.—J. Rzeszewicz	50
Dolphin	75	8	4	2		12/10/50	Mafia Channel, E. Africa—A. Conan-Doyle	80
Flounder (Summer)	20		3	1	32	9/ 7/48	Oak Beach, N. Y.—F. H. Kessel	20
Kingfish	76	8	5	3	31	5/22/52	Bimini, Bahamas—R. E. Maytag	130
Marlin (Blue)	756		14			4/24/56	San Juan, F.R.—A. Sherman (See Photo 50 p. 176)	
Marlin (Pacific Bl'k)	1,560		14	6	81	8/ 4/53	Cabo Blanco, Peru—A. Glassell, Jr.	130
Marlin (Silver)	755		13	7¾	65¼	11/21/53	Pinas Bay, Panama—R. Dugan, Jr.	130
Marlin (Striped)	692		13	5		8/18/31	Balboa, Calif.—A. Hamann	80
Marlin (White)	161		8	8	33	3/20/38	Miami Beach, Fla.—L. F. Hooper	80
Permit	42	4	3	7	33½	9/11/53	Boca Grande, Fla.—R. H. Martin	12
Pollack	32	4	3	8	26¾	4/25/53	Belmar, N. J.—J. Wolf	50
Roosterfish	100		4	6	32	1/12/54	Cabo Blanco, Peru—M. Barrenechea	130
Sailfish (Atlantic)	123		10	4	32¾	4/25/50	Walker Cay, Bahamas—H. Teetor	50
Sailfish (Pacific)	221		10	9		2/12/47	Santa Cruz, Galapagos Is.—Stewart	130
Sawfish	736		14	7		9/ 4/38	Galveston, Texas—G. Pangarakis	130
Shark (Mako)	1,000		12			3/14/43	Mayor Island, N. Z.—B. D. H. Ross	130

NAME	WEIGHT		LENGTH		GIRTH	DATE	LOCATION AND ANGLER	LINE
	lbs.	Ozs.	Ft.	Ins.	Inches			Lbs.
Shark (Man-Eater or White)	2,536		16	9	111	4/11/55	Denial Bay, Australia—A. Dean	180
Shark (Porbeagle)	260		11	4	68¾	2/ 5/49	Durban, S. Africa—J. L. Daniel	80
Shark (Thresher)	922					3/21/37	Bay of Islands, N. Z.—W. W. Dowding	130
Shark (Tiger)	1,382		13	10	93	2/22/39	Sydney Heads, Australia—L. Bagnard	130
Snook or Robalo	50	8	4	7		1/ 2/44	Gatun Spillway, Panama—J. Anderson	130
Swordfish	1,182		14	11¼	78	5/ 7/53	Iquique, Chile—L. Marron	130
Tarpon	247		7	5½		3/24/38	Panuco River, Mexico—H. W. Sedgwick	130
Tuna (Allison or Yellowfin)	265		6	1	53	7/31/37	Makua, T. H.—J. W. Harvey	80
Tuna (Big Eyed)	368		7	5	63½	3/26/53	Cabo Blanco, Peru—H. Woodward	130
Tuna (Bluefin)	977		9	8	94½	9/ 4/50	St. Ann Bay, N. S.—D. McI. Hodgson	130
Wahoo	136		6	4½	34½	4/ 8/55	East Boynton Inlet, Fla.—R. J. Geyer	80
Weakfish	17	8	3	10	19	9/30/44	Mullica River, N. J.—A. Weisbecker, Jr.	50
Weakfish (Spotted)	15	3	2	10½	20½	1/13/49	Ft. Pierce, Fla.—C. W. Hubbard	50
Yellowtail	105	12½	5	5	40	4./30/55	Bahia de Topolambopo, Mex.—M. A. Yant	50

WORLD RECORDS (FRESH-WATER) (as confirmed by Field and Stream Magazine)

SPECIES	WT.	LENGTH	PLACE	DATE	
Black Bass, Largemouth	22¼ lbs.	32½"	Montgomery Lake, Ga.	June	2, 1932
Black Bass, Smallmouth	11 lbs. 15 oz.	27"	Dale Hollow Lake, Ky.	July	9, 1955
Bluegill, Sunfish	4¾ lbs.	15"	Ketona Lake, Ala.	Apr.	9, 1950
Bullhead, Black	8 lbs.	24"	Lake Waccabuc, N. Y.	Aug.	1, 1951
Carp	55 lbs. 5 oz.	42"	Clearwater Lake, Minn.	July	10, 1952
Catfish, Blue	94½ lbs.	56"	James River, S. D.	May	22, 1949
Catfish, Channel	55 lbs.	50"	James River, S. D.	May	18, 1949
Charr, Arctic	11½ lbs.	30"	Richmond Gulf, Hudson Bay	Aug.	10, 1950
Gar, Alligator	279 lbs.	93"	Rio Grande River, Tex.	Dec.	2, 1951
Muskellunge	69 lbs. 11 oz.	63½"	Chippewa Flowage, Wis.	Oct.	20, 1949
Perch, White	4 lbs. 12 oz.	19½"	Messalonskee Lake, Me.	June	4, 1949
Perch, Yellow	4 lbs. 3½ oz.		Bordentown, N. J.	May	1865
Pickerel, Eastern Chain	9 lbs.	30"	Green Pond, N. J.	Jan.	5, 1948
Pike, Northern	46 lbs. 2 oz.	52½"	Sacandaga Reservoir, N. Y.	Sept.	15, 1940
Pike, Walleyed	22 lbs. 4 oz.	36¼"	Fort Erie, Ontario	May	26, 1943
Salmon, Atlantic	79 lbs. 2 oz.		Tanalev, Norway		1928
Salmon, Chinook	83 lbs.		Umpqua River, Ore.		1910
Salmon, Landlocked	22½ lbs.	36"	Sebago Lake, Me.	Aug.	1, 1907
Salmon, Silver	31 lbs.		Cowichan Bay, B. C.	Oct.	11, 1947
Trout, Brook	14½ lbs.		Nipigon River, Ontario	July	1916
Trout, Brown	39½ lbs.		Loch Awe, Scotland		1866
Trout, Cut-throat	41 lbs.	39"	Pyramid Lake, Nev.	Dec.	1925
Trout, Dolly Varden	32 lbs.	40½"	L. Pend Oreille, Ida.	Oct.	27, 1949
Trout, Golden	11 lbs.	28"	Cook's Lake, Wyo.	Aug.	5, 1948
Trout, Lake	63 lbs. 2 oz.	51½"	Lake Superior	May	25, 1952
Trout, Rainbow	37 lbs.	40½"	L. Pend Oreille, Ida.	Nov.	25, 1947
Trout, Sunapee	11 lbs. 8 oz.	33"	Lake Sunapee, N. H.	Aug.	1, 1954

ARCHERY

EARLIEST REFERENCES

Palaeolithic drawings of archers indicate that bows and arrows are an invention of at least 20,000 years ago. Archery developed as an organized sport at least as early as the fifth century A.D. The oldest archery body in the British Isles is the Royal Company of Archers, the Sovereign's bodyguard for Scotland, dating from 1676, though the Ancient Scorton Arrow meeting in Yorkshire was first staged in 1673.

FLIGHT SHOOTING

The world's greatest distances were achieved in Turkey, near Istanbul, in 1798, when a distance of 967 yards was attained by Sultan Selim.

The modern world flight shooting freestyle record is 774 yards by Charles Pierson of Cincinnati, made at Oxford, Ohio, in August 1955.

The regular style (standing stance) record is 640 yards by J. Stewart at Austin, Texas, in 1949.

MOST TITLES

The greatest number of world (Fédération Internationale de Tir à l'Arc) titles (instituted 1911), won by a man is 5 by H. Deutgen (Sweden) from 1947-1950 and 1952. The greatest number won by a woman is also 5 by Janina Kurkowska (Poland) winning the last in 1946.

MOST U.S. TITLES

The most U. S. archery titles have been won by R. P. Elmer who was the American round champion in 1911-1914, the York round champion in 1914 and the aggregate champion in 1915-16, 1919-20 and 1922 making 10 titles in all. The winner of most women's titles was Mrs. M. C. Howell who won the titles (National rounds) of 1883, 1885-86, 1890-93, 1895-96, 1898-1900, 1902-05 and 1907, making 17 titles in all.

ATHLETICS—TRACK AND FIELD

EARLIEST REFERENCES

Track and field athletics date from the ancient Olympic Games. The earliest recorded Olympiad dates from July 21st or 22nd, 776 B.C., at which celebration Coroebas won the foot race. Their earliest origins are believed to date from c.1370 B.C.

The earliest meetings in the British Isles were probably those at the Royal Military Academy, Sandhurst, c. 1810. The race with the longest history is the Rugby School Crick Run which has records back to 1837. The oldest athletic club in the world is Exeter College A.C., Oxford, which was founded in the autumn of 1850.

FASTEST RUNNER

In May, 1949, Melvin Patton (U.S.A.), co-holder of the world's 100 yards record, running the last stage of a sprint relay, was timed to cover a flying 100 yards in 8.3 seconds, giving an average of 24.64 m.p.h. However, there is evidence that another Californian sprinter, Harold Davis, well surpassed 25 m.p.h. in the latter half of the Amateur Athletics Union 100 metre championship final in New York on June 20th, 1943.

HIGHEST JUMPER

There are several reported instances of high jumpers exceeding the official world record height of 7 feet 0⅝ inch. The earliest of these came from unsubstantiated reports of Watussi tribesmen in Central Africa clearing up to 8 feet 2½ inches, probably however, from inclined take-offs. The greatest height cleared above an athlete's own head is the 13 inches by E. A. Ifeajuna (Nigeria), at Vancouver on July 31st, 1954, when winning the British Empire Title at 6 feet 8 inches. The highest cleared by a woman above her own head is 2¼ inches by Mary Donaghy (New Zealand), at Paeroa, New Zealand, on March 29th, 1955, when jumping 5 feet 4¼ inches.

MOST OLYMPIC GOLD MEDALS

Ray C. Ewry (U.S.A.), between 1900 and 1908, won 8 individual Olympic gold medals. His standing long jump record of 11 feet 4⅞ inches at St. Louis in August, 1904, remains unsurpassed. Paavo Johannes Nurmi (Finland) won 4 individual and 3 team race gold medals between 1920 and 1928. The greatest number of medals won in a single celebration is 4 by A. C. Kraenzelin (U.S.A.) in 1900, by P. J. Nurmi (Finland) in 1924, V. Ritola (Finland) in 1924, J. C. Owens (U.S.A.) (100 and 200 metres, the long jump and first stage in the 4 x 100 metre relay) at Berlin in 1936, and the 4 of Francina E. Blankers-Koen (Netherlands), (100 and 200 metres, 80 metre hurdles, and last stage in the women's 4 x 100 metre relay) at Wembley, London, in 1948.

EARLIEST LANDMARKS

The first time 10 seconds ("even time") was bettered under championship conditions was in the 1890 A.A.U. Championships at Analostan Island, Washington, by John Owen who recorded 9 4/5th seconds. The first recorded instance of 6 feet being cleared in the high jump was on March 17th, 1876, at Marston, near Oxford, England, by the Hon. Marshall Jones Brooks with 6 feet ⅛ inches. The breaking of the "4 minute barrier" in the one mile was first achieved at 6:10 p.m. on May 6th, 1954, on the Iffley Road track, Oxford, by Dr. Roger Gilbert Bannister, C.B.E. (Great Britain) with 3 minutes 59.4 seconds. See Photo No. 49, p. 176.

WORLD'S RECORDS (MEN)

The complete list of World's Records for the fifty scheduled men's events passed by the International Amateur Athletic Federation as of August 1st, 1956.   * = awaiting ratification

RUNNING

EVENT	Mins. Secs.		PLACE	DATE
	9.3	Melvin Emery Patton (U.S.A.)	Fresno, Cal.	May 15, 1948
	9.3	Hector Dennie Hogan (Australia)	Sydney, Australia	Mar. 3, 1954
	9.3	James J. Golliday (U.S.A.)	Evanston, Ill.	May 14, 1955
100 yards	9.3*	Leamon King (U.S.A.)	Fresno, Cal.	May 12, 1956
	9.3*	David William Sime (U.S.A.) See Photo No. 48, p. 176	Raleigh, S. C.	May 19, 1956
	9.3*	Michael Agostina (Trinidad)	Long Beach, Cal.	May 5, 1956
	9.3*	David William Sime (U.S.A.)	Sanger, Cal.	June 9, 1956
220 yards	20.0*	David William Sime (U.S.A.)	Sanger, Cal.	June 9, 1956
440 yards	45.8*	James Lea (U.S.A.)	Modesto, Cal.	May 26, 1956
880 yards	1:47.5	Lonnie Spurrier (U.S.A.)	Berkeley, Cal.	Mar. 26, 1955
1 mile	3:58.0	John Michael Landy (Australia)	Turku, Finland	June 21, 1954
2 miles	8:33.4	Sándor Iharos (Hungary)	London, England	May 30, 1955
3 miles	13:14.2	Sándor Iharos (Hungary)	Budapest, Hungary	Oct. 23, 1955
6 miles	27:43.8	Sándor Iharos (Hungary)	Budapest, Hungary	July 15, 1956
10 miles	48:12.0	Emil Zátopek (Czechoslovakia)	Stara Boleslav, CSR.	Sept. 29, 1951
15 miles	1H14:01.0	Emil Zátopek (Czechoslovakia)	Prague, CSR.	Oct. 29, 1955
	10.1*	William Williams (U.S.A.)	Berlin, Germany	Aug. 3, 1956
100 metres	10.1*	Ira Murchison (U.S.A.)	Berlin, Germany	Aug. 4, 1956
	10.1*	William Williams (U.S.A.)	Berlin, Germany	Aug. 5, 1956
200 metres	20.0*	David William Sime (U.S.A.)	Sanger, Cal.	June 9, 1956
400 metres	45.2*	Louis Jones (U.S.A.)	Los Angeles, Cal.	June 30, 1956

RUNNING

EVENT	Mins. Secs.		PLACE	DATE
800 metres	1:45.7	Roger Moens (Belgium)	Oslo, Norway	Aug. 3, 1955
1,000 metres	2:19.0	Audun Boysen (Norway)	Göteborg, Sweden	Aug. 30, 1955
	2:19.0	István Rozsavölgyi (Hungary)	Budapest, Hungary	Sept. 21, 1955
1,500 metres	3:40.6*	István Rozsavölgyi (Hungary)	Tata, Hungary	Aug. 3, 1956
2,000 metres	5:02.2	István Rozsavölgyi (Hungary)	Budapest, Hungary	Oct. 2, 1955
3,000 metres	7:52.8	Douglas Alistair Gordon Pirie (G.B.)	Malmo, Sweden	Sept. 4, 1956
5,000 metres	13:36.8*	Douglas Alistair Gordon Pirie (G.B.)	Bergen, Norway	June 19, 1956
10,000 metres	28:42.8*	Sándor Iharos (Hungary)	Budapest, Hungary	July 15, 1956
20,000 metres	59:51.8	Emil Zátopek (Czechoslovakia)	Stara Boleslav, CSR.	Sept. 29, 1951
25,000 metres	1H16:34.6	Emil Zátopek (Czechoslovakia)	Prague, CSR.	Oct. 29, 1955
30,000 metres	1H35:23.8	Emil Zátopek (Czechoslovakia)	Stara Boleslav, CSR.	Oct. 26, 1952
1 hr. (12m. 809 yd.) 20,052m.		Emil Zátopek (Czechoslovakia)	Stara Boleslav, CSR.	Sept. 29, 1951

RELAYS

EVENT	Mins. Secs.		PLACE	DATE
4 x 110 yards	40.1*	Texas University (U.S.A.)	Lawrence, Kan.	April 21, 1956
		(George Schneider, Jerry Prewitt, Robert Whilden, Frank Daugherty)		
4 x 220 yards and	1:24.0	University of Southern California (U.S.A.)	Los Angeles, Cal.	May 20, 1949
		(George Pasquali, Ronald Frazier, Norman Stocks, Patton)		
4 x 200 metres	1:24.0*	Abilene Christian College (U.S.A.)	Modesto, Cal.	May 26, 1956
		(Bill Woodhouse, James Segrest, Don Conder, Robert Morrow)		
4 x 440 yards	3:08.8	Amateur Athletic Union Team (U.S.A.)	London, England	Aug. 9, 1952
		(Gerald Eugene Cole, John William Mashburn, Reginald Pearman, Whitfield)		
4 x 880 yards	7:25.2*	South Pacific A.A.U. (U.S.A.)	Modesto, Cal.	May 26, 1956
		(Jerome Walters, Hal Butler, Daniel Schweikart, William Weiss)		
4 x 1 mile	16:41.0	Great Britain and Northern Ireland Team	London, England	Aug. 1, 1953
		(C. J. Chataway, G. W. Nankeville, D. C. Seaman, R. G. Bannister)		
4 x 100 metres	39.8	United States Olympic Games Team	Berlin, Germany	Aug. 9, 1936
		(Owens, Ralph H. Metcalfe, Foy Draper, Frank C. Wykoff)		
4 x 400 metres	3:03.9	Jamaican Olympic Games Team	Helsinki, Finland	July 27, 1952
		(Arthur Stanley Wint, Leslie Alphanzo Laing, Herbert McKenley, George Rhoden)		
4 x 800 metres	7:15.8*	Belgian Team	Brussels, Belgium	Aug. 8, 1956
		(A. Ballieux, A. Langenus, F. Leva, R. Moens)		
4 x 1,500 metres	15:14.8	Budapest Honved Sport Egyesulet	Budapest, Hungary	Sept. 29, 1955
		(Ferenc Mikes, László Tábori Talabercsuk, István Rózsavölgyi, Sándor Iharos)		

HURDLING

EVENT	Mins. Secs.		PLACE	DATE
120 yards (3'6")	13.4*	Jack W. Davis (U.S.A.)	Bakersfield, Cal.	June 22, 1956
220 yards (2'6")	22.2*	David William Sime (U.S.A.)	Durham, N. C.	May 5, 1956
440 yards (3'0")	51.3	Yuriy Nikolayvich Lituyev (U.S.S.R.)	London, England	Oct. 13, 1954
110 metres (3'6")	13.4*	Jack W. Davis (U.S.A.)	Bakersfield, Cal.	June 22, 1956
200 metres (2'6")	22.2*	David William Sime (U.S.A.)	Durham, N. C.	May 5, 1956
400 metres (3'0")	49.5*	G'enn Davis (U.S.A.)	Los Angeles, Cal.	June 29, 1956
3,000 metres S'chase	8:39.8*	Semyon Rzhishchin (U.S.S.R.)	Moscow, U.S.S.R.	Aug. 14, 1956

FIELD EVENTS

EVENT	Ft. Ins.	Metres		PLACE	DATE
High Jump	7' 0⅝"*	(2.149 m.)	Charles Dumas (U.S.A.)	Los Angeles, Cal.	June 29, 1956
Pole Vault	15' 7¾"	(4.77 m.)	Cornelius Anthony Warmerdam (U.S.A.)	Modesto, Cal.	May 23, 1942
Long Jump	26' 8¼"	(8.13 m.)	James Cleveland Owens (U.S.A.)	Ann Arbor, Mich.	May 25, 1935
Hop, Step and Jump	54' 3¾"	(16.56 m.)	Adhemar Ferriera da Silva (Brazil)	Mexico City	Mar. 16, 1955
Shot Putt	62' 6¼"	(19.07 m.)	William Parry O'Brien (U.S.A.)	Pasadena, Cal.	Sept. 1, 1956
Discus Throw	194' 6"	(59.28 m.)	Fortune Everette Gordien (U.S.A.)	Pasadena, Cal.	Aug. 22, 1953
Hammer Throw	217' 9½"*	(66.38 m.)	Mikhail Petrovich Krivonosov (U.S.S.R.)	Minsk, U.S.S.R.	July 8, 1956
Javelin Throw	274' 5¾"*	(83.66 m.)	Janusz Sidio (Poland)	Milan, Italy	June 30, 1956
Decathlon		7,980 points.	Rafer Johnson (U.S.A.)	Kingsburg, Cal.	June 10-11, 1955

1st day: 100 m. 10.5; Long Jump 24'6¾"; Shot Putt 45'3¼"; High Jump 6'¾"; 400 m. 49.7.
2nd day: 110 m. Hurdles 14.5; Discus 154'10¾"; Pole Vault 12'8½"; Javelin 193'10⅜"; 1,500 m. 5:01.5.

WORLD'S RECORDS (WOMEN)

The complete list of Women's World's Records passed by the International Amateur Athletic Federation as at August 1st, 1956.

RUNNING

EVENT	Mins. Secs.		PLACE	DATE
100 yards	10.4	Marjorie Jackson (Australia)	Sydney, Australia	Mar. 8, 1952
220 yards	23.6*	Mariya Leontivna Itkina (U.S.S.R.)	Kiev, U.S.S.R.	July 21, 1956
880 yards	2:06.6*	Nina Grigorievna Otkalenko (1) (U.S.S.R.)	Moscow, U.S.S.R.	June 9, 1956
60 metres	7.3	Stanislava Walasiewiczowna (Poland)	Lemberg, Poland	Sept. 24, 1933
100 metres	11.4	Marjorie Jackson (Australia)	Gifu, Japan	Oct. 4, 1952
200 metres	23.4	Marjorie Jackson (Australia)	Helsinki, Finland	July 25, 1952
800 metres	2:05.0	Nina Grigorievna Otkalenko (1) (U.S.S.R.)	Zagreb, Jugoslavia	Sept. 25, 1955

See Photo No. 47, p. 176

47. Nina Otkalenko
48. David W. Sime

49. Roger Bannister
50. Blue Marlin

RELAYS

EVENT	Mins. Secs.		PLACE	DATE
4 x 110 yards	45.8*	Eastern German Team	Rostock, Germany	July 29, 1956
4 x 220 yards	1:36.4*	Eastern German Team	Rostock, Germany	July 29, 1956
3 x 880 yards	6:36.2	Hungarian National Team	Tata, Hungary	July 21, 1954
		(Anna Bacskai, Agnes Oros, Aranka Kazi)		
4 x 100 metres	45.2*	U.S.S.R. Team	Kiev, U.S.S.R.	July 29, 1956
		(Vera Krepkina, O. Kotcheleva, Mariya Itkina, J. Botchkarev)		
4 x 100 metres	45.2*	East German Team	Erfurt, Germany	Aug. 12, 1956
		(Henning, Christa Stubnick, Gisela Köhler, Barbell Mayer)		
4 x 200 metres	1:36.4	U.S.S.R. National Team	Bucharest, Rumania	Aug. 9, 1953
		(Vyera Kalashnikova, Zinaida Safronova, Flora Kazantseva, Nadezhda Dvalishvili (2))		
3 x 800 metres	6:27.6	U.S.S.R. National Team	Moscow, U.S.S.R.	Sept. 11, 1955
		(A. Lapshina, Ludmila Lysenko, Nina Grigorievna Otkalenko (1))		

HURDLES

EVENT	Secs.		PLACE	DATE
80 metres	10.6*	Centa Gastl (East Germany)	Cologne	July 28, 1956

FIELD EVENTS

EVENT	Ft. Ins.	Metres		PLACE	DATE
High Jump	5' 8¾"	(1.75 m.)	Iolanda Balas (Rumania)	Bucharest, Rumania	July 14, 1956
Long Jump	20' 10"*	(6.35 m.)	Elzbieta Krzesinska-Dunska (Poland)	Budapest, Hungary	Aug. 20, 1956
Shot Putt	53' 6¼"	(16.32 m.)	Galina Ivanovna Zybina (U.S.S.R.)	Stalinabad, U.S.S.R.	Oct. 24, 1955
Discus Throw	187' 1"	(57.04 m.)	Nina Dumbadze (U.S.S.R.)	Tbilisi, U.S.S.R.	Oct. 18, 1952
Javelin Throw	182' 0"	(55.48 m.)	Nadezhda Efimova Konyayeva (U.S.S.R.)	Kiev, U.S.S.R.	Aug. 6, 1954

PENTATHLON

			PLACE	DATE
4,977* points		Nina Martyenko (U.S.S.R.)	Leningrad, U.S.S.R.	July 8, 1955

(200 metres 25.8; 80 metre H. 11.3; High Jump 1.62 m. (5'3¾"); Long Jump 5.92 m. (19' 5⅛"); Shot Putt 13.54 m. (44'5⅛").)
(1) nee Pletnyeve, (2) nee Khnykina, (3) now Mme. Popov.

The longest recorded pull was that of 2 hours 41 minutes between "H" Company and "E" Company of the 2nd Derbyshire Regiment at Jubbulpore, India, on August 12th, 1889.

LONGEST TUG OF WAR

The fastest recorded time for a 100 yards three-legged race is 11.0 seconds made at Brooklyn, New York, by Harry L. Hillman and Lawson Robertson on April 24th, 1909.

THREE-LEGGED RACE

The 21-foot long, 230-pound Braemar Caber defied all comers until it was successfully tossed at the Braemar Gathering of September 6th, 1951, by George Clark.

GREATEST CABER TOSS

UNITED STATES BEST PERFORMANCES

EVENT	Mins. Secs.		PLACE	DATE
	9.3	Melvin Patton	Fresno, Calif.	May 15, 1948
	9.3	James Golliday	Evanston, Ill.	May 14, 1955
	9.3*	Leamon King	Fresno, Calif.	May 12, 1956
100 Yards	9.3*	David Sime	Raleigh, S. C.	May 19, 1956
	9.3*	David Sime	Stockton, Calif.	June 2, 1956
	9.3*	David Sime	Sanger, Calif.	June 9, 1956
220 Yards (Straight)	20.0*	David Sime	Sanger, Calif.	June 9, 1956
220 Yards (Turn)	20.6	Andrew Stanfield	Philadelphia, Pa.	May 26, 1951
440 Yards	45.8*	James Lea	Modesto, Calif.	May 26, 1956
880 Yards	1:47.5	Lonnie Spurrier	Berkeley, Calif.	Mar. 26, 1955
880 Yards (4 turns)	1:47.6	Arnold Sowell	Boulder, Colo.	June 25, 1955
1 Mile	4:00.5	Wesley Santee	Austin, Texas	Apr. 2, 1955
2 Miles	8:49.6	Horace Ashenfelter	Compton, Calif.	June 3, 1955
3 Miles	13:51.8	Charles Capozzoli	London, England	Aug. 4, 1952
6 Miles	29:28.2*	Gordon McKenzie	New York, N. Y.	June 9, 1956
10 Miles	52:32.4	Fred Faller	Brooklyn, N. Y.	Oct. 25, 1919
15 Miles	1H23:24.2	Charles Pores	New York City	June 1, 1919
20 Miles	1H58:27.6	James Clark	Celtic Park, N. Y.	Nov. 14, 1909
100 metres	10.1	William Williams	Berlin, Germany	Aug. 3, 1956
	10.1	Ira Murchison	Berlin, Germany	Aug. 4, 1956
200 Metres	20.0*	David Sime	Sanger, Calif.	June 9, 1956
400 Metres	45.2*	Louis Jones	Los Angeles, Calif.	June 30, 1956
800 Metres	1:46.4*	Thomas Courtney	Los Angeles, Calif.	June 29, 1956
1,000 Metres	2:20.8	Mal Whitfield	Eskilstuna, Sweden	Aug. 16, 1953
1,500 Metres	3:42.8	Wesley Santee	Compton, Calif.	June 4, 1954
2,000 Metres	5:10.0	Fred Dwyer	Boras, Sweden	July 29, 1955
3,000 Metres	8:12.2	Fred Wilt	Turku, Finland	July 20, 1950
5,000 Metres	14:26.8	Fred Wilt	Helsinki, Finland	June 29, 1950
10,000 Metres	30:33.4	Curtis Stone	Long Beach, Calif.	June 20, 1952
Marathon	2H14:33.0	John Kelley	Boston, Mass.	April 19, 1956
120 Yards Hurdles	13.4*	Jack Davis	Bakersfield, Calif.	June 22, 1956
220 Yards Hurdles	22.2*	David Sime	Durham, N. C.	May 5, 1956
440 Yards Hurdles	51.5*	Edward Southern	Houston, Texas	June 9, 1956
110 Metres Hurdles	13.4*	Jack Davis	Bakersfield, Calif.	June 22, 1956
200 Metres Hurdles	22.2*	David Sime	Durham, N. C.	May 5, 1956

EVENT	Mins. Secs.		PLACE	DATE
400 Metres Hurdles	49.5*	Glenn Davis	Los Angeles, Calif.	June 29, 1956
3,000 Metres Steeplechase	8:45.4	Horace Ashenfelter	Helsinki, Finland	July 25, 1952
(4 x 100 meters, 4 x 110 yards, 4 x 200 metres, 4 x 220 yards, 4 x 440 yards Relays records as per World Records)				
4 x 400 Metres Relay	3:04.0	U. S. Olympic Team	Helsinki, Finland	July 27, 1952
(Olle Matson, Eugene Cole, Charles Moore, Malvin Whitfield)				
4 x 800 Metres Relay as per world 4 x 880 yards Relay				
4 x 1,500 Metres Relay	16:36.7	New York A.C.	Chicago, Ill.	June 30, 1933
(Frank Nordell, Joseph McCluskey, Gene Venzke, Joseph Mangan)				
4 x 1 Mile Relay	16:52.6	U. S. Team	London, England	Aug. 4, 1952
(J. Montes, Warren Druetzler, Wesley Santee, John Barnes)				
Sprint Medley	3:20.2	University of Kansas	Austin, Tex.	Apr. 3, 1954
(440, 220, 220, 880)				
(F. Cindrich, R. Moody, Richard Blair, Wesley Santee)				
Distance Medley	9:50.4	University of Kansas	Des Moines, Iowa	Apr. 24, 1954
(½, ¼, ¾, 1 mile)				
(F. Cindrich, L. Koby, Arthur Dalzell, Wesley Santee)				
High Jump	7' 0⅝"*	Charles Dumas	Los Angeles, Calif.	June 29, 1956
Pole Vault	15' 7¾"	Cornelius Warmerdam	Modesto, Calif.	May 23, 1942
Broad Jump	26' 8¼"	Jesse Owens	Ann Arbor, Mich.	May 25, 1935
Hop, Step and Jump	51' 4¾"*	Ira Davis	Los Angeles, Calif.	June 30, 1956
Shot Putt	62' 6¼"	Parry O'Brien	Pasadena, Cal.	Sept. 1, 1956
Discus Throw	194' 6"	Fortune Gordien	Pasadena, Calif.	Aug. 22, 1953
Hammer Throw	216' 4¾"*	Cliff Blair	Needham, Mass.	July 4, 1956
Javelin Throw	268' 2½"	Franklin Held	Pasadena, Calif.	May 21, 1955
Decathlon (as world record)				

WOMEN'S TRACK AND FIELD

100 Yards	10.7	Mae Faggs	Ponca City, Okla.	June 18, 1955
100 Metres	11.5	Barbara Jones	Mexico City, Mex.	Mar. 16, 1955
200 Metres	24.3	Catherine Hardy	Georgia	July 4, 1952
220 Yards	24.6	Betty McDonnell	Boston, Mass.	June 19, 1954
80 Metre Hurdles	11.1	Bertha Diaz	Philadelphia, Penn.	Aug. 18, 1956
High Jump	5' 6½"	Mildred McDaniel	Ponca City, Okla.	June 18, 1955
Broad Jump	19' 3½"	Mabel Landry	Helsinki, Finland	July 23, 1952
Shot Putt (8 lbs.)	45' 0"	Erlene Brown	Philadelphia, Penn.	Aug. 18, 1956
Discus	133' 2"	Lillian Copeland	Los Angeles, Calif.	Aug. 2, 1932
Javelin	161' 3"	Karen Anderson	Mexico City, Mex.	Mar. 18, 1955

BOSTON MARATHON

Outside of the Olympic marathon, that staged annually by the Boston Athletic Association is the world's leading classic over the 26 miles 385 yards route. The event, run each Patriot's Day (April 19th), was inaugurated in 1897. The greatest number of wins is 7 by Clarence DeMar who won in 1911, 1922-24, 1927-28 and 1930. The record time is the world's fastest recorded time for a point to point course of 2 hours 14 minutes 14.0 seconds set by the Finn, Antti Viskari, in the 1956 race.

MOST TEAM CHAMPIONSHIPS

The greatest number of outdoor A.A.U. team championships (instituted 1888) have been won by New York A.C. with 30, including a record streak of 11 consecutive wins from 1893 to 1903. The greatest number of team championships (instituted 1906) in the A.A.U. Indoor Championships is 27 again by New York A.C., including a record streak of 11 between 1932 and 1942.

WIDEST AND NARROWEST MARGINS

Outdoors the record margin was in 1899 at Boston, Mass., when New York A.C. won the team title by 98½ points. Indoors, the widest margin is 48 points when Irish-American A.C. defeated New York A.C., 84 to 36 points, in 1908. The narrowest wins are outdoors—1926 when both Illinois A.C. and New York A.C. scored 45 points and indoors—1931, when Illinois A.C. beat Penn, 16 points to 15.

BADMINTON

The game reached Canada in 1890 but never gained a permanent footing in the United States until 1929.

MOST TITLES

The greatest number of U. S. titles have been won by David G. Freeman with 7 singles titles in 1939-42, 1947-48 and 1953; 5 shares in the doubles title in 1940-42 and 1947-48 and 3 shares in the mixed doubles title in 1940-42 making 14 in all. The greatest number of women's titles have been won by Ethel Marshall with 7 singles from 1947 to 1953 and one share in a doubles title in 1952 making 8 all told.

BASEBALL

(Note: Exhaustive records of Baseball are so readily available in many publications that the Compilers have here confined themselves to a basic treatment.)

ORIGINS

Baseball is a totally American derivative of the English game of cricket (first recorded in the U. S. in 1747) and the now little played English game of rounders. The game evolved from the beginning of the nineteenth century. Haphazard versions of the so-called Town Ball Game grew up in Boston, New York and Philadelphia during the period 1820 to 1833. Rules were first codified in 1845 in New York by Alexander Cartwright.

The earliest match on record was that of June 19, 1846, in Hoboken, New Jersey, where the "New York Nine" defeated the Knickerbockers 23 to 1 in 4 hands or innings. The earliest all-professional team to be sponsored was that of the Cincinnati Red Stockings in 1869.

EARLIEST MATCHES

The World Series (National League v. American League) was started in 1903.

The score after 52 series stands at 33 to 19 in favor of the American League.

World Series

The most successful single club has been the New York Yankees (American League) with 16 victories in a record 21 appearances in 1923, 1927-28, 1932, 1936-39, 1941, 1943, 1947 and 1949-53. The most successful National League club has been the St. Louis Cardinals with 6 victories in 1926, 1931, 1934, 1942, 1944 and 1946.

CLUBS

The largest score in a game is the 22 when the Yankees (18) met the Giants (4) on October 2nd, 1936.

The longest game was one of 3 hours 28 minutes for the 12 inning match between Detroit AL and the Brooklyn Dodgers on October 8th, 1945. The shortest game was one of 1 hour 25 minutes between Chicago NL and Detroit AL on October 14th, 1908.

SCORES

Since 1903 to January 1st, 1956, the total attendance has been 10,973,000 and the total receipts $50,645,000. The largest attendance at any one series has been 389,763 at the 1947 7-game series between Brooklyn NL and New York AL. The smallest is 62,232 in the 1906 5-game series between Chicago AL and Chicago NL. The largest attendance at a single game is 86,288 at the Municipal Stadium at Cleveland on October 10th, 1948.

The largest receipts for any series are $2,979,269 (including broadcasting) for the 6-game 1953 series. The largest receipts from a single game are $480,085 on October 2nd, 1954, in the match between New York NL and Cleveland AL at Cleveland. The record receipts for a winning player are $9,768 by the Brooklyn Dodgers in 1955.

RECEIPTS AND ATTENDANCE

The most times any player has been on a world championship club is 9 by Joe Di Maggio of New York AL in 1936-39, 1941, 1947, 1949-51.

The record for the most series played is 10 by George H. 'Babe' Ruth (1915-16, 1918 with Boston AL and 1921-23, 1926-28, 1932 with New York AL) and 10 by Di Maggio (as above plus 1942).

The record for the number of games played is 52 by Phillip F. Rizzuto (New York AL). The most times at bat is 199 by Di Maggio with New York AL from 1936 to 1951.

PLAYERS

The World Series home run record is 15 by Ruth between 1921 (1) and 1932 (2) with 4 in 1926. Ruth also holds the game record of 3 set on October 6th, 1926, and again on October 9th, 1928, on both occasions with 2 in successive innings.

Ruth set the record of series with a batting record of .300 or better at six between 1921 and 1932 with .625 in 1928.

HOME RUNS

The most putouts in a series is 91 in the 8-game series of 1921 by first baseman Walter C. Pipp of New York AL. The record for a game is 19 by George L. Kelley of New York NL on October 15th, 1923.

The putout record for a catcher in a series is 59 by Gordon Cochrane of Philadelphia AL in 1929 (5 games) and 59 by Lawrence P. Berra, New York AL in 1952 (7 games). The record for a game is 15 by Herold D. Ruel of Washington AL on October 4th, 1924, in 12 innings.

FIELDING

The most shutout games pitched in a total series is 4 by Christy Mathewson of New York NL in 1905 (a record 3) and 1913 (1). Mathewson also holds the record for the most innings pitched with 101⅔ for New York NL in 1905, 1911-13. The most innings pitched in a game is 44 by C. Philippe of Pittsburgh NL in an 8-game series in 1903. The most strikeouts have been scored by Allie P. Reynolds of New York AL with 62 from 1947 to 1953. The most strikeouts by a pitcher in one game is 14 by Carl D. Erskine of Brooklyn NL on October 2nd, 1953.

PITCHING

The most pennants won by a club is 21 by the New York Yankees in the American League. The New York Giants hold the National League record with 15. In the Major League All-Star Games (inaugurated 1933) the American Leaguers have won 13 to the National League's 9 games.

PENNANTS

Major League All-Time Records

BATTING RECORDS

The lifetime batting leader is left-handed Tyrus R. Cobb (Detroit AL 1905-26 and Philadelphia AL 1927-28) who made 4,191 hits in 11,429 times at bat over 24 years for a .367 average. Cobb also holds the record for leading the league for 12 years from 1907-15 and from 1917-19. Cobb batted .300 or better for the record of 23 years from 1906-28. The season record average is .438 by Hugh Duffy of Boston AL with 236 hits in 539 times at bat in 1894.

The durability record is 2,130 consecutive league games between 1925 and 1939 by Henry Gehrig of New York AL. The record total of league games is 3,033 by Cobb from 1905 to 1928 during which time he was 11,429 times at bat making a record of 2,244 runs and a record of 4,191 base hits. The most runs in a game is 7 by Guy Hecker of Louisville AA on August 15th, 1886, and the most in a season 196 by William R. Hamilton of Philadelphia NL in 131 games in 1894. The most runs batted in a game is 12 by James Bottomley of St. Louis NL on September 16th, 1924. The season record is 190 by Lewis R. Wilson of Chicago NL in 155 games in 1930. The most base hits in a season is 257 by George Sisler of St. Louis AL in 1920.

The record number of consecutive games hitting safely is 56 by Joe Di Maggio in 1941.

LONG HITTING

The lifetime record of long hits (doubles, triples and home runs) is 1,356 by George 'Babe' Ruth with 1,356 between 1914 and 1935 with a season record of 119 in 1921.

Ruth's 5,793 total bases in 8,399 times at bat (1914-35) gave him the record slugging percentage of .690.

HOME RUNS

The lifetime home run record is 714 by Ruth with a record 60 for New York AL in 151 games in 1927. Babe led the league a record 12 years in 1918 (tied), 1919-21, 1923-24, 1926-30, 1931 (tied).

The record of 4 home runs in a game, 7 times achieved, was first done by Robert Lowe of Boston NL on May 30th, 1894.

Longest

The longest measured home run is one of 565 feet at the Griffith Stadium, Washington (deepest spot 457 feet) by Mickey Mantle of the New York Yankees on April 17th, 1953. See Photo No. 53, p. 185.

PITCHING

The most games pitched in a lifetime is 906 by Cy Young with 906 between 1890 and 1911. See Photo No. 52, p. 185. The most pitched in a season is still 75 by William White of Cincinnati NL in 1879.

Denton holds the record for the most games won with 511. The season record is 60 by Charles Radbourne of Providence NL in 1884.

The record for shutout games is 113 by Walter P. Johnson of Washington AL between 1907 and 1927. The season record is 16 by Grover Alexander of Philadelphia AL in 1920.

The lifetime strikeout record is 3,497 also by Johnson. The record for a season is 505 by Matthew Kilroy of Baltimore AA in 1886 with a 50-foot pitching distance. The modern season record is 348 by Bob Feller of Cleveland AL in 1946. The most strikeouts in a game (9 innings) is 19 by Charles Sweeney (Providence NL) and Hugh Dailey (Chicago UA) in 1884. The modern record is 18 by Feller for Cleveland AL v. Detroit on October 2nd, 1938.

Of the six recorded perfect games with no batter reaching first base, the earliest was by John Richmond of Worcester v. Cleveland on June 12th, 1880, and the most recent by Charley Robertson of the White Sox on April 30th, 1922. The champion no-hit pitchers with 3 hitless games are Larry Corcoran in 1880, 1882 and 1884; Cy Young in 1897, 1904 and 1908 and Bob Feller in 1940, 1946 and 1951.

LONGEST THROW

The longest measured baseball throw is one of 443 feet 3½ inches at Chattanooga, Tenn., by the Southern Association outfielder Don Grate during exercises on August 23rd, 1953.

OLDEST AND YOUNGEST PLAYERS

The youngest major league player of all-time was the Cincinnati pitcher Joe Nuxhall who started his career on June 10th, 1944, aged 15 years 10 months 11 days. Currently the youngest on the 1956 spring roster is the Kansas City infielder Alex George, aged 18 on September 27th, 1956, while the oldest is the St. Louis pitcher Ellis Kinder, 42 on July 26th, 1956.

The National Basketball Association's Championship series was established in 1947. Prior to 1949, when it joined with the National Basketball League, the professional circuit was known as the Basketball Association of America.

The most successful team has been the Minneapolis Lakers who have won the professional title in 1949-50, 1952-54.

The most decisive play-off results have been in 1947 when the Philadelphia Warriors defeated Chicago 4 games to 1 and in 1953 when the Lakers defeated Syracuse by the same margin.

Both George Mikan of the Lakers (1949-51) and Neil Johnston of the Warriors (1953-55) have won 3 N.B.A. top-scoring titles. Mikan's 1,932 points in 1951 is the record. Bob Cousy of the Boston Celtics set the assists record at 557 in 1955 and H. Gallatin of New York the rebounds record of 1,098 in 1954.

Most Points (Single Game)
    Joe Fulks (Philadelphia v. Indianapolis) February 10th, 1949.................................. 63
Highest Score (2-team aggregate)
    Syracuse (125) v. Anderson (123) with 5 overtime periods November 24th, 1949....248
Highest Score (Regulation Time) (2-team aggregate)
    Sheboygan (141) v. Denver (104) March 10th, 1950.......................................245
Most Field Goals (Single Game)
    Joe Fulks, February 10th, 1949.. 27
Most Field Goals (2-team aggregate)
    Sheboygan (107) v. Denver (46) March 10th, 1950.......................................107
Most Fouls Shot (Single Game)
    Frank Selvy (Milwaukee v. Minneapolis) December 2nd, 1954.................................. 24
Most Fouls Shot (2-team aggregate)
    Syracuse (59) v. Anderson (67) with 5 overtime periods November 24th, 1949......116

The world record attendance at a basketball game is 75,000 in the Olympic Stadium, Berlin, Germany, to see the Harlem Globetrotters in 1951.

The record attendance in the U. S. is 36,256 in the Memorial Coliseum, Los Angeles, to see a "World Series" game on April 8th, 1953.

The record aggregate attendance for a "World Series" between the Globetrotters and the All-Stars was 308,451 for 21 games in 1953.

The N.C.A.A. tournament was instituted in 1939. Most wins have been secured by Kentucky with 3 in 1948, 1949 and 1951. The greatest margin of victory in any final was in 1940 when Indiana beat Kansas 60-42 and the narrowest margin was in 1953 when Indiana beat Kansas 69-68. The highest scoring final was in 1954 when La Salle beat Bradley 92-76. The record highest scorer in the tournament has been the Olympic player, Clyde Lovellette of Kansas, who scored 141 points in the 1952 season.

The top scoring team in the 8 major conferences are:—
Big Seven (since 1929) 16—Kansas—1931-34, 1936, 1937*, 1938, 1940*, 1941*, 1942*, 1943, 1946, 1950*, 1952-3, 1954*.
Big Ten (since 1906) 13—Wisconsin—1907*, 1912*, 1913-14, 1916, 1918, 1921*, 1923*, 1924*, 1929*, 1935*, 1941, 1947.
Ivy or Eastern (since 1902) 12—Columbia—1904-5, 1911-12, 1914*, 1926, 1930-31, 1936, 1947-48, 1951.
Missouri Valley (since 1908) 15—Oklahoma A & M—1931*, 1936*, 1937-38, 1939*, 1940, 1942*, 1944-46, 1948-49, 1951, 1953-54.
Pacific Coast (since 1916) 10—California—1916*, 1921*, 1924-27, 1929, 1932, 1944*, 1946.
Southeastern (since 1933) 16—Kentucky   1933, 1937, 1939-40, 1942, 1944-52, 1954-55.
Southern (since 1930) 6—N. C. State—1947-52.
Southwest (since 1915) 13—Arkansas—1926-30, 1935*, 1936, 1938, 1941, 1942*, 1944*, 1949*, 1950*.
        *Title shared

The record major college scorer is Frank Selvy of Furman with an average of 41.7 points per game in 1954. The minor college record is 46.5 points per game by Bevo Francis of Rio Grande in 1954.

The major college career record is 2,587 points in the 4 seasons 1952-55 by Dickie Hemric of Wake Forest. The highest career average among top-scorers is 32.5 points per game by Frank Selvy of Furman (1952-54) who amassed 2,538 points in 3 seasons. The minor college career record is 2,959 points in the 4 seasons 1952-55, by Carl Hartman of Alderson-Broaddus.

MOST A.A.U.
TITLES

The A.A.U. Basketball Championship was instituted in 1897. The greatest number of championships have been won by Phillips 66 of Bartlesville, Oklahoma, with wins in 1943-48, 1950 and 1955. Nash played on the 5 winning teams in 1943, 1945, 1946, 1947 and 1948.

In the women's championship instituted in 1926, 3 teams have recorded 3 wins.
Tulsa Business College, Oklahoma...1934-36
Nashville Goldblames 1946, 1948-49
Hanes Hosiery Mills, Winston-Salem, North Carolina.................................1951-53

MOST
OLYMPIC WINS

Basketball, staged as the demonstration sport at the St. Louis Olympics of 1904, was not added to the Olympic program until 1936. The U. S. has won each of the 3 subsequent contests at Berlin (1936), London (1948) and Helsinki (1952).

TALLEST
PLAYER

The tallest basketball player of all time was "Tiny" Reichert of House of David, Tennessee, who played center during 1936 when he measured 8 feet 1 inch in height.

BILLIARDS

EARLIEST
MENTION

The earliest mention of Billiards was in a poem of the Frenchman Marot (d. 1544) while the earliest mention in England was in 1591 by Spenser. The first recorded public billiard room in England was the Piazza, Covent Gardens, in the early part of the last century. Slate-beds came in in 1827 and rubber cushions in 1835.

The earliest mentions of the game in the United States date from the year 1800 but the earliest matches on record date from 1854 and the earliest championship from 1859.

MOST TITLES

Willie Hoppe won 51 assorted 'world' titles between 1906 and his retirement in 1952 including 12 3-cushion titles. The most 'world' pocket billiards titles have been won by Alfredo De Oro with 16 between 1888 and 1913.

HIGH RUN
RECORDS

The high run record in the 3 cushion game is 25 in an exhibition by Willie Hoppe in 1928. The high run record in pocket billiards is 309 in exhibition by Irving Crane in 1939 and by Willie Mosconi in 1945.

BOBSLEDDING

MOST WORLD
TITLES

The world championships were inaugurated in 1924. Switzerland (1924, 1936, 1939, 1940, 1954, 1955) and the United States (1928, 1932, 1948-50, 1953) have most titles with 6 each.

Switzerland has most 2-man bob titles (instituted 1931) with 7 in 1935, 1947-50, 1953 and 1955. The Swiss Felix Endrix (1948-49, 1953) and Fritz Feierabend (1947, 1950, 1955) are the only 3 time winners.

BOWLING

Bowling is a sport of great antiquity, having originated in the cloisters of abbeys and monasteries in Germany before the 5th century A.D. The number of pins later varied between 3 to as high as 17 but 9 became standard about 1550. The game was introduced into this country by the Dutch and had been long established before its first mention in 1818. The chaotic rules began to be standardized with the formation of the American Bowling Congress on September 9th, 1895.

A.B.C.
RECORDS

The A.B.C. Championship was inaugurated in 1901 at Chicago. The record entry is 8,180 five-man teams and a total of 43,000 bowlers at the 50th Meeting again at Chicago in 1953.

The record number of A.B.C. titles won by a bowler is 4 by John Koster (Nyack, N. Y.) who won the All-Events in 1902; the Team titles in 1902 and 1912 and the Doubles title in 1913 and 4 by Joseph Wilman (Berwyn, Ill.) who won the All-Events in 1939 and 1946 and the Team titles in 1942 and 1954.

The only bowler ever to win two singles titles is Larry Sutton (Rochester) in 1909 and 1912.

Highest Singles Total—755—Lee Jouglard (Detroit) at St. Paul, 1951 (242, 255, 278)

Highest All-Event Total—2,070—Max Stein (Belleville, Ill.) in New York, 1937 (658 team, 707 doubles, 705 singles)

Highest Doubles Total—1,453—John Klares (255, 222, 278—755) and Steve Nagy (Cleveland) in Milwaukee, 1952 (256, 236, 206—698)

Highest Team Total—3,234—Birk Bros. (Chicago) in Chicago, 1938; George Geiser (255, 174, 211—640); Leo Krisch (224, 185, 190—599); George Notz (243, 203, 266—712); Joe Traubenik (206, 164, 245—615); Jule Lellinger (201, 244, 223—668)

The only 300 games (perfect scores) rolled in A.B.C. title victories were by Leo Rollick (Santa Monica) at Buffalo in 1946 and by Tony Sparando (Rego Park, N. Y.) at Seattle in 1954.

The highest scores ever set in sanctioned A.B.C. tournaments are:
Singles (3 games)—886 (297, 289, 300) by Allie Brandt (Lockport, N. Y.) in 1939.

Doubles (3 games)—1,494 (267, 223, 246) for 736 by Charles Lausche; (266, 202, 290) for 758 by Frank Franz (Cleveland) in 1938.

Team (1 game)—1,342—Hook Grips—Pete Kavalski (296), Sam Vitola (276), Tony Lakawicz (266), Stixie Mulick (266) and Stan Niemiec (238) (Lodi, N. J.) in 1950.

Team (3 games)—3,797—Herman Undertakers—Buzz Wilson (709), Ray Holmes (792), Fred Taff (766), Bob Wills (771) and Sam Garafalo (759) (St. Louis) in 1937.

All-Events—2,259 (267, 255, 234 for 756 Singles), (225, 225, 279 for 729 Doubles) and (227, 267, 280 for 774 Team) by Frank Benkovic (Milwaukee) in 1932.

The Women's International Bowling Congress Championships were inaugurated in 1918. The winner of most individual titles is Mrs. E. Jaeger with 3 Singles titles in 1921, 1922 and 1923 and 4 All-Events titles in 1918, 1921, 1928 and 1929, making 7 in all. Most five-woman team titles have been won by Alberti Jewellers, Chicago, in 1928, 1931, 1933 and 1935.

The highest championship scores are:—
        Singles—712—by Marie Clemensen (1934).
        Doubles—1,251—by V. Focozio and P. Dusher (1946).
        All-Events—1,911—by Marie Warmbier (1935).
        5-Woman Team—2,987—by Kornitz Pure Oil (1947).

Duck-pin bowling developed in Baltimore, Maryland, in April, 1900, with the first leagues in 1903. The National Duck-Pin Bowling Congress was formed on September 8th, 1927.

The greatest number of hand-pin titles won is 5, by Nick Tronsky of Willimantic, Conn., with the singles title in 1934 and 1939 and the all events title in 1939-41.

The most women's individual hand-pin titles have been won by Lorraine Gulli of Washington, D. C., with one singles title in 1951 and 6 all event titles in 1930, 1934-35, 1938 and 1946-47.

The men's individual single game record is 239 by Eddie Funaro of New Haven, Conn., on January 11th, 1941 and the 100 game set (continuous bowling) record 12,466 by Gordon McIlwee of Winchester, Va., on December 18th, 1940.

The women's individual single game record is 232 by Vivian Walsh of Washington, D. C., on February 24th, 1954.

With acknowledgment to Nat S. Fleischer and the 'Ring' for part of the following material.

The origins of fist-fighting belong to Greek mythology. The earliest prize-ring code of rules was formulated in England in 1743 by the champion pugilist Broughton. Boxing, which had in 1865 come under the Queensberry Rules, was not established as a legal sport in Britain until April 24th, 1901.

Earliest World Title Fight

The first world heavyweight title fight, with gloves, and 3-minute rounds, was on September 7th, 1892, between John L. Sullivan and James J. Corbett in New Orleans, U.S.A.

Longest Fight

The longest recorded fight with gloves was between Andy Bowen and Jack Burke on April 6th, 1893, at New Orleans, U.S.A. The fight lasted 110 rounds and 7 hours 19 minutes but was declared a no contest. The record duration for a bare knuckle fight was 6 hours 15 minutes between James Kelly and Jack Smith at Melbourne, Australia, on October 19th, 1856.

Shortest Fight

The extreme case is recorded of a knockout in 10½ seconds (including a 10 second count) on September 24th, 1946, when Al Couture struck Ralph Walton while the latter was adjusting a gum shield in his corner. If the time was accurately taken it is clear that Couture must have been more than half-way across the ring from his own corner at the opening bell.

The shortest world heavyweight title occurred in Dublin, Ireland, on March 17th, 1908, when Tommy Burns knocked out Jem Rocke in 1 minute 28 seconds. The shortest world title fight was on April 6th, 1914, when Al McCoy knocked out George Chip for the middleweight crown in New York in 45 seconds.

Tallest and Heaviest

The tallest boxer of all time was the Canadian negro Harry Gunson who boxed from 1898 to 1900. He was 7 feet 2 inches tall.

The heaviest boxer ever is the 7 feet 1 inch Ewart Potgieter (South Africa) who has weighed in at 326 lbs.

WORLD HEAVYWEIGHT CHAMPIONS Longest and Shortest Reigns

The longest reign of any world heavyweight champion is the 11 years 8 months 9 days of Joe Louis from June 22nd, 1937, when he knocked out Jim Braddock in the eighth round at Chicago. During his reign Louis made a record number of 25 defenses of his title. The shortest reign was by Primo Carnera (Italy) at 350 days from June 29th, 1933, to June 14th, 1934. However, if the disputed title claim of Marvin Hart is allowed, his reign from July 3rd, 1905, to February 23rd, 1906, is only 235 days.

Heaviest and Lightest

The heaviest world champion was Primo Carnera of Italy who won the title on June 29th, 1933, at Long Island, U.S.A. He was scaled 270 lbs. The lightest champion was Bob Fitzsimmons (b. Cornwall, England, June 4th, 1862), who won the title on March 17th, 1897, at Carson City, Nevada, U.S.A., at 167 lbs.

The greatest differential in a fight was the 94 lbs. between Carnera (270 lbs.) and Tommy Loughran (U.S.A.) (186 lbs.) when the former won on points at Miami, U.S.A., on March 1st, 1934. The greatest "tonnage" in a world title fight was 488¾ lbs. when Carnera (259½ lbs.) fought Uzcudun (229½ lbs.) on October 22nd, 1933, in Rome.

Tallest and Shortest

The tallest world champion was the 6 feet 6¾ inches tall Jess Willard (U.S.A.) who won the title by knocking out Jack Johnson in the 26th round at Havana, Cuba, on April 5th, 1915. The shortest was Tommy Burns (1881-1955), world champion from 1906-08, at 5 feet 7 inches.

Youngest

The youngest age at which the world title has been won is 23 years 1 month by Joe Louis (b. May 13th, 1914) on June 22nd, 1937.

WORLD CHAMPIONS (any weight)
Longest and Shortest Reign

Joe Louis's heavyweight record stands for all divisions. The shortest reign was 47 days by the flyweight Emile Pladner.

Youngest and Oldest

The youngest at which any world title has been claimed is 18 years 8 months 6 days by the featherweight Abe Attell in 1901. The oldest world champion was Bob Fitzsimmons who held his light-heavyweight title till December 20th, 1905, when he was 43 years 6 months old. Fitzsimmons also had the longest career of any official world title-holder with 33 years from 1882-1914.

Longest Fight

The longest world title fight (under Queensberry Rules) was that between the lightweight Joe Gans and Battling Nelson at Goldfield, Nevada, on September 3rd, 1906, which was terminated in the 42nd round when the former was declared the winner after a foul.

Biggest Weight Span

The only man to hold world titles at 3 weights simultaneously was Henry Armstrong (U.S.A.) at featherweight, lightweight and welterweight in 1938.

51. Rocky Marciano

52. Cy Young

53. Mickey Mantle

54. Don Hutson

Most Knockdowns	Max Baer knocked down Primo Carnera 12 times in 11 rounds in their heavyweight title fight in New York on June 14th, 1934, before the referee stopped the fight.
Biggest Purse	The greatest purse was the $990,445 received by Gene Tunney for his fight against Jack Dempsey in Chicago on September 22nd, 1927.
BIGGEST GATE	This was accumulated at the above fight at Soldiers' Field, Chicago, when receipts totalled $2,658,660. The promoter, Ted Rickard, took a profit of $475,690.
HIGHEST ATTENDANCES	The greatest paid attendance at any boxing fight was the 120,757 at the Sesquicentennial Stadium, Philadelphia, on September 23rd, 1926, for the Tunney v. Dempsey world heavyweight title fight. The highest non-paying attendance is 135,132 at the Tony Zale v. Billy Prior fight at Milwaukee, Wisconsin, U.S.A., on August 18th, 1941.
HIGHEST EARNINGS IN CAREER	The largest fortune made in a fighting career is the $4,626,721.69 amassed by Rocky Marciano (born Rocco Marchegiano at Brockton, Mass., on September 1st, 1924) in 49 bouts (43 won by K.O., 6 by decision) from 1947 to 1955. See Photo No. 51, p. 185. Including $3,000,000 earnings for refereeing, Jack Dempsey has grossed over $6,100,000.
MOST KNOCK-DOWNS	The greatest recorded number of knock-downs in a fight is 38. This occurred in the fight between Joe Jeanette (27) and Sam McVey (11) in Paris on April 17th, 1907.
Greatest Number of Knock-outs	The greatest number of knock-outs in a career is 127 by "Young" Stribling (William Lawrence) (1921-1933).
Greatest Number of Fights	The greatest number of fights in a career is the 1,309 fought by Abe the Newsboy (U.S.A.) (Abraham Hollandersky) in the fourteen years from 1905 to 1918.
Biggest Weight Difference	The greatest weight difference recorded in a major bout is at Brooklyn, U.S.A., on April 30th, 1900, between Bob Fitzsimmons (172 lbs.) and Ed Dunkhorst (312 lbs.). Fitzsimmons won in two rounds.
MOST A.A.U. TITLES	The most A.A.U. titles won by any boxer is 6 by W. Rodenbach (New West Side A.C., New York) with 5 at 158 lbs. (as above) at the 1901 heavyweight title.
MOST OLYMPIC TITLES	Of the 17 countries who have supplied Olympic Champions, most have come from the United States with 19 winners between 1904 and 1952. The only champions to win a second gold medal have been: O. L. Kirk (U.S.A.)—1904 Bantamweight (115 lbs.), 1904 Featherweight. Harry Mallin (Great Britain)—1920 Middleweight, 1924 Middleweight. Laszlo Popp (Hungary)—1948 Middleweight, 1952 Light Middleweight.

CANOEING

Canoeing as a sport was founded with the formation of the Royal Canoe Club in London, England, on July 26th, 1865, by John Macgregor. The premier American club, the New York Canoe Club, was founded in 1871 and the American Canoe Association in August 1880.

MOST TITLES

The greatest number of National Paddling singles titles has been won by E. Riedel (Pendleton Canoe Club) who won the One Man single blade title in 1938 and the One Man double blade titles of 1935, 1937-38, 1940-41 and 1946-48, making nine in all.

CHESS

ORIGINS

Chess, derived from the Persian word *shah*, spread from India in the seventh century A.D., reaching England c.1255. The *Fédération Internationale des Echecs* was established in 1924.

LONGEST GAMES

The most protracted chess match on record was one drawn on the 191st move between H. Pilnik (Argentina) and M. Czerniak (Israel) at Mar del Plata, Argentina, in April, 1953. The total playing time was 20 hours. A game of 21½ hours but drawn on the 171st move (average over 7½ minutes per move) was played between the Russians Makagonov and Chekover at Baku in 1945.

MOST OPPONENTS

Records by chess masters for numbers of opponents tackled simultaneously depend very much whether or not all the opponents are replaced as defeated, are in relays, or whether they are taken on in a simultaneous start.

The greatest number tackled on a replacement basis is 400 (379 defeated) by the Swedish master G. Stahlberg in 36 hours' play in Buenos Aires, Argentina, in 1946.

The blindfold record is 45 opponents (43 defeated) in Buenos Aires in 1947 by the Argentinian Miguel Najdorf. The exact conditions of this record are not clear, but in 1937 in Glasgow, G. Koltanowski (Belgium, now of U.S.A.) tackled 34 opponents blindfold in a simultaneous start.

LONGEST REIGN

The longest tenure of the title of world champion is 28 years by the Austrian Wilhelm Steinitz (1866-1894). The only U. S. world champion has been Paul Morphy (1858-1862) of New Orleans.

CONTRACT BRIDGE

EARLIEST REFERENCES

Bridge (a corruption of Biritch) is of Levantine origin, being played in Greece in the early 1880's. The game was known in London, England, in 1886 under the title of "Biritch or Russian Whist."

HIGHEST POSSIBLE SCORES

Opponents bid 7 of any suit or No Trumps doubled and redoubled and vulnerable. Opponents make no trick.			Bid 7 no trumps, double and redouble, vulnerable.		
Above Line	1st undertrick	400	Below Line	1st trick (40 x 4)	160
				6 tricks (30 x 6 x 4)	720
	12 subsequent undertricks		Above Line	*2nd game of 2-Game	
	at 600 each	7,200		Rubber (worth)	350
	All Honors	150		Grand Slam	1,500
		———		All Honors (4 aces)	150
		7,750			———
		———	(Highest Possible Positive Score)		2,880

In practice, the full bonus of 700 points is awarded after the completion of the 2nd game rather than 350 after each game.

MOST CHAMPIONSHIPS

The greatest number of U. S. national championships have been won by Charles H. Goren with 37 in the 22-year period 1935 to 1956. Goren has also won the record number of 5 titles in the single year of 1943.

MOST MASTER POINTS

Bridge players are ranked according to the number of master points won in organized competition. Those accumulating over 300 points are accorded the rank of Life Master. The highest total accumulated is 5,202 master points by Charles H. Goren who has won the McKenney Trophy 8 times since 1937 for the player winning most master points in the year. The leading woman player is Life Master Mrs. Helen Sobel with 3,250 points.

HIGHEST ODDS

The odds against dealing 13 cards of one suit are 158,758,389,000 to 1 while the odds against receiving a "perfect deal" consisting of all 13 spades are 635,013,559,000 to 1. The probability of this latter is nearly 1 million times as remote as a Royal Flush in poker at 649,739 to 1.

COURT TENNIS

(Sometimes known as "Real" or "Royal" Tennis).

LONGEST REIGN

The longest reign of any of the 15 world champions since Clerge is that of Pierre Etchebaster who won the title in Paris in 1928, last defended it in New York (winning 7-0) in 1950 and retired undefeated in 1954 after 26 years. Etchebaster also holds the record for the greatest number of successful defenses of his title with seven.

MOST U.S. TITLES

The greatest number of U. S. Amateur Court Tennis titles have been won by the 1914 world champion Joy Gould of Philadelphia, who won every year from 1906 to 1917 and from 1920 to 1925, making a total of 19 titles.

CRICKET

The earliest references to cricket in the U. S. date from 1747 while in May 1751 a New York team defeated a team from London, England, in New York City. The game lost ground to baseball from 1860 onwards.

HIGHEST INNINGS

The highest individual innings made by an American is 344 by J. Barton King of the Belmont Club, Philadelphia, in 1906.

CURLING

The game, played with granite stones on an ice rink, is of Scottish origin, dating from c.1520. The sport reached Canada c.1810 and the United States 10 years later. The world governing body, the Royal Caledonian Curling Club, was formed in 1842, and the first international match between Scotland and the United States took place in 1902.

MOST
TITLES

The greatest number of American titles won in the Championships, inaugurated in 1891, is 11 by R. H. Dunbar between 1900 and 1928.

CYCLING

Earliest Race

The earliest recorded bicycle race was a velocipede race at the Parc de St. Cloud, Paris, on May 31st, 1868, over two kilometres.

Fastest Speed

The highest speed ever achieved on a bicycle is 109.12 m.p.h. by Jose Meiffret of France using a 275-inch gear behind a windshield on a racing car near Bordeaux in October, 1951.

The greatest distance ever covered in one hour is 76 miles 504 yards by Leon Vanderstuyft (Belgium) on the Montlhéry Motor Circuit, France, in September, 1928. This was achieved from a standing start paced by a motor cycle.

MOST OLYMPIC
TITLES

Cycling has been on the Olympic program since the revival of the Games in 1896. The greatest number of gold medals won is three by P. Masson (France) 333.3 m. 2 kms. and 10 kms. in Athens in 1896 and three by F. Verri (Italy) 333.3 m., 1,000 m. and 5 kms. in the 1906 Games also at Athens.

TOUR DE FRANCE

The only 3 times winner of the Continental Tour de France race (inaugurated in 1903) is Louison Bobet who won in 1953, 1954 and 1955.

U.S. RECORDS

Amateur Road Competition—Scratch.

1 mile	2m. 02.0s.	R. L. Guthridge	Westfield, N. J.	Aug. 8, 1908
		S. C. Haberle		
25 miles	1 hr. 02m. 14.0s.	Charles Thomas	Tonawanda, N. Y.	Sept. 6, 1937
50 miles	2 hr. 02m. 00.0s.	Leo Adams	Buffalo, N. Y.	July 14, 1935
100 miles	4 hr. 33m. 25.2s.	Louis Maltese	Union City, N. J.	June 6, 1926

The only 3 time winner of the Senior Amateur Road title has been Ted Smith, in 1945, 1947 and 1948.

EQUESTRIAN SPORTS

ORIGIN

Evidence of horse-riding dates from an Egyptian statuette dated c.2000 B.C. Pignatelli's academy of horsemanship at Naples dates from the sixteenth century.

Equestrian events have been included in the Olympic Games since 1912.

MOST OLYMPIC
MEDALS

The greatest number of Olympic Gold Medals by a horseman is four by Lt. C. F. Pahud de Mortanges (Netherlands) who won the individual three-day event in 1928 and 1932 and was in the winning team in 1924 and 1928.

MOST TEAM
WINS

The most team wins in the Prix de Nations is three by Sweden in 1912, 1920 and 1924.

No rider has yet succeeded in retaining an individual Olympic Prix de Nations. The lowest score obtained by a winner was by F. Ventura (Czechoslovakia) at Amsterdam in 1928 with no faults.

JUMPING

The official Fédération Equestre Internationale high jump record is 8 feet 1¼ inches by Huaso ridden by Capt. A. L. Morales (Chile) at Santiago, Chile, on February 5th, 1949.

At the Diamond Jubilee Show, Tenterfield, New South Wales, in March, 1937, Lookout cleared a measured 8 feet 3 inches. In 1946 at Cairns, Queensland, "Gold Meade", ridden by Jack Martin, cleared 8 feet 6 inches. On June 25th, 1937, Lady Wright of Durley set the best ever recorded height for an equestrienne on Jimmy Brown at 7 feet 4 inches.

FENCING

The sport of fencing grew up with the prohibition of duelling. In England this occurred c.1842.

MOST OLYMPIC
TITLES

The greatest number of individual Olympic gold medals won is three by Nedo Nadi (Italy) 1912 and 1920 (2) and Ramon Fonst (Cuba) 1900, 1904 (2).

The U. S. Championships were inaugurated in 1892 and the Women's Championship in 1913.

The greatest number of foils titles is 6 by George C. Calman (1925-28, 1930-31) and by Joseph L. Levis (Fencers Club, New York) (1929, 1932-33, 1935, 1937 and 1954). Calman also won the 1923 épée title.

The greatest number of épée titles is 5 by Leo G. Nunes (1922, 1924, 1926, 1928 and 1932). Nunes also won the saber title in 1922, 1926 and 1929. The greatest number of titles in any division is 10 by Norman C. Armitage in saber (1930, 1934-36, 1939-43 and 1945).

The most women's titles (foil only) have been won by Helene Mayer with 8 (1934-35, 1937-39, 1941-42 and 1946).

The origin of football stems from the "Boston Game" as played at Harvard University which was itself a handling code of mob football. Harvard declined to participate in the inaugural meeting of the Intercollegiate Football Association in New York City on October 19th, 1873, on the grounds that the proposed rules were based on the non-handling "Association" code of English football. Instead, Harvard accepted a fixture proposal from McGill University of Montreal, Canada, who played the more closely akin English code of Rugby Football. The first football match under the Harvard Rules was thus played against McGill at Cambridge, Mass., on May 14th, 1873. On November 23rd, 1876, a new Intercollegiate Football Association, based on the handling code, was inaugurated at Springfield, Mass., with a pioneer membership of five colleges.

Professional football dates from the Latrobe v. Jeannette match at Latrobe, Pennsylvania, on August 31st, 1895. The National Football League, who maintain the professional records, was founded in Canton, Ohio, in 1920.

Most in a Season	(Collegiate)	253	Mayes McClain (Haskell)	1926
	(Major College)	166	Art Luppino (Arizona) See Photo No. 55, p. 192	1954
	(Professional)	138	Don Hutson (Green Bay) See Photo No. 54, p. 185	1942
Most in a Game	(Collegiate)	100	Leo Schlick (St. Viator) (12 touchdowns, 28 pts. after)	1916
	(Professional)			
Most in a Career	(Collegiate)	465	Willie Heston (Michigan) (93 touchdowns)	1901-2-3-4
		465	Leo Lewis (Lincoln, Mo.)	1951-2-3-4
	(Professional)	825	Don Hutson (Green Bay)	1935-45
Most in a Game	(Collegiate) (Professional)	12	Leo Schlick (St. Viator) v. Lane	1916
Most in a Season	(Collegiate)	30	John Imlay (Missouri Mines)	1914
	(Major College)	24	Art Luppino (Arizona)	1954
	(Professional)	18	Steve Van Buren (Philadelphia)	1945
Most in a Career	(Professional)	105	Don Hutson (Green Bay)	1935-45
Most in a Game	(Collegiate)	17	Forest Peters (Montana) v. Billings Poly	1924
	(Professional)			
Most in a Season	(Major Collegiate)	13	Charles Brickley (Harvard)	1913
	(Professional)	23	Lou Groza (Cleveland)	1953
Most in a Career	(Collegiate)	34	Charles Brickley (Harvard)	1911-12-13
	(Professional)	81	Lou Groza (Cleveland)	1950-54
Most in a Season	(Collegiate)	64	Frank Acker (St. Louis U.)	1906
	(Major College)	48	Bob Fuller (Arizona State)	1950
	(Professional)	54	Bob Waterfield (Los Angeles)	1950
Most in a Career	(Professional)	315	Bob Waterfield (Los Angeles)	1946-52

PROFESSIONAL CHAMPIONS

The National Football League Championship was instituted in 1921. Between 1921 and 1932 the title depended upon final standings but in 1933 inter-divisional play-offs were inaugurated.

The most titles have been won by the Chicago Bears (formerly the Chicago Staleys) with 7 victories in 1921, 1932-1933, 1940-41, 1943, 1946. The record attendance at a Championship Play-off is 87,695 at Los Angeles in 1955.

ALL-STAR GAME

The reigning N.F.L. Champions first met an All-Star College selection in the annual August series in Chicago in 1934. Two of the 22 games have been ties (1934 and 1936) and of the remaining 20 the professionals have won 13 and lost 7. The highest scoring match was that of 1940 in which Green Bay beat the All Stars 45-28. The biggest professional win was that of 1949 when Philadelphia won 38-0 and the biggest All Stars win was that of 1943 when Washington was defeated 27-7.

KICKING RECORDS

The following kicking records have been recorded in collegiate football:

Longest Field Goal (Placed)—65 yds.—James T. Haxall (Princeton) v. Yale, 1882

Longest Field Goal (Drop-kick)—63 yds.—Mark Payne (Dakota Wesleyan) v. Spearfish Norman, 1915

Longest Punt—89 yds.—Albert Braga (San Franciso) v. Montana, 1937

OTHER RECORDS

Longest Run from a Scrimmage—115 yds. (from behind goal-line)—Wyllys Terry (Yale) v. Wesleyan, 1884

Longest Kick-off Return—110 yds.—Robert Hill (Army) v. New York University, 1907

Longest Punt Return—110 yds.—Oscar Morgan (Trinity) v. Wesleyan, 1904
                 110 yds.—Ben Boynton (William) v. Hamilton, 1920

Longest Scoring Forward Pass—67 yds.—John Woerner to Maynard Schultz (Oregon State) v. Nebraska 1935

MAJOR CONFERENCE CHAMPIONS

	Instituted	Most Titles	Wins Shared	
Ivy League	1872	Yale	18- 8	Between 1872-1954 (tie)
Big Ten	1896	Michigan	8-10	Between 1898-1950
Southern Conference	1933	Duke*	10- 0	Between 1933-1952
Southeastern Conference	1922‡	Alabama	7- 2	Between 1924-1953
†Missouri Valley Inter-collegiate A.A.	1907	Nebraska	22- 0	Between 1907-27 (in M.V.C.) to 1940
Missouri Valley	1928	Tulsa	10- 2	Between 1935 (tie)-1951
Southwest Conference	1923	Texas	8- 1	Between 1920-1953 (tie)
Border Conference	1931	Texas Tech.	11- 1	Between 1932-1954
Mountain States	1938	Utah	8- 1	Between 1938-1953
Pacific Coast	1916	S. California	10- 3	Between 1927 (tie)-1952

*Now in Atlantic Coast Conference formed in 1953.

†Operated as Big Six after 1928 and Big Seven after 1948 since when Oklahoma has won 7 straight.

‡Only independent of the Southern Conference from 1933.

ALL AMERICA SELECTIONS MOST-TIMES CHAMPION

The earliest All-America selections were in 1889, made by Casper Whitney of "The Week's Sport" and later of "Harper's Weekly."

There is no official national college championship. National supremacy has, however, been established by polls—from 1924-30 for the Rissman Trophy; from 1931-35 for the Knute Rockne Trophy and from 1936 by the Associated Press, supplemented in 1950 by the United Press.

The most successful college has been Notre Dame (7 times) in 1924, 1929-30, 1943, 1946-47, 1949.

LONGEST STREAKS

The longest winning streak is 48 straight by Yale from 1885 to 1889. The longest unbeaten streak is 63 games (59 won, 4 tied) by Washington from 1907 to 1917.

The earliest Bowl Game was that of January 1st, 1902, between Stanford and Michigan as an attraction for Pasadena's Tournament of Roses. The most successful teams have been:

	Instituted	Team	Titles	Years
Rose Bowl	1902	S. California	9	1923, 1930, 1932-33, 1939-40, 1944-45, 1953
Sugar Bowl	1935	Georgia Tech.	3	1944, 1953-54
Orange Bowl	1935	Georgia Tech.	3	1940, 1948, 1952
Cotton Bowl	1937	Texas	3	1943-44, 1946
		Rice	3	1938, 1950, 1954
Gator Bowl	1946	Maryland	2	1948, 1950

The most successful team in the whole post-season Bowl series have been the Trojans of Southern California with 9 wins in 12 appearances.

The oldest series is that between Princeton and Rutgers dating from 1869 or 7 years before the passing of the Springfield rules. The most regularly contested series is that between Lafayette and Lehigh who have closed 90 times since 1884.

The longest service coach was Amos Alonzo Stagg who served Springfield in 1890-91, Chicago from 1892 to 1932 and College of Pacific from 1933 to 1946, making a total of 57 years.

The most successful team of those who have been in representative football for over 50 years is Notre Dame with a winning percentage of 81.

ALL-TIME INDIVIDUAL SEASON RECORDS

Total Offense

(Collegiate)	2,400 yds.	Johnny Bright (Drake)	1950

Most Rushing and Passing Plays

(Collegiate)	400	Davey O'Brien (T.C.U.)	1937

Most Times Carried

(Collegiate)	270	Frank Goode (Hardin-Simmons)	1951
(Professional)	271	Eddie Price (New York)	1951

Yards Gained Rushing

(Collegiate)	1,570 yds.	Fred Wendt (Texas Mines)	1948
(Professional)	1,146 yds.	Steve Van Buren (Philadelphia)	1949

Highest Average Gain per Rush

(Collegiate)	11.51 yds.	Glenn Davis (Army)	1945

Most Passes Completed

(Collegiate)	159	Don Klosterman (Loyola, L. A.)	1951
(Professional)	210	Sammy Baugh (Washington)	1947

Most Touchdown Passes

(Collegiate)	23	'Babe' Pavilli (Kentucky)	1950
(Professional)	28	Sid Luckman (Chicago Bears)	1943

Highest Complete Percent

(Collegiate)	64.1%	Paul Larson (California) (125 from 195)	1954
(Professional)	56.7%	Sammy Baugh (Washington)	1945

Most Yards Gained Passing

(Collegiate)	2,005 yds.	Stan Heath (Nevada)	1948
(Professional)	2,938 yds.	Sammy Baugh (Washington)	1947

Most Passes Caught

(Collegiate)	57	Ed. Brown (Fordham).	1952
(Professional)	84	Tom Fears (Los Angeles)	1950

55. Art Luppino

56. Don Perry

57. Guy Zimmerman

58. Bobby Jones

Most Yards Gained on Catches

(Collegiate)	864 yds.	Ed. Barker (Washington State)	1951
(Professional)	1,495 yds.	Elroy Hirsch (Los Angeles)	1951

Most Touchdown Passes Caught

(Collegiate)	15	Vito Ragazzi (William & Mary)	1949
(Professional)	17	Don Hutson (Green Bay)	1942

Most Passes Intercepted By

(Collegiate)	13	George Shaw (Oregon)	1951

FOOTBALL (GAELIC)

EARLIEST REFERENCES

The game developed from inter-parish "free for alls" with the formation on November 1st, 1884, of the Gaelic Athletic Association in Thurles, Ireland.

MOST TITLES

The greatest number of All-Ireland Championships won by one team is the seventeen by Kerry (1903-53). The greatest number of successive wins is four by Wexford (1915-18) and four by Kerry (1929-32).

HIGHEST SCORE

The highest score in an All-Ireland final was in 1911 when Cork (6 goals, 6 points) beat Antrim (1 goal, 2 points).

MOST APPEARANCES

The most appearances in All-Ireland finals are by Dan O'Keefe (Kerry) with ten, of which seven were on the winning side.

GOLF

The earliest international match was on Leith Links in 1657 between James, Duke of York and John Paterson representing Scotland v. two English peers and resulted in a win for Scotland.

CLUBS

The oldest club of which there is written evidence is the Gentlemen Golfers (now the Honourable Company of Edinburgh Golfers) formed in March, 1744—10 years prior to the Institution of the Royal and Ancient. The oldest club in America is St. Andrew's, New York, founded in 1888.

Largest

The largest club in the world is the Johannesburg Country Club in South Africa with a membership of 4,500.

COURSES
Highest

The highest golf course in the world is that of the La Paz Golf Club, La Paz, Bolivia, 12,000 feet above sea level. Golf, however, has been played in Tibet at an altitude of over 16,000 feet.

Lowest

The lowest golf club in the world is at Kallia, on the north eastern shores of the Dead Sea, 1,250 feet below sea level.

Longest Hole

The two longest holes in the world are at Cohanzick Country Club, New Jersey, and the Hot Springs Golf Club, Arkansas, U.S.A., which both have 700 yard holes.

LOWEST SCORES
9 holes and
18 holes

The lowest recorded score on an 18 hole course is the 55 (15 under bogey) of A. E. Smith, the Woolacombe professional on his home course in England on January 1st, 1936. The course measured 4,248 yards and had a bogey 70. The detail was 4, 2, 3, 4, 2, 4, 3, 4, 3 = 29 out and 2, 3, 3, 3, 3, 2, 5, 4, 1 = 26 in. The last 9 were also a record low. The lowest recorded score on a long course (6,000 yards) is 58 by J. L. Black of Claremont, California, on June 18th, 1914.

The U. S. tournament play 18 holes record is 60 (30-30) by Al Brosch in the Texas Open at Brackenridge Park on February 10th, 1951 and 60 (31-29) by William Navy in the El Paso Open at the El Paso Country Club, Texas, on February 9th, 1952.

72 holes

The lowest recorded score on a first class course is 259 (21 under par) by Byron Nelson (U.S.A.) in the Seattle Open Championship at the par-70 6,200 yard long Broadmoor Course, Washington, on October 11-14, 1945, with rounds of 62, 68, 63, 66, and 259 by Ben Hogan (U.S.A.) in the Greenbriars Tournament at the Old White par-70 6,368 yard course at White Sulphur Springs on May 2-7, 1950, with 64, 64, 65, 66.

The lowest 72 holes in a national championship is 262 by Percy Alliss (G.B.) in the Italian Open Championship at San Remo in 1935 with 67, 66, 66, 63.

The most shots recorded for a hole in a professional tournament is variously 21 or 23 for the 17th by the 1927 American Open Champion T. Armour in the Shawnee Open Championship of that year.

FASTEST ROUNDS

With such variations in the lengths of courses, speed records even for rounds under par are of little comparative value. It is recorded that on September 20th, 1938, K. Bousfield completed the 18 holes of the Burnham Beeches course, England, in 91 minutes, scoring 69, one over the course record, to complete 6 rounds in 3 minutes outside a 12 hour target. In 1939 a large team of players propelled a ball round the famous Tam O'Shanter Course at Niles, Illinois, in 17 minutes 20 seconds, hence maintaining an average of 57.8 seconds per hole.

LONGEST DRIVE

In long-driving contests 280 yards is rarely surpassed. However, under freak conditions of wind, slope, parched or frozen surfaces or ricochet from a stone or flint much greater distances are achieved. The greatest recorded, and the only drive in excess of a ¼ mile, is that by E. C. Bliss (1863-1917), a 12 handicap player, at the 9th hole of the Old Course, Herne Bay, Kent, England, in August, 1913, at 445 yards. Bliss, 6 feet tall and over 182 lbs., drove to the back of the green on the left-handed dog-leg. The drive was measured by a government surveyor, Capt. Lloyd, who also measured the drop from tee to resting place as 57 feet.

U.S. ORIGINS

There is no evidence that the so-called Golf Clubs of the 18th century in Georgia and North and South Carolina were anything more than social clubs. The game was introduced to this country from Scotland by Joseph M. Fox of Philadelphia in 1885 but the initial nucleus of pioneers were those who, in April, 1888, laid out a six-hole course at North Broadway and Shonnard Place, New York. The United States Golf Association (U.S.G.A.) was formed from a meeting of December 22nd, 1894.

U.S. OPEN MOST TITLES

The United States Open was inaugurated in 1895 and decided, since 1898, on 72-hole medal scores.

There have been three 4-time winners:

William Anderson—1901, 331-85; 1903, 307-82; 1904, 303; 1905, 314.

Robert T. (Bobby) Jones, Jr. (amateur)—1923, 296-76; 1926, 293; 1929, 294-141; 1930, 287. See Photo No. 58, p. 192.

Ben Hogan—1948, 276; 1950, 287-69; 1951, 287; 1953, 283.

RECORD SCORES

The record low score is 276 (average 69) by Hogan at Los Angeles in 1948. The record high score is 331 (average 82 plus) by Anderson and Alex. Smith at Hamilton, Mass., from which Anderson won the play-off, 85-86. The greatest margin of victory was 9 strokes at Baltimore, Maryland, in 1899 by Willie Smith (315) over George Low, Val Fitzjohn and W. H. Way (all 326) and at Chevy Chase, Maryland, in 1921, by James Barnes (289) over Walter Hagen and Fred McLeod (both 298). The most closely contested title was that of 1931 at Toledo, Ohio. Billy Burke and George Von Elm tied at 292 and then both returned 149 in a 36-hole play-off. In the second 36-hole play-off, Burke won by a single stroke, 148-149, making 589 strokes against 590.

LOWEST SCORES

The lowest 18-hole round ever recorded by a woman golfer is 64 by Patty Berg (U.S.A.) at Richmond, Calif., on April 29th, 1952 with 30 out and 34 home, being 8 strokes under the men's par. The 72 hole women's record is 286 by Marlene Hagge at Virginia Beach, June 1956.

U.S. AMATEUR

The United States Amateur Championship was inaugurated in 1895 as a match-play tournament.

MOST TITLES

The only five-time winner has been:

Robert T. (Bobby) Jones, Jr.—1924 (9-6), 1925 (8-7), 1927 (8-7), 1928 (10-9), 1930 (8-7).

The greatest margin of victory has been 12 and 11 in the first championship at Newport, R. I., in 1895, when C. B. Macdonald beat C. E. Sands. Since then, the greatest margin has been 11 up and 9 to play at Mamaroneck, N. Y., when R. D. Chapman beat W. B. McCullough in 1940. Margins of 1 up on the last green have been registered in 1911, 1923, 1936, 1946, 1950, 1953 and most recently in 1954 when at Latrobe, Pa., Arnold Palmer beat Robert Sweeney.

The U.S. Public Links Championship was inaugurated in 1922 on a match-play basis. The only 3 time winner has been Carl F. Kauffmann who won in 1927 (1 up), 1928 (8-7) and 1929 (4-3).

U.S. PUBLIC
LINKS

The Masters Tournament, golf's top invitational event, staged annually at Augusta National Golf Club, Augusta, Georgia, was inaugurated in 1934. There have been two 3-time winners:

Jimmy Demaret—1940 (280), 1947 (281) and 1950 (283).

Sam Snead—1949 (282), 1952 (286) and 1954 (289).

The record score is 274 by Ben Hogan in 1953. The widest margin of victory of 8 strokes was in 1955 when Cary Middlecoff (279) beat Hogan (287).

MASTERS
TOURNAMENT

The Professional Golfer's Association annual championship was instituted in 1916. The only 5-time winner has been Walter Hagen in 1921 and 1924-7. The widest margin in the match-play event was in 1938 when Paul Runyan beat Sam Snead 8-7 at Shawnee-on-Delaware, Pennsylvania.

P.G.A.
CHAMPIONSHIP

The record total for the P.G.A. money-winning title was set at $65,891.24 by Bob Toski in 1954.

PRIZE MONEY

The Ryder Cup arose from an informal team match between American and British professionals in England in 1926. The first of the formal biennial series (4 foursomes and 8 singles) was in 1927 at Worcester, Mass., Country Club. The United States has won 8 of the 10 contests with the widest margin of victory 11-1 at Portland, Oregon, in 1947. Great Britain's best win was that of 7-5 at Moortown, England, in 1929.

RYDER CUP

The Walker Cup was established in 1922 between United States and British amateurs. After 1924, it has been contested biennially in alternate countries with the U. S. winning all but 1 of the 15 contests. The widest margin of victory was 11-1 at Chicago Golf Club, Wheaton, Ill., in 1928 and the narrowest 6½-5½ in 1923 and 1926 both at St. Andrews, Scotland. Britain's win was by 7½-4½ at St. Andrews in 1938.

WALKER CUP

The U. S. Women's amateur championship was inaugurated in 1895 as a medal-play contest. Since 1896, it has been a match play test with Mrs. Glenna Collett Vare winning 6 times in 1922, 1925, 1928-30 and 1935. The greatest margin of victory was in 1928 when Glenna Collett defeated the 1932-34 winner, Virginia Van Wie, 13 and 12 at Hot Springs, Virginia.

U.S. WOMEN'S
AMATEUR

The U.S. Women's Open was instituted in 1946 by the Women's P.G.A. The only 3-time winner has been Mrs. Mildred Didrikson Zaharias in 1948, 1950 and 1954. The low scoring record of 284 was set by Louise Suggs at Philadelphia in 1952.

U.S. WOMEN'S
OPEN

The Curtis Cup was presented in 1932 for competition between the women amateurs of the U. S. and Britain. The series consists of 3 foursomes and 6 twosomes staged every two years in alternate countries. The U. S. has won 6 of the 9 contests with 4½-4½ tie at Gleneagles, Scotland, in 1936. The British Isles won 5-4 at Muirfield, Scotland, in 1952, and 5-4 at Sandwich, England, in 1956.

CURTIS CUP

The largest entry for the U. S. Open Championship is 1,411 in 1948. The record for the U. S. Amateur Championship is 1,220, also in 1948.

LARGEST
ENTRIES

The world's largest tournament was the "Morning Post" Tournament of 1938 organized in Great Britain at 1,056 clubs for 50,000 players.

LARGEST
TOURNAMENT

The largest prize fund in the world is the $50,000 for the winner of the Tam O'Shanter Country Club tournament held annually in Illinois.

LARGEST
PRIZE FUND

The lowest 9 holes ever scored in the U. S. Amateur is 30 by Frances Ouimet on September 14th, 1932.

AMATEUR

Len Richardson (South Africa) played round the 6,248 yard Mowbray Course, Cape Town, South Africa, in November, 1931, in 31 minutes 22 seconds.

SUBSTITUTE
FASTEST ROUND

The greatest prize money from a single meeting is the $22,500 (£8,035) won by Lloyd Mangrum during the 1948 Tam O'Shanter tournaments.

Highest Prize
Money

MOST TITLES

The most titles won in the world's major championships are as follows:—

British Open	H. Vardon	6	1896-98-99, 1903, 1911-14.
British Amateur	John Ball	7	1888-90-92-94-99, 1907-10.
American Open	W. Anderson	4	1901-03-04-05.
	R. T. Jones	4	1923-26-29-30.
American Amateur	R. T. Jones	5	1924-25-27-28-30.
British Ladies'	Miss C. Leitch	4	1914-20-21-26.
	Miss J. Wethered	4	1922-24-25-29.
	(now Lady Heathcoat-Amory)		

LONGEST
HOLE IN ONE

The longest hole ever driven in one is the par four (425 yards) ninth hole at Hillcrest Golf Club, Winston-Salem, North Carolina, U.S.A., by Cardwell, in 1939. This green has many times been driven in one in dry weather particularly with, as on this occasion, a strong following wind.

Most
Holes in One

The greatest number of holes in one in a career is 23 by C. T. Chevalier between June, 1918 and 1954.

There is no recorded instance of a golfer performing three consecutive holes in one but there are three cases of aces being achieved in two consecutive holes:—

A. Duthie	Vancouver Golf and Country Club, Canada	1911
Cpl. R. Halverty	Recreation Park, Long Beach, California, U.S.A.	Aug. 1945
W/Cdr. T. R. Vickers	Changi Golf Course, Singapore	June 1950

Youngest
and Oldest

The youngest golfer recorded to have shot a hole in one was Peter Toogood, aged 8, at the 7th (110 yards) at Kingston Beach Golf Club. The oldest golfer to have performed the feat is T. S. South, aged 91, at the seventh (110 yards) at Highcliffe Castle Golf Club, Hampshire, England, in 1952.

The oft-repeated claim for a 435 yard hole in one in 1953 at the first hole of the Hermitage Country Club, Richmond, Virginia, U.S.A., was in fact achieved by a ball-testing driving machine built by the Achushnet Co.

GYMNASTICS

EARLIEST
REFERENCES

Gymnastics were widely practiced in Greece during the period of the ancient Olympic Games (776 B.C. to 392 A.D.). They were not, however, revived until c.1780.

MOST OLYMPIC
WINS

Italy has won most Olympic team titles with four victories in 1912, 1920, 1924 and 1932.

The most individual gold medals have been won by Anton Heida (U.S.A.) with four (All-round title, long horse, side horse and horizontal bar) all in 1904. At Helsinki in 1952 Viktor Tchoukarine (U.S.S.R.) won three gold medals for Combined Exercises, Pommelled Horse and Long Horse and two silver medals for Parallel Bars and Rings.

ROPE CLIMBING

The American Amateur Athletic Union records are tantamount to world records: 20 feet (hands alone) 2.8 seconds, Don Perry (U.S.A.) at Champaign, Ill., on April 3rd, 1954 (See Photo No. 56, p. 192), and Sandford Werner (U.S.A.) at Detroit, May 4th, 1951. 25 feet (hands alone), 4.7 seconds, Garvin S. Smith at Los Angeles, April 19th, 1947.

CHINNING
THE BAR

It is recorded that the professionals A. Cutler (England) achieved twelve successive chins with one arm in 1878 and A. Lewis (England) 78 chins with both arms in 1913.

GREATEST
TUMBLER

The greatest tumbler of all-time is Dick Browning (U.S.A.) who in April 1954 at Santa Barbara, California, made a backward somersault over a 7 feet 6 inch bar. In his unique repertoire is a "Round-off," backward handspring, backward somersault with half-twist, walk-out tinsica tigna round-off, backward handspring, double backward somersault.

LARGEST
GYMNASIUM

The world's largest gymnasium is Yale University's Payne Whitney Gymnasium at New Haven, Connecticut, U.S.A., completed in 1932 and valued at $18 million. The building, known as the "Cathedral of Muscle," has nine stories with wings of five stories each. It is equipped with four basketball courts, three rowing tanks, twenty-eight squash courts, twelve handball courts, a roof jogging track and twenty-five yard by forty-two foot swimming pool on the first floor and a fifty-five yards long pool on the third floor.

MOST TITLES

The greatest number of titles won in any division of the A.A.U. Gymnastic Championships (instituted 1885) is 11 by J. D. Gleason on the Rings, 1908-15, 1919-20, 1922.

The lightest winner ever recorded was Kitchener who won the Chester Cup on "Red Deer" in 1844 at 3 stone 7 lb. He died in 1872.

Sir Gordon Richards (G.B.) won the last race on October 3rd, 1933, all the six next day and the first five on October 5th—total twelve. The U. S. record for one day is 7 winners in 8 races by Joe Sylvester at Ravenna Park, Ohio, on October 18th, 1930.

Dolly Byers (U.S.A.) starting in 1916 rode in 446 steeplechases and won 152 races.

"Devineress", a three-year-old, travelled the 5 furlongs of the Belmont Handicap at Epsom, England, on June 2nd, 1933, in 54.6 seconds = 41.2 m.p.h.

In eight races at the National Hunt meeting at Worcester, England, on March 16th, 1955, 361 horses were engaged.

The most in a flat race meeting was the seven races at Nottingham, England, on October 11th, 1941, when 346 horses were engaged.

(Flat) 214 in seven races at Newmarket, England, June 15th, 1915.
(National Hunt) 158 in six races at Wetherby, England, January 20th, 1951.

66 (a world record) in the Grand National on March 22nd, 1929, Aintree, Eng.
58 in the Lincolnshire Handicap on March 13th, 1948, is the flat racing record.

Instituted in 1837 (under present conditions in 1839), the Grand National is a steeplechase for six year olds and over. The course at Aintree, near Liverpool, England, is 4 miles 856 yards and over 30 jumps.

No horse has won three times but six share the record of two wins:

Peter Simple	1849 and 1853	The Colonel	1869 and 1870
Abd-el-Kader	1850 and 1851	Manifesto	1897 and 1899
The Lamb	1868 and 1871	Reynoldstown	1935 and 1936

Poethlyn won in 1919 having won the war-time Gatwick race in 1918.

Manifesto was entered eight times between 1895 and 1904—winning twice, coming third three times and fourth once.

Golden Miller, a seven-year-old ridden by G. Wilson, carrying 12 stone 2 lb. owned by Miss D. Paget, won by 5 lengths from a field of 30 with odds of 8 to 1 in 9 minutes 20.4 seconds (28.82 m.p.h.) in 1934.

The "Open Ditch", the 15th Jump, is 5 feet 2 inches high, 3 feet 9 inches wide. The ditch on take-off side is 6 feet wide, guard rail in front of ditch 1 foot 6 inches in height.

The largest field was the 66 starters in 1929 and the smallest 6 in the inaugural race of 1837.

The longest recorded horse race was one of 1,200 miles in Portugal, won by a horse Emir bred from Egyptian-bred Blunt Arab stock. The holder of the world's record for long distance racing and speed is Champion Crabbet who covered 300 miles in 52 hours 33 minutes carrying 17½ stone in 1920.

The highest recorded odds secured by a backer was the 60,640 : 1 secured on June 15th, 1951, by Mr. Pratley, of Coventry, England, on a 1s. (19c) each-way accumulator which built up to £3,032 ($8,489). His wins were on "Guerrier," "Val d'Assa," "Pun" and "Donore."

The world record odds on a "double" are 24,741 : 1 secured by Mr. Montague Harry Parker of Windsor, England, for £1 ($2.80) each-way "double" on "Ivernia" and "Golden Sparkle".

The American Pari-Mutuel record pay-off is the $941.75 : 1 on "Wishing Ring" at Laytonia, Kentucky, in 1912.

The shortest ever odds, quoted on any race horse is the 100 : 1 on, on the American horse "Man O'War" on three separate occasions in 1920.

HORSESHOE PITCHING

ORIGINS

Throwing quoits for accuracy as opposed to length was a sport originating in the Middle East in or before the 3rd Century B.C. The fashioning of horse shoes was an art first employed about the 5th Century A.D. In the United States horseshoe pitching was known as a sport before the Colonial War of Liberation (1812).

EARLIEST CLUB

The first organized club dates from 1900 and was formed at Long Beach, Calif. The earliest governing body for the sport was the Grand League of American Horseshoe Pitchers Association formed on May 16th, 1914, at Kansas City, Kansas.

The first tournament with competition open to the world was at Bronson, Kansas, in 1909. The first official World Championship Tournament was at Kansas City, Kansas, on Ocober 23-24, 1915.

MOST TITLES

The greatest number of title wins is 14 by Frank Jackson of Iowa, from 1909-1915 (10 unofficial titles) and official champion 1915, 1920, 1921 and 1926.

The greatest number of official world titles is 7 by the Mexican Fernando Isais of Los Angeles, Calif., who won in 1941, 1947-1952. The youngest world champion was Harold Falor of Akron, Ohio, who won at St. Petersburg, Fla., on February 24th, 1923, aged 15.

HIGHEST SCORES

The record ringer percentage in a world championship final is 86.3% by the 6 time champion Ted Allen of Alhambra, Calif. In a tie at Des Moines, Iowa, on August 25th, 1940, Theodore 'Ted' Allen of Boulder, Colo., and Guy Zimmermann of Danville, Calif., both scored 88.4%. Zimmermann set a record of a perfect game (100%) at Milwaukee in 1948. See Photo No. 57, p. 192. The record for consecutive ringers is 67 by Ray Gatewood at the Exposition Park Horseshoe Club, Los Angeles, on July 7th, 1946.

HURLING

EARLIEST REFERENCE

A game of very ancient origin, hurling only became standardized with the formation of the Gaelic Athletic Association in Thurles, Ireland, on November 1st, 1884.

MOST TITLES

The greatest number of All-Ireland Championships won by one team is twenty by Cork (1890-1954). The greatest number of successive wins is four by Cork (1941-44).

HIGHEST SCORE

The highest score in an All-Ireland final was in 1896 when Tipperary (8 goals, 14 points) beat Dublin (0 goals, 4 points).

MOST APPEARANCES

The most appearances in All-Ireland finals is nine by Christie Ring (Cork) of which eight were on the winning side.

ICE HOCKEY

The game probably originated in 1855 at Kingston, Ontario, Canada, but Montreal and Halifax also lay claims as the originators. Twenty-two countries were members of the international body—Ligue Internationale de Hockey sur Glace—at the time of the last Winter Olympic Games at Cortina, 1956.

MOST OLYMPIC CHAMPIONSHIPS

Canada has won the Olympic title six times—that is at every Winter Olympic celebration except in 1936 when Great Britain won at Garmisch-Partenkirchen, Germany.

STANLEY CUP RECORDS

(This cup became emblematic of world professional team supremacy several years after the first contest in 1893.)

MOST WINS

Eight times by the Montreal Canadiens: 1916, 1924, 1930, 1931, 1944, 1946, 1953, 1956.

LONGEST MATCH

2 hours 56 minutes 30 seconds at Montreal when Detroit Red Wings eventually beat Montreal Maroons 1-0 in the sixth period of overtime.

MOST GOALS

(a) By one side: 11, when Montreal Canadiens beat Toronto.

(b) Aggregate: 13, when Montreal Canadiens beat Toronto 10-3 on March 29th, 1945.

Most cup goals in a season: Maurice Richard of Montreal Canadiens—54 goals.

The all time N.H.L. scoring record is held by Maurice Richard (Montreal Canadiens) who had scored 422 goals entering the 1956 season. His single season record was 50 goals in 1944-45. The individual goal scoring record in one game is 7 by Joe Malone of the Quebec Bulldogs v. Toronto St. Patricks on January 31st, 1920.

59. Lester Stoefen

60. Jack Kelly

61. Ralph Miller

62. Sonja Henie

N.H.L. RECORDS
MOST GOALS

The most goals scored by one side is 15 when Detroit Red Wings beat New York Rangers 15-0 at Detroit on January 23rd, 1945. The most goals (aggregate) was 21 when Montreal Canadiens beat Toronto 14-7 on January 10th, 1920.

FASTEST
SCORING

The fastest scoring record is eight goals in 4 minutes 52 seconds by Toronto v. N. Y. Americans when winning 8-5 on March 19th, 1938. The individual record for 3 goals is 21 seconds by Bill Mosienko (Chicago) v. N. Y. Rangers on March 23rd, 1952.

MOST WORLD
TITLES

The F.I.H.G. (Fédération Internationale de Hockey sur Glace) World Championships were instituted in 1930. Most titles have been won by Canada with 10 victories in 1930-31, 1934-35, 1937-39, 1950-51 and 1955. The United States only win was in 1933.

MOST N.H.L.
TITLES

The most N.H.L. titles (instituted 1917) have been won by the Detroit Red Wings. The first victory was in 1933-34 while that of 1954-55 was their 11th.

MOST COLLEGIATE
TITLES

Michigan University has won 5 National Collegiate titles with wins in 1948, 1951-53 and 1955. The highest scoring final was in 1950 when Colorado C. defeated Boston University 13-4.

ICE SKATING

ORIGINS

The earliest reference to ice skating is that of a Danish writer dated 1134. The earliest English account of 1180 refers to skates made of bone. Metal blades date from probably c.1600. The oldest skating club is the Edinburgh Skating Club formed in 1642. The earliest artificial ice rink in the world was built in Chelsea, London, in 1876.

LARGEST RINK

The world's largest artificial ice rink is the Pan-Pacific Auditorium, Los Angeles, California, U.S.A. It has an ice area of 300 x 100 feet.

SPEED RECORDS

Men	500 m.	40.8	Jurij Sergyer (U.S.S.R.)	Alma Ata	Jan. 19, 1955
	10,000 m.	16 32.6	Hjalmar Andersen (Norway)	Hamar	Feb. 10, 1952

MOST TITLES

The greatest number of world speed skating titles (instituted 1893) won by any skater is five by O. Mathisen (Norway) 1908-09, 1912-14, and Clas. Thunberg (Finland) 1923, 1925, 1928-29, 1931. The most Ladies' titles is thre by Mlle. M. Isakova (U.S.S.R.).

MOST U.S.
SPEED TITLES

The U. S. Outdoor Speed-Skating Championships were introduced in 1891. The greatest number of titles have been won by Ken Bartholomew (Minneapolis) with 10 in 1939, 1941-42, 1947, 1950-55.

FIGURE SKATING

The greatest number of world figure skating titles (instituted 1896) is ten by U. Salchov between 1901 and 1911. The women's record is ten titles by Frk. Sonja Henie (Norway), (1927-36). See Photo No. 62, p. 201.

The most world titles by an American is 5 straight by Richard Button (1948-1952).

MOST U.S.
FIGURE TITLES

The greatest number of U. S. figure-skating titles (instituted 1914) have been won by Roger Turner (1928-34) and Richard Button (1946-1952) each with 7 straight. The most girl's titles have been won by Maribel Y. Vinson with 9 from 1928-33 and 1935-37.

MOST OLYMPIC
TITLES

The greatest number of gold medals won is 4 by C. Thunberg of Finland in speed skating with 500 metres 1924 (tie), 1,500 metres 1924 and 1928 and 5,000 metres 1924.

The most won in a single celebration is 3 by Ivan Ballangrad of Norway for the 500; 5,000 and 10,000 metres in 1936 and by Hjalmar Andersen of Norway for the 1,500; 5,000 and 10,000 metres in 1952.

The greatest number of figure-skating gold medals is 3 by Gillis Grafström of Sweden in 1920, 1924 and 1928 and 3 by Frk. Sonja Henie of Norway in 1928, 1932 and 1936.

LACROSSE

ORIGINS

Lacrosse is derived from the Canadian-Indian mob game of baggataway. The earliest reference to white settlers playing the game is in 1839.

MOST TITLES

The leading lacrosse championship is the U. S. Intercollegiate Lacrosse Association Championship instituted in 1881. Most titles have been won by Johns Hopkins of Baltimore, Maryland, with 17 in 1906-09, 1911, 1913, 1915 and 1919 (all-tied) and in 1923, 1926-28, 1941, 1947-48, 1949 (tie) and 1950.

ORIGIN

'Bowling on the green' has been traced back to, at least, the thirteenth century in England. The Southampton Town Bowling Club was formed in 1299. Public bowling greens were established in London in 1455 but the game soon fell into disrepute.

In the United States, the game is recorded in Connecticut and Massachusetts as early as 1615. The lease of ground for lawn bowling at the lower end of Broadway in New York City was dated 1732.

The American Lawn Bowling Association was admitted to the International Bowling Board in 1938.

MOST TITLES

The only two-time winner of the National Open Singles Trophy is Richard Folkins of Redlands, California, who won in 1950 and 1954. The only three-time winners of the Doubles Championship (California Trophy) has been Hugh Folkins and Richard Folkins (Skip) of California who won in 1950, 1952 and 1954.

MODERN PENTATHLON

Modern Pentathlon (Riding, Fencing, Shooting, Swimming and Running) was inaugurated into the Olympic Games at Stockholm in 1912.

OLYMPIC TITLES

Swedes have won 7 of the 8 titles contested but no individual has retained a title. The highest United States placings have been silver medals by Lt. (now Col.) Charles L. Leonard in 1936 at Berlin and by Major (now Lt. Col.) George B. Moore in 1948 in London. Individual sport winners from the U. S. teams have been:

1932—Fencing—Lt. (now Brig. Gen.) R. W. Mayo

1936—Fencing—Col. F. R. Weber
   Shooting—Lt. (now Col.) Charles L. Leonard (200 possible in pistol competition)

1952—Running—Private 1st Class Thad McArthur

MOST WORLD TITLES

The only pentathlete to have retained a world modern pentathlon title is Lars Hall (Sweden), the 1952 Olympic Champion, who won in Bern, Switzerland in 1950 and again at Halsingborg, Sweden, in 1951.

MOTOR CYCLING

OLDEST RACE

The oldest motorcycle races in the world are the A.-C.U. Tourist Trophy series, first held on a 15¾-mile course in the Isle of Man in 1907 and still run in the Island, on the 37¾-mile "Mountain" circuit and the 10¾-mile Clypse circuit.

Motorcycling developed as a sport in the United States in 1914 and the American Motorcycle Association was formed in 1921.

LONGEST CIRCUIT

The "Mountain" circuit, over which the two main T.T. races are run, is the longest used for a "classic" motorcycle race.

FASTEST CIRCUIT

The fastest circuit is the 4¾-mile Hockenheim track near Heidelberg in Germany, lapped by G. E. Duke on a 500 c.c. Italian Gilera at 123.8 m.p.h. in May, 1955.

Of the Grand Prix races, the French, run over the 5.2 mile Rheims circuit, is the fastest, Duke having lapped there in 1955 at 116.7 m.p.h. The Senior T.T. in the Isle of Man is the longest, covering seven laps of the "Mountain" course (264¼ miles) and is generally regarded as the most difficult.

The 2⅜-mile Barcelona circuit over which the Spanish Grand Prix is run is the most fatiguing, however, for it consists almost entirely of corners and the 500 c.c. race covers no fewer than 53 laps. The lap record, held in 1955 by C. Bandirola, on an Italian M.V.-Agusta, stands at 69.5 m.p.h.

MOST SUCCESS-FUL RIDERS

With 10 T.T. victories between 1923 and 1939, the Irishman S. Woods has a record which has still to be beaten in the Isle of Man.

Since 1949, the Fédération Internationale Motocycliste has conducted World Championships. Duke, five times a T.T. winner, has won the 500 c.c. championship four times and the 350 c.c. title twice, giving him the highest total of successes. He and the sidecar driver, E. S. Oliver are the only men to have held one title for three consecutive seasons.

MOST SUCCESS-FUL MACHINES

Since he first T.T. was run, the British Norton factory has won 32 races in the series, more than any other make. In the past few years, however, the Italian Gilera has been outstanding, with five 500 c.c. Championship wins out of seven.

U.S. RECORDS

Half-Mile Dirt Track—45 c.i. Motor

    5 miles 70.58 mph—Don Hutchinson, Belleville, Kan., H-D, Aug. 29, 1954
   10 miles 66.99 mph—Buck Brigance, Weaverville, N. C., H-D, Sept. 28, 1952

Mile Dirt Track—45 c.i. Motor

    5 miles 85.81 mph—Kenny Eggers, Springfield, Ill., H-D, Aug. 19, 1951
   10 miles 87.89 mph—Joe Leonard, San Mateo, Calif., H-D, Sept. 11, 1954
   25 miles 88.36 mph—Bobby Hill, Springfield, Ill., Indian, Aug. 19, 1951
   50 miles 76.42 mph—Lester Hillbish, Syracuse, N. Y., Indian, Aug. 26, 1939

Dirt Track Speedway—45 c.i. Motor

  100 miles 92.52 mph—Brad Andres, Langhorne, Pa., H-D, April 9, 1955

Straightaway One Mile—Both Directions Class C

   $7\frac{1}{2}$ c.i. 71.706 mph—Bobby Michael, Rosamund Dry Lake, Calif., N.S.U., July 18, 1954
(100 c.c.)
   15 c.i. 92.378 mph—Bobby Michael, Rosamund Dry Lake, Calif., N.S.U., July 18, 1954
   40 c.i. 132.16 mph—Blackie Bullock, Bonneville, Utah, Triumph, Sept. 13, 1951
   61 c.i. 147.58 mph—Marty Dickerson—Bonneville, Utah, Vincent, June 9, 1953
   74 c.i. 128.11 mph—Denny Grammar, Bonneville, Utah, H-D, March 9, 1954

Straightaway One Mile—Both Directions Class A

   15 c.i. 104.68 mph—Mike Ward, Bonneville, Utah, Triumph, Feb. 9, 1954
   40 c.i. 192.30 mph—John Allen, Bonneville, Utah, Triumph, Sept. 25, 1955
   61 c.i. 160.739 mph—Rollie Free, Bonneville, Utah, Vincent, Oct. 9, 1953
   74 c.i. 139.49 mph—Robert Kucera, Bonneville, Utah, H-D, Sept. 9, 1953

Non Competitive Record Against Time

   24 hours—1,825.2 miles—Fred J. Ham, Maroc Dry Lakes, Calif., H-D, April 8, 1937
   H-D—Harley-Davidson

WORLD
RECORDS

    The fastest speed ever attained on a motor cycle is the 210.64 m.p.h. achieved by Wilhelm Herz (Germany) on a 500 c.c. N.S.U. on Bonneville Salt Flats, Utah, on August 4th, 1956.

    The fastest speed achieved with the smallest recognized engine is $93\frac{1}{2}$ m.p.h. for the flying kilometre achieved by H. Baumm on a 49 c.c. N.S.U. near Munich on May 10th, 1955.

    The longest listed motorcycle record is the 30,998 miles in 19 days at an average speed of 68 m.p.h. set by a group of French Army officers on a Gnôme et Rhône "Yacco" machine at Montlhéry from June 19th to July 8th, 1939.

MOTOR RACING

OLDEST RACE

    The oldest motor race in the world still being regularly run is the R.A.C. Tourist Trophy—first held in the Isle of Man in 1905. It is currently run on the Dundrod course outside Belfast, Northern Ireland.

    The oldest Continental races are the French Grand Prix and the Targa Florio, which both began in 1906.

LONGEST
CIRCUIT

    The longest motor racing circuit in the world is the Mille Miglia which has been run in Italy since 1927. The 1955 course measured 992.37 miles, starting and finishing at Brescia. The record average speed attained on the course, which is held on public roads is 97.96 m.p.h. by Stirling Moss (G.B.) driving a Mercedes Benz in 1955. On the last 85 miles of the race from Cremona to Brescia, Moss averaged 123 m.p.h.

FASTEST
CIRCUITS

    The fastest motor racing circuit in the world is the Avus track near Berlin. In 1937, Rosemeyer (Germany) in a 6 litre Auto Union lapped at a record speed of 171 m.p.h.

TOUGHEST
CIRCUITS

    The Targa Florio is acknowledged to be the most difficult and arduous circuit. Held in Sicily on the Madonie Circuit it is 45 miles in length and over the eight laps of the race it involves the negotiation of approximately 6,800 corners, over severe mountain gradients and narrow rough roads. The lap record is 57.82 m.p.h. by E. Castellotti (Italy) in a sports Lancia in 1955.

The most difficult Grand Prix circuit is generally regarded to be the Monaco, run through the streets of Monte Carlo. It is 1.9 miles in length and has ten pronounced corners and several sharp changes of gradient. The race is run over 100 laps and involves on average some 1,500 gear changes. The record lap stands at 68.70 m.p.h. by J. M. Fangio (Argentina) in a Mercedes Benz in 1955.

The most important sports car race is the Le Mans 24 hours Grand Prix d'Endurance held on the 8.35 mile Sarthe circuit in France. The longest distance ever covered is 2,594.58 miles by M. Hawthorn and I. Bueb in a Jaguar in 1955. Their average speed for the whole distance was 107.072 m.p.h. The fastest speed ever recorded in the race was 181.57 m.p.h. over the measured kilometre by J. M. Fangio in a Mercedes Benz in 1955.

Since its inception in 1923 it has been won five times by Bentley (U.K.) cars in 1924-27-28-29 and 1930 (more than any other single make).

LONGEST AND FASTEST

Based on the World Drivers' Championships inaugurated in 1950, the most success-ful driver is J. M. Fangio (Argentine) who has won four times, 1951-4-5-6.

MOST SUCCESSFUL DRIVERS

Before the inception of the Drivers' Championship there was no official basis for comparison, but of major races Nuvolari (Italy) won 42 between 1927-46, A. Ascari 45 between 1947-55, R. Caracciola (Germany) 27 between 1926-39, J. M. Fangio 35 between 1949-55.

The most successful land speed record breaker was Sir Malcolm Campbell. He broke the record nine times between 1924, with 146.16 m.p.h. in a Sunbeam and 1935 with 301.13 m.p.h. in the Rolls Royce engined "Bluebird."

LAND SPEED RECORDS

The land speed record now stands at 394.196 m.p.h. achieved by John Cobb. (See page 145.)

The longest duration world record is the 300,000 kilometre (186,410 miles) covered in 133 days 17 hours 37 minutes 38.64 seconds, an average of 58.08 m.p.h. achieved at Montlhéry, France, in March-July 1933 by a Citröen car with a team of eight drivers.

The world speed record for compression ignition engined cars is 169.3 m.p.h. by Dana Fuller, Jr., in the Fuller Diesel 6/71 on September 11th, 1953, at Bonneville Salt Beds, U.S.A.

The slowest international class record is the "J" class (up to 350 c.c.) 2,000 kilometres (1,242.7 miles) held by a Citröen-Barbot at 52.8 m.p.h. and achieved at Montlhéry in 1953.

The earliest celebration of the ancient Olympic Games of which there is a record is that of July 776 B.C. The ancient Games were terminated by decree of the Roman Emperor Theodosius in 394 A.D.

OLYMPIC GAMES

The Olympic Games of the modern era were inaugurated in Athens in April, 1896.

Celebrations have been allocated as follows:—

I	Athens	1896	IX	Amsterdam	1928
II	Paris	1900	X	Los Angeles	1932
III	St. Louis	1904	XI	Berlin	1936
	†Athens	1906	XII	*Tokyo, then Helsinki	1940
IV	London	1908	XIII	*London	1944
V	Stockholm	1912	XIV	London	1948
VI	*Berlin	1916	XV	Helsinki	1952
VII	Antwerp	1920	XVI	Melbourne	1956
VIII	Paris	1924	XVII	Rome	1960

*Cancelled due to World Wars.   †Intercalated Celebration.

The Winter Olympics were inaugurated in 1924 and have been allocated as follows:—

I	Chamonix	1924	V	St. Moritz	1948
II	St. Moritz	1928	VI	Oslo	1952
III	Lake Placid	1932	VII	Cortina, Italy	1956
IV	Garmisch-Partenkirchen	1936	VIII	Squaw Valley	1960

PIGEON RACING

EARLIEST REFERENCES

Pigeon Racing was the natural development of the use of homing pigeons for the carrying of messages—a quality utilized in the ancient Olympic Games (776 B.C.-392 A.D.). The earliest major long-distance race was from Crystal Palace, South London, in 1871. The earliest recorded occasion on which 500 miles was flown in a day was by "Motor" (owned by G. P. Pointer of Alexander Park Racing Club) which released from Thurso, Scotland, on June 30th, 1896, covered the 501 miles at a speed of 1,454 yards per minute (49½ m.p.h.).

LONGEST DURATION

The greatest recorded homing flight was that by a pigeon, owned by the Duke of Wellington, which was released from a sailing ship off the Ichabo Islands, West Africa, on June 1st, 1845. It dropped dead a mile from its loft at Nine Elms, London, 55 days later, having flown an airline route of 5,400 miles but an actual flight of probably 7,000 miles to avoid the Sahara Desert.

BEST SPEEDS

The fastest speed recorded in any race is 2,744 yards per minute (93.55 m.p.h.) by H. Mussen's winner of the 1914 Malahide (Ulster Federation) Race over 80 miles.

The world's 24 hour record is 751 miles by Edfeldt and Wahlström's winner of the 1951 Lulea Race to Ystrad, Sweden—liberated 1 a.m., flying time 15 hours 52 minutes, velocity 47.25 m.p.h.

POLO

EARLIEST GAMES

There is record of polo being played in Persia in 525 B.C. though the name is derived from the Tibetan word *pula*. The game was introduced into England from India in 1869 and the earliest match was that on Hounslow Heath, West of London, in July, 1871, between 9th Lancers and the 10th Hussars. The first All-Ireland Cup match was at Phoenix Park, Dublin, in 1878. The earliest international match, England v. America, was in 1886.

The game is played on the largest pitch of any ball game in the world. A ground measures 300 yards long by 160 yards wide with side boards or, as in India, 200 yards wide without boards.

HIGHEST HANDICAP

The highest handicap based on eight 7½ minute "chukkers" is 10 goals. The top handicap players currently are R. Cavanagh and E. Alberdi in Argentina; S. Igleheart, C. Smith and R. Skene (Australia) in U.S.A. all at 10.

HIGHEST SCORE

The highest score in an international match is 23 goals in the second match of the 1930 Westchester Cup at Meadow Brook, U.S.A., in which U.S.A. won, 14 goals to England's 9.

HIGHEST PRICED PONY

The highest price ever paid for a polo pony is $22,000 (£7,600) for Mr. L. Lacey's Argentine pony "Jupiter" by Mr. Sandford in America in 1928.

U.S. CHAMPIONSHIPS

The United States Championships were inaugurated in 1904. The team with most victories is Meadow Brook with 7 in 1914 (as Magpies), 1916, 1919-20, 1923, 1928 and 1953. The highest number of goals in a final was 25 in 1933 when Aurora defeated Greentree 14-11. The greatest margin of victory was 13 goals when Tampleton beat Greentree 16-3 in 1932.

RODEO

ORIGIN

Rodeo came into being with the early days of the American cattle industry. The earliest references to the sport are from Santa Fe, New Mexico, in 1847.

MOST WORLD TITLES

All Around Champion	3	Gene Rambo (Shandon, Cal.) 1946, 1948-49
Bareback	3	Eddy Akridge (Pampas, Texas) 1953-55
Saddle Bronc	5	Casey Tibbs (Ft. Pierre, S. Dak.) 1949, 1951-54
Calf-Roping	7	Toots Mansfield (Bandera, Texas) 1939-41, 1943, 1945, 1948, 1950
Bull-Riding	5	Dick Griffiths (Scottsdale, Ariz.) 1939-42, 1946
Steer-Wrestling	6	Homer Pettigrew (Chandler, Ariz.) 1940, 1942-45, 1948

The highest total of titles is 8 by Casey Tibbs who has won 5 saddle bronc titles (as above), the 1951 bareback title and the all-around cowboy titles of 1951 and 1955. Tibbs also holds the record for the highest amount of winnings in a year with $42,065 in 1955.

Records for timed events, such as calf-roping and steer-wrestling, are meaningless, because of the widely varying conditions due to the size of arenas and amount of start given the stock. The fastest time recorded in 1955 for roping a calf was 10.0 seconds by Marlin Stephenson of Mobridge, South Dakota, and the fastest time for overcoming a steer was 2.4 seconds by James Bynum of Marietta, Oklahoma.

TIME RECORDS

The standard required time to stay on in bareback events is 8 seconds and in saddle bronc riding 10 seconds. In the now obsolete ride to a finish events, rodeo riders have been recorded to have survived 90 minutes or more until the horse quit bucking altogether.

ROWING

The earliest established sculling race is the Doggett's Coat and Badge which was first rowed on August 1st, 1715, on a course from London Bridge to Chelsea on the River Thames, England, and is still being rowed every year over the same course, under the administration of the Fishmongers' Company.

OLDEST RACE

The annual regatta at Henley-on-Thames was inaugurated on March 26th, 1839.

HENLEY ROYAL
REGATTA

The course, except in 1923, has been 1 mile 550 yards since 1839. Prior to 1922 there were two slight angles. Classic Records:—(Year in brackets, date instituted)

			Min. Secs.
Grand Challenge (1839)	8 oars	Leander Club 1952	6 : 38
Ladies' Plate (1846)	8 oars	Lady Margaret 1949	6 : 43
Thames Challenge (1868)	8 oars	Princeton U.S.A. 1953	6 : 45
Stewards' Challenge (1841)	4 oars	Trinity, Oxford 1949	7 : 13
Visitors' Challenge (1847)	4 oars	Pembroke, Cambridge 1952	7 : 15
Silver Goblets (1895)	Pair oar	R. Baetens and M. Knuysen (Belgium) 1953	7 : 51
Diamond Challenge (1844)	Sculls	R. George (Belgium) 1953	8 : 0

The only American two-time winners of the Diamond Skulls are Joseph W. Burk (1938 and 1939) and John B. Kelly, Jr. (1947 and 1949).

The greatest number of U. S. Single Skulls titles have been won by John B. Kelly, Jr., with 7 in 1946, 1948, 1950, 1952-55. See Photo No. 60, p. 201.

U.S. SINGLES
TITLES

The annual Yale-Harvard crew race over 4 miles on the Thames at New London, Conn., is the longest established fixture in United States sport, having been inaugurated in 1852 and in its present form 1878. Entering 1956, the series score stands at 47-43 in Harvard's favor. The record winning streak is 10 by Harvard from 1936 to 1948.

YALE-HARVARD

The downstream and course record is 19 minutes 21.4 seconds by Harvard in 1948. The upstream record is 19 minutes 52.8 seconds by Yale in 1949.

SHOOTING

Free Pistol—50 m. 6 x 10 shot series Poss. 600—559
    T. E. Ullman (Sweden)—Berlin, August, 1936
Free Rifle—300 m. 3 x 40 shot series Poss. 1,200—1,133
    A. Bogdanov (U.S.S.R.)—Caracas, November, 1954
Small Bore Rifle—50 m. 3 x 40 shot series Poss. 1,200—1,174
    A. Bogdanov (U.S.S.R.)—Caracas, November, 1954
Bench Rest .22 Rifle: ten shots put through a hole .2402 in dia. at 100 yards
    by O. A. Rinehart (U.S.A.)

WORLD RECORDS

The world's record stag, shot near Moritzburg, Germany, in 1699 by Frederick I, was a 66-pointer.

The record bag for one gun in a day is 1,070 grouse by Lord Walsingham at Blubberhouse, Yorkshire, England, in September, 1888.

Rabbits	6,943	5 guns	Blenheim, Oxfordshire, Eng.	Oct. 7, 1898
Partridge	2,119	6 guns	Rothwell, Lincs., Eng.	Oct. 12, 1952
Pheasants	3,937	7 guns	Hall Barn, Bucks., Eng.	Dec. 18, 1913

The National All-Bore Championship, instituted in 1935, now held annually at Dallas, Texas, is the sport's top event. Most titles have been won by T/Sgt. Glenn W. Van Buren of Texas in 1948, 1949 and 1951. Perfect scores of 250 have been required to win in 8 of the 10 post war contests.

SKEET-SHOOTING

63. Victor Barna   64. Butch Rosenberg   65. Paul Anderson

The U. S. Small Bore Championships were instituted in 1919. The only 3 time winner has been William B. Wooding in 1936, 1937 and 1938.

SMALL-BORE

The U. S. Pistol Shooting Championships were instituted in 1936. The winner of most titles has been Lieutenant Harry Reeves of the Detroit Police with 6 in 1940-41, 1946, 1948, 1953-54.

PISTOL SHOOTING

The Grand American Handicap, instituted in 1900, held annually at Dayton, Ohio, is the premier trapshooting contest. No marksman has ever won the title twice. The youngest winner was the 1954 victor, Nick Egan of Long Island, N. Y., at the age of 14. The record score is 100 hits in 1910 by R. Thompson off 19 yards, by C. A. Young in 1926 off 23 yards, by F. G. Carroll in 1937 off 19 yards by Peter Donat in 1949 off 20 yards and by Oscar Scheske in 1950 off 19 yards. The record entry was 2,024 competitors in 1955.

TRAP SHOOTING

SKIING

The earliest mention of skiing exists in a work by Procopius c.550 A.D. The earliest recorded competition was in Norway in 1767. The Winter Olympics were inaugurated in 1924.

ORIGINS

The most Olympic gold medals won by an individual for skiing is three by Torleif Haug (Norway) who, in 1924, won the Skiing Combined Event, the 18 kilometre and the 50 kilometre event and Toni Sailer (Austria) who in 1956 won the Slalom, Giant Slalom and downhill events. The only woman to have won two gold medals is Mrs. Andrea Mead Lawrence (U.S.A.) who at Oslo in 1952 won both the Slalom and the Giant Slalom.

MOST OLYMPIC MEDALS

Event	Instituted	Times	Name	Years
Jumping	1935	2	Art Tokle	1951, 1953
Downhill	1935	2	Toni Matt	1939, 1941
		2	Dick Durrance	1937, 1940
		2	Ernie McCulloch (Canada)	1951, 1952
Slalom	1935	2	Dick Durrance	1937, 1941
		2	Friedl Pfeifer (Austria)	1939, 1940
		2	Jack Reddish	1950 (tie), 1952
		2	Chiharu Igaya (Japan)	1953, 1954
Cross-Country		3	Tauno Pulkkinen	1953, 1954, 1955
Alpine Combined		3	Dick Durrance	1937, 1939, 1940
Nordic Combined		2	Ralph Townsend	1947, 1949
Total (Men's)		7	Dick Durrance	(as above)
Women's Downhill		3	Mrs. Andrea Mead Lawrence	1949, 1952, 1955
Women's Slalom		3	Mrs. Andrea Mead Lawrence	1949, 1952, 1955
Alpine Combined		3	Mrs. Andrea Mead Lawrence	1949, 1952, 1955
Total (Women's)		9	Mrs. Andrea Mead Lawrence	(as above)

MOST U.S. TITLES

The fastest recorded speed attained on ski is 109.11 m.p.h. by Ralph Miller (U.S.A.) at Portillos, Chile, in July, 1955. See Photo No. 61, p. 201.

FASTEST SPEED

The world's greatest ski-jump was achieved on the Obersdorf Jump in Bavaria on March 3rd, 1951, by the nineteen-year-old Finn, Tauno Luiro, who covered 456 feet (139 metres). The vertical height of the run is 161 metres (528.2 feet).

LONGEST JUMP

There is no national or world governing body or authority for depth records in skin diving.

SKIN DIVING

The greatest recorded depths are as follows:

Salt water free diving (fins and mask)
128 feet (World record)—Ramando Bucher, Italy—1954
90 feet (U.S. record)—Herb Sampson, Santa Catalina Island—1953

Salt water diving with oxygen-helium mixture
350 feet (U.S. record)—John Clark-Samazan, Santa Catalina Island—1954

Fresh water diving with lung
230 feet in Green Lake, Wisconsin, Robert Domkowski, Ron Domkowski, Don Hue, Dick Guerine—Chicago Submarine Exploration Group—1954

Salt water diving with lung (women)
270 feet—Mrs. Barbara Jones, Florida—1955

Largest fish ever taken underwater
Giant Black Grouper (804 pounds)—Don Pinder, Miami Triton Club—1953

SOCCER

MOST U.S.
TITLES

In the U. S. the sport is strongly supported only in the Eastern industrial cities. The National Challenge Cup Championship open to all teams was inaugurated in 1914. The most victories have been by Bethlehem Steel with 5 in 1915-16, 1918-19, and 1926.

The National Amateur Challenge Cup Championship was instituted in 1924. The most victories have been by Ponta Delgarda of Fall River, Mass., with 4 in 1938, 1946-48.

SPORTS AWARDS

A.P.

The only men to have been repeat winners of the Associated Press of America poll (instituted 1933) are Donald Budge (lawn tennis) in 1937 and 1938 and Byron Nelson (golf) in 1944 and 1945. The most female awards have gone to Mrs. Mildred Didrikson Zaharias with 5 in 1945-47, 1950 and 1954.

SULLIVAN
TROPHY

The only woman to have won the A.A.U. award instituted in 1930 is the swimmer Ann Curtis in 1944. Confined to amateur sports, the greatest number of awards have been won by track and field athletes with 16.

SQUASH RACKETS

EARLIEST
CHAMPION

Although the game was evolved in the middle of the last century at Harrow School (England) there was no recognized champion of any country until J. A. Miskey of Philadelphia won the American Amateur Singles Championship in 1906.

MOST
TITLES

The most men's singles titles (instituted 1907) have been won by Stanley W. Pearson of Philadelphia with 6 in 1915-17, 1921-23. Most women's titles have been won by Miss Cecile Bowes with 4 in 1938, 1940, 1941 and 1948.

SWIMMING

EARLIEST
REFERENCES

Competitive swimming originated in London c.1837 at which time there were 5 or more pools.

MOST WORLD
RECORDS

Men, 31, Arne Borg (Sweden) 1921-1929.
Women, 41, Ragnild Hveger (Denmark) 1936-1941.

MOST OLYMPIC
TITLES

The record number of individual Olympic gold medals by a swimmer is the four won by C. M. Daniels (U.S.A.) in 1904, 1906 and 1908. The greatest individual number on the current program on the four year cycle is three in 1924 and 1928 by J. Weissmuller (U.S.A.) who also won two further gold medals in relays.

DIVES
Easiest
Most Difficult

The dive with the lowest tariff (degree of difficulty 1.0) is the "jump forward standing straight" from the 1 metre (1 yard 3¼ inches) board while that with the highest tariff (degree of difficulty 2.7) is the "three and a half somersaults forward with pike" from the 10 metre (32 feet 9 inches) board. The Mexican diver Joaquin Capilla has performed a 4½ somersaults from a 10 metre board but this dive is not on the International tariff.

PLUNGING
RECORDS

No world records are recognized in plunging but the following British records (limit of 60 seconds from the start of the dive) are the best known records:
Men: 86 feet 8 inches. F. Parrington (Liverpool) Bootle September 20th, 1933.
Women: 71 feet 3½ inches. Miss E. Todd (Everton) Seacombe, November 17th, 1937.

WORLD RECORDS

(as recognized by the Fédération Internationale de Natation Amateur)

Distance	Name	Time	Date	Venue	Length of course
MEN:		**FREESTYLE**			
100 yards	R. Moore (U.S.A.)	48.9	5/19/56	Stanford	25 yards
100 metres	R. Cleveland (U.S.A.)	54.8	4/ 1/54	New Haven	25 metres
200 metres	J. C. Wardrop (G.B.)	2 03.4	3/ 4/55	Columbus	25 yards
220 yards	J. C. Wardrop (G.B.)	2 03.4	3/ 4/55	Columbus	25 yards
400 metres	F. H. Konno (U.S.A.)	4 26.7	4/ 3/54	New Haven	25 yards
440 yards	J. B. Marshall (Australia)	4 28.1	2/17/51	New Haven	25 yards
800 metres	F. H. Konno (U.S.A.)	9 30.7	7/ 7/51	Honolulu	100 metres
880 yards	M. Rose (Australia)	9 34.3	1/18/50	Sydney	55 yards
1,500 metres	G. Breen (U.S.A.)	18 05.9	3/29/56	New Haven	50 metres
1,760 yards	G. Breen (U.S.A.)	19 40.4	4/ 5/56	New Haven	55 yards

Distance	Name	Time	Date	Venue	Length of course
		BREAST STROKE			
100 yards	M. Furakawa (Japan)	1 01.4	10/ 1/55	Tokyo	25 metres
100 metres	M. Furakawa (Japan)	1 08.3	10/ 1/55	Tokyo	25 metres
200 metres	M. Furakawa (Japan)	2 31.0	10/ 1/55	Tokyo	25 metres
220 yards	M. Furakawa (Japan)	2 31.9	10/ 1/55	Tokyo	25 metres
		BUTTERFLY STROKE			
100 yards	A. Wiggins (U.S.A.)	54.4	1/21/56	Columbus	25 yards
100 metres	A. Wiggins (U.S.A.)	1 01.5	4/ 2/56	New Haven	25 metres
200 metres	W. Yorzyk (U.S.A.)	2 16.7	4/14/56	Winchendon	25 yards
220 yards	W. Yorzyk (U.S.A.)	2 18.7	4/14/56	Winchendon	25 yards
		BACK STROKE			
100 yards	Y. Oyakawa (U.S.A.)	55.7	2/27/54	Columbus	25 yards
100 metre.	G. Bozon (France)	1 02.1	2/27/55	Troyes	25 metres
200 metres	G. Bozon (France)	2 18.3	6/26/53	Algiers	25 metres
220 yards	VACANT. Basic time 2 mins. 20.0 secs.				
		INDIVIDUAL MEDLEY			
400 yards	J. C. Wardrop (G.B.)	4 36.9	4/ 1/55	New Haven	25 yards
400 metres	V. Stroujanov (U.S.S.R.)	5 15.4	10/ 2/54	Minsk	25 metres
		FREESTYLE RELAY			
4 x 100 yards	Yale University (U.S.A.)	3 21.3	2/ 1/55	New Haven	25 yards
	(K. Donovan, H. Gideonse, D. Armstrong, J. Niles)				
4 x 100 metres	National Team (Japan)	3 46.8	8/16/55	Tokyo	50 metres
	(H. Suzuki, A. Tani, N. Goto, M. Kogo)				
4 x 200 yards	Yale University (U.S.A.)	7 39.9	2/14/53	New Haven	25 yards
	(W. Moore, J. McLane, M. Smith, D. Sheff)				
4 x 200 metres	Yale University (U.S.A.)	8 29.4	2/16/52	New Haven	25 metres
	(W. Moore, J. McLane, D. Sheff, R. Thomas)				
		MEDLEY RELAY			
4 x 100 yards	North Carolina (U.S.A.)	3 46.0	4/ 7/56	New Haven	25 yards
	(W. Sonner, R. Fadgen, J. Nelson, D. McIntyre)				
4 x 100 metres	National Team (Japan)	4 15.7	8/13/55	Tokyo	50 metres
	(K. Hasi, M. Furakawa, T. Ishimoto, M. Kogo)				
WOMEN:		**FREESTYLE**			
100 yards	D. Frazer (Australia)	56.9	8/25/56	Townsville	25 yards
100 metres	C. Gastelaars (Netherlands)	1 04.0	4/14/56	Schiedam	25 metres
200 metres	L. Crapp (Australia)	2 19.3	8/25/56	Townsville	25 yards
220 yards	L. Crapp (Australia)	2 20.5	8/25/56	Townsville	25 yards
400 metres	L. Crapp (Australia)	4 50.8	8/25/56	Townsville	25 yards
440 yards	L. Crapp (Australia)	4 52.4	8/25/56	Townsville	25 yards
800 metres	L. Crapp (Australia)	10 30.9	1/14/56	Sydney	55 yards
880 yards	L. Crapp (Australia)	10 34.6	1/14/56	Sydney	55 yards
1,500 metres	L. de Nijs (Netherlands)	20 46.5	7/22/55	Utrecht	50 metres
1,760 yards	L. de Nijs (Netherlands)	22 05.5	8/12/55	Utrecht	50 metres
		BREAST STROKE			
100 yards	VACANT. Basic time 1 min. 09.2 secs.				
100 metres	VACANT. Basic time 1 min. 18.2 secs.				
200 metres	VACANT. Basic time 2 min. 48.5 secs.				
220 yards	VACANT. Basic time 2 min. 50.0 secs.				
		BUTTERFLY STROKE			
100 yards	S. Mann (U.S.A.)	1 04.1	4/ 7/56	Daytona Beach	25 yards
100 metres	A. Voorbij (Netherlands)	1 11.9	2/ 5/56	Velsen	25 metres
200 metres	S. Mann (U.S.A.)	2 44.4	7/ 6/56	Tyler	25 yards
220 yards	VACANT. Basic time 2 min. 49.5 secs.				
		BACK STROKE			
100 yards	G. Wielema (Netherlands)	1 04.6	3/13/50	Hilversum	25 metres
100 metres	C. Kint (Netherlands)	1 10.9	9/22/39	Rotterdam	25 metres
200 metres	G. Wielema (Netherlands)	2 35.3	4/ 2/50	Hilversum	25 metres
220 yards	VACANT. Basic time 2 min. 37.0 secs.				
		INDIVIDUAL MEDLEY			
400 yards	M. Kok (Netherlands)	5 10.5	12/10/55	Isleworth	33⅓ yards
400 metres	E. Szekely (Hungary)	5 40.8	7/13/55	Budapest	33⅓ metres
		FREESTYLE RELAY			
4 x 100 yards	Lafayette (U.S.A.)	3 56.8	4/ 6/56	Daytona Beach	25 yards
	(L. Crocker, B. Love, H. Hughes, J. Rosazza)				
4 x 100 metres	National Team (Hungary)	4 24.4	8/ 1/52	Helsinki	50 metres
	(I. Novak, J. Temes, E. Novak, K. Szoke)				
		MEDLEY RELAY			
4 x 100 yards	Walter Reed S.C. (U.S.A.)	4 23.0	3/ 8/56	Detroit	25 yards
4 x 100 metres	National Team (Hungary)	4 57.8	9/ 3/55	Budapest	50 metres
	(E. Pajor, E. Szekely, R. Szekely, K. Szoke)				

CHANNEL
SWIMMING

The first cross English Channel swim (without a life jacket) was achieved on August 24th-25th, 1875, by Capt. Matthew Webb (G.B.) from Dover, England, to Cape Gris Nez, France, in 21 hours 45 minutes. Webb swam an estimated 38 miles to make the 21 mile crossing. The first reverse crossing from France to England was achieved by Enrique Tiriboschi (Argentina) in 16 hours 33 minutes on August 11th, 1923.

The first woman to succeed was Gertrude Ederle (U.S.A.) from France to England on August 6th, 1926, in the then record time of 14 hours 31 minutes. The first woman to swim from England to France was Florence Chadwick (U.S.A.) in 16 hours 22 minutes on September 11th, 1951, having on August 8th, 1950, already achieved France to England in 13 hours 23 minutes.

The first man to complete a crossing both ways was Edward H. Temme (G.B.) who swam from France to England (14 hours 29 minutes) on August 5th, 1927, and England to France (15 hours 54 minutes) on August 19th, 1934.

Fastest

The cross-channel record is the 10 hours 50 minutes set by the Egyptian Hassan Abd-el-Rheim on August 22nd, 1950, on which day 8 other swimmers succeeded.

An unrecognized claim of 10 hours 45 minutes was made by Vencesles Spacek (Austria) in 1927.

The official record for the England to France crossing is 13 hours 55 minutes by Miss Florence Chadwick (U.S.A.) on October 11th, 1955.

Slowest

The slowest crossing was the 3rd ever made when Henry Sullivan (U.S.A.) on August 5th-6th, 1923, was in the water for 27 hours 25 minutes.

Most in a Day

The record number of successful crossings in a day is 18 on August 16th, 1951 (12 men, 6 women) all from France to England with the fastest time by Mareeh H. Hamad (Egypt) at 12 hours 12 minutes.

MOST
SYNCHRONIZED
TITLES

The greatest number of titles won in the A.A.U. Synchronized Swimming Championships (instituted 1946) are:

Solo Outdoor	4	Beulah Gundling	1950-53
Duet Outdoor	3	Marilyn Stanley	1947-48, 1950
Team Outdoor	4	St. Clair Synchronettes	1948-51
Solo Indoor	4	June Taylor	1950-53
Team Indoor	3	St. Clair Recreation Center (later Synchronettes)	1948-50
	3	Athens Water Follies	1953-55
Team Combined	4	Athens Water Follies	1952-55

The most difficult stunt is the Flamingo, full twist with a degree of difficulty of 2.1.

TABLE TENNIS

EARLIEST
REFERENCE

The earliest evidence relating to a game resembling table tennis has been found in the catalogs of London sports goods manufacturers in the 1880's. The old Ping Pong Association was formed in 1902 but the game proved only a temporary craze until resuscitated in 1921.

MOST WINS
IN WORLD
CHAMPIONSHIPS
(Instituted 1926-27)

Event	Holder	Times	Date
Men's Singles (St. Bride's Vase)	G. Viktor Barna (Hungary) See Photo No. 63, p. 208	5	1930, 32, 33, 34, 35
Women's Singles (G. Geist Prize)	Angelica Roseanu (Rumania)	6	1950, 51, 52, 53, 54, 55
Men's Doubles	G. Viktor Barna (Hungary) with 3 different partners	8	1929, 30, 31, 32, 33, 34, 35, 39
Women's Doubles	M. Mednyanszky (Hungary) with 3 different partners	8	1927, 29, 30, 31, 32, 33, 34, 35
Mixed Doubles (Men)	Ferenc Sido (Hungary)	4	1949, 50, 52, 53
(Women)	M. Mednyanszky (Hungary)	6	1927, 28, 30, 31, 33 34

G. Viktor Barna gained a personal total of 15 world titles, while 19 have been won by Mlle. M. Mednyanszky.

MOST
TEAM
TITLES

Event	Holder	Times	Date
Men's Team (Swaythling Cup)	Hungary	11	1927, 28, 29, 30, 31, 33, 34, 35, 38, 49, 52
Women's Team (Marcel Corbillon Cup)	Rumania	4	1951, 52, 54, 55

MOST U.S.
TITLES

Most U. S. men's singles titles have been won by Richard Miles of New York City with 10 between 1945 and 1955. Most women's singles titles have been won by Sally Green with 5 from 1940 to 1945.

The longest recorded match occurred in the 1935 Swaythling Cup final between M. Haguenauer (France) *v.* Marina (Rumania) which was unfinished after 7 hours' play. In the same meeting A. Ehrlich (Poland) played Paneth (Rumania) for over 125 minutes for a single point.

LONGEST
MATCH

The shortest title match on record was in the 1955 world men's single final when T. Tanaka (Japan) beat Z. Dolinar (Jugoslavia) in 3 straight games in a total time of 13 minutes including the time spent retrieving balls and changing ends.

SHORTEST
MATCH

The modern game is generally agreed to have started with Major W. Wingfields patent for "sphairistike" taken out in February, 1874. This game soon became known as Lawn Tennis.

TENNIS

The game was introduced into the United States from Bermuda in March, 1874, by Miss Mary Ewing Outerbridge to the Staten Island Cricket and Baseball Club but did not become established there until 1880. The U. S. Lawn Tennis Association was founded in 1881.

The greatest number of games ever played in a singles match is 100. J. Drobny (Egypt) and J. E. Patty (U.S.A.) divided their match on an indoor court at Lyons, France, on February 20th, 1955, with the score at 21-19, 8-10, 21-21 (Drobny's score first) after four hours' play.

ALL TIME RECORDS
MOST GAMES
Singles Match

The greatest number of games ever played in a doubles match is 135. F. R. Schroeder and R. Falkenburg beat R. A. Gonzalez and H. W. Stewart (all U.S.A.) 36-34, 3-6, 4-6, 6-4, 19-17 at Los Angeles, U.S.A., on May 15th, 1949, after 4¾ hours of play.

Doubles Match

The most games played in a mixed doubles match was 71 when, in the semi-finals of the American Championship of 1948, W. F. Talbert and Mrs. W. du Pont (U.S.A.) beat R. Falkenburg and Miss G. Moran (U.S.A.) 27-25, 5-7, 6-1.

Mixed Doubles
Match

The most games ever recorded in a set is the 70 in the first set of the 1949 Los Angeles doubles match quoted above. For singles, the most games in a set was 54 when J. Coughlin beat E. Miles 28-26 in the 1933 American Inter-Collegiate Championships.

Set

At Beaulieu on the French Riviera in 1937, Mme. R. Mathieu (France) took two hours to win a first set 7-5 against Mrs. H. Sperling (Germany).

LONGEST SET

It took six hours playing time for F. G. Lowe (G.B.) to beat A. J. Zerlendi (Greece) in the second round of the Olympic Games singles championship at Antwerp in 1920. The match was subjected to interruptions owing to the weather. The score was 14-12, 8-10, 5-7, 6-4, 6-4.

LONGEST
MATCH

Miss Huiskamp, having won her previous round 6-0, 6-0 in the Washington State Championships in 1910, was beaten by Miss Hazel V. Hotchkiss (now Mrs. George Wightman), then the American champion, 6-0, 6-0, without winning a single point.

MOST DECISIVE
DEFEAT

The fastest service of any player was that of the U. S. Davis Cup player Lester Stoefen who, in 1935, was measured to drive a ball at 131 m.p.h. See Photo No. 59, p. 201.

FASTEST
SERVICE

The greatest crowd at a tennis match was 25,578 at the first day of the Davis Cup Challenge Round between Australia and the United States at White City, Sydney, on December 27th, 1954.

GREATEST
CROWD

(This international knock-out team championship was instituted in 1900 and has been contested to date by no less than 49 nations).

DAVIS CUP
RECORDS

The greatest number of games in a Davis Cup singles rubber was 78, when J. Drobny (Czechoslovakia) beat A. K. Quist (Australia) in the 1948 Inter-Zone final at Boston, Mass., U.S.A., 6-8, 3-6, 18-16, 6-3, 7-5.

MOST GAMES
Singles

The greatest number of games in a Davis Cup doubles rubber was 81 when W. T. Tilden and R. N. Williams (U.S.A.) beat J. O. Anderson and J. B. Hawkes (Australia) 17-15, 11-13, 2-6, 6-3, 6-2, in the Challenge Round at Forest Hills, U.S.A., on September 1st, 1923, and again when J. D. Hackett and M. Murphy (Ireland) beat V. Skonecki and J. Chytrowski (Poland) 10-8, 8-10, 12-14, 7-5, 6-1, in the third round of the European Zone at Warsaw in 1950.

Doubles

The most games in any set in a Davis Cup match was 34 in the 1948 Inter-Zone final (see above).

Set

LONGEST SPAN

Dr. J. C. Gregory (G.B.) who first played for England in 1926 and finally for Great Britain in 1952—26 years later, holds this record. Gregory came into the game in 1952 because of an injury to G. L. Paish, and partnered by A. J. Mottram, won the doubles in the fifth set against Yugoslavia in Belgrade.

MOST DECISIVE RUBBERS

On 6 occasions, a rubber has been won 6-0, 6-0, 6-0. In March, 1955, at Rangoon, Burma, the Philippines secured the necessary three rubbers to win the tie with the loss of only 4 games against the Burmese Ko Ko and Maung-Maung in the two singles. A Burmese pair failed to register a single game in the doubles.

TIES
Longest

In 1946, at Paris, Yugoslavia, having lost the two opening singles in the fifth set, then went on to win the tie 3-2 by winning the doubles and reverse singles each in the fifth set. The total number of games was 261.

Shortest

Argentina, in 1931, on March 26-28 beat Paraguay at Asuncion, 5-0, losing only 15 games. Paraguay has not entered the competition since. On April 2-4, 1931, at Buenos Aires, Argentina beat Uruguay 5-0 again also losing only 15 games.

Most Representations

G. von Cramm (Germany) played 102 rubbers (between 1932 and 1953) winning 82 and losing only 20 matches.

WIMBLEDON RECORDS
MOST GAMES
Singles

(The first Championship was in 1877).
The most games in a singles match at Wimbledon was 93 when J. Drobny (Egypt) beat J. E. Patty (U.S.A.) 8-6, 16-18, 3-6, 8-6, 12-10 in the 3rd round on June 25th, 1953.

Doubles

The most games in a doubles match at Wimbledon was 94 when J. E. Patty and M. A. Trabert (U.S.A.) beat K. McGregor and F. A. Sedgman (Australia) 6-4, 31-29, 7-9, 6-2 in the quarter finals of 1950.

Set

The most games in a set at Wimbledon was 60—also the longest time taken by a set which was 2½ hours—in the record doubles match mentioned above.

LONGEST MATCH

The longest Wimbledon match was the 4¼ hours required by the 1953 Drobny v Patty match (see above).

YOUNGEST CHAMPIONS

The youngest ever champion at Wimbledon was Miss Charlotte Dodd (b. September 29th, 1871) who was 15 when she won in 1887.

The youngest male champion was Wilfred Baddeley (b. January 11th, 1872) who won the Wimbledon title in 1891 at the age of 19.

The youngest doubles champions were the 18-year-old Australian Lewis A. Hoad (b. November 23rd, 1934) and his partner Kenneth R. Rosewall, who was born only 3 weeks before, who won the title in 1953.

MOST APPEARANCES

Jean Borotra (France) first entered Wimbledon in 1922 (the wettest-ever Wimbledon) and appeared without a break to 1956, except for the years 1946-1947—27 appearances in all.

MOST WINS

Miss Elizabeth Ryan (U.S.A.) won her first title in 1914 and her ninetenth in 1934 (12 women's doubles with 5 different partners and 7 mixed doubles with 5 different partners).

The greatest number of wins by a man at Wimbledon was by William C. Renshaw (G.B.) who won 7 singles titles (1881-2-3-4-5-6-9) and 7 doubles (1880-1-4-5-6-8-9) partnered by his twin brother Ernest.

The greatest number of singles wins were those of Mrs. Helen Wills-Moody (U.S.A.) (now Mrs. Roark) who won her 8th singles title in 1938.

The greatest number of singles wins by a man were those of William C. Renshaw as quoted above.

The greatest number of doubles wins by men was 8 by R. F. and H. L. Doherty, brothers. They won each year from 1897 to 1905 except for 1902.

The most women's doubles titles won were the 12 by Miss Elizabeth Ryan mentioned above.

The greatest number of mixed doubles wins were the 7 times by Miss Elizabeth Ryan as noted above. E. Victor Seixas (U.S.A.) 1953-54-55-56 is the only man who has won four.

MOST U.S. TITLES

The greatest number of U. S. titles won is:

Richard D. Sears	7	1881-1887		MEN'S SINGLES
William A. Larned	7	1901-02, 1907-11		
William T. Tilden, II	7	1920-25, 1929		
Molla Bjurstedt Mallory	8	1915-18, 1920-22, 1926		WOMEN'S SINGLES
Richard D. Sears	6	1882-87		MEN'S DOUBLES
Holcombe Ward	6	1899-1901, 1904-06		
Margaret Osborne du Pont	11	1941-50, 1955		WOMEN'S DOUBLES

WALKING

WORLD RECORDS

	hrs.	mins.	secs.	Holder	Country	Date	Place
2 miles		12	45.0	W. Hardmo	Sweden	Sept. 1, 1945	Sweden
5 miles		34	32.8	J. Dolezal	Czechoslovakia	Oct. 15, 1955	England
7 miles		48	15.2	W. Hardmo	Sweden	Sept. 9, 1945	Sweden
10 miles	1	10	45.8	J. Dolezal	Czechoslovakia	Apr. 30, 1954	Czechoslovakia
20 miles	2	33	09.4	J. Dolezal	Czechoslovakia	May 14, 1954	Czechoslovakia
30 miles	4	12	03.4	L. Moc	Czechoslovakia	June 21, 1956	Czechoslovakia
3,000 metres		11	51.8	W. Hardmo	Sweden	Sept. 1, 1945	Sweden
5,000 metres		20	26.8	W. Hardmo	Sweden	July 31, 1945	Sweden
10,000 metres		42	39.6	W. Hardmo	Sweden	Sept. 9, 1945	Sweden
15,000 metres	1	05	59.6	J. Dolezal	Czechoslovakia	Apr. 30, 1954	Czechoslovakia
20,000 metres	1	27	58.2	M. Lavrov	U.S.S.R.	Aug. 13, 1956	Moscow
25,000 metres	1	56	43.0	J. Dolezal	Czechoslovakia	May 14, 1955	Czechoslovakia
30,000 metres	2	21	38.6	J. Dolezal	Czechoslovakia	Oct. 12, 1952	Czechoslovakia
50,000 metres	4	05	12.2	G. Klimov	U.S.S.R.	Aug. 10, 1956	Moscow
1 hour	8 m. 1,025 yds.			J. F. Mikaelsson	Sweden	Sept. 1, 1945	Sweden
2 hours	15 m. 1,708 yds.			J. Dolezal	Czechoslovakia	May 14, 1955	Czechoslovakia

The unofficial 24 hour record is 125 miles 1,591 yards by Claud Hubert (France) at Motspur Park on July 4th-5th, 1953.

WATER SKIING

ORIGINS

The sport of water skiing was pioneered by Fred Waller of Long Island, N. Y., who rode skis of his own design behind his own boat on Long Island Sound in 1924. The earliest meeting for aquaplanists which included a jumping event was at Massapequa, N. Y., in 1936. The American Water Ski Association (A.W.S.A.) was founded in 1939.

LONGEST JUMP

The world record jump stands at 125 feet by Butch Rosenberg, made on August 28th, 1955, at Lake Hollingsworth, Lakeland, Florida. See Photo No. 64, p. 208.

LONGEST NONSTOP RUN

The greatest distance travelled non-stop is 276 miles by Joseph Balcao and Hubert Miller of Stockton, California. The run took from 7:35 a.m. from Aquatic Park beach, San Francisco to a 5:15 p.m. landing at Stockton on October 9th, 1955.

The long distance record is 400 miles on a measured course over Lake of the Ozarks in 15 hours 35 minutes by Lyle Lee of Galatia, Illinois, on September 5th, 1955.

MOST TITLES

The greatest number of national titles won by a water skier is 8 by Willa McGuire of Cypress Gardens, Florida.

WEIGHTLIFTING

ORIGINS

Amateur weightlifting is of comparatively modern origin, having been introduced in the Olympic Games at Athens in 1896. Prior to that time weightlifting consisted of professional exhibitions in which some of the advertised poundages were open to doubt.

GREATEST EVER LIFT

The greatest weight ever raised by a human being is 4,133 lbs. (1.84 tons) by the 350 lb. French-Canadian, Louis Cyr (1863-1912) in Chicago in 1896 in a back-lift (weight raised off trestles). Cyr had a 60½ inch chest and 22 inch biceps.

The greatest overhead lift ever made by a woman, also professional, is 282 lbs. by Katie Sandwena (Germany) c.1926 in a continental clean and jerk. This is equivalent to seven 40 pound office typewriters.

MOST OLYMPIC WINS

The only lifters to win two Olympic gold medals are L. Hostin (France) who won the light-heavyweight title in 1932 and 1936 and J. Davis (U.S.A.) who won the heavyweight title in 1948 and 1952. Davis was the youngest lifter to win a world title when he took the 1938 light-heavyweight title in Vienna aged 17 years.

WORLD RECORDS

		lbs.			lbs.
Bantam weight					
Press	V. Stogov, U.S.S.R.	235¾	Jerk	Chen Tsin-kai, China	292
Snatch	C. Vinci, U.S.A.	225¾	Total	V. Stogov, U.S.S.R.	738
Feather weight					
Press	E. Minayev, U.S.S.R.	251	Jerk	R. Chimishkyan, U.S.S.R.	315
Snatch	R. Chimishkyan, U.S.S.R.	242½	Total	R. Chimishkyan, U.S.S.R.	771
Light weight					
Press	R. Khabutinov, U.S.S.R.	270	Jerk	I. Shams, Egypt	338¼
Snatch	N. Kostilev, U.S.S.R.	271	Total	N. Kostilev, U.S.S.R.	843
Middle weight					
Press	T. Kono, U.S.A.	295½	Jerk	T. Kono, U.S.A.	371¼
Snatch	Y. Duganov, U.S.S.R.	293	Total	F. Bogdanovsky, U.S.S.R.	914¼
Light heavy weight					
Press	T. Kono, U.S.A.	317½	Jerk	T. Lomakin, U.S.S.R.	381¼
Snatch	Y. Duganov, U.S.S.R.	300¾	Total	T. Kono, U.S.A.	958¾
Middle heavy weight					
Press	D. Sheppard, U.S.A.	321½	Jerk	N. Schemansky, U.S.A.	399
Snatch	A. Vorobyev, U.S.S.R.	315¼	Total	A. Vorobyev, U.S.S.R.	1013¾
Heavy weight					
Press	P. Anderson, U.S.A. See Photo No. 65, p. 208	408¾	Jerk	P. Anderson, U.S.A.	440
Snatch	P. Anderson, U.S.A.	335	Total	P. Anderson, U.S.A.	1,175

Class	Champion	Times	Years
123¼ lbs.	Joseph De Pietro	8	1942-43, 1946-51
132¼ lbs.	Richard Bachtell	6	1929-31, 1934-35, 1937
148¾ lbs.	Anthony Terlazzo	11	1933, 1935, 1937-45
165 lbs.	John Terpak	8	1937-42, 1944-45
181 lbs.	{ William Good	5	1930-33, 1937
	{ Stan Stanczyk	5	1948-51, 1953
Middle Heavyweight	Norbert Schemansky	3	1951-53
Heavyweight	John Davis	10	1941-43, 1946-48, 1949-53

MOST A.A.U. TITLES

The lifter with most A.A.U. titles is Anthony Terlazzo with 11 at 148¾ lbs. (as above) and 2 at 132¼ lbs. (1932 and 1936) making a total of 13.

The earliest occasion on which a total of 1,000 lbs. was achieved in an official contest was at the Middle Atlantic Championship of 1941 by Steve Stanko who raised 1,002 lbs.

WRESTLING

EARLIEST REFERENCES

Wrestling holds and falls, depicted on the walls of the Egyptian tombs of Beni Hasan, prove that wrestling dates from 3000 B.C. or earlier. It was introduced into the ancient Olympic Games in the 18th Olympiad c.704 B.C. The Greco-Roman style is of French origin and arose about 1860.

MOST OLYMPIC TITLES

Two wrestlers have won 3 Olympic Gold medals.

Ivar Johansson (Sweden) 1932 Freestyle middleweight

1932 Greco-Roman welterweight

1936 Greco-Roman middleweight

Carl Westergren (Sweden) 1920 Greco-Roman middleweight

1924 Greco-Rcman light heavyweight

1932 Greco-Roman heavyweight

The A.A.U. Wrestling Championships were instituted in 1889. The greatest number of titles won in each division are:

Class	Times	Champion	Date
115 lbs.	4	G. Mehnert	1902-04, 1908
	4	G. Bauer	1905-07, 1909
125 lbs.	4	I. Niflot	1901-04
135 lbs.	4	Lowell Lange	1946-47, 1949-50
145 lbs.	4	M. Wiley	1899-1901, 1908
165 lbs.	3	Bill Smith	1950-52
175 lbs.	3	K. Kunert	1918-20
	3	A. Crawford	1937-39
	3	C. S. Swift	1949-50, 1952
191 lbs.	6	Henry Wittenberg	1943-44, 1946-48, 1952
Heavyweight	3	J. Gunderson	1907-08, 1913
	3	Richard Vaughan	1937, 1944-45
Team Champions (instituted 1935)	3	Oklahoma A.&M.	1935-36, 1938
	3	West Side Y.M.C.A.	1940-41, 1943

MOST A.A.U. TITLES

The longest recorded bout was in the light-heavyweight division in the Olympic Games at Stockholm in 1912, when A. Ahlgren (Sweden) and F. Boling (Finland) wrestled for over 9 hours in the final with no decision.

LONGEST BOUT

YACHTING

The highest authenticated speed attained by any yacht is 16.5 knots by the schooner "Rainbow" in 1898. A 17-foot sliding-seat canoe, sailed and designed by Uffa Fox (G.B.), has attained 16.3 knots over a measured half mile.

HIGHEST SPEED

The most successful racing yacht in history was the Royal Yacht "Britannia" (1893-1935) owned by King George V which in 625 starts won 231 races.

The America's Cup races, open to challenge by any nation's yachts, began in 1870 with the unsuccessful attempt by J. Ashbury's "Cambria" (G.B.) to capture the trophy from the "Magic" owned by F. Osgood (U.S.A.). Since then the cup has been challenged by Great Britain in sixteen contests but the American or Canadian (in 1876 and 1881) holders have never been defeated.

In Olympic yachting events, which were inaugurated in 1904, the only two yachts to win gold medals twice were the "Llanoria" (U.S.A.) 6 metre class, in 1948 and 1952 and the "Pan" (Norway) Dragon class, also in 1948 and 1952.

MOST SUCCESSFUL

The first Transatlantic Race was in 1866, when three starters sailed from Sandy Hook to the Isle of Wight. The winner, James Gordon Bennett's schooner "Henrietta" (U.S.A.), 107 feet overall, took 13 days 21 hours 45 minutes. Since then there have been eleven races at irregular intervals.

Shortest elapsed time was that of Wilson Marshall's 185 feet overall schooner "Atlantic" (U.S.A.) in 1905, from Sandy Hook to Lizard Light in 12 days 4 hours 1 minute, which still stands as the record.

Longest race was that in 1951, when the ketch "Malabar III" (Kennen Jewett, U.S.A.) sailed from Havana, Cuba, to San Sebastian, Spain, in 29 days and 26 minutes.

The smallest yachts ever to take part in transatlantic races were the 32 feet overall sloops "Cohoe" and "Samuel Pepys". "Cohoe", owned by Adlard Coles (Great Britain), won the 1950 race on handicap, sailing from Bermuda to Plymouth in 21 days 9 hours 14 minutes. The Royal Naval Sailing Association yacht "Samuel Pepys", captained by Lt. Cmdr. Errol Bruce, was also successful in winning the 1952 race, from Bermuda to Plymouth in 17 days 5 hours 4 minutes.

TRANSATLANTIC RACE

The 635 miles Bermuda Cup Race from Newport, Rhode Island, to Bermuda inaugurated in 1906, is a biennial event. The greatest number of victories is 3 by J. G. Alden who was in the 54 foot schooner "Malabar VII" in 1926 and the 58 foot schooner "Malabar X" in 1930 and 1932. The fastest elapsed time made for the 628 miles from Montauk Point to Bermuda is 71 hours 35 minutes 43 seconds in 1932 by the 62 foot sloop "Highland Light" owned by Frank C. Paine (average 8.77 knots).

BERMUDA CUP

GUINNESS —A BRIEF HISTORICAL NOTE

In 1759 Arthur Guinness of Dublin took a lease of a brewery at St. James's Gate in that city for a period of nine thousand years at a rent of £45 a year. He thus became the founder of the vast concern of Arthur Guinness Son & Co. Ltd., of which Rupert Guinness, Lord Iveagh, is the present chairman and the great-great-grandson of the founder. During that period Guinness has become a household word as a beverage the world over. As early as 1801 Guinness was brewing specially for export to the New World. One of the earliest recorded references to Guinness has been found in the diary of a cavalry officer after he was severely wounded in the Battle of Waterloo in June, 1815. He wrote, "When I was sufficiently recovered to be permitted to take some nourishment, I felt the most extraordinary desire for a glass of Guinness, which I knew could be obtained without difficulty. Upon expressing my wish to the doctor, he told me I might take a small glass . . . It was not long before I sent for the Guinness and I shall never forget how much I enjoyed it. I thought I had never tasted anything so delightful . . ."

THE GUINNESS HARP

"The best-known of Irish harps, the so-called 'Brian Boru Harp', known all over the world as the trade mark of one of the most celebrated beverages in public demand, modern descendant of the famous BEOIR CUALANN, the beer of the Dublin Mountains and of our Celtic ancestors."

L. S. GOGAN, Keeper of Fine Art, National Museum of Ireland

The Angel Falls in Venezuela, highest waterfall in the world with a total drop of 3,312 feet.

INDEX